Longman

Effective Guide to 'O' Level Physics

2nd Edition

Poh Liong Yong

Pearson Education South Asia Pte Ltd
23/25, First Lok Yang Road, Singapore 629733

Associated companies, branches and
representatives throughout the world

© Pearson Education South Asia Pte Ltd 2002, 2007

All rights reserved. No part of this publication may be
reproduced, stored in a retrieval system, or transmitted in
any form or by any means, electronic, mechanical,
photocopying, recording, or otherwise, without the prior
permission of the Copyright owner.

First published 2002
Second edition 2007
Fourth reprint 2009

ISBN   978-981-06-0013-6
ISBN 10   981-06-0013-5

Produced by Pearson Education South Asia Pte Ltd
Printed in Singapore

The
publisher's
policy is to use
paper manufactured
from sustainable forests

CONTENTS

Introduction		iv
Syllabus		v
Chapter 1	Physical Quantities, Units and Measurement	1
Chapter 2	Kinematics	15
Chapter 3	Dynamics	30
Chapter 4	Mass, Weight and Density	41
Chapter 5	Turning Effect of Forces	49
Chapter 6	Pressure	57
Chapter 7	Energy, Work and Power	66
Chapter 8	Kinetic Model of Matter	75
Chapter 9	Transfer of Thermal Energy	85
Chapter 10	Temperature and Thermal Properties of Matter	92
Chapter 11	General Wave Properties	107
Chapter 12	Light	115
Chapter 13	Electromagnetic Spectrum	131
Chapter 14	Sound	137
Chapter 15	Static Electricity	144
Chapter 16	Current of Electricity and D.C. Circuit	157
Chapter 17	Practical Electricity	175
Chapter 18	Magnetism	181
Chapter 19	Electromagnetism	187
Chapter 20	Electromagnetic Induction	198
Specimen Examination Paper		209
Answers		218

INTRODUCTION

The Longman Effective Guide to 'O' Level Physics was first published in 2002. Over the years, students and teachers have found the book to be very effective in the teaching and learning of 'O' Level Physics.

The **new edition** retains all the best characteristics of the previous edition such as
- Systematic and comprehensive notes illustrated with accurate and well-labelled diagrams
- Examples which are qualitative and quantitative in nature
- Questions – multiple choice and structured questions
- Hints and answers to questions

These characteristics aims to enable students to acquire scientific expertise and understanding. Students learn problem solving skills, effective communication skills and understand the physical phenomena around us.

The **new edition** is based on the 2007 GCE 'O' Level Physics syllabus. Changes had been made not only to the content to suit the requirements of the **new syllabus**. The new content includes
- Magnitude of sizes of common objects
- Effect of air resistance in kinematics
- Free-body diagram in dynamics
- Kinetic model to explain the behaviour of gases
- Thermocouple thermometers
- Internal energy
- Effects of electromagnetic waves on cells and tissue
- Electric field
- Potential divider circuit
- Thermistor and light-dependent resistor
- Use of cathode-ray oscilloscope

The **new features** in the books includes
- **Problem solving technique** – strategy that the student should follow in solving each type of problem
- **Self Evaluation** at the end of each subtopic which serves to check that the student understands. The student will be able to move on to the next section after completing the Self Evaluation questions.
- **New multiple choice and structured questions** in the **Revision Exercises** expose students to questions that involved both familiar and unfamiliar situations.
- **Data-based questions** had been included so that students are familiar with the latest requirement of the syllabus.
- **All numerical answers** are provided, with detailed answers for the more difficult questions. Answers, including drawings that can be found from the notes, are not provided for the more routine questions. The rationale for not providing full solutions at the back of the book is that students have to do their homework.

This book complements the Physics textbook and is a **must have** for students in their daily learning experience and it can serve as a **quick revision** tool before the examinations.

Poh Liong Yong

PHYSICS

GCE ORDINARY LEVEL (Syllabus 5058)

Introduction

The 'O' level physics syllabus provides students with a coherent understanding of energy, matter, and their interrelationships. It focuses on investigating natural phenomena and then applying patterns, models (including mathematical ones), principles, theories and laws to explain the physical behaviour of the universe. The theories and concepts presented in this syllabus belong to a branch of physics commonly referred to as classical physics. Modern physics, developed to explain the quantum properties at the atomic and sub-atomic level, is built on knowledge of these classical theories and concepts.

Students should think of physics in terms of scales. Whereas the classical theories such as Newton's laws of motion apply to common physical systems that are larger than the size of atoms, a more comprehensive theory, quantum theory, is needed to describe systems that are very small, at the atomic and sub-atomic scales, or that move very fast, close to the speed of light. It is at this atomic and sub-atomic scale that physicists are currently making new discoveries and inventing new applications.

It is envisaged that teaching and learning programmes based on this syllabus would feature a wide variety of learning experiences designed to promote acquisition of scientific expertise and understanding, and to develop values and attitudes relevant to science. Teachers are encouraged to use a combination of appropriate strategies to effectively engage and challenge their students. It is expected that students will apply investigative and problem-solving skills, effectively communicate the theoretical concepts covered in this course and appreciate the contribution physics makes to our understanding of the physical world.

Aims

These are not listed in order of priority. The aims are to:
1. provide, through well-designed studies of experimental and practical Physics, a worthwhile educational experience for all students, whether or not they go on to study science beyond this level and, in particular, to enable them to acquire sufficient understanding and knowledge to
    1.1 become confident citizens in a technological world, able to take or develop an informed interest in matters of scientific import;
    1.2 recognise the usefulness, and limitations, of scientific method and to appreciate its applicability in other disciplines and in everyday life;
    1.3 be suitably prepared and stimulated for studies beyond Ordinary Level in Physics, in applied sciences or in science-dependent vocational courses.
2. develop abilities and skills that
    2.1 are relevant to the study and practice of science;
    2.2 are useful in everyday life;
    2.3 encourage efficient and safe practice;
    2.4 encourage effective communication.

3. develop attitudes relevant to science such as
    3.1 concern for accuracy and precision;
    3.2 objectivity;
    3.3 integrity;
    3.4 enquiry;
    3.5 initiative;
    3.6 inventiveness.
4. stimulate interest in and care for the local and global environment.
5. promote an awareness that
    5.1 the study and practice of science are co-operative and cumulative activities, and are subject to social, economic, technological, ethical and cultural influences and limitations;
    5.2 the applications of science may be both beneficial and detrimental to the individual, the community and the environment;
    5.3 science transcends national boundaries and that the language of science, correctly and rigorously applied, is universal;
    5.4 the use of information technology (IT) is important for communications, as an aid to experiments and as a tool for the interpretation of experimental and theoretical results.

Assessment Objectives

A Knowledge with Understanding

Students should be able to demonstrate knowledge and understanding in relation to:
1. scientific phenomena, facts, laws, definitions, concepts, theories;
2. scientific vocabulary, terminology, conventions (including symbols, quantities and units contained in *'Signs, Symbols and Systematics 16-19'*, Association for Science Education, 2000);
3. scientific instruments and apparatus, including techniques of operation and aspects of safety;
4. scientific quantities and their determination;
5. scientific and technological applications with their social, economic and environmental implications.

The subject content defines the factual knowledge that candidates may be required to recall and explain. Questions testing those objectives will often begin with one of the following words: *define*, *state*, *describe*, *explain* or *outline*. (See the glossary of terms.)

B Handling Information and Solving Problems

Students should be able – in words or by using symbolic, graphical and numerical forms of presentation – to:
1. locate, select, organise and present information from a variety of sources;
2. translate information from one form to another;
3. manipulate numerical and other data;
4. use information to identify patterns, report trends and draw inferences;
5. present reasoned explanations for phenomena, patterns and relationships;
6. make predictions and propose hypotheses;
7. solve problems.

These assessment objectives cannot be precisely specified in the subject content because questions testing such skills may be based on information which is unfamiliar to the candidate. In answering such questions, candidates are required to use principles and concepts that are within the syllabus and apply them in a logical, reasoned or deductive manner to a novel situation. Questions testing these objectives will often begin with one of the following words: *predict*, *suggest*, *calculate* or *determine*. (See the glossary of terms.)

C Experimental Skills and Investigations

Students should able to:
1. follow a sequence of instructions;
2. use techniques, apparatus and materials;
3. make and record observations, measurements and estimates;
4. interpret and evaluate observations and experimental results;
5. plan investigations, select techniques, apparatus and materials;
6. evaluate methods and suggest possible improvements.

Weighting of Assessment Objectives

Theory Papers (Papers 1 and 2)

A Knowledge with Understanding, approximately **55%** of the marks with approximately **20%** allocated to recall.
B Handling Information and Solving Problems, approximately **45%** of the marks.

School-Based Science Practical Assessment (SPA) (Paper 3)

C Experimental Skills and Investigations, 100% of the marks.

Scheme of Assessment

Candidates are required to enter for Papers 1, 2 and 3.

Paper	Type of Paper	Duration	Marks	Weighting
1	Multiple Choice	1 h	40	30%
2	Structured and Free Response	1 h 45 min	80	50%
3	School-based Science Practical Assessment (SPA)	–	96	20%

Theory papers

Paper 1 (1 h, 40 marks), consisting of 40 compulsory multiple choice questions

Paper 2 (1 h 45 min, 80 marks), consisting of two sections.

Section A (50 marks), consisting of a variable number of compulsory structured questions.

Section B (30 marks), consisting of three questions. The first two questions are compulsory questions, one of which will be a data-based question requiring candidates to interpret, evaluate or solve problems using a stem of information. This question will carry 8–12 marks. The last question will be presented in an either/or form and will carry 10 marks.

SUBJECT CONTENT

SECTION I: MEASUREMENT

Overview

In this section, we examine how a small set of base physical quantities and units is used to describe all other physical quantities. These precisely defined quantities and units, with accompanying order-of-ten prefixes (e.g. milli, centi and kilo) can then be used to describe the interactions between objects in systems that range from celestial objects in space to sub-atomic particles.

1. Physical Quantities, Units and Measurement

Content

1.1 Physical quantities
1.2 SI units
1.3 Prefixes
1.4 Scalars and vectors
1.5 Measurement of length and time

Learning Outcomes:

Candidates should be able to:
(a) show understanding that all physical quantities consist of a numerical magnitude and a unit
(b) recall the following base quantities and their units: mass (kg), length (m), time (s), current (A), temperature (K), amount of substance (mol)
(c) use the following prefixes and their symbols to indicate decimal sub-multiples and multiples of the SI units: nano (n), micro (μ), milli (m), centi (c), deci (d), kilo (k), mega (M)
(d) show an understanding of the orders of magnitude of the sizes of common objects ranging from a typical atom to the Earth
(e) state what is meant by scalar and vector quantities and give common examples of each
(f) add two vectors to determine a resultant by a graphical method
(g) describe how to measure a variety of lengths with appropriate accuracy by means of tapes, rules, micrometers and calipers, using a vernier scale as necessary
(h) describe how to measure a short interval of time including the period of a simple pendulum with appropriate accuracy using stopwatches or appropriate instruments

SECTION II: NEWTONIAN MECHANICS

Overview

In this section, we examine important concepts in mechanics which include speed, velocity, acceleration, force, gravitational field and energy conversion and conservation. Analysis of the motion of an object is performed using free-body and vector diagrams, graphical analysis as well as mathematical formulas. Examples of the effects of forces introduced include the moment of a force and pressure. The law of conservation of energy and two important physical quantities, work and power, are introduced to study and explain the interactions between objects in a system.

2. Kinematics

Content

2.1 Speed, velocity and acceleration
2.2 Graphical analysis of motion
2.3 Free-fall
2.4 Effect of air resistance

Learning Outcomes:

Candidates should be able to:
(a) state what is meant by speed and velocity
(b) calculate average speed using $\dfrac{\text{distance travelled}}{\text{time taken}}$
(c) state what is meant by uniform acceleration and calculate the value of an acceleration using $\dfrac{\text{change in velocity}}{\text{time taken}}$
(d) interpret given examples of non-uniform acceleration
(e) * plot and * interpret a distance-time graph and a speed-time graph
(f) * deduce from the shape of a distance-time graph when a body is: (i) at rest; (ii) moving with uniform speed; (iii) moving with non-uniform speed
(g) * deduce from the shape of a speed-time graph when a body is (i) at rest; (ii) moving with uniform speed; (iii) moving with uniform acceleration; (iv) moving with non-uniform acceleration
(h) * calculate the area under a speed-time graph to determine the distance travelled for motion with uniform speed or uniform acceleration
(i) state that the acceleration of free fall for a body near to the Earth is constant and is approximately 10 m/s^2
(j) describe the motion of bodies with constant weight falling with or without air resistance, including reference to terminal velocity

* indicates learning outcomes where information technology might be made used of

3. Dynamics

Content

3.1 Balanced and unbalanced forces
3.2 Free-body diagram
3.3 Friction

Learning Outcomes:

Candidates should be able to:
(a) describe the effect of balanced and unbalanced forces on a body
(b) describe the ways in which a force may change the motion of a body
(c) * identify forces acting on an object and draw free body diagram(s) representing the forces acting on the object (for cases involving forces acting in at most 2 dimensions)
(d) * solve problems for a static point mass under the action of 3 forces for 2-dimensional cases (a graphical method would suffice)
(e) *recall and apply the relationship *resultant force = mass × acceleration* to new situations or to solve related problems
(f) explain the effects of friction on the motion of a body

4. Mass, Weight and Density

Content

4.1 Mass and weight
4.2 Gravitational field and field strength
4.3 Density

Learning Outcomes:

Candidates should be able to:
(a) state that mass is a measure of the amount of substance in a body
(b) state that the mass of a body resists a change in the state of rest or motion of the body (inertia)
(c) state that a gravitational field is a region in which a mass experiences a force due to gravitational attraction
(d) define gravitational field strength g as *gravitational force per unit mass*
(e) recall and apply the relationship *weight = mass × gravitational field strength* to new situations or to solve related problems
(f) distinguish between mass and weight
(g) recall and apply the relationship $density = \dfrac{mass}{volume}$ to new situations or to solve related problems

5. Turning Effect of Forces

Content

5.1 Moments
5.2 Centre of gravity
5.3 Stability

Learning Outcomes:

Candidates should be able to:
(a) describe the moment of a force in terms of its turning effect and relate this to everyday examples
(b) recall and apply the relationship *moment of a force (or torque) = force × perpendicular distance from the pivot* to new situations or to solve related problems
(c) state the principle of moments for a body in equilibrium
(d) apply the principle of moments to new situations or to solve related problems
(e) show understanding that the weight of a body may be taken as acting at a single point known as its centre of gravity
(f) describe qualitatively the effect of the position of the centre of gravity on the stability of objects

6. Pressure

Content

6.1 Pressure
6.2 Pressure differences
6.3 Pressure measurement

Learning Outcomes:

Candidates should be able to:
(a) define the term pressure in terms of force and area
(b) recall and apply the relationship $pressure = \frac{force}{area}$ to new situations or to solve related problems
(c) describe and explain the transmission of pressure in hydraulic systems with particular reference to the hydraulic press
(d) recall and apply the relationship *pressure due to a liquid column = height of column × density of the liquid × gravitational field strength* to new situations or to solve related problems
(e) describe how the height of a liquid column may be used to measure the atmospheric pressure
(f) describe the use of a manometer in the measurement of pressure difference

7. Energy, Work and Power

Content

7.1 Energy conversion and conservation
7.2 Work
7.3 Power

Learning Outcomes:

Candidates should be able to:
(a) show understanding that kinetic energy, elastic potential energy, gravitational potential energy, chemical potential energy and thermal energy are examples of different forms of energy
(b) state the principle of the conservation of energy
(c) apply the principle of the conservation of energy to new situations or to solve related problems
(d) state that kinetic energy $E_k = \frac{1}{2} mv^2$ and gravitational potential energy $E_p = mgh$ (for potential energy changes near the Earth's surface)
(e) apply the relationships for kinetic energy and potential energy to new situations or to solve related problems
(f) recall and apply the relationship *work done = force × distance moved in the direction of the force* to new situations or to solve related problems
(g) recall and apply the relationship $power = \frac{work\ done}{time\ taken}$ to new situations or to solve related problems

SECTION III: THERMAL PHYSICS

Overview

In this section, we examine how changes in temperature or state of matter are related to internal energy and heat (or more precisely, thermal energy transfer). The kinetic model of matter is used to explain and predict the physical properties and changes of matter in terms of the microscopic molecular interactions level. The different processes of thermal energy transfer are introduced, together with the thermal properties, such as specific heat capacity and latent heat, of matter.

8. Kinetic Model of Matter

Content

8.1 States of matter
8.2 Brownian motion
8.3 Kinetic model

Learning Outcomes:

Candidates should be able to:
(a) compare the properties of solids, liquids and gases
(b) *describe qualitatively the molecular structure of solids, liquids and gases, relating their properties to the forces and distances between molecules and to the motion of the molecules
(c) infer from Brownian motion experiments the evidence for the movement of molecules
(d) describe the relationship between the motion of molecules and temperature
(e) explain the pressure of a gas in terms of the motion of its molecules
(f) recall and explain the following relationships using the kinetic model (stating of the corresponding gas laws is not required):
    (i) a change in pressure of a fixed mass of gas at constant volume is caused by a change in temperature of the gas
    (ii) a change in volume occupied by a fixed mass of gas at constant pressure is caused by a change in temperature of the gas
    (iii) a change in pressure of a fixed mass of gas at constant temperature is caused by a change in volume of the gas
(g) use the relationships in (f) in related situations and to solve problems (a qualitative treatment would suffice)

9. Transfer of Thermal Energy

Content

9.1 Conduction
9.2 Convection
9.3 Radiation

Learning Outcomes:

Candidates should be able to:
(a) show understanding that thermal energy is transferred from a region of higher temperature to a region of lower temperature
(b) describe, in molecular terms, how energy transfer occurs in solids
(c) describe, in terms of density changes, convection in fluids
(d) explain that energy transfer of a body by radiation does not require a material medium and the rate of energy transfer is affected by:
    (i) colour and texture of the surface
    (ii) surface temperature
    (iii) surface area
(e) apply the concept of thermal energy transfer to everyday applications

10. Temperature

Content

10.1 Principles of thermometry
10.2 Thermocouple thermometers

Learning Outcomes:

Candidates should be able to:
(a) explain how a physical property which varies with temperature may be used to define temperature scales and state examples of such properties
(b) explain the need for fixed points and state what is meant by *ice point* and *steam point*
(c) discuss the action of a thermocouple thermometer
(d) explain the use of a thermocouple for measuring high temperatures and temperatures which vary rapidly

11. Thermal Properties of Matter

Content

11.1 Internal energy
11.2 Specific heat capacity
11.3 Melting, boiling and evaporation
11.4 Specific latent heat

Learning Outcomes:

Candidates should be able to:
(a) describe a rise in temperature of a body in terms of an increase in its internal energy (random thermal energy)
(b) define the terms *heat capacity* and *specific heat capacity*
(c) recall and apply the relationship *thermal energy = mass × specific heat capacity × change in temperature* to new situations or to solve related problems
(d) describe melting/solidification and boiling/condensation as processes of energy transfer without a change in temperature
(e) explain the difference between boiling and evaporation
(f) define the terms *latent heat* and *specific latent heat*
(g) recall and apply the relationship *thermal energy = mass × specific latent heat* to new situations or to solve related problems
(h) explain latent heat in terms of molecular behaviour
(i) *sketch and interpret a cooling curve

SECTION IV: WAVES

Overview

In this section, we examine the nature of waves and wave propagation and its uses by studying the properties of light, electromagnetic waves and sound, and their applications in communication, home appliances, and medical and industrial use.

12. General Wave Properties

Content

12.1 Describing wave motion
12.2 Wave terms
12.3 Longitudinal and transverse waves

Learning Outcomes:

Candidates should be able to:
(a) describe what is meant by wave motion as illustrated by vibrations in ropes and springs and by waves in a ripple tank
(b) show understanding that waves transfer energy without transferring matter
(c) define *speed, frequency, wavelength, period* and *amplitude*
(d) state what is meant by the term *wavefront*
(e) recall and apply the relationship *velocity = frequency × wavelength* to new situations or to solve related problems
(f) * compare transverse and longitudinal waves and give suitable examples of each

13. Light

Content

13.1 Reflection of light
13.2 Refraction of light
13.3 Thin lenses

Learning Outcomes:

Candidates should be able to:
(a) recall and use the terms for reflection, including *normal, angle of incidence* and *angle of reflection*
(b) state that, for reflection, the angle of incidence is equal to the angle of reflection and use this principle in constructions, measurements and calculations
(c) recall and use the terms for *refraction*, including *normal, angle of incidence* and *angle of refraction*
(d) recall and apply the relationship $\frac{\sin i}{\sin r}$ = constant to new situations or to solve related problems
(e) define *refractive index* of a medium in terms of the ratio of speed of light in vacuum and in the medium
(f) explain the terms *critical angle* and *total internal reflection*
(g) identify the main ideas in total internal reflection and apply them to the use of optical fibres in telecommunication and state the advantages of their use
(h) describe the action of a thin lens (both converging and diverging) on a beam of light
(i) define the term *focal length* for a converging lens
(j) * draw ray diagrams to illustrate the formation of real and virtual images of an object by a thin converging lens

14. Electromagnetic Spectrum

Content

14.1 Properties of electromagnetic waves
14.2 Applications of electromagnetic waves
14.3 Effects of electromagnetic waves on cells and tissue

Learning Outcomes:

Candidates should be able to:
(a) state that all electromagnetic waves are transverse waves that travel with the same speed in vacuo and state the magnitude of this speed (3×10^8 m s^{-1})
(b) describe the main components of the electromagnetic spectrum
(c) state examples of the use of the following components:
 (i) radio waves in radio and television communication
 (ii) microwaves in microwave oven and satellite television
 (iii) infra-red in remote controllers and intruder alarms
 (iv) light in optical fibres for medical uses and telecommunications
 (v) ultra-violet in sunbeds and sterilisation
 (vi) X-rays in radiological and engineering applications
 (vii) gamma rays in medical treatment
(d) describe the effects of absorbing electromagnetic waves, e.g. heating, ionisation and damage to living cells and tissue

15. Sound

Content

15.1 Sound waves
15.2 Speed of sound
15.3 Echo
15.4 Ultrasound

Learning Outcomes:

Candidates should be able to:
(a) describe the production of sound by vibrating sources
(b) describe the longitudinal nature of sound waves in terms of the processes of compression and rarefaction
(c) explain that a medium is required in order to transmit sound waves and the speed of sound differs in air, liquids and solids
(d) describe a direct method for the determination of the speed of sound in air and make the necessary calculation
(e) relate loudness of a sound wave to its amplitude and pitch to its frequency
(f) describe how the reflection of sound may produce an echo, and how it is used for measuring distances
(g) define *ultrasound* and describe one use of ultrasound, e.g. quality control and pre-natal scanning

SECTION V: ELECTRICITY AND MAGNETISM

Overview

In this section, we examine the interaction and effects of electric charges; the relationship between current flow, resistance, potential difference, charge, energy and power in electrical circuits; effects of magnetism and applications of electromagnetism and electromagnetic induction. The concepts of electric and magnetic fields are introduced as regions of space in which electric charges and magnets experience a force respectively.

16. Static Electricity

Content

16.1 Laws of electrostatics
16.2 Principles of electrostatics
16.3 Electric field
16.4 Applications of electrostatics

Learning Outcomes:

Candidates should be able to:

(a) state that there are positive and negative charges and that charge is measured in coulombs
(b) state that unlike charges attract and like charges repel
(c) * describe an electric field as a region in which an electric charge experiences a force
(d) * draw the electric field of an isolated point charge and recall that the direction of the field lines gives the direction of the force acting on a positive test charge
(e) * draw the electric field pattern between two isolated point charges
(f) show understanding that electrostatic charging by rubbing involves a transfer of electrons
(g) describe experiments to show electrostatic charging by induction
(h) describe examples where electrostatic charging may be a potential hazard
(i) describe an application of electrostatic charging such as a photocopier and a laser printer

17. Current of Electricity

Content

17.1 Conventional current and electron flow
17.2 Electromotive force
17.3 Potential Difference
17.4 Resistance

Learning Outcomes:

Candidates should be able to:

(a) state that current is a rate of flow of charge and that it is measured in amperes
(b) distinguish between conventional current and electron flow
(c) recall and apply the relationship *charge = current × time* to new situations or to solve related problems
(d) define *electromotive force* (e.m.f.) as the work done by a source in driving a unit charge around a complete circuit
(e) calculate the total e.m.f. of several sources (cells and batteries) arranged in series

(f) state that the e.m.f. of a source and the potential difference (p.d.) across a circuit component is measured in volts
(g) define the p.d. across a component in a circuit as the work done to drive a unit charge through the component
(h) state the definition that $resistance\ R = \dfrac{\text{potential difference }V}{\text{current }I}$
(i) apply the relationship $R = \dfrac{V}{I}$ to new situations or to solve related problems
(j) describe an experiment to determine the resistance of a metallic conductor using a voltmeter and an ammeter, and make the necessary calculations
(k) recall and apply the formulae for the effective resistance of a number of resistors in series and in parallel to new situations or to solve related problems
(l) recall and apply the relationship $\left(R = \dfrac{\rho l}{A}\right)$ of the proportionality between resistance R and the length l and cross-sectional area A of a wire to new situations or to solve related problems
(m) state Ohm's Law
(n) describe the effect of temperature increase on the resistance of a metallic conductor
(o) * sketch and interpret the I/V characteristic graphs for a metallic conductor at constant temperature, for a filament lamp and for a semiconductor diode
(p) understand how a diode is used as a rectifier

18. D.C. Circuits

Content

18.1 Current and potential difference in circuits
18.2 Series and parallel circuits
18.3 Potential divider circuit
18.4 Thermistor and light-dependent resistor
18.5 Use of cathode-ray oscilloscope

Learning Outcomes:

Candidates should be able to:
(a) * draw circuit diagrams with power sources (cell or battery), switches, lamps, resistors (fixed and variable), fuses, ammeters and voltmeters, bells, light-dependent resistors, thermistors and light-emitting diodes
(b) state that the current at every point in a series circuit is the same and apply the principle to new situations or to solve related problems.
(c) state that the sum of the potential differences in a series circuit is equal to the potential difference across the whole circuit and apply the principle to new situations or to solve related problems.
(d) state that the current from the source is the sum of the currents in the separate branches of a parallel circuit and apply the principle to new situations or to solve related problems
(e) state that the potential difference across the separate branches of a parallel circuit is the same and apply the principle to new situations or to solve related problems
(f) recall and apply the relevant relationships, including $R = \dfrac{V}{I}$ and those for current, potential differences and resistors in series and in parallel circuits, in calculations involving a whole circuit
(g) describe the action of a variable potential divider (potentiometer)
(h) describe the action of thermistors and light-dependent resistors and explain their use as input transducers in potential dividers

(i) solve simple circuit problems involving thermistors and light-dependent resistors
(j) describe the use of a cathode-ray oscilloscope (c.r.o.) to display waveforms and to measure p.d.'s and short intervals of time (detailed circuits, structure and operation of the c.r.o. are not required)
(k) interpret c.r.o. displays of waveforms, p.d.'s and time intervals to solve related problems

19. Practical Electricity

Content

19.1 Electric power and energy
19.2 Dangers of electricity
19.3 Safe use of electricity in the home

Learning Outcomes:

Candidates should be able to:
(a) describe the use of the heating effect of electricity in appliances such as electric kettles, ovens and heaters
(b) recall and apply the relationships $P = VI$ and $E = VIt$ to new situations or to solve related problems
(c) calculate the cost of using electrical appliances where the energy unit is the kWh
(d) state the hazards of using electricity in the following situations: (i) damaged insulation; (ii) overheating of cables; (iii) damp conditions
(e) explain the use of fuses and circuit breakers in electrical circuits and of fuse ratings
(f) explain the need for earthing metal cases and for double insulation
(g) state the meaning of the terms *live*, *neutral* and *earth*
(h) describe the wiring in a mains plug
(i) explain why switches, fuses, and circuit breakers are wired into the live conductor

20. Magnetism

Content

20.1 Laws of magnetism
20.2 Magnetic properties of matter
20.3 Magnetic field

Learning Outcomes:

Candidates should be able to:
(a) state the properties of magnets
(b) describe induced magnetism
(c) describe electrical methods of magnetisation and demagnetisation
(d) * draw the magnetic field pattern around a bar magnet and between the poles of two bar magnets
(e) describe the plotting of magnetic field lines with a compass
(f) distinguish between the properties and uses of temporary magnets (e.g. iron) and permanent magnets (e.g. steel)

21. Electromagnetism

Content

21.1 Magnetic effect of a current
21.2 Applications of the magnetic effect of a current
21.3 Force on a current-carrying conductor
21.4 The d.c. motor

Learning Outcomes:

Candidates should be able to:

(a) * draw the pattern of the magnetic field due to currents in straight wires and in solenoids and state the effect on the magnetic field of changing the magnitude and/or direction of the current
(b) describe the application of the magnetic effect of a current in a circuit breaker
(c) describe experiments to show the force on a current-carrying conductor, and on a beam of charged particles, in a magnetic field, including the effect of reversing (i) the current (ii) the direction of the field
(d) deduce the relative directions of force, field and current when any two of these quantities are at right angles to each other using Fleming's left-hand rule
(e) * describe the field patterns between currents in parallel conductors and relate these to the forces which exist between the conductors (excluding the Earth's field)
(f) explain how a current-carrying coil in a magnetic field experiences a turning effect and that the effect is increased by increasing (i) the number of turns on the coil (ii) the current
(g) discuss how this turning effect is used in the action of an electric motor
(h) describe the action of a split-ring commutator in a two-pole, single-coil motor and the effect of winding the coil on to a soft-iron cylinder

22. Electromagnetic Induction

Content

22.1 Principles of electromagnetic induction
22.2 The a.c. generator
22.3 The transformer

Learning Outcomes:

Candidates should be able to:

(a) * deduce from Faraday's experiments on electromagnetic induction or other appropriate experiments:
    (i) that a changing magnetic field can induce an e.m.f. in a circuit
    (ii) that the direction of the induced e.m.f. opposes the change producing it
    (iii) the factors affecting the magnitude of the induced e.m.f.
(b) describe a simple form of a.c. generator (rotating coil or rotating magnet) and the use of slip rings (where needed)
(c) * sketch a graph of voltage output against time for a simple a.c. generator
(d) describe the structure and principle of operation of a simple iron-cored transformer as used for voltage transformations
(e) recall and apply the equations $\frac{V_P}{V_S} = \frac{N_P}{N_S}$ and $V_P I_P = V_S I_S$ for an ideal transformer to new situations or to solve related problems
(f) describe the energy loss in cables and deduce the advantages of high voltage transmission

SUMMARY OF KEY QUANTITIES, SYMBOLS AND UNITS

Students should be able to state the symbols for the following physical quantities and, where indicated, state the units in which they are measured. Students should be able to define those items indicated by an asterisk (*).

Quantity	Symbol	Unit
length	$l, h \ldots$	km, m, cm, mm
area	A	m^2, cm^2
volume	V	m^3, cm^3
weight*	W	N*
mass	m, M	kg, g, mg
time	t	h, min, s, ms
period*	T	s
density*	ρ	g/cm^3, kg/m^3
speed*	u, v	km/h, m/s, cm/s
acceleration*	a	m/s^2
acceleration of free fall	g	m/s^2, N/kg
force*	F, f	N
moment of force*		N m
work done*	W, E	J*
energy	E	J, kW h*
power*	P	W*
pressure*	p, P	Pa*, N/m^2
atmospheric pressure		use of millibar
temperature	$\theta \ldots$	°C, K
heat capacity	C	J/°C, J/K
specific heat capacity*	c	J/(g °C), J/(kg K)
latent heat	L	J
specific latent heat*	l	J/kg, J/g
frequency*	f	Hz
wavelength*	λ	m, cm, …
focal length*	f	cm
angle of incidence	i	degree (°)
angles of reflection, refraction	r	degree (°)
critical angle	c	degree (°)
potential difference*/voltage	V	V*, mV
current*	I	A, mA
charge	q, Q	C, A s
e.m.f.*	E	V
resistance	R	Ω

BRIEF GLOSSARY OF TERMS USED IN PHYSICS PAPERS

The glossary has been deliberately kept brief not only with respect to the number of terms included but also to the descriptions of their meanings. Candidates should appreciate that the meaning of a term must depend in part on its context. They should also note that the number of marks allocated for any part of a question is a guide to the depth of treatment required for the answer.

1. **Define** *(the term(s) ...)* is intended literally. Only a formal statement or equivalent paraphrase, such as the defining equation with symbols identified, are required.
2. **Explain/What is meant by** ... normally implies that a definition should be given, together with some relevant comment on the significance or context of the term(s) concerned, especially where two or more terms are included in the question. The amount of comment should correspond with the indicated mark value.
3. **State** implies a concise answer with little or no supporting argument, e.g. a numerical answer that can be obtained 'by inspection'.
4. **List** requires a number of points with no elaboration. Where the number of points is specified in the question, this should not be exceeded.
5. **Describe** requires candidates to state in words (using diagrams where appropriate) the main points of the topic. It is often used with reference either to particular phenomena or to particular experiments. In the former instance, the term usually implies that the answer should include reference to (visual) observations associated with the phenomena. The amount of description should correspond with the indicated mark value.
6. **Discuss** requires candidates to give a *critical* account of the points involved in the topic.
7. **Predict** *or* **deduce** implies that candidates are not expected to produce the required answer by recall but by making a logical connection between other pieces of information. Such information may be given in the question or may depend on answers to an earlier part of the question.
8. **Suggest** is used in two main contexts. It may either imply that there is no unique answer or that candidates are expected to apply their general knowledge to a situation that may not be 'in the syllabus'.
9. **Calculate** is used when a numerical answer is required. In general, working should be shown.
10. **Measure** implies that the quantity concerned can be directly obtained from a suitable measuring instrument, e.g. length, using a rule, or angle, using a protractor.
11. **Determine** often implies that the quantity concerned cannot be measured directly but is obtained by calculation, substituting measured or known values of other quantities into a standard formula.
12. **Show** is used when an algebraic deduction has to be made to prove a given equation. It is important that the candidates state the terms being used explicitly.
13. **Estimate** implies a reasoned order of magnitude statement or calculation of the quantity concerned. Candidates should make such simplifying assumptions as may be necessary about points of principle and about the values of quantities not included in the question.
14. **Sketch**, when applied to graph work, implies that the shape and/or position of the curve need only be qualitatively correct. However, candidates should be aware that, depending on the context, some quantitative aspects may be looked for, e.g. passing through the origin, having an intercept, asymptote or discontinuity at a particular value. On a sketch graph it is essential that candidates clearly indicate what is being plotted on each axis.
    Sketch, when applied to diagrams, implies that a simple, freehand drawing is acceptable. Nevertheless, care should be taken over to draw to proportion and show clearly the important details.

CHAPTER 1
Physical Quantities, Units and Measurement

1.1 Physical Quantities

1. A **physical quantity** is a quantity that can be measured.
2. A physical quantity is made up of a **numerical magnitude** and a unit.
3. Examples of physical quantities.

Physical quantity	Example	Numerical magnitude	Unit
Length	10 m	10	m
Mass	5 kg	5	kg
Time	30 s	30	s

4. The **unit** of a physical quantity is a **standard magnitude** of the physical quantity which is used to compare other magnitudes of the same physical quantity.
5. *'The length of a room is 10 m'* means that the length of the room is 10 times the length of a standard metre rule.

> **Self Evaluation 1.1**
> 1. Group the following into physical quantity and non-physical quantity.
>   Mass, love, fear, length, beauty, weight

1.2 SI Units

1. The *International System of Units* (abbreviated as SI) is the system of units that was established in 1968 and is used by most countries.
2. The advantages of a single and internationally accepted system of units are
   - that it facilitates international trade and communications and
   - that it encourages the transfer and exchange of scientific findings and information.

3. In the SI system, seven physical quantities are chosen as **base quantities**.

Base quantity (symbol)	Base unit (symbol)
Length (l)	metre (m)
Mass (m)	kilogram (kg)
Time (t)	second (s)
Temperature (T)	kelvin (K)
Electric current (I)	ampere (A)
Amount of substance (n)	mole (mol)
Luminous intensity (I_V)	candela (cd)

4. The units for the other physical quantities can be derived using the relationship between the physical quantities and the base quantities.

Physical quantity	Derived unit
Area = length × width	m^2 (from m × m)
Volume = length × width × height	m^3 (from m × m × m)
Density = $\frac{mass}{volume}$	$kg\ m^{-3}$ (from $\frac{kg}{m^3}$)
Speed = $\frac{distance}{time}$	$m\ s^{-1}$ (from $\frac{m}{s}$)
Acceleration = $\frac{change\ of\ velocity}{time}$	$m\ s^{-2}$ (from $\frac{m\ s^{-1}}{s}$)
Force = mass × acceleration	$kg\ m\ s^{-2}$ (from $kg \times \frac{m\ s^{-1}}{s}$)
Work = force × displacement	$J = kg\ m^2\ s^{-2}$ (from N × m = $kg\ m\ s^{-2}$ × m)
Power = $\frac{work\ done}{time\ taken}$	$W = kg\ m^2\ s^{-3}$ (from $\frac{J}{s} = \frac{kg\ m^2\ s^{-2}}{s}$)
Pressure = $\frac{force}{area}$	$Pa = kg\ m^{-1}\ s^{-2}$ (from $\frac{N}{m^2} = \frac{kg\ m\ s^{-2}}{m^2}$)

Note: There must be a space between two different units.

Self Evaluation 1.2

1. Write down the unit for each of the quantities defined below in terms of m, s, kg, K, and A.

   (a) $\dfrac{\text{mass}}{\text{time}}$ (e) current × time

   (b) $\dfrac{\text{mass}}{\text{area}}$ (f) density × volume

   (c) $\dfrac{\text{volume}}{\text{time}}$ (g) $\dfrac{\text{change in speed}}{\text{time}}$

   (d) $\dfrac{\text{change in temperature}}{\text{mass}}$

2. In a remote settlement in the Amazon jungle, sugarcane cultivators use the "hand" to measure the length of the sugar cane that they sell (see poster below).

   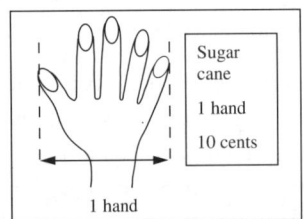

   (a) What is meant by a unit of a physical quantity?
   (b) Explain whether the "hand" is suitable as a unit for length.

1.3 Prefixes

PREFIXES FOR SI UNITS:

Prefix (symbol)	Factor	Example
Tera (T)	10^{12}	Tm = 10^{12} m
Giga (G)	10^{9}	Gm = 10^{9} m
Mega (M)	10^{6}	Mm = 10^{6} m
kilo (k)	10^{3}	km = 10^{3} m
deci (d)	10^{-1}	dm = 10^{-1} m
centi (c)	10^{-2}	cm = 10^{-2} m
milli (m)	10^{-3}	mm = 10^{-3} m
micro (μ)	10^{-6}	μm = 10^{-6} m
nano (n)	10^{-9}	nm = 10^{-9} m
pico (p)	10^{-12}	pm = 10^{-12} m

One of the advantages of the SI system of units is that only one unit is used for a physical quantity. When the numeric part of the quantity is very big or very small, prefixes which are multiples of ten or decimals are used.

> **Note:** There should not be any space between the prefix and the unit.
>
> **Example**
> ms = millisecond
>   = 10^{-3} s and not m s
> m s = metre second

Example
The dimensions of a box are 20 cm × 25 cm × 5 cm. Calculate the volume of the box in (a) cm³, (b) mm³ and (c) m³.

Solution
(a) Volume of the box = (20 cm)(25 cm)(5 cm)
  = 2500 cm³

(b) Volume of the box = (200 mm)(250 mm)(50 mm)
  = 2 500 000 mm³

(c) Volume of the box = (0.20 m)(0.25 m)(0.05 m)
  = 0.0025 m³

Example
The density of water is 1.0 g cm⁻³. What is its density in kg m⁻³?

Solution
$$1 \text{ kg} = 10^3 \text{ g}$$
$$1 \text{ g} = \frac{1}{10^3} \text{ kg} = 10^{-3} \text{ kg}$$
$$1 \text{ m} = 10^2 \text{ cm}$$
$$1 \text{ cm} = \frac{1}{10^2} \text{ m} = 10^{-2} \text{ m}$$
$$1 \text{ cm}^3 = \left(\frac{1}{10^2}\right)^3 \text{ m}^3 = \frac{1}{10^6} \text{ m}^3$$
$$1.0 \text{ g cm}^{-3} = \frac{1.0 \text{ g}}{\text{cm}^3}$$
$$= \frac{1.0 \times 10^{-3} \text{ kg}}{10^{-6} \text{ m}^3}$$
$$= 1.0 \times 10^3 \text{ kg m}^{-3}$$

Note: To convert the units of density from $g\,cm^{-3}$ to $kg\,m^{-3}$, one need to multiply by 10^3.

$1.0\,g\,cm^{-3} = 1.0 \times 10^3\,kg\,m^{-3}$
$2.0\,g\,cm^{-3} = 2.0 \times 10^3\,kg\,m^{-3}$

Standard Form

For very large or very small numbers, it is convenient to write them in the standard form. The standard form is denoted by $a \times 10^n$, where $1 < a < 10$ and n is an integer.

Examples
(a) $1\,100\,000 = 1.1 \times 10^6$
(b) $0.000\,0090 = 9.0 \times 10^{-6}$

Example
Express the following quantities in their base units. Give your answers in standard form up to 3 significant figures.
(a) Density = $200\,mg\,cm^{-3}$
(b) Speed = $45\,\mu m\,ns^{-1}$
(c) Work done = $700\,kN \times 28\,Mm$

Solution
(a) Density = $200\,mg\,cm^{-3}$
$= \dfrac{200 \times 10^{-3}\,g}{(10^{-2}\,m)^3}$ ($1\,mg = 10^{-3}\,g$; $1\,cm = 10^{-2}\,m$)
$= \dfrac{(200 \times 10^{-3})(10^{-3}\,kg)}{10^{-6}\,m^3}$
$= 200\,kg\,m^{-3}$ ($\because 1\,g = 10^{-3}\,kg$)
$= 2.00 \times 10^2\,kg\,m^{-3}$

(b) Speed = $45\,\mu m\,ns^{-1}$
$= \dfrac{45 \times 10^{-6}\,m}{10^{-9}\,s}$ ($\because 1\,\mu m = 10^{-6}\,m$; $1\,ns = 10^{-9}\,s$)
$= 4.50 \times 10^4\,m\,s^{-1}$

(c) Work done
$= 700\,kN \times 28\,Mm$ ($\because 1\,kN = 10^3\,N$;
$= (700 \times 10^3\,N)(28 \times 10^6\,m)$ $1\,Mm = 10^6\,m$)
$= 19\,600 \times 10^9\,N\,m$ ($1\,J = 1\,N\,m$)
$= 1.96 \times 10^{13}\,J$

Approximate values of the size of some common objects

Diameter of a hydrogen atom	10^{-10} m
Size of a cell of a living organism	10^{-5} m
Height of a room	3 m
Radius of the Earth	6×10^6 m
Distance from the Earth to the Moon	4×10^8 m
Distance from the Earth to the Sun	2×10^{11} m

Approximate values of the mass of some common objects

Mass of the electron	9×10^{-31} kg
Mass of a hydrogen atom	2×10^{-27} kg
Mass of a man	50 kg
Mass of a car	2×10^3 kg
Mass of the Earth	6×10^{24} kg
Mass of the Sun	2×10^{30} kg

Example
The number of particles in a mole of a substance is known as Avogadro's number N_A. The value of N_A is 6.02×10^{23} per mole. The mass of a mole of copper is 64 g. How many copper atoms are there in 8.0 g of copper?

Solution
In 1 mole (64 g) of copper, the number of copper atoms = N_A
Therefore in 8.0 g of copper, the number
of copper atoms = $\left(\dfrac{8.0}{64}\right)(N_A)$
$= \left(\dfrac{8.0}{64}\right)(6.02 \times 10^{23})$
$= 7.53 \times 10^{22}$

Self Evaluation 1.3

1. Calculate the volume of a slab of copper measuring 20 cm × 25 cm × 8.0 mm in (a) mm^3, (b) cm^3 and (c) m^3.
   Give your answer in standard form.

2. An astronomical unit (AU) is defined as the average distance between the Earth and the Sun, that is 1.50×10^{11} m. One light-year is the distance travelled by the light in a year.
   (a) If the speed of light is 3.00×10^8 m s^{-1}, what is the distance of a light-year in metre?
   (b) How many AU are there in one light-year?

1.4 Scalars and Vectors

1. A **scalar** is a physical quantity that has only magnitude. Mass, time, length, energy and density are scalar quantities.
2. A **vector** is a physical quantity that has both magnitude and direction. Displacement, velocity, force and momentum are examples of vector quantities.
3. The sum of two vectors is also a vector known as the **resultant**.
   (a) Addition of two vectors in the *same direction*.

   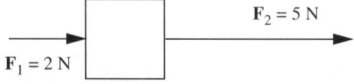

   The resultant of the two forces $F_1 = 2$ N and $F_2 = 5$ N acting in the same direction is **F**, a force that acts in the direction of F_1 and F_2.

   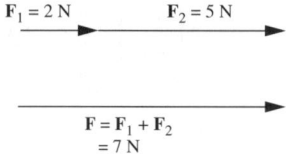

   (b) Addition of two vectors in the *opposite directions*.

   The resultant of the two forces $F_1 = 12$ N and $F_2 = 4$ N which act in the opposite directions is **F**, a force that acts in the direction of the greater force among F_1 and F_2.

   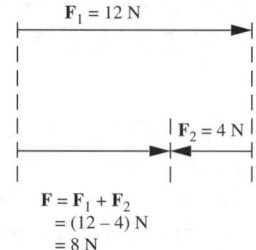

   (c) The addition of two vectors whose directions are not parallel to each other can be determined by graphical methods, i.e. either by
   (i) drawing a triangle or
   (ii) drawing a parallelogram.

(I) Triangle method

Example
A plane flies a distance of 500 km east from point O, it then turns counterclockwise by 60° and flies 600 km further. Determine the resultant displacement from O.

Solution
Step 1. Draw a line OA 2.5 cm long to represent the displacement $S_1 = 500$ km east.

O ———————(STEP 1)———————> A
$S_1 = 500$ km

Note: All lengths and angles must be measured accurately to scale.

Step 2. From point A draw a line AB 3.0 cm long at an angle of 60° in the counterclockwise direction to the original direction to represent the displacement $S_2 = 600$ km.

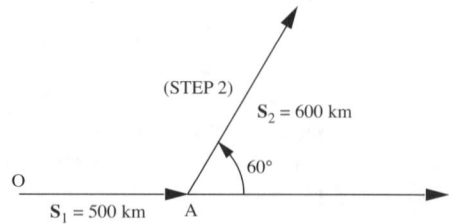

Step 3. Complete the triangle OAB.

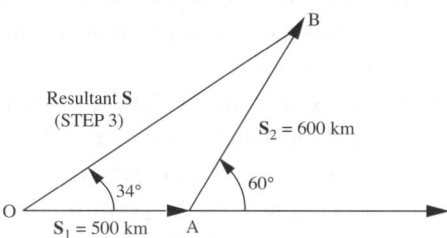

The resultant displacement **S** is represented both in **magnitude and direction** by the line OB. Measure the length of OB and the angle BOA. Resultant displacement **S** is 950 km in a direction 34° to the original displacement.

(II) Parallelogram method

Example

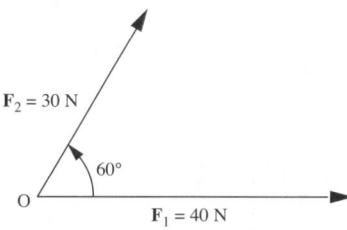

Two forces $F_1 = 40$ N and $F_2 = 30$ N act on a point O at an angle of 60° to each other. Determine the resultant force.

Solution

Step 1. Draw the line OA = 4.0 cm to represent the force $F_1 = 40$ N.

Step 2. Draw the line OB = 3.0 cm at an angle of 60° to F_1 to represent the force $F_2 = 30$ N.

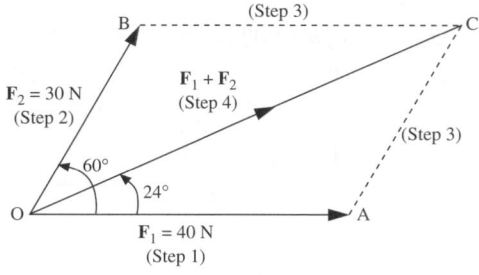

Step 3. Complete the parallelogram OACB by drawing (i) the line BC parallel to OA and (ii) the line AC parallel to OB.

Step 4. Draw the diagonal OC, which represents the magnitude and direction of the resultant force. Measure the length of OC and the angle AOC. The resultant force is 60 N at an angle of 24° to F_1.

Problem Solving Technique

Do not mix up the **triangle method** and the **parallelogram method**.

Triangle method

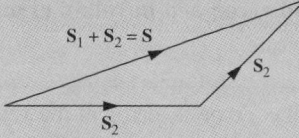

The arrows of S_1 and S_2 point in the same direction round the triangle and the arrow for **S** points in the opposite direction.

Parallelogram method

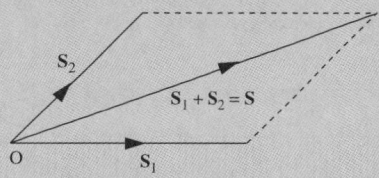

All the vectors S_1, S_2, and **S** start from the same point O.

Self Evaluation 1.4

1. Forces of 4.0 N and 3.0 N act at right angle on a point. By means of a scale diagram, find the resultant force.

2. In still water, the velocity of a boat crossing the river is 1.2 m s^{-1}. Draw a scale diagram to find the resultant velocity of the boat when there is a current flowing down the river at a speed of 0.9 m s^{-1}.

3. Two forces of 8 N and 6 N act a body. What is
   (a) the maximum resultant force;
   (b) the minimum resultant force?

1.5 Measurement of Length and Time

1. The base SI unit for length is the **metre** (m).

2. Other units for the length:
   cm = 10^{-2} m
   mm = 10^{-3} m
   μm = 10^{-6} m
   nm = 10^{-9} m
   km = 10^{3} m
3. Avoid **end error** and **parallax error** when using the metre rule.

> 1. Parallax error — error in the reading due to incorrect position of the eye.
> 2. To avoid parallax error, your line of vision should be perpendicular to the scale.

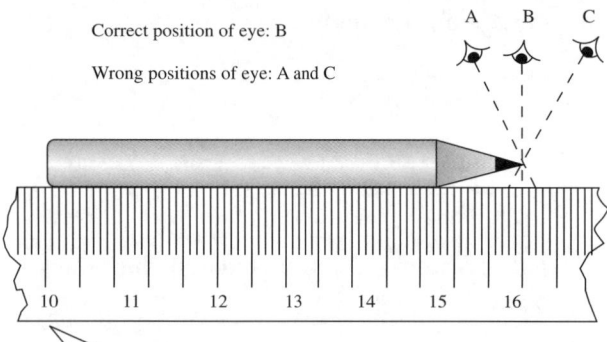

> 1. To avoid **end error**, start from the 10.0 cm mark.
> 2. To avoid **parallax error**, place pencil in contact with the scale.

4. All readings from the metre rule must be taken up to the first decimal place of a centimetre, for example, one should take the reading of 10.0 cm and **not** 10 cm.
5. **Vernier calipers**

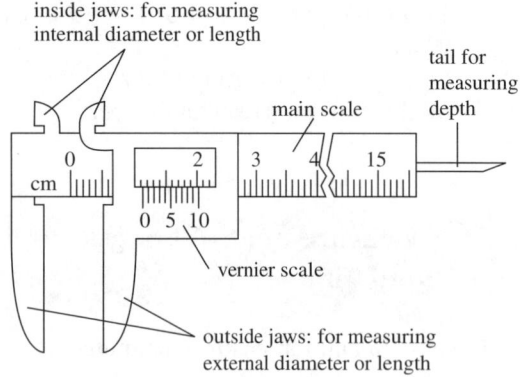

   (a) 10 divisions on the vernier scale = 0.9 cm. Hence 1 division on the vernier scale is 0.09 cm.

   (b) To read the vernier calipers.
      (i) Note the reading on the main scale just before the zero mark on the vernier scale, i.e. 1.1 cm
      (ii) The second decimal place is given by the reading on the vernier scale that is *exactly in line* with the main scale, i.e. 3.
      (iii) Hence the reading given by the vernier calipers is 1.13 cm.
   (c) The vernier calipers gives readings up to the second decimal place of a centimetre.
6. To check for zero error (or end error), close the jaws of the calipers.
   (a) No zero error if the '0' on both the main scale and vernier scale are exactly in line.

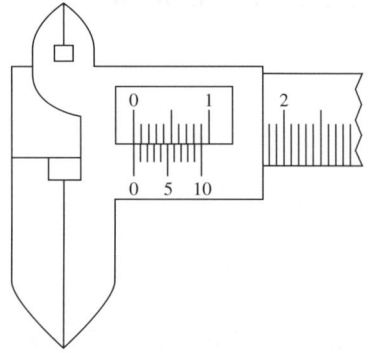

   (b) Zero error = +0.02 cm

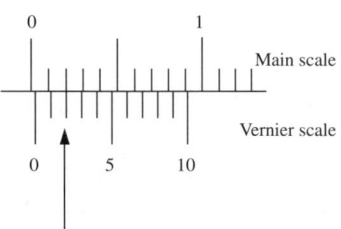

   (c) Zero error = –0.02 cm

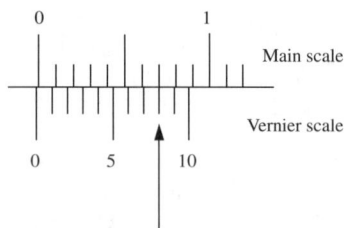

   Correct reading = scale reading – zero error

Examples
(a) If zero error = +0.01 cm
    Correct reading = (1.23 – 0.01) cm
                    = 1.22 cm

(b) If zero error = –0.02 cm
Correct reading = (1.23 – (–0.02)) cm
= 1.25 cm

7. **Micrometer screw gauge**

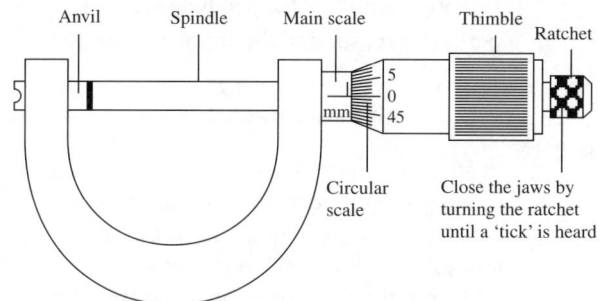

(a) For a complete turn of the thimble, the spindle moves through 0.5 mm and the circular scale moves through 50 divisions.
(b) 50 divisions on the circular scale = 0.5 mm
$$1 \text{ division} = \frac{0.5}{50} \text{ mm}$$
$$= 0.01 \text{ mm}$$
(c) The micrometer screw gauge gives readings up to the *second* decimal place of a millimetre.

8. Zero error.
(a) Zero error = 0.00 mm

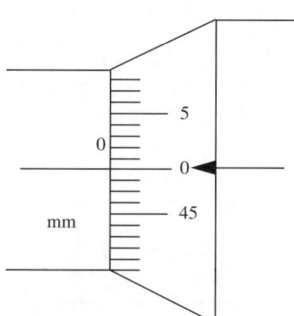

(b) Zero error = + 0.01 mm

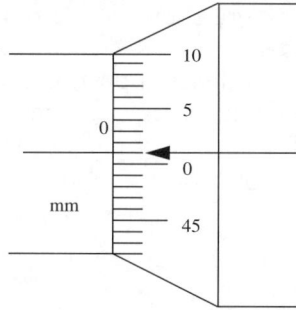

(c) Zero error = –0.01 mm

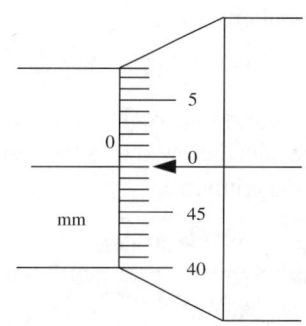

9. To read the micrometer scale.

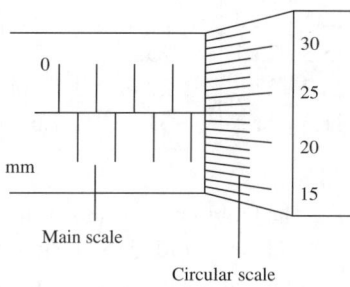

(a) Read the main scale: 3.5 mm
(b) Read the circular scale: 0.23 mm
(c) Micrometer reading = (3.5 + 0.23) mm
= 3.73 mm

10. Measurement of time.
(a) A **stopwatch** is used to measure an interval of time.
(b) **Simple Pendulum**

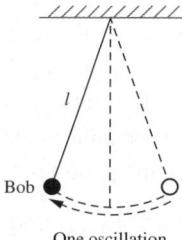

One oscillation

To measure the period T of a simple pendulum.
(i) Measure time for 20 oscillations t_{20}.
(ii) Calculate the period using $T = \frac{t_{20}}{20}$.
(c) The period T of a simple pendulum is *independent* of
(i) the amplitude of oscillation,
(ii) the mass of the bob.

(d) The period T depends on the length l of the pendulum.

$$T = 2\pi\sqrt{\frac{l}{g}}$$

where g is the acceleration due to gravity.

(e) The table below shows the results obtained in an experiment

l (cm)	Time for 20 oscillations t_{20} (s)			T (s)	$\sqrt{l}$ (cm$^{1/2}$)
	t_1 (s)	t_2 (s)	Average (s)		
10.0	12.8	12.7	12.8	0.640	3.16
20.0	17.9	17.9	17.9	0.895	4.47
30.0	22.5	22.3	22.4	1.12	5.48
40.0	25.2	25.1	25.2	1.26	6.32
50.0	28.2	28.2	28.0	1.40	7.07
60.0	31.3	31.5	31.4	1.57	7.75

Note:
(i) The length which is measured using a mm scale is recorded to the first decimal place of a centimetre i.e. 0.1 cm.
(ii) The time for 20 oscillations t_{20} which is measured using a stopwatch is recorded to the first decimal place of a second.
(iii) For each value of l, two readings for t_{20} are taken and the average values are calculated to the first decimal of a second. Repeated readings are taken to eliminate random error, such as mistake made when the watch is read.
(iv) The value of the period T and $\sqrt{l}$ are calculated to 3 significant figures because the values of t_{20} and l are recorded to 3 significant figures.
Since the period is given by the expression $T = 2\pi\sqrt{\frac{l}{g}}$, a graph of T against $\sqrt{l}$ is plotted to obtain a straight line graph (see below).

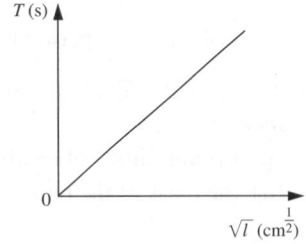

(f) The frequency f of the simple pendulum is the number of complete oscillations it makes in one second. Hence frequency $f = \frac{1}{T}$, where T is the period of oscillation.

(g) When the length of the pendulum increases, the period increases and the frequency decreases.

Self Evaluation 1.5

1. In an experiment, a student is required to measure the length, width and thickness of a piece of aluminium of about 20 cm long, 2 cm wide and 2 mm thick.
   (a) Name the measuring instruments that the student should use.
   (b) Give a sample reading for each measurement, indicating the degree of accuracy of the instrument.

2. What are the readings of the vernier scales shown below?

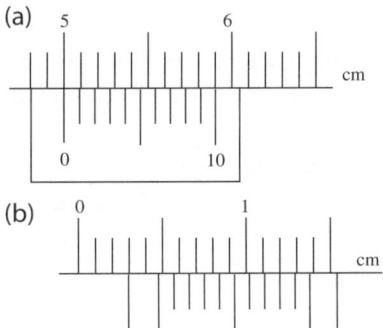

3.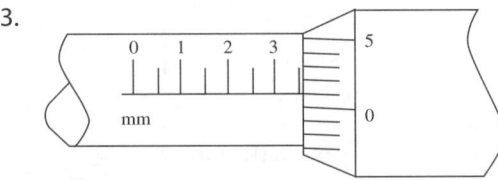

The figure shows a micrometer screw gauge.
(a) Each division on the circular scale represents _____ mm.
(b) The reading of the micrometer screw gauge is _____ mm.

4. The figure shows a simple pendulum.

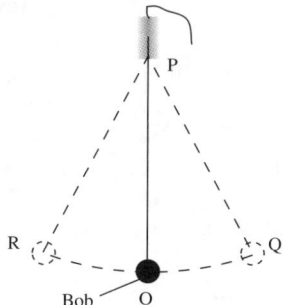

The points X, Y, and Z are at the top, centre and bottom of the pendulum bob.
(a) The length of the pendulum is the distance from the point P to _____.
   A: X
   B: Y
   C: Z
(b) The period of the simple pendulum is the time taken by the bob to move _____.
   A: from Q to O
   B: from Q to R
   C: from Q to R and back
(c) If the length of the pendulum is shortened, the frequency of the pendulum _____.
   A: increases
   B: decreases
   C: remains the same

REVISION EXERCISE 1

Multiple Choice Questions

1. The order of magnitude of the diameter of an atom is _____.
   A 100 dm
   B 0.01 mm
   C 10 μm
   D 0.10 nm

2. The volume of liquid in a bottle is 700 ml. What is its volume in m³?
   A 7.00×10^{-2} m³
   B 7.00×10^{-3} m³
   C 7.00×10^{-4} m³
   D 7.00×10^{-5} m³

3. The speed of a car is 20 m s⁻¹. What is its speed in km h⁻¹?
   A 18 km h⁻¹
   B 60 km h⁻¹
   C 72 km h⁻¹
   D 120 km h⁻¹

4. Which of the following diagrams shows that the resultant of the vectors **a** and **b** is **c**?

   A 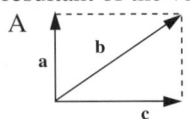   B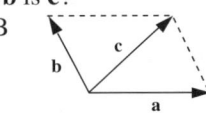

   C 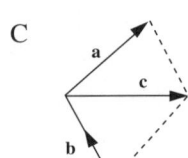   D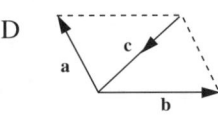

5. The possible maximum and minimum magnitudes of the resultant of two forces are 14 N and 6 N respectively. The two forces are of magnitudes _____ respectively.
   A 4 N and 10 N
   B 8 N and 6 N
   C 10 N and 6 N
   D 20 N and 8 N

6. The figure shows the two forces W and T on the bob of a simple pendulum.

   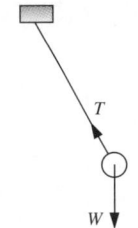

   Which of the figures below shows correctly the direction of the resultant force F relative to T and W?

   A 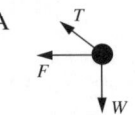   B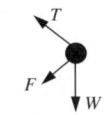

   C 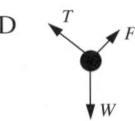   D

7. The figure shows a vernier scale.

   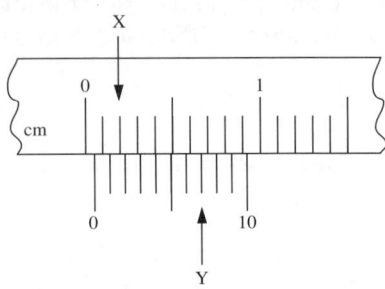

   What is the distance between the lines X and Y?
   A 0.47 cm
   B 0.51 cm
   C 0.67 cm
   D 0.77 cm

8. A wire is about 50 cm long and about 1 mm in diameter. What measuring instruments should be used to measure the length and the diameter?

	Length	Diameter
A	Vernier caliper	Micrometer
B	Micrometer	Vernier caliper
C	Metre rule	Vernier caliper
D	Metre rule	Micrometer

9. The figure shows a simple pendulum.

   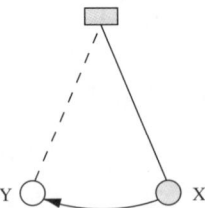

   Which method would be the most accurate way to measure the period of the simple pendulum using a stopwatch?
   A Time the motion from X to Y.
   B Time the motion from X to Y and back.
   C Time 20 oscillations and multiple by 20.
   D Time 20 oscillations and divide by 20.

10. The period T of a simple pendulum is measured for different lengths l. Which of the following graphs shows correctly the variation of the period T with the length l?

A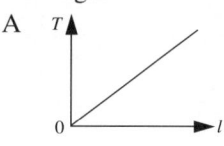
B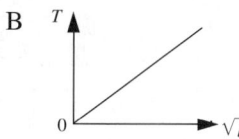
C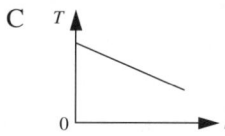
D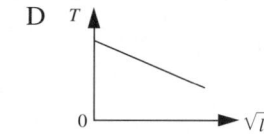

Structured Questions

Section A

1. A granular of sand measures 2 mm × 3 mm × 1 mm.
   (a) Calculate the volume of a granular of sand
       (i) in mm³ and (ii) in m³.
   (b) Estimate the number of sand granular in a volume of 1.0 m³. Give your answer in standard form.

2. Here are values of five lengths.

   10 m, 0.01 nm, 6 Mm, 20 km, 0.2 mm

   Fill the table below with the values given above.

Diameter of an atom	
Radius of the Earth	
Thickness of a piece of paper	
Height of a double-storey house	
Northeast MRT line from Punggol to Harbour Front	

3. (a) Name the instrument used to obtained the readings shown in the table below

Reading	Instrument
20.0 cm	
5.46 mm	
3.89 cm	

   (b) Name the instrument used to measure each of the quantities shown below.

Physical Quantity	Instrument
Internal diameter of a test tube	
Length of this book	
Thickness of a piece of paper	

4. The figure shows how a student measures the diameter of a cylinder using a mm scale.

   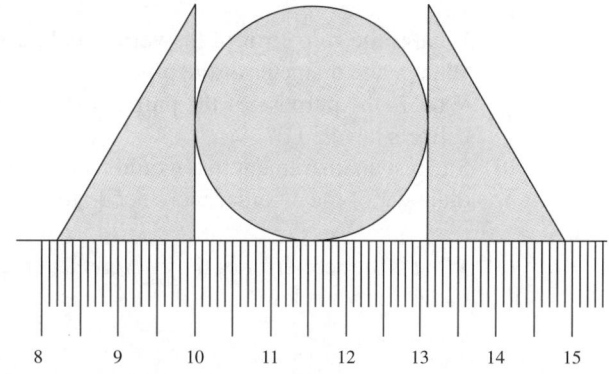

   (a) What is the diameter of the cylinder?
   (b) What is the purpose of using the two set squares?
   (c) State a procedure that would eliminate random error.

5. Figure (a) shows a pair of vernier calipers with its jaws closing and figure (b) shows that the vernier calipers is used to measure the diameter of a pipe.

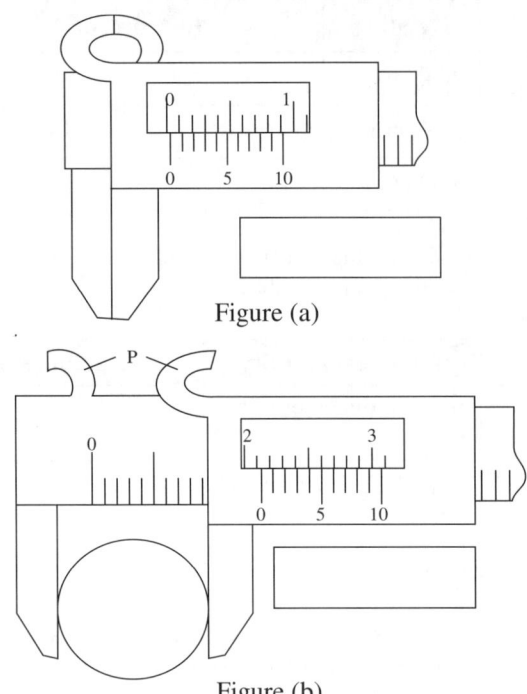

Figure (a)

Figure (b)

(a) What is the zero error of the vernier calipers?
(b) What is the diameter of the pipe?
(c) What is the purpose of the part of the vernier calipers labelled P?
(d) Suggest an instrument that would measure the diameter of the cylinder more accurately.

6. (a) What is the zero error of the micrometer screw gauge shown below?

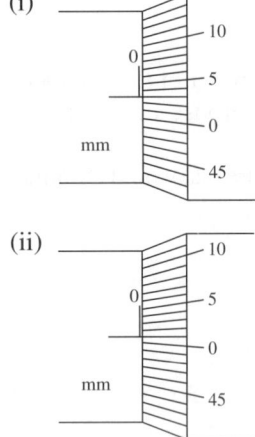

(b) The micrometer screw gauge in (a) (i) is then used to measure three lengths, and the scales are as shown below.

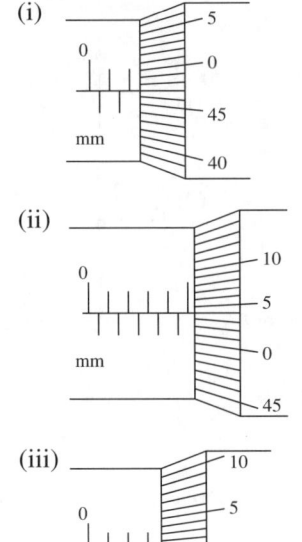

Write down the readings and the corrected readings.

	Reading	Corrected reading
(i)		
(ii)		
(iii)		

Section B

1. The figure shows a simple pendulum.

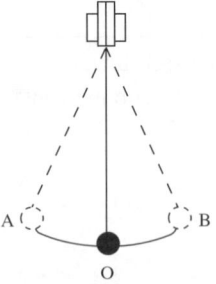

(a) With the aid of the above diagram, explain what is meant by the *period* of the simple pendulum.

(b) The period of a simple pendulum is about 1 s. State clearly how you would determine the period of the pendulum as accurately as possible using a stopwatch accurate to within 0.1 s.
(c) Discuss how the period of the pendulum would change
  (i) when a bob of larger mass is used,
  (ii) when the length of the pendulum is increased,
  (iii) when the amplitude of oscillation is smaller,
  if the other quantities remain constant.

2. (a) Distinguish between a scalar quantity and a vector quantity.
(b) In the list of physical quantities below, group the quantities into scalar quantity and vector quantity respectively.

| Distance | Velocity | Acceleration |
| Energy | Force | Time |

(c) A large vessel is towed by two tugs P and Q. Tug P exerts a force of 5000 N and tug Q exerts a force of F. The ropes from the tugs make an angle of 90°. The vessel moves in the direction Ox.

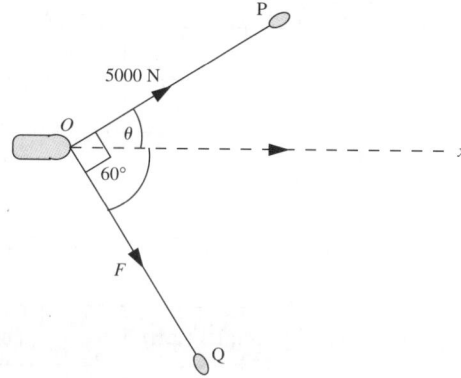

By drawing a suitable scale diagram, determine
(i) the angle θ;
(ii) the force F;
(iii) the resultant force on the vessel.
State the scale used for your diagram.

Data-based Question

3. A student uses three methods to measure the period of a simple pendulum using a stopwatch. The tables below are prepared by the student to record his readings.

Method 1

| Length (cm) | Time for 5 oscillations (s) | | | Period T (s) |
	First reading	Second reading	Average	

Method 2

Length (cm)	Time for 20 oscillations (s)	Period T (s)

Method 3

Length (cm)	Time for 100 oscillations (s)	Period T (s)

(a) The student measures the time for 5 oscillations in method 1, 20 oscillations in method 2, and 100 oscillations in method 3.
Which method is the most appropriate? Explain why the other two methods are not appropriate.

(b) In method 1, the student takes repeat readings. Explain why this is a good experimental procedure.

(c) Suggest how to improve method 2. Explain how the period T is calculated from the readings obtained in the improved method that you had suggested.

CHAPTER 2
Kinematics

2.1 Speed, Velocity and Acceleration

1. **Speed** is the distance travelled divided by time.

   $$\text{Speed} = \frac{\text{distance travelled}}{\text{time taken}}$$

   The SI unit of speed is metres per second (m s^{-1}).

2. **Velocity** is the distance travelled **in a given direction** (or **displacement**) divided by the time taken.

   $$\text{Velocity} = \frac{\text{displacement}}{\text{time taken}}$$

   The SI unit of velocity is metres per second (m s^{-1}).

3. Two objects travelling with the same speed by in different directions have different velocities.

4. Since velocity has both magnitude and direction, it is a **vector quantity**.

5. **Acceleration** is the rate of change of velocity.

   $$\text{Acceleration} = \frac{\text{change in velocity}}{\text{time taken}}$$
   $$= \frac{\text{final velocity} - \text{initial velocity}}{\text{time taken}}$$

6. The acceleration is *uniform* if the rate of change of velocity is *constant*.

7. In **linear motion**, a body travels in a straight line. The direction of motion does not change. Any change in the velocity is due to the change in speed.
   Hence the acceleration is

   $$\text{acceleration} = \frac{\text{change in speed}}{\text{time taken}}$$

Example
When the speed of a car changes from 5 m s^{-1} to 20 m s^{-1} in 5.0 s,

$$\text{acceleration} = \frac{\text{change in speed}}{\text{time taken}}$$
$$= \frac{(20 \text{ m s}^{-1} - 5 \text{ m s}^{-1})}{5.0 \text{ s}}$$
$$= 3.0 \text{ m s}^{-2}$$

8. When the velocity decreases, the acceleration is *negative*. Negative acceleration is known as **deceleration** or **retardation**.

Example
A car travelling at 20 m s^{-1} takes 10 s to stop after the brakes are applied. What is its retardation?

Solution

$$\text{Acceleration} = \frac{\text{final velocity} - \text{initial velocity}}{\text{time taken}}$$
$$= \frac{0 \text{ m s}^{-1} - 20 \text{ m s}^{-1}}{10 \text{ s}}$$
$$= -2.0 \text{ m s}^{-2}$$
$$\text{Retardation} = 2.0 \text{ m s}^{-2}$$

9. **Non-uniform acceleration** – the rate of change of velocity is not constant, instead it changes with time.

Problem Solving Technique

Step 1: Collect and summarise the data from the question.
Look for keys words.
'Starts' means when time = 0
'From rest' means initial speed = 0
'Stops' means final speed = 0

Step 2: Understand what the question wants.

Step 3: Select and apply the relevant equation(s). The equation(s) should involve the quantities given, the data provided and the quantity that you are required to find.

Step 4: Reflect on your answer.
– A numerical answer must have a unit.
– Is the value of the calculated quantity reasonable?

Example
In a 100 m sprint event a runner starts from rest and his speed is 10.0 m s^{-1} after 5.0 s. He then completes the rest of the race at a constant speed of 10.0 m s^{-1}.
(a) Calculate his average acceleration in the first 5.0 s.
(b) What is the distance covered in the first 5.0 s?
(c) What is the time taken by the runner to run the 100 m race?
(d) Is the acceleration uniform for the whole race? Explain your answer.

Solution
Step 1: Initial speed = 0
When time = 5.0 s, speed = 10.0 m s^{-1}.
For time greater than 5.0 s, speed is constant.
Constant speed = 10.0 m s^{-1}

(a) Step 2: Required to find average acceleration.

Step 3: Select and apply the equation.
Average acceleration

$$= \frac{\text{change in velocity}}{\text{time taken}}$$

$$= \frac{10.0 \text{ m s}^{-1} - 0 \text{ m s}^{-1}}{5.0 \text{ s}}$$

$$= 2.00 \text{ m s}^{-2}$$

Step 4: Reflect on the answer.
- Unit of acceleration: m s^{-2}
- Values of the acceleration: 2.00 m s^{-2} is reasonable.

Try to identify step 2, 3 and 4 for the rest of the solution.

(b) Distance travelled in the first 5.0 s
= average speed × time
$= \frac{1}{2}$(initial speed + final speed) × time
$= \frac{1}{2}$(0 m s^{-1} + 10.0 m s^{-1})(5.0 s)
= 25.0 m

(c) The speed (= 10.0 m s^{-1}) is constant for the distance (100 – 25) m.

Time taken to run 75 m $= \frac{75 \text{ m}}{10.0 \text{ m s}^{-1}}$

= 7.5 s
Total time taken = 5.0 s + 7.5 s
= 12.5 s

(d) The acceleration is non-uniform because in the first 5.0 s the acceleration is 2.0 m s^{-2} and the acceleration is zero for the rest of the time.

Self Evaluation 2.1

1. A car starts from rest and accelerates uniformly. After 5.0 s, its speed is 20.0 m s^{-1}.
   (a) What is the acceleration of the car?
   (b) What is its speed after 2.0 s?
   (c) What is the distance travelled in the first 2.0 s?

2. A bus was travelling at 20 m s^{-1} when the driver saw an obstacle in the middle of the road 120 m ahead. The reaction time of the driver is 0.6 s. During this interval of 0.6 s, the bus was travelling at 20 m s^{-1}. After the brakes were applied, the bus travelled a distance of 100 m before stopping.
   (a) Calculate the distance travelled by the bus during the reaction time of the driver?
   (b) Calculate the deceleration of the bus.
   (c) Explain whether the bus collided into the obstacle.

2.2 Graphical Analysis of Motion

1. **Displacement-time graph**.
   (a) Deduction from the graph
      (i) Horizontal line — body at rest.
      (ii) Straight line with positive gradient — uniform velocity.
      (iii) Straight line with negative gradient — uniform velocity in the opposite direction.
      (iv) Curve — non-uniform velocity.
   (b) The gradient of the graph is the velocity.

Example

(a) Body at rest

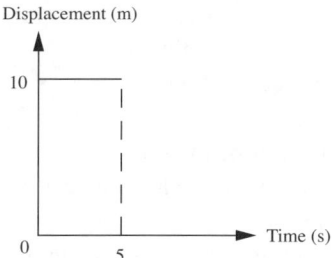

(b) Uniform velocity

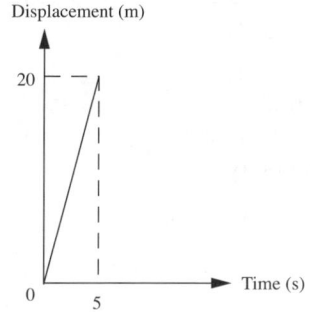

Velocity = gradient
$$= \frac{20 \text{ m}}{5 \text{ s}}$$
$$= 4 \text{ m s}^{-1}$$

(c) Uniform velocity in the opposite direction

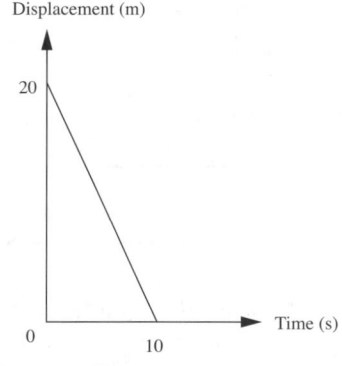

Velocity = gradient
$$= \frac{0 \text{ m} - 20 \text{ m}}{10 \text{ s}}$$
$$= -2 \text{ m s}^{-1}$$

(d) Non-uniform velocity

(i)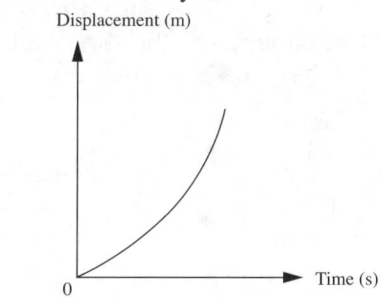

Gradient of graph is increasing.
Deduction: velocity keeps increasing.

(ii)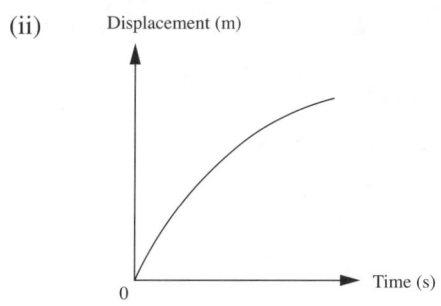

Gradient of graph is decreasing.
Deduction: velocity keeps decreasing.

Problem Solving Technique

1. The gradient of the displacement-time graph = speed.

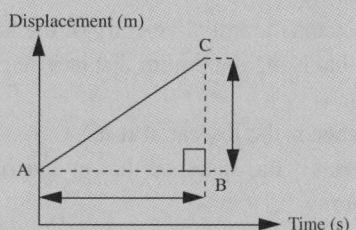

2. To determine the gradient of a straight line:
   (i) draw a suitable right angle triangle ABC.
   (ii) gradient = $\dfrac{CB}{AB}$

3. (a) The gradient of a line parallel to the time-axis = 0, hence velocity = 0.

(b) The gradient of a straight line is constant, and the same at all point on the graph

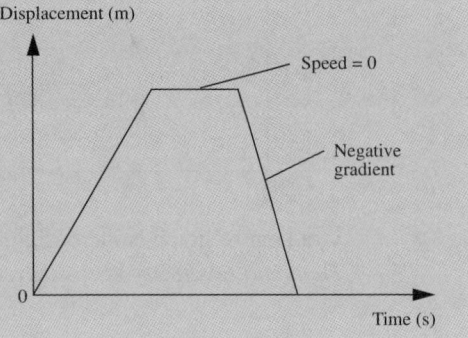

Example

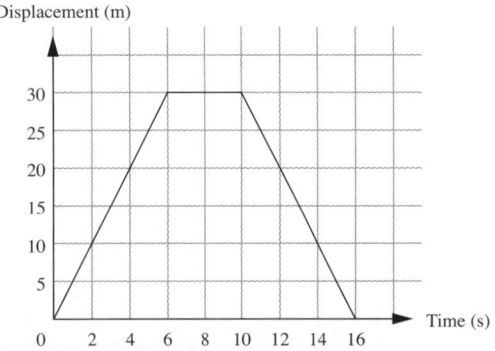

The figure above is the displacement-time graph of a toy car.
(a) What is the initial velocity of the toy car?
(b) What is the maximum displacement of the toy car?
(c) When is the toy car at rest?
(d) What is the speed of the toy car on its return journey?

Solution
(a) Initial velocity = gradient of the curve
$$= \frac{30 \text{ m}}{6 \text{ s}}$$
$$= 5.0 \text{ m s}^{-1}$$

(b) Maximum displacement = 30 m

(c) The car is at rest from $t = 6$ s to $t = 10$ s.

(d) Velocity on its return journey
$$= \frac{0 \text{ m} - 30 \text{ m}}{16 \text{ s} - 10 \text{ s}}$$
$$= -5.0 \text{ m s}^{-1}$$
Speed = 5.0 m s^{-1}

2. **Velocity-time graph**
The following deductions can be made from the velocity-time graph.
– Gradient of graph is the acceleration of the body.
– Area under the graph gives the displacement of the body.

Example
(a) Body at rest
Velocity = 0

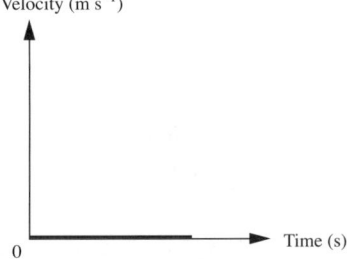

(b) Body moves with uniform velocity of 5 m s^{-1}.

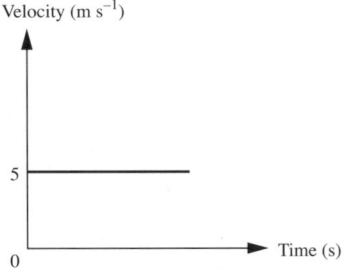

(c) Body moves from rest with uniform acceleration.

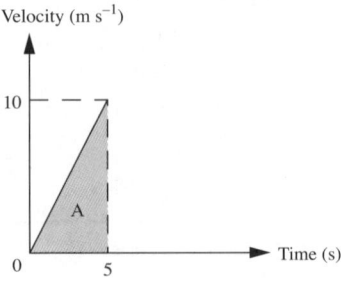

Acceleration = gradient
$$= \frac{10 \text{ m s}^{-1}}{5 \text{ s}}$$
$$= 2 \text{ m s}^{-2}$$
Displacement = area A
$$= \frac{1}{2}(5 \text{ s})(10 \text{ m s}^{-1})$$
$$= 25 \text{ m}$$

(d) Initial velocity $\neq 0$

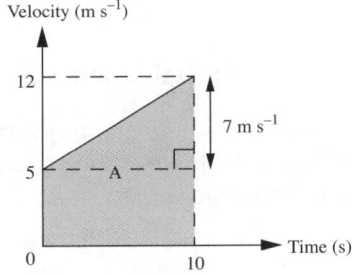

At $t = 0$, velocity = 5 m s^{-1}.
Acceleration = gradient
$$= \frac{7 \text{ m s}^{-1}}{10 \text{ s}}$$
$$= 0.70 \text{ m s}^{-2}$$
Displacement = area A of trapezium
$$= \frac{1}{2}(\text{sum of parallel sides})(\text{height})$$
$$= \frac{1}{2}(5 \text{ m s}^{-1} + 12 \text{ m s}^{-1})(10 \text{ s})$$
$$= 85 \text{ m}$$

(e) Graph with negative gradient

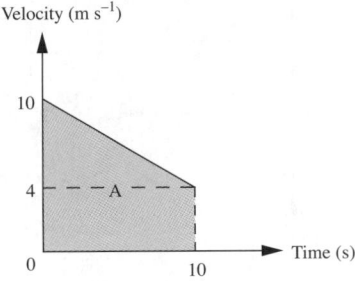

At $t = 0$, velocity = 10 m s^{-1}.
Gradient of the graph is negative implies that the velocity is decreasing.
$$\text{Retardation} = \frac{(10 \text{ m s}^{-1} - 4 \text{ m s}^{-1})}{10 \text{ s}}$$
$$= 0.6 \text{ m s}^{-2}$$

Displacement = area A
$$= \frac{1}{2}(10 \text{ m s}^{-1} + 4 \text{ m s}^{-1})(10 \text{ s})$$
$$= 70 \text{ m}$$

(f) Non-uniform acceleration
(i)

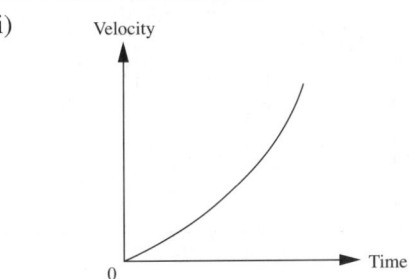

Gradient of the graph is increasing, this implies that the acceleration is increasing.

(ii)

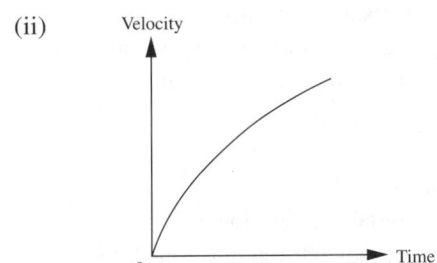

Gradient of the graph is decreasing, this implies acceleration decreases as the velocity increases.

Problem Solving Technique

1. The gradient of the speed-time graph is
$$\text{acceleration} = \frac{a}{b}$$

2. Area under the speed-time graph = distance travelled

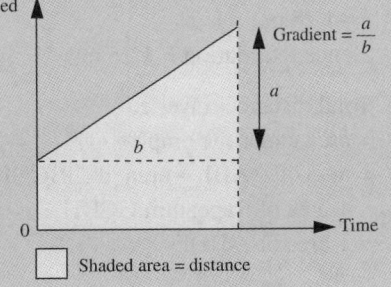

Example

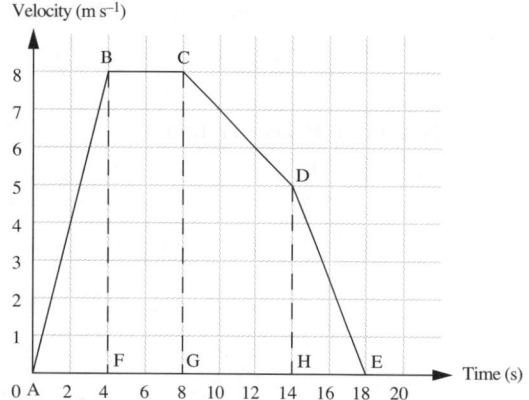

The velocity-time graph of a cyclist is as shown above. Calculate
(a) the initial acceleration of the cyclist;
(b) the distance travelled before the maximum velocity is reached;
(c) the retardation just before stopping;
(d) the total distance travelled;
(e) the average speed.

Solution

(a) Initial acceleration
= gradient of graph from A to B
$$= \frac{8 \text{ m s}^{-1} - 0 \text{ m s}^{-1}}{4 \text{ s} - 0 \text{ s}}$$
$$= 2.0 \text{ m s}^{-2}$$

(b) Distance travelled while accelerating
= area under the graph from $t = 0$ s to $t = 4$ s
$$= \frac{1}{2}(4 \text{ s})(8 \text{ m s}^{-1})$$
$$= 16 \text{ m}$$

(c) Acceleration just before stopping
= gradient of graph from $t = 14$ s to $t = 18$ s
$$= \frac{0 \text{ m s}^{-1} - 5 \text{ m s}^{-1}}{18 \text{ s} - 14 \text{ s}}$$
$$= -1.25 \text{ m s}^{-2}$$
Hence retardation = 1.25 m s^{-2}

(d) Total distance travelled
= area under the graph
= area of △ABF + area of □BCGF
+ area of trapezium GCDH
+ area of △HDE
$$= \frac{1}{2}(4 \text{ s})(8 \text{ m s}^{-1}) + (4 \text{ s})(8 \text{ m s}^{-1})$$
$$+ \frac{1}{2}(8 \text{ m s}^{-1} + 5 \text{ m s}^{-1})(6 \text{ s})$$
$$+ \frac{1}{2}(4 \text{ s})(5 \text{ m s}^{-1})$$
$$= 97 \text{ m}$$

(e) Average speed = $\frac{\text{total distance travelled}}{\text{time taken}}$
$$= \frac{97 \text{ m}}{18 \text{ s}}$$
$$= 5.39 \text{ m s}^{-1}$$

Self Evaluation 2.2

1. The distance-time graphs for the motion of four objects are as shown. Describe the motion of each object.

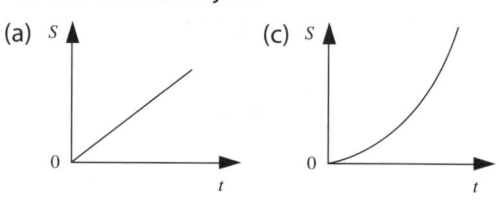

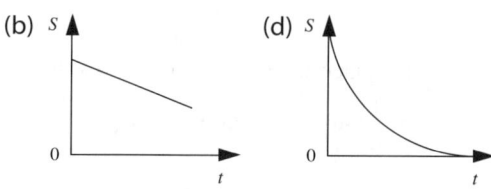

2. The velocity-time graphs of the motion of three objects are shown.

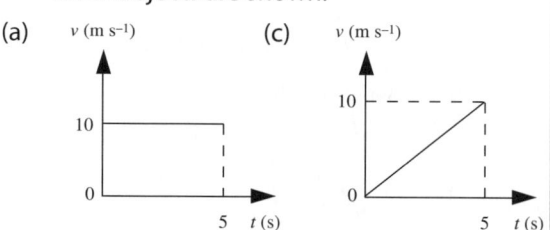

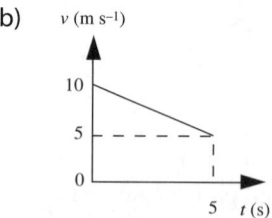

From each of the graphs, determine
(i) the speed when time $t = 2.5$ s.
(ii) the average speed.
(iii) the distance travelled in 5.0 s.
(iv) the acceleration.

2.3 Free Fall

1. The gravitational force of the Earth pulls all objects towards the centre of the Earth.
2. A body is in free fall motion if it moves under the influence of the Earth's gravity alone.
3. Without air resistance a body in free fall has an acceleration known as the acceleration of free fall g.
4. The acceleration of free fall for a body close to the Earth's surface is approximately 10 m s^{-2}.
5. For a body which is released from rest, its initial speed is 0 m s^{-1}.
   Every second its speed increases by 10 m s^{-1}.
6. After 1.0 s, its speed = $(0 + 10) \text{ m s}^{-1}$
   $= 10 \text{ m s}^{-1}$
   After 2.0 s, its speed = $(10 + 10) \text{ m s}^{-1}$
   $= (10 \times 2) \text{ m s}^{-1}$
   $= 20 \text{ m s}^{-1}$
   After 3.0 s, its speed = $(20 + 10) \text{ m s}^{-1}$
   $= (10 \times 3) \text{ m s}^{-1}$
   $= 30 \text{ m s}^{-1}$
   After time t, its speed = $10t \text{ m s}^{-1}$
7. The velocity-time graph and distance-time graph for a body under free fall from rest are as shown below.

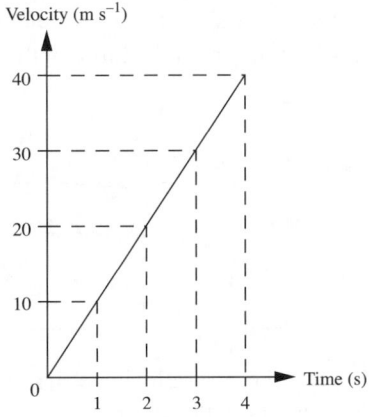

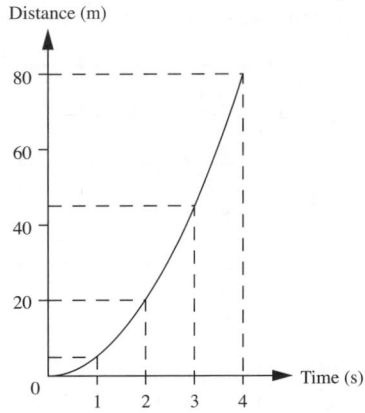

8. When an object is projected vertically upwards, the direction of the acceleration of free fall g is in the opposite direction of the motion of the object. Hence the speed of the object **decreases** at a rate of 10 m s^{-1}.
9. The figure below shows the motion of a object which is projected vertically upwards with an initial speed of 40 m s^{-1}.

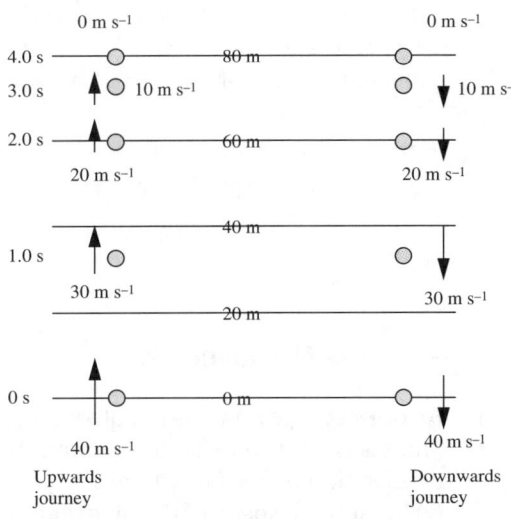

10. The speed-time graph and the distance-time graph for the upwards motion of the object are as shown below.

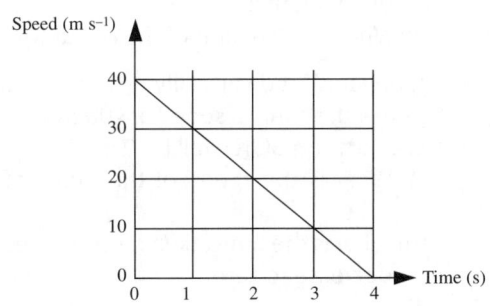

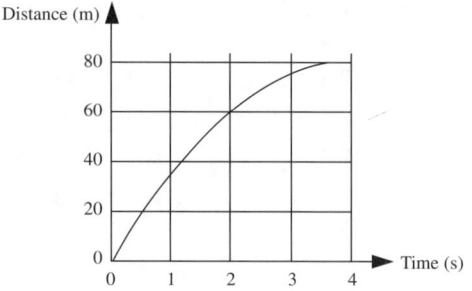

Example

A brick falls from the top of a building and takes 4.0 s to reach the ground. If the acceleration of free fall g is 10 m s^{-2}, calculate
(a) the speed of the brick when it reaches the ground;
(b) the height from which it falls.

Solution

(a) Initial speed of brick = 0 m s^{-1}
Acceleration of brick = g = 10 m s^{-2}, which means that its velocity increases by 10 m s^{-1} every second.
After 4.0 s, its speed = 4(10 m s^{-1}) = 40 m s^{-1}

(b) Height = distance travelled
= average speed × time
= $\frac{1}{2}$(0 m s^{-1} + 40 m s^{-1})(4.0 s)
= 80 m

Self Evaluation 2.3

1. An object drops from the top of a building and takes 5.0 s to reach the ground. The acceleration of free fall is 10 m s^{-2}.
   (a) What is the speed of the object after
   (i) 1.0 s, (ii) 2.0 s, (iii) 5.0 s?
   (b) What is the distance travelled after
   (i) in the first second,
   (ii) in the next second?
   (c) What is the height of the building?

2. A bullet is fired vertically upwards from a gun with an initial speed of 100 m s^{-1}. The acceleration of free fall is 10 m s^{-2}.
   (a) What is the speed of the bullet after 1.0 s?
   (b) What is the time taken for the speed to decrease to zero?
   (c) What is the speed of the bullet when it reaches the highest point?
   (d) What is the average speed of the bullet for the whole journey upwards?
   (e) What is the maximum height reached by the bullet?

2.4 Effect of Air Resistance

1. When an object falls through the air, it experiences air resistance, which opposes its motion.
2. Because of air resistance, the acceleration of an object falling in air is less than the acceleration of free fall.
3. The air resistance increases when the velocity of the object increases.
4. For an object which is released from rest and falls in air:
   – initially its velocity increases;
   – as its velocity increases, the air resistance increases;
   – the acceleration decreases;
   – finally the acceleration becomes zero, and it falls at a constant velocity known as the **terminal velocity**.
5. The graph below shows how the velocity of sphere varies with time as it falls through the air.

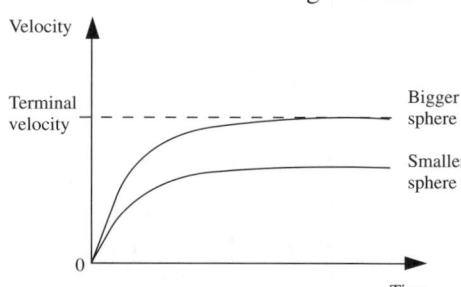

6. A bigger sphere would have a larger terminal velocity than a smaller sphere as shown in the above graph.

Example

(a) Without opening his parachute, a sky diver jumps from a plane.
   (i) Describe the motion of the sky diver as he falls through the air.
   (ii) Explain why he spread himself wide.
(b) Explain why he is able to land safely after the parachute is opened?

Solution

(a) (i) As the sky diver falls through the air:
- his velocity increases;
- the air resistance increases;
- his acceleration decreases;
- when the acceleration is zero, he falls with his terminal velocity.

(ii) The sky diver spread himself wide to increase his cross-sectional area. When the cross-sectional area increases, the air resistance increases and the terminal velocity is smaller.

(b) With the parachute opened, there is a large increase in the cross-sectional area. The air resistance becomes very large and a much lower terminal velocity is achieved.

Self Evaluation 2.4

1. The variation of the velocity v of an object falling in air with time t is as shown in the table.

t (s)	0	1.0	2.0	3.0	4.0	5.0	6.0
v (m s^{-1})	0	9.5	15.0	19.0	21.5	23.0	23.0

   (a) Calculate the average acceleration of the object
      (i) from $t = 0$ to $t = 1.0$ s;
      (ii) from $t = 1.0$ s to $t = 2.0$ s.
   (b) Explain for the difference in the acceleration in (a) (i) and (ii) above.
   (c) What is the terminal velocity?
   (d) Sketch an acceleration-time graph for the motion of the object.

REVISION EXERCISE 2

Multiple Choice Questions

1. A bus was travelling at a constant speed of 15 m s^{-1} when it passed a car which was starting the journey from rest with a constant acceleration of 2.0 m s^{-2}. After 10 s,
   A the bus was ahead of the car by 50 m.
   B the bus was ahead of the car by 130 m.
   C the car was ahead of the bus by 5 m.
   D the car was ahead of the bus by 100 m

2. The speed of a rocket increases from 500 m s^{-1} to 1500 m s^{-1} in 5.0 s. What is the distance travelled by the rocket in the 5.0 s interval?
   A 2500 m C 5000 m
   B 7500 m D 10 000 m

3. Identical blocks P and Q are placed on top of the smooth inclined planes as shown below.

    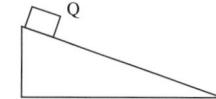

   The blocks slide down the inclined planes from rest. Which graph best represents the variation of the speeds of P and Q with time?

   A 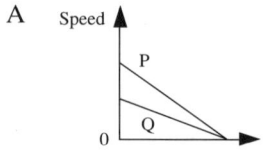   C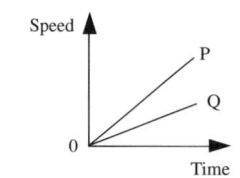

   B 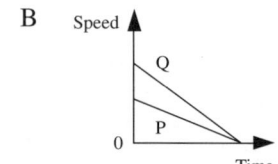   D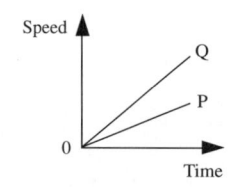

4. The distance-time graph of a body is as shown below.

   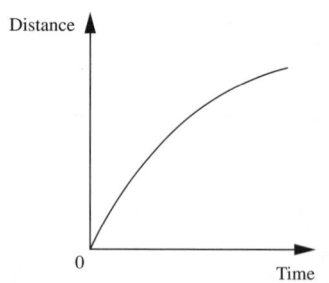

   Which of the following deductions from the graph is correct?
   A The speed of the body is constant.
   B The body is accelerating.
   C The body is decelerating.
   D The body is travelling at the terminal speed.

5. The speed-time graphs for three vehicles X, Y and Z are as shown.

   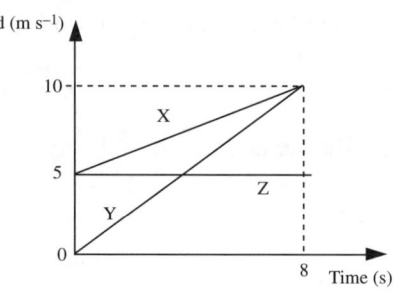

   If x, y and z are the distance travelled by X, Y and Z respectively in 8 s, which of the following comparisons is correct?
   A $x > y = z$
   B $x > y > z$
   C $x = y < z$
   D $x < z < y$

6. The distance-time graph of a body is as shown.

   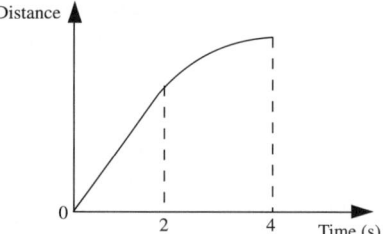

   The speed-time graph of the body is

   A 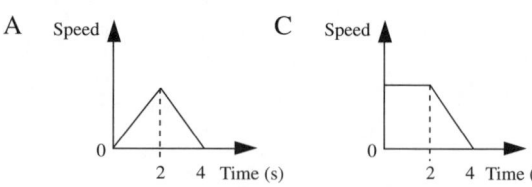 C

   B 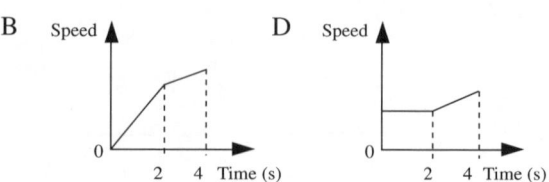 D

7. A stone is released from rest and falls freely due to gravity. If the acceleration of free fall is 10 m s^{-2}, which of the following is true?
   A The stone takes the same time to fall through the same distances.
   B After 2.0 s the acceleration is 20 m s^{-2}.
   C The time taken to fall through the first 10 m is 1.0 s.
   D For the first interval of 1.0 s, the average speed is 5 m s^{-1}.

8. A ball is projected upwards. If the air resistance is negligible, which is the distance-time graph for the up and down motion of the ball?

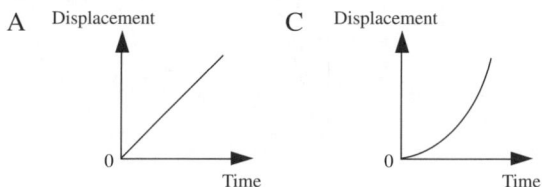

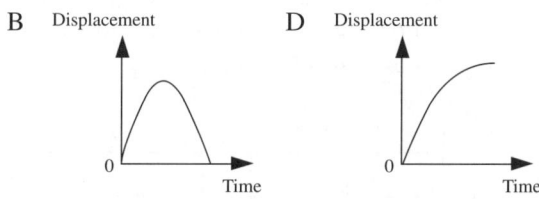

9. A raindrop falls under gravity and experiences air resistance as it falls. Which statement is true?
   A Initially, the acceleration of the raindrop is constant.
   B The speed of the raindrop decreases as it falls.
   C When the raindrop is falling with its terminal velocity, its acceleration is 10 m s^{-2}.
   D The speed becomes maximum when the raindrop is falling with its terminal velocity.

10. A body falls with air resistance near the surface of the Earth. Which quantity remains constant when the terminal velocity is reached?
    A Acceleration
    B Height above the ground
    C Air resistance
    D Resultant force

Structured Questions

Section A

1. (a) Figure 1(a) shows two cars P and Q 1400 m apart travelling toward each other along a straight road at a speed of 15 m s^{-1} and 20 m s^{-1} respectively.

   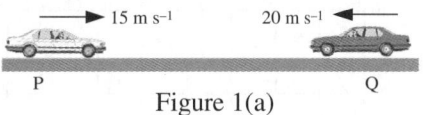
   Figure 1(a)

   (i) Calculate the time that the cars have to travel before meeting each other.
   (ii) What is the distance travelled by each car before meeting each other?

   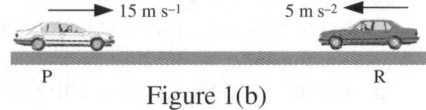
   Figure 1(b)

   (b) Figure 1(b) shows another car R at a distance of 1400 m from car P. Car R accelerates from rest at 5.0 m s^{-2} towards P.
      (i) Calculate the time that the cars P and R have to travel before meeting each other.
      (ii) What is the distance travelled by each car before meeting each other?

2. A ball is projected vertically upwards and reached the maximum height after 4.0 s and then falls back. The graph below shows the height h of the ball above the ground during its motion.

   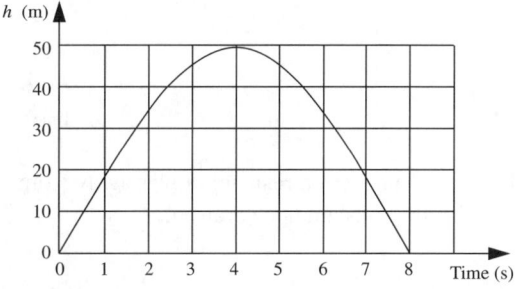

   From the graph,
   (a) determine the greatest height reached by the ball.
   (b) describe how the speed of the ball changes over the first 4.0 s of its motion. Given a reason for your answer.
   (c) determine the average speed of the ball over the first 1.0 s of the motion.
   (d) find the speed of the ball at the highest point.
   (e) determine the time taken for the ball to fall back to the ground from the highest point.

3. The distance s of an object from a point at various time t is as shown in the graph.

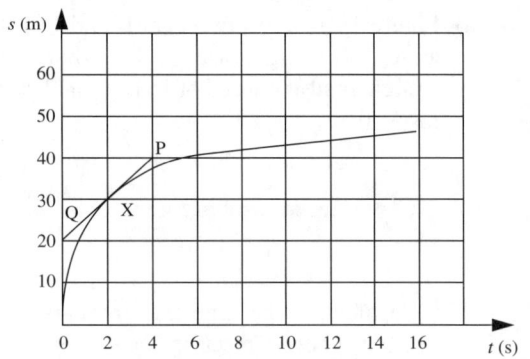

(a) The line PQ is tangential to the curve at the point X.
   (i) What physical quantity is represented by the gradient of the line PQ?
   (ii) Use the graph to determine the value of this quantity.
(b) Calculate the speed of the object during the last 10 s of its motion.
(c) Describe how the speed of the object changes during the motion
(d) On the axes below, sketch the speed-time for the motion of the object.

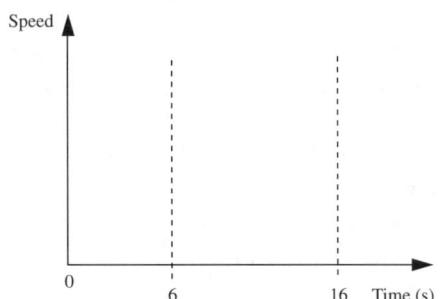

4. A car starts from rest and moves away from a point O with constant acceleration.

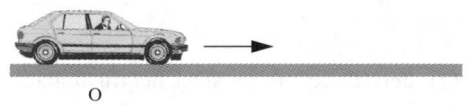

On the axes provided, sketch graphs that describe the motion of the car.

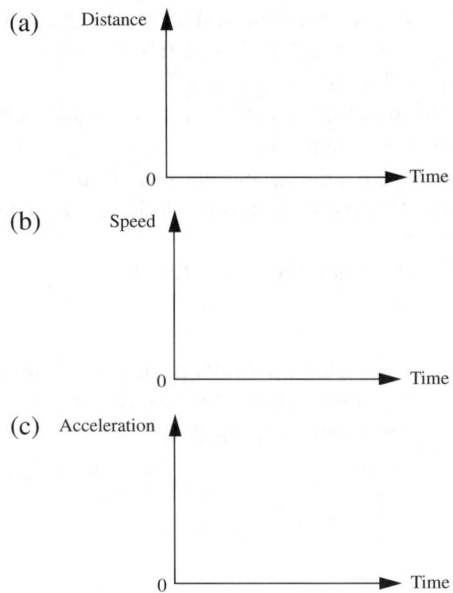

(a) Distance vs Time
(b) Speed vs Time
(c) Acceleration vs Time

5. A parcel attached to a parachute is released from a plane flying at a height h. The figure shows the speed-time graph of the parcel. The parcel takes 16 s to reach the ground.

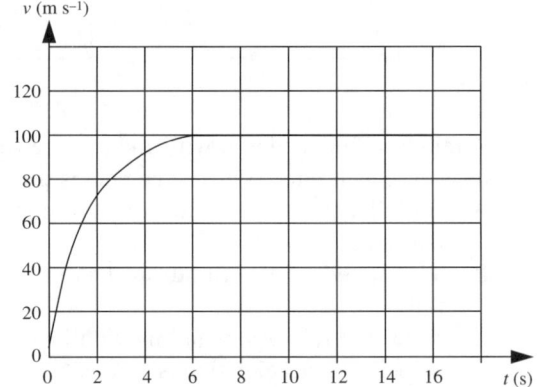

(a) Describe and explain the changes in
   (i) the speed of the parcel;
   (ii) the acceleration of the parcel.
(b) What is the terminal velocity of the parcel?
(c) Use the information in the graph to calculate an approximate value of h.
(d) Copy the above figure and on the same axes, sketch the speed-time graph of the parcel if it is released from the plane without a parachute. Label your curves clearly.
(e) Account for any change in the speed-time graph.

Section B

1. The telegraph poles beside a railway track are uniformly spaced at a distance of 20 m apart. A student in a train notes down the time that the train passes each pole as the train moves from rest. The readings are recorded in the table below.

Pole number	0	1	2	3	4	5	6	7
Distance travelled (m)	0	20	40					
Time taken (s)	0	3.2	4.5	5.5	6.3	7.1	7.7	8.4

   (a) Complete the table by filling in the distance travelled by the train when it passes each telegraph pole. The first three readings had been filled for you.
   (b) Draw a distance-time graph for the motion of the train.
   (c) From the shape of the graph you draw, explain the change in the speed of the train.
   (d) Calculate an average speed of the train when it moves from the sixth telegraph pole to the seventh pole.

2. (a) A plane P is at rest at one end of the runway. It accelerates at 12 m s^{-2} and must attain a speed of 108 m s^{-1} before it can take off.

   Calculate
   (i) the time taken for the plane to reach the take-off speed;
   (ii) the minimum length of the runway.
   (b) Another plane Q has the same acceleration, but required twice the speed to take off. What is the minimum length of the runway required by plane Q?
   (c) From your answers to (a)(ii) and (b) above, deduce how the minimum length L of the runway depends on the take-off speed v.

Data-based Question

3.

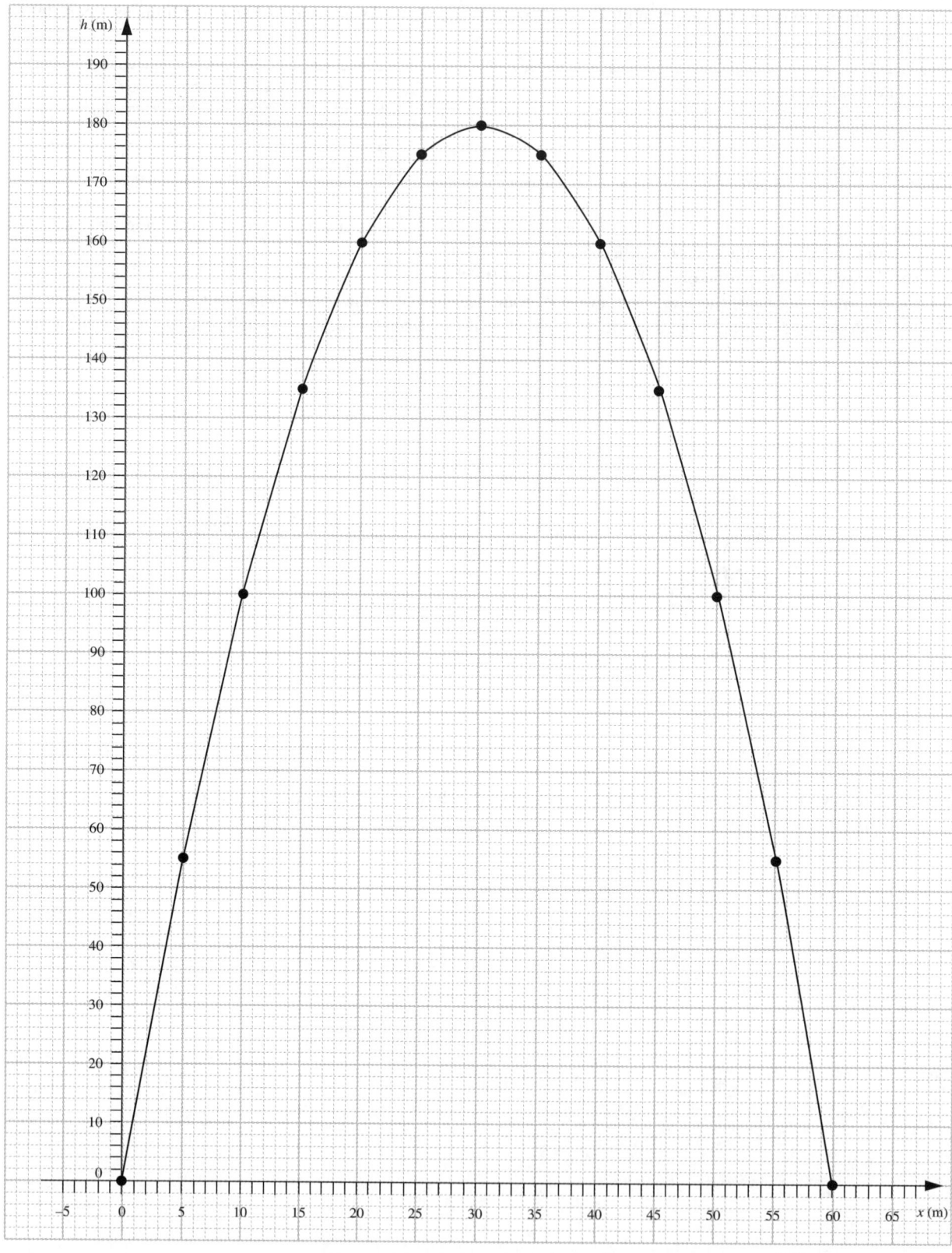

The figure above is a multi-flash photograph of a ball which is projected at an angle to the horizontal. The position of the ball is captured every 1.0 s.

(a) Read from the graph, the horizontal distance x and the height h of the ball above the ground when the time $t = 0$ s, 1 s, 2 s, 3 s, ..., 12 s. Record the readings in the table below.

t (s)	0	1	2	3	4	5	6	7	8	9	10	11	12
x (m)													
h (m)													

(b) From the values of x recorded in the table, what can you deduce about the horizontal distance travelled by the ball in each interval of 1 s? Give a numerical value for the horizontal distance travelled per second.

(c) From the values of h recorded in the table, what can you deduce about the vertical speed of the ball during the upwards motion? Suggest a reason for the change in the vertical speed of the ball.

(d) At the highest point in the motion of the ball, what is
 (i) the horizontal speed of the ball;
 (ii) the vertical speed of the ball?

CHAPTER 3
Dynamics

3.1 Forces

1. A force is a push or a pull.
2. Force is a vector quantity. It has both magnitude and direction.
3. The unit of force is the newton (N).
4. In general a body can have several forces acting on it at the same time.

Balanced Forces

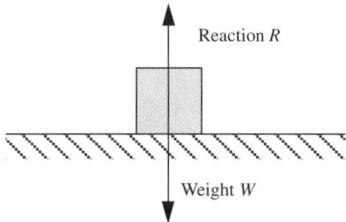

Resultant force = $R - W = 0$

5. An object on the table experiences:
   (i) a downwards force due to gravity known as its weight W and;
   (ii) an upwards force, which is the reaction R of the table on the object.
6. The reaction R and the weight W have the same magnitude but act in opposite directions. Hence the resultant force on the body is zero.
7. The forces W and R acting on the body are **balanced forces**.
8. One **effect** of balanced force as shown in this example is that the body **remains stationary**.

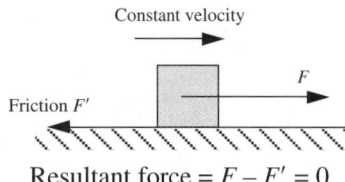

Resultant force = $F - F' = 0$

9. The above figure shows a block on a table moving with a constant velocity when it is pulled by a force F.
10. The frictional force F' between the block and the table has the same magnitude as F but is in the opposite direction. Therefore F and F' are balanced forces.
11. Hence another effect of balanced forces on a body is that the **body moves with constant velocity**.
12. In general the forces acting on a body are balanced if the **resultant force** is zero. The body is said to be in **equilibrium**.

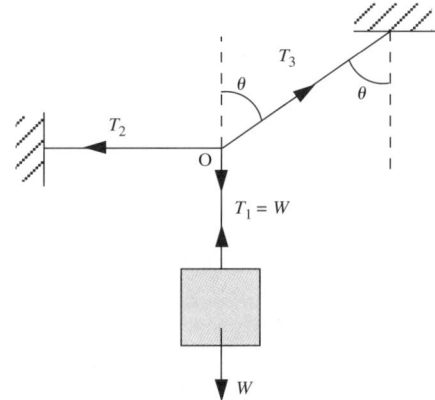

13. When a block of weight W hangs in equilibrium as shown above, the force T_1 is
$$T_1 = W$$
14. Since the point O is stationary, the forces T_1, T_2 and T_3 in the strings are in equilibrium. Then the vector sum is
$$\mathbf{T}_1 + \mathbf{T}_2 + \mathbf{T}_3 = 0$$
15. The vector diagram below shows the vectors $\mathbf{T}_1$, $\mathbf{T}_2$ and $\mathbf{T}_3$ forming a closed triangle.

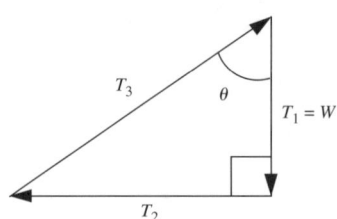

16. Using $\tan\theta = \dfrac{T_2}{W}$, $T_2 = W\tan\theta$

    $\cos\theta = \dfrac{W}{T_3}$, $T_3 = \dfrac{W}{\cos\theta}$

> ### Problem Solving Technique
> When three forces act on a point are in equilibrium, the three forces can be represented in magnitude and directions by the sides of a triangle.
>
> Tips for drawing the triangle of forces.
> 1. Start with the force which is either horizontal or vertical – example T_1 in the above figure.
> 2. Continue with the second force, the directions of the forces must follow – T_2
> 3. Complete the triangle, change the lengths of the sides if necessary so that the directions of the forces in the triangle are parallel with their respective directions.
> 4. Mark the angle θ correctly in the triangle.
> 5. Use sine, cosine or tangent functions to find the unknown forces.

Example
A block of weight 12 N is stationary on a smooth inclined plane when a horizontal force F acts on it. The plane is inclined at an angle of 30° to the horizontal.

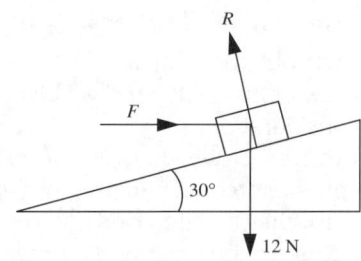

By drawing a vector diagram, find the magnitude of
(a) the force F, and;
(b) the reaction R of the plane on the block.

Solution

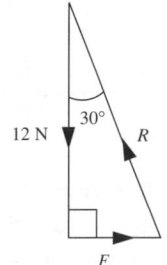

(a) $\tan 30° = \dfrac{F}{12\text{ N}}$

   $F = (12\text{ N})(\tan 30°)$
   $= 6.9\text{ N}$

(b) $\cos 30° = \dfrac{12\text{ N}}{R}$

   $R = \dfrac{12\text{ N}}{\cos 30°}$
   $= 14\text{ N}$

Unbalanced forces

17. Forces acting on a body are unbalanced if the resultant force is **not zero**.
18. The effects of unbalanced forces on an object are as shown in the figures below.
    (a) Object is at rest initially.

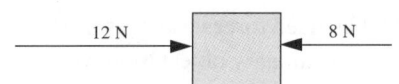

Resultant force = (12 N − 8 N) = 4 N
Effect: Object accelerates from rest in the direction of the resultant force.

(b) Moving object.
    (i)

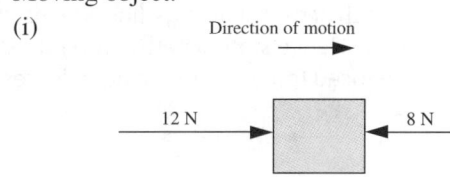

Resultant force = (12 N − 8 N) = 4 N
Effect: Object accelerates.

(ii)

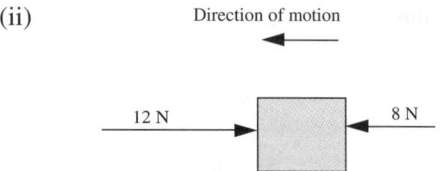

Resultant force = (12 N − 8 N) = 4 N
Effect: Object decelerates because the resultant force opposes the motion of the object.

(iii)

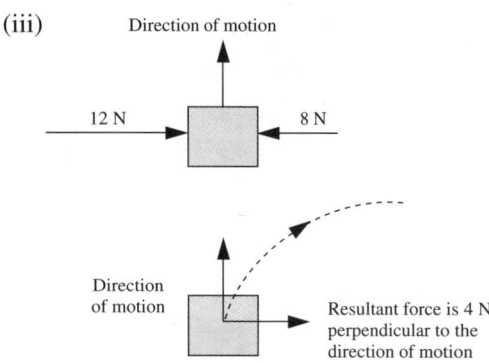

Effect: Direction of motion changes.

19. Unbalanced forces can change the motion of an object.
Unbalanced forces can cause:
– a stationary object to move;
– the speed of an object to increase;
– the speed of an object to decrease;
– the direction of motion to change.

Self Evaluation 3.1

1. In each of the followings, find the resultant force. Hence state whether the forces are balanced forces or unbalanced forces.

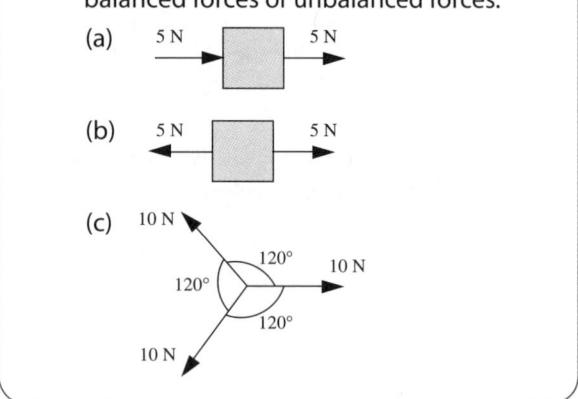

2. A load of 6.0 N hanging from a string is pulled by a force F until the string makes an angle of 60° with the vertical as shown in the figure.

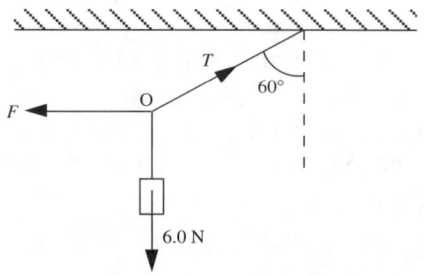

By drawing a vector diagram to scale, determine the magnitude of (a) the force F and (b) the tension T in the string.

3.2 Free-body Diagram

1. The effect of unbalanced forces on an object is summarised by **Newton's second law of motion**.

   Resultant force = mass × acceleration
   $$F = ma$$

2. To apply the equation $F = ma$, we draw a free-body diagram. A **free-body diagram** shows all the forces that act on the body, isolated from other bodies.

> ### Problem Solving Technique
> In solving problems using $F = ma$,
> (i) – draw a free-body for the object under consideration.
> – the free-body diagram should not contain forces acting on other objects.
> – mark the direction of the acceleration a to be in the positive direction, which is the direction of motion.
> (ii) apply the equation $F = ma$, where F is the resultant force on the mass m in the direction of the acceleration.

Example
Each of the diagrams shows the forces on an object of mass 2.0 kg. Find the acceleration of the object.

(a)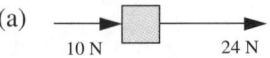

(b)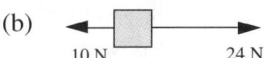

(c)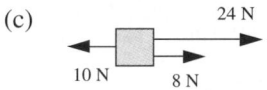

Solution
(a)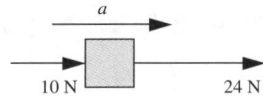

$$F = ma$$
$$24 \text{ N} + 10 \text{ N} = (2.0 \text{ kg})a$$
$$\text{Acceleration } a = \frac{34 \text{ N}}{2.0 \text{ kg}}$$
$$= 17 \text{ m s}^{-2}$$

(b)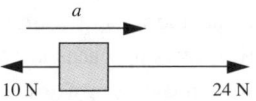

$$F = ma$$
$$24 \text{ N} - 10 \text{ N} = (2.0 \text{ kg})a$$
$$\text{Acceleration } a = \frac{14 \text{ N}}{2.0 \text{ kg}}$$
$$= 7 \text{ m s}^{-2}$$

(c)

$$F = ma$$
$$24 \text{ N} + 8 \text{ N} - 10 \text{ N} = (2.0 \text{ kg})a$$
$$\text{Acceleration } a = \frac{22 \text{ N}}{2.0 \text{ kg}}$$
$$= 11 \text{ m s}^{-2}$$

Example
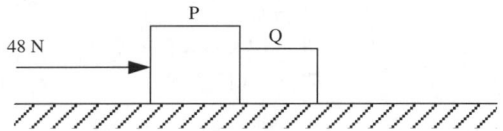

Two blocks P and Q of mass 8 kg and 4 kg respectively rest on a smooth surface. A force of 48 N pushes on block P.
(a) Find the acceleration of the blocks.
(b) Calculate the force that P pushes on Q.

Solution
(a) To find the common acceleration, consider P and Q as a single block of mass (8 + 4 = 12 kg). The free-body diagram is as shown below.

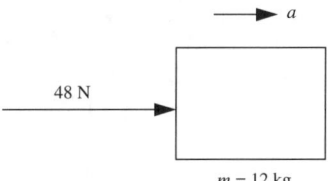

$$F = ma$$
$$48 \text{ N} = (12 \text{ kg})a$$
$$\text{Acceleration } a = 4.0 \text{ m s}^{-2}$$

(b) F is the force of P on Q and the force of Q on P is F' which is of the same magnitude as F but in the opposite direction.

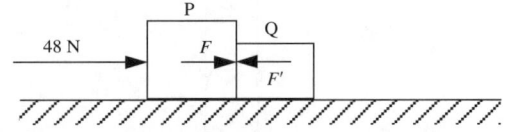

The free-body diagrams for P and Q are as shown below.

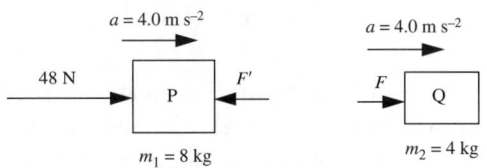

Using the free-body diagram for P

$$F = ma$$
$$48 \text{ N} - F' = (8 \text{ kg})(4.0 \text{ m s}^{-2})$$
$$F' = 16 \text{ N}$$

Alternatively, using the free-body diagram for Q

$$F = ma$$
$$F = (4 \text{ kg})(4.0 \text{ m s}^{-2})$$
$$F' = 16 \text{ N}$$

Example
Two loads P and Q of mass 6 kg and 4 kg respectively are attached to the ends of a string that passes over a smooth pulley as shown in the figure. The system is released from rest.

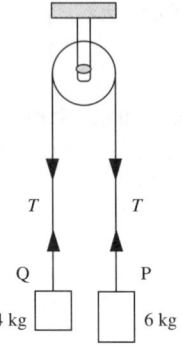

Calculate
(a) the acceleration of the masses;
(b) the tension T in the string.

Solution
The figure shows all the forces on the system.

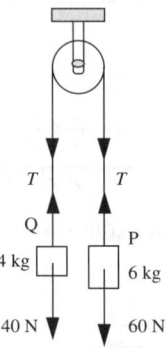

(a) Since the weight of P is greater, it accelerates downwards and Q accelerates upwards with acceleration of the same magnitude a. To determine the value of a, consider P and Q together. The tension T in the string is an internal force. The resultant force on the total mass of $(6 + 4)$ kg is $(60 - 40)$ N.

$$F = ma$$
$$(60 \text{ N} - 40 \text{ N}) = (10 \text{ kg})a$$
$$\text{Acceleration } a = 2.0 \text{ m s}^{-2}$$

(b) The separate free-body diagrams for P and Q are as shown below.

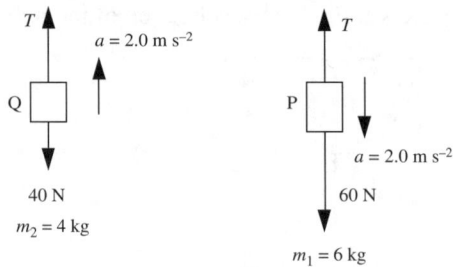

Using the free-body diagram for Q,

$$F = ma$$
$$T - 40 \text{ N} = (4 \text{ kg})(2.0 \text{ m s}^{-2})$$
$$\text{Tension } T = 48 \text{ N}$$

Alternatively, using the free-body diagram for P,

$$F = ma$$
$$60 \text{ N} - T = (6 \text{ kg})(2.0 \text{ m s}^{-2})$$
$$\text{Tension } T = 48 \text{ N}$$

Example
A spring balance is used to measure the weight of an apple of mass 200 g in a lift.
What is the reading of the spring balance
(a) when the lift is stationary?
(b) when the lift accelerates upwards at 2.0 m s^{-2}?
(c) when the lift moves upwards at constant speed?
(d) when the lift is moving upwards but decelerates at 3.0 m s^{-2}?
(Use acceleration of free fall $g = 10$ m s^{-2})

Solution
(a) The reading of the spring balance T is the tension in the string.

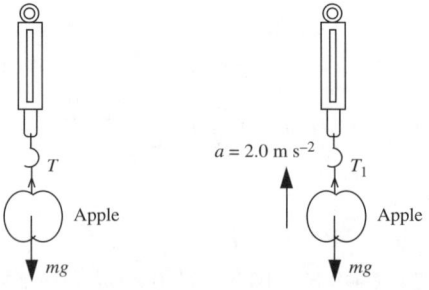

(i) When the lift is stationary
(ii) When the acceleration of the lift is a upwards.

When the lift is stationary,
$T = mg$ (200 g = 0.200 kg)
$= (0.200 \text{ kg})(10 \text{ m s}^{-2})$
$= 2.00 \text{ N}$

(b) When the lift accelerates upwards at the rate of 2 m s^{-2}
Using $F = ma$
$$T_1 - mg = ma$$
$$T_1 = m(g + a)$$
$$= (0.200 \text{ kg})(10 \text{ m s}^{-2} + 2.0 \text{ m s}^{-2})$$
$$= 2.40 \text{ N}$$

(c) When the speed is constant, acceleration, $a = 0$.
From (b) above,
$$T - mg = ma$$
$$T - mg = 0$$
$$T = mg$$
$$= 2.00 \text{ N (from (a))}$$

(d)

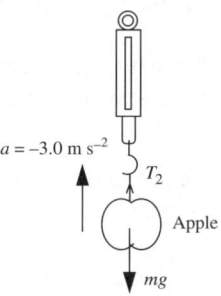

When the deceleration of the lift is a

When the lift decelerates at a rate of 3.0 m s^{-2},
$$a = -3.0 \text{ m s}^{-2}$$
$$F = ma$$
$$T_2 - mg = m(-3.0 \text{ m s}^{-2})$$
$$T_2 = m(g - 3.0 \text{ m s}^{-2})$$
$$T_2 = (0.200 \text{ kg})(10 \text{ m s}^{-2} - 3.0 \text{ m s}^{-2})$$
$$T_2 = 1.40 \text{ N}$$

Self Evaluation 3.2

1.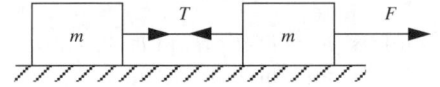

Two equal masses m are connected by an inextensible string and move across a smooth horizontal surface with uniform acceleration, when pulled by a force F. The tension T in the connecting string is

A zero. B F. C $\dfrac{F}{2}$. D $2F$.

2. A 2 kg mass and a 3 kg mass are connected by an inextensible string and pulled by a force of 20 N on a horizontal surface.

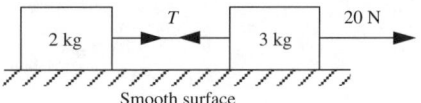

What is the tension T in the connecting string?

A 8 N   B 12 N   C 10 N   D 20 N

3.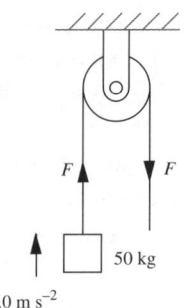

A mass of 50 kg is raised vertically using a smooth pulley. What is the force F which is required to move the mass up with an acceleration of 4.0 m s^{-2}? ($g = 10$ m s^{-2})

A 200 N   C 300 N
B 500 N   D 700 N

3.3 Friction

1. **Friction** is the force that opposes the relative motion of one surface over another.
2. Friction between two surfaces depends on:
   - the nature of surfaces in contact. Friction is greater if the surfaces are rough.
   - the force pressing on the surface together. On a horizontal surface, the weight of the object presses the object onto the horizontal surface.
3. Friction is independent of:
   - the area of contact between the surfaces;
   - the relative velocity between the two surfaces.

4. Friction is needed:
   - to prevent motion.
     Friction can prevent an object on an incline plane from sliding down.

     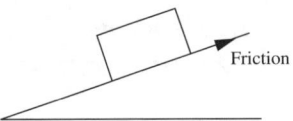

   - to produce motion.
     Friction between the wheels of a car and the road enables the car to move forward. When you walk, friction between your feet and the floor enables you to move forward.

5. Methods of reducing friction.
   (a) Lubricate the surfaces in contact with oil or grease.
   (b) Use ball bearings or rollers.
   (c) Separate the surfaces with a cushion of air.

6.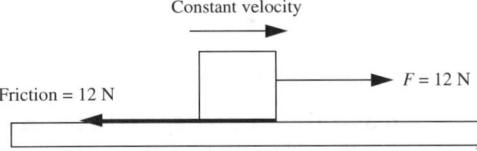

When an object is pulled by a force F and it moves at a constant velocity across a rough surface, the frictional force on the object equals the applied force F but acts in the opposite direction.

Example
When a table of mass 20 kg is pushed across the floor with a force of 80 N, it moves at a uniform velocity. Calculate the force required to push the table across the floor with an acceleration of 0.40 m s^{-2}.

Solution

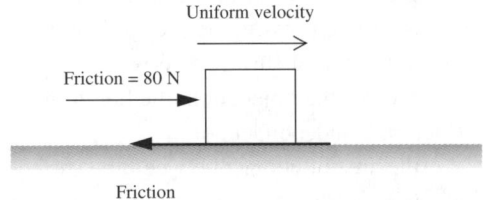

When the table is pushed across the floor with uniform velocity,
friction = force applied
= 80 N

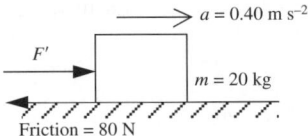

When the acceleration a is 0.40 m s^{-2},
$$F = ma$$
$$F' - 80 \text{ N} = (20 \text{ kg})(0.40 \text{ m s}^{-2})$$
Force required $F' = 80 \text{ N} + 8 \text{ N}$
$$= 88 \text{ N}$$

Self Evaluation 3.3

1. A worker pushes a heavy box of mass 80 kg at a uniform velocity of 0.20 m s^{-1} across the floor with a force of 200 N.
   (a) What is the frictional force acting on the box?
   (b) What force is required to push the box at an acceleration of 0.20 m s^{-2} across the floor?

2. Give three examples in everyday life where friction is beneficial.

3.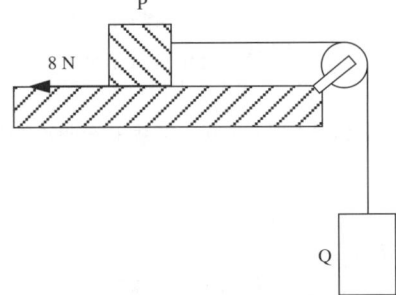

   A block P of mass 2.0 kg which is on a table is connected to a block Q of mass 4.0 kg by an inelastic string. Friction between the block P and the table is 8 N. The system is released from rest.
   Calculate
   (a) the acceleration of blocks P and Q;
   (b) the tension in the string.

REVISION EXERCISE 3

Multiple Choice Questions

1. A point is subjected to three forces F_1, F_2 and F_3 which are in equilibrium. Which triangle represents the equilibrium of the three forces?

   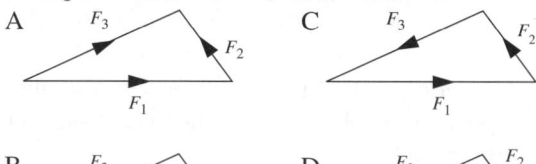

   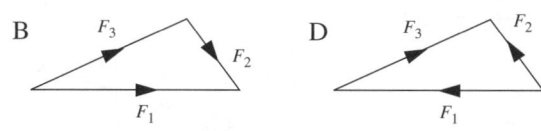

2. Which of the following objects is under the action of balanced forces?
   A An object moving with constant velocity.
   B An object moving with constant acceleration.
   C An object moving in a circle with constant speed.
   D An object moving from rest.

3. Which statement is true about an object which is under the action of three unbalanced forces?
   A The resultant force is zero
   B The object accelerates.
   C The object remains stationary.
   D The object moves with constant velocity.

4. A load of weight W hangs from a string as shown in the figure below.

   The balanced forces W, F and T is represented by the triangle

   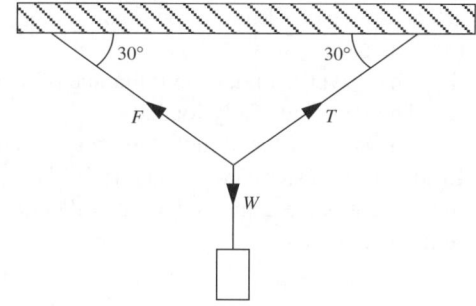

   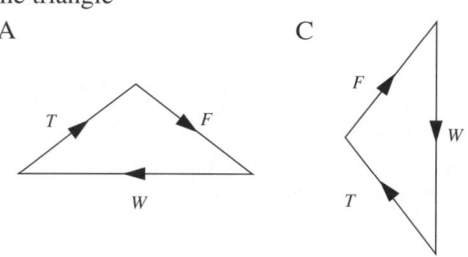

   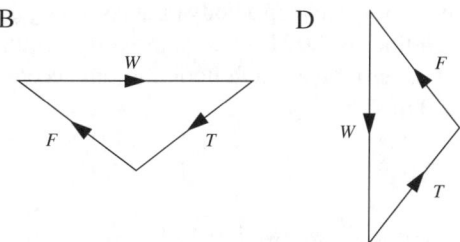

5. Two bodies P and Q on a smooth table are of masses 2.0 kg and 3.0 kg respectively. They are connected by an inelastic string and Q is pulled by a force of 15.0 N. The tension T in the string is
   A 2.0 N.   C 6.0 N.
   B 4.0 N.   D 10.0 N.

6. A block P is pulled with a spring balance at a constant velocity of 0.20 m s^{-1} on the table. The spring balance reads 8.0 N. An identical block is placed on top of P and the blocks are pulled at a constant velocity of 0.10 m s^{-1} on the table. What is the reading of the spring balance?
   A 4.0 N   C 12.0 N
   B 8.0 N   D 16.0 N

7. The frictional force between the tyres of a car and the road increases when
   A there are more passengers in the car.
   B the speed of the car increases.
   C the surface area of the tyres in contact with the road increases.
   D the road is wet.

8. The frictional force between two solid surfaces can be reduced by
   A decreasing the surface area in contact.
   B having a layer of air between the surfaces.
   C decreasing the relative velocity between the surfaces.
   D increasing the pressure between the surfaces.

9. The friction between a body of mass 3.5 kg and the rough floor is 4.0 N. What is the force required to push it across the rough floor with an acceleration of 2.0 m s^{-2}?
   A 3.0 N   C 11.0 N
   B 7.0 N   D 14.0 N

10. The figure shows two blocks P and Q of the same mass being pushed across a rough horizontal surface by a constant force F. After some time t_1, the block Q drops off but the force remains the same.

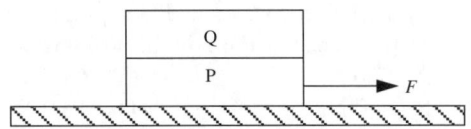

Which graph shows correctly how the speed v of the block P varies with time t?

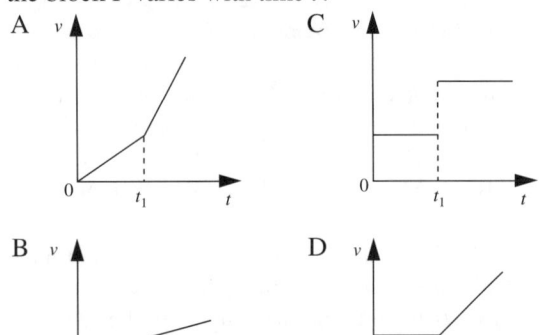

Structured Questions

Section A

1. A light spring balance is attached to two strings that passes over smooth pulleys as shown in the figure. Loads of masses m_1 and m_2 are attached to the ends of the strings.

   What is the reading of the spring balance
   (a) if $m_1 = m_2 = 4.0$ kg?
   (b) if $m_1 = 6.0$ kg and $m_2 = 4.0$ kg?
   (Acceleration of free fall $g = 10$ m s^{-2})

2. Two forces of 6 N act on a point.
   (a) With the help of a labelled diagram, explain how the two forces must act to produce a resultant force of magnitude
       (i) 0 N;   (ii) 12 N and; (iii) 6 N.
   (b) Explain why it is not possible to obtain a resultant force of 15 N from the two forces of 6 N.

3. A set of traffic lights is suspended from the mid-point of a cable AC across the road as shown in the figure below.

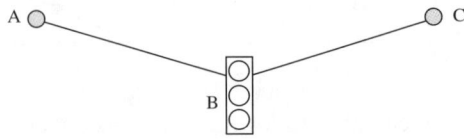

   (a) Explain why the sections AB and BC of the cable cannot be horizontal.
   (b) The weight of the set of traffic lights is 150 N and the angle between the two sections AB and BC of the cable is 120°. Draw a scale vector diagram to determine the tension in each section of the cable.

4. The reaction time of a driver is the time interval between the instant that he sees the traffic lights turning red and the instant that he steps on the brakes. The stopping distance of a vehicle is the total distance travelled during the reaction time of the driver plus the distance travelled by the vehicle after the brakes are applied.
   Explain how the stopping distance of a vehicle is affected in each of the followings.
   (a) The road is wet.
   (b) The driver is under the influence of alcohol.
   (c) The vehicle is fully loaded.
   (d) The tyres of the vehicle are under inflated.
   In all the cases, assume that the initial speed of the vehicle is the same and all the other conditions remain unchanged.

5. Describe and explain the effect of the forces on each of the bodies shown below.
   (a) Stationary body

   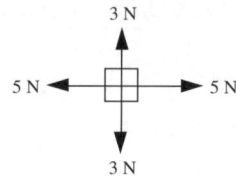

   (b) Direction of motion

   5 N ← □ → 5 N

   (c) Direction of motion

   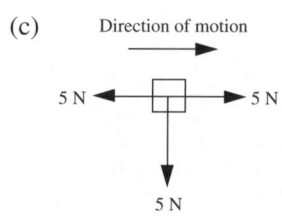

   (d) Direction of motion

   8 N ← □ → 5 N

Section B

1. A car of mass 800 kg moves along a horizontal road at a constant velocity of 10 m s^{-1}. The driving force of the car is 500 N.
   (a) What is the combined air resistance and friction that oppose the motion of the car?
   (b) The driving force is then increased to 900 N. Determine the acceleration of the car.
   (c) The driving force is kept constant at 900 N and the velocity-time graph of the car is as shown below.

   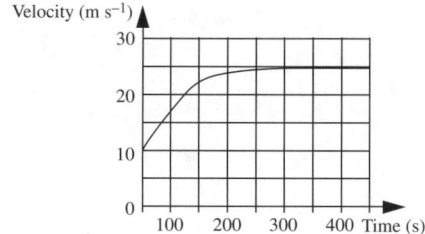

   (i) From the velocity-time graph describe and explain how the acceleration of the car varies with time.
   (ii) What is the terminal velocity of the car?
   (iii) What is the value of the combined air resistance and friction when the car travels with its terminal velocity?
   (iv) Suggest change(s) to the design of the shape of the car so that the terminal velocity of the car is greater.

2. (a) The figure below shows a horizontal force of 12 N acting on a body of mass 2.5 kg on a rough horizontal surface.

   (i) Explain why the body does not move under the action of the force of 12 N.
   (ii) Draw a free-body diagram showing all the forces on the body. Label the forces clearly and give the magnitude of each force.
   (b) The body is then pushed along the surface from A to C by a constant force of 15 N. Along the section AB, the body moves with constant velocity. There is a thin layer of oil over the section BC.

   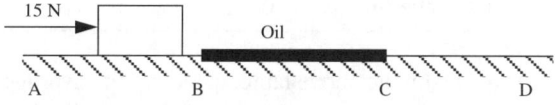

   (i) State and explain how the velocity of the body changes as it moves over the section BC.
   (ii) Once the body enters the section CD, the force of 15 N is removed. Discuss the subsequent motion of the body.

Data-based question

3. An object is released from rest from the point A on a rough inclined plane AB. It moves down the incline with constant acceleration. The object then moves along the frictionless horizontal surface BC before continuing its motion up the rough incline plane CD. The distance of the object from the point A at different time is shown in Table 1.

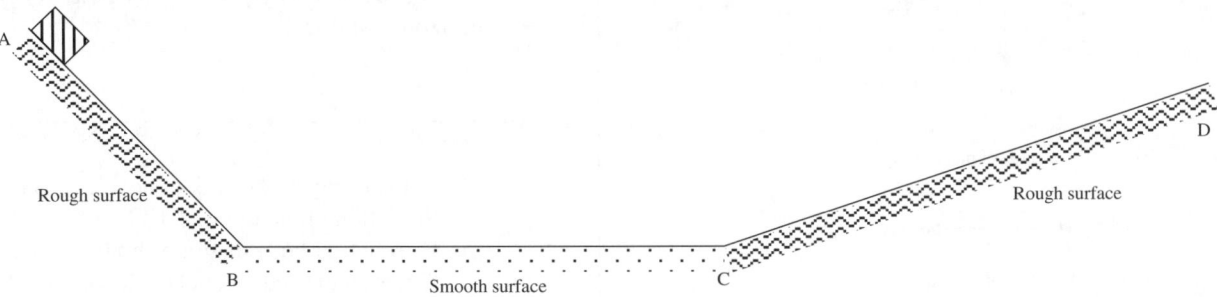

Table 1

	Along AB			Along BC		Along CD			
Time (s)	0	1	2	3	4	5	6	7	8	9
Distance (m)	0	0.2	0.8	1.8	3.0	4.2	5.3	6.2	6.9	7.4

(a) From the above table, calculate the average speed of the object for each successive 1.0 s interval when the object moves along (i) AB and (ii) CD. Write your answers in the space provided in Table 2.

Table 2

	Average speed in successive 1.0 s interval (m s^{-1})		
(i) Along AB			
(ii) Along CD			

(b) From your answers in Table 2, deduce the acceleration of the object
 (i) along AB and (ii) along CD.
(c) What is the speed of the object along BC?
(d) Draw the free-body diagram of the object when it is moving
 (i) along AB, (ii) along BC and (iii) along CD.

CHAPTER 4
Mass, Weight and Density

4.1 Mass

1. The **mass** of an object is the amount of substance in the object.
2. The mass of an object is constant. It does not change even when the object is on the Moon's surface in which the gravitational pull on the object changes.
3. The mass of an object is a measure of the inertia of the object.
4. The inertia of an object is its resistance to change in its state of rest or motion.
5. Hence the larger the mass of the object, the greater is its inertia.

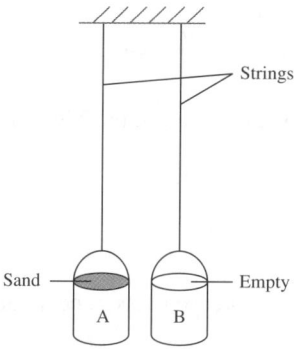

6. In the above figure, when both tins are pushed with the same force, it is easier to move the empty tin B than tin A that is filled with sand.
7. Tin A, which has a larger mass, has a larger resistance to change in its state of rest.
8. When both the tins A and B are left to swing freely, it is more difficult to stop tin A. Hence it shows that the greater the mass, the greater is the inertia.
9. Because of its inertia, an object which is at rest will remain at rest unless it is acted upon by an external force. Similarly, a moving object will continue to move in a straight line with uniform speed unless it is acted upon by an external force. This is **Newton's first law of motion**.
10. Below are situations which can be explained using the idea of inertia – the resistance to change in the state of rest or motion of an object.
    (a) When a car suddenly speeds off, its passenger is pushed back against the seat.
       – Initially the passenger is at rest.
       – When the car suddenly speeds off, the passenger tends to remain in a state of rest.
       – He is pushed by the seat.
    (b)

    A coin on top of the card falls into the glass when the card beneath it is quickly pulled away.
       – Initially the coin is at rest.
       – Because of its inertia, it remains at rest when the card is pulled away quickly beneath it.
       – Hence the coin falls into the glass.
    (c) A passenger in a fast moving car is thrown forward when the car suddenly brakes.
       – Initially the passenger is moving.
       – When the car suddenly stops, the passenger tends to continue moving because of his inertia.
       – Hence he is thrown forward.

Self Evaluation 4.1

1. A body at rest resists to change its state of rest. Which property of the body is responsible for this resistance?
   A Weight C Inertia
   B Density D Volume

2. Which of the following quantities is a measure of the inertia of a body?
   A Mass C Weight
   B Speed D Velocity

3. Which of the following has the greatest inertia?
   A A boy is running the 100 m race in 10 s.
   B A stationary car of mass 1500 kg.
   C A football is moving at a speed of 10 m s^{-1}.
   D A trolley of mass 2 kg is moving down an incline plane.

4. Lorry P is empty and a similar lorry Q is fully loaded. Between P and Q, which one would accelerate more easily? Which would be easier to stop, if both are moving at the same speed?

	Easier to accelerate	Easier to stop
A	Lorry P	Lorry Q
B	Lorry Q	Lorry P
C	Lorry Q	Lorry Q
D	Lorry P	Lorry P

4.2 Gravitational Field and Field Strength

1. When a ball is released, it drops to the floor due to the gravitational pull of the Earth.
2. There is a **gravitational field** around the Earth. A **gravitational field** is the region within which a mass experiences a force of attraction.
3. The gravitational field strength g is the *gravitational force per unit mass*.
4. On the Earth's surface, the gravitational field strength g is approximately 10 N kg^{-1}.
5. The gravitational force on
   (i) 1 kg mass is 10 N.
   (ii) 2 kg mass is 20 N.
   (iii) 3 kg mass is 30 N.
   (iv) m kg mass is mg.

6. The gravitational force on a mass is known as its **weight**. Hence the weight of a mass m is given by

   $$\text{weight} = \text{mass} \times \text{gravitational field strength}$$
   $$= mg$$

7. The gravitational field strength of the Earth decreases as the altitude increases.
8. On the surface of the Moon, the gravitational field strength is about $\frac{1}{6}$ the value of g on the Earth's surface.
9. Hence the weight W ($= mg$) of an object is not constant but changes when the value of g changes.

Example

The weight of an astronaut of mass 80 kg on the Earth's surface is

$$W = mg$$
$$= (80 \text{ kg})(10 \text{ N kg}^{-1})$$
$$= 800 \text{ N}$$

On the surface of the Moon the gravitational field strength is $g' = \frac{10}{6}$ N kg^{-1}

Weight of astronaut on the Moon is
$$= (80 \text{ kg})\left(\frac{10}{6} \text{ N kg}^{-1}\right)$$
$$= 133 \text{ N}$$

10. From the equation,

    $$\text{force} = \text{mass} \times \text{acceleration}$$

    An object of mass m experiences a gravitational force of F, which is equal to mg.
    Hence $mg = \text{mass} \times \text{acceleration}$.

    $$\frac{\text{Acceleration of object}}{\text{on the Earth's surface}} = \frac{\text{weight}}{\text{mass}}$$
    $$= \frac{mg}{m}$$
    $$= g$$
    $$= 10 \text{ m s}^{-2}$$

11. The acceleration of an object that falls freely under the action of gravitational force is known as the **acceleration due to gravity** g.
    On the Earth's surface, $g = 10 \text{ m s}^{-2}$.

Example

A stone of mass 100 g is released from rest and falls to the ground.
(a) What is the weight of the stone?
(b) What is its speed
   (i) after 1.0 s;
   (ii) after 1.0 min?
(c) If the stone takes 1.0 s to reach the ground, what is the height from which the stone is released?

Solution

(a) Weight = mg
    = $(0.100 \text{ kg})(10 \text{ N kg}^{-1})$
    = 1.0 N
(b) (i) Initial speed = 0
        Acceleration = 10 m s^{-2}
        After 1 s, speed = 10 m s^{-1}
    (ii) After 60 s,
        speed = $(60 \text{ s})(10 \text{ m s}^{-2})$
        = 600 m s^{-1}
(c) Height = average speed × time
    = $\frac{1}{2}(0 \text{ m s}^{-1} + 10 \text{ m s}^{-1})(1.0 \text{ s})$
    = 5 m

Self Evaluation 4.2

1. The gravitational field strength is the ratio
   A $\frac{\text{mass}}{\text{volume}}$.
   B $\frac{\text{gravitational force}}{\text{weight}}$.
   C $\frac{\text{gravitational force}}{\text{mass}}$.
   D $\frac{\text{mass}}{\text{weight}}$.

2. On a planet, the gravitational force on a mass of 5 kg is 20 N. The gravitational field strength on the planet is
   A 4 N kg^{-1}.   C 20 N kg^{-1}.
   B 10 N kg^{-1}.   D 100 N kg^{-1}.

3. The gravitational field strength on the Moon is 1.6 m s^{-2}. What are the acceleration of free fall for a body of mass of 2 kg and a body of mass 5 kg respectively on the Moon?

	2 kg	5 kg
A	0.8 m s^{-2}	0.32 m s^{-2}
B	1.6 m s^{-2}	1.6 m s^{-2}
C	3.2 m s^{-2}	8.0 m s^{-2}
D	2.0 m s^{-2}	5.0 m s^{-2}

4. An astronaut on the Moon has
   A the same weight and mass as on the Earth.
   B the same weight but less mass as on the Earth.
   C less weight but the same mass as on the Earth.
   D less weight and less mass as on the Earth.

5. A metal sphere is placed on a newton balance X and then on a beam balance Y. This is repeated on the surface of the Moon.

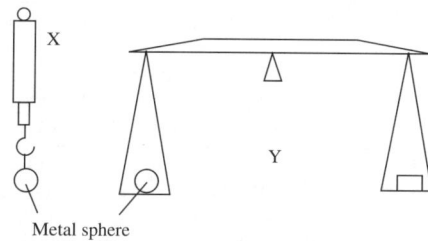
Metal sphere

On the Moon, what happen to the readings of X and Y?

	Reading of X	Reading of Y
A	no change	no change
B	decreases	no change
C	decreases	decreases
D	no change	decreases

6. A stone is released from rest from a height h. On the surface of the Earth it takes a time t to reach the ground and its speed on reaching the ground is v. When it is released from the same height h on the Moon, the time taken is t_1 and the speed is v_1. If the gravitational field strength on the Moon is $\frac{1}{6}$ that on the Earth, which of the followings is true?
   A $t_1 > t$ and $v_1 > v$
   B $t_1 < t$ and $v_1 > v$
   C $t_1 < t$ and $v_1 = v$
   D $t_1 > t$ and $v_1 < v$

4.3 Density

1. The **density** of a material is its *mass per unit volume*.

$$\text{Density} = \frac{\text{mass}}{\text{volume}}$$

$$\rho = \frac{m}{V}$$

2. Density is measured in g cm^{-3} or kg m^{-3}.
   1 g cm^{-3} = 1000 kg m^{-3}

3. **Density of common materials**

Material	Density	
	g cm^{-3}	kg m^{-3}
Water	1.0	1000
Ice	0.9	900
Air	0.0013	1.3
Petrol	0.67	670
Aluminium	2.70	2700
Mercury	13.6	13 600

4. To measure the density of a solid such as a stone.

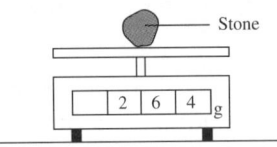

(a) Measure its mass m with a balance.

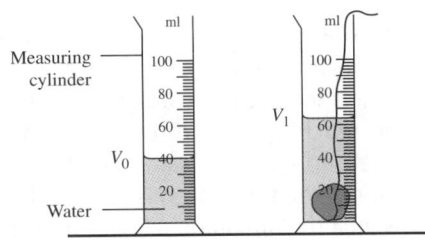

(b) Use a measuring cylinder to measure its volume.
Volume of the stone = $V_1 - V_0$

(c) Density of stone = $\dfrac{\text{mass}}{\text{volume}}$
$= \dfrac{m}{V_1 - V_0}$

5. To measure the density of a liquid.

(a)

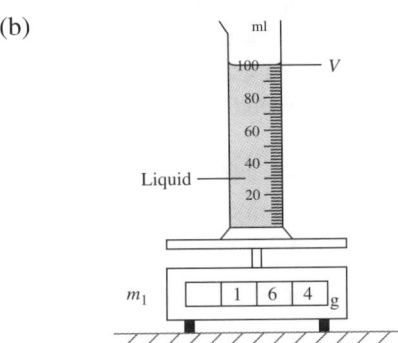

Measure the mass m_0 of an empty measuring cylinder

(b)

Fill the measuring cylinder with a volume V of the liquid and measure its mass m.
Mass of liquid = $m_1 - m_0$

(c) Density of liquid = $\dfrac{\text{mass}}{\text{volume}}$
$= \dfrac{(m_1 - m_0)}{V}$

Example
The measurements shown in the figures below were taken by a student to measure the density of sand.

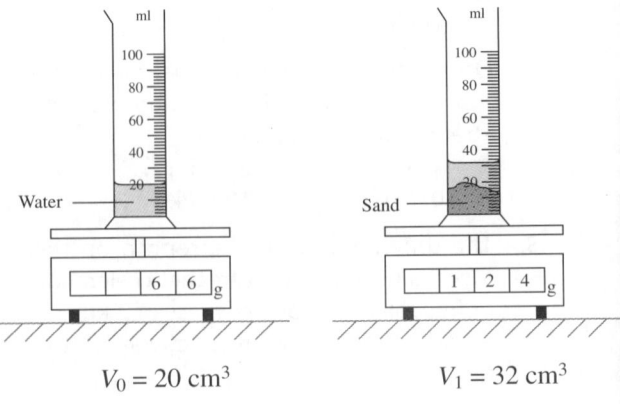

$V_0 = 20$ cm^3 $V_1 = 32$ cm^3

Calculate the density of sand.
(Density of water = 1.0 g cm^{-3})

Solution

Mass of sand m = 124 g − 66 g
   = 58 g
Volume of sand V = 32 cm^3 − 20 cm^3
   = 12 cm^3
Density of sand = $\dfrac{\text{mass}}{\text{volume}}$
   = $\dfrac{58 \text{ g}}{12 \text{ cm}^3}$
   = 4.8 g cm^{-3}

Example
A closed thin-walled plastic bottle is of mass 15 g and volume 100 cm^3. What is the **maximum** mass of sand which may be added into the bottle so that it floats freely in a liquid of density 1.2 g cm^{-3}?

Solution
When the mass of sand added is the maximum for the bottle to float freely, the density of the filled bottle is equal to the density of the liquid.
Density of (bottle + sand) = density of liquid

$$\dfrac{15 \text{ g} + m}{100 \text{ cm}^3} = 1.2 \text{ g cm}^{-3}$$
$$15 \text{ g} + m = (1.2 \text{ g cm}^{-3})(100 \text{ cm}^3)$$

Maximum mass of sand m = 105 g.

Self Evaluation 4.3

1. The mass of a measuring cylinder with its contents is determined using the balance shown in the figure below.

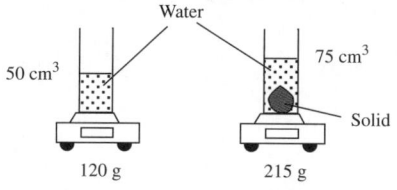

   What is the density of the solid?
   A 1.9 g cm^{-3} C 2.9 g cm^{-3}
   B 2.4 g cm^{-3} D 3.8 g cm^{-3}

2. The density of a liquid is determined by taking the measurements shown in the figure.

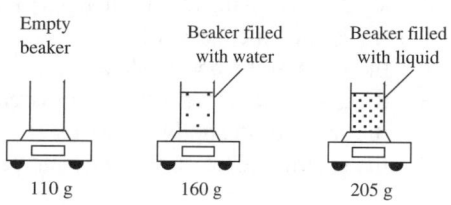

   The density of the liquid is
   A 0.90 g cm^{-3}.   C 1.90 g cm^{-3}.
   B 1.11 g cm^{-3}.   D 2.20 g cm^{-3}.

3. A metal cylinder is 25.0 cm long and its diameter is 2.00 cm. The density of the metal is 8.9 g cm^{-3}.
   (a) Name the instrument that can be used to measure
      (i) the length;
      (ii) the diameter of the cylinder.
   (b) Calculate
      (i) the volume;
      (ii) the mass of the cylinder.

REVISION EXERCISE 4

Multiple Choice Questions

1. A body that is moving resists changes to its motion. This resistance increases when
   A the mass of the body increases.
   B the gravitational field strength increases.
   C the speed of the body increases.
   D the external force on the body increases.

2. The weight of a body is given by
   A weight = density × volume.
   B weight = mass × gravitational field strength.
   C weight = mass × acceleration.
   D weight = velocity × time.

3. The gravitational field strength on the Moon is $\frac{1}{6}$ that on the Earth. When a ball is thrown vertically upwards on the Earth, the maximum height reached is H. When the ball is thrown vertical upwards with the same speed on the Moon, the maximum height reached is
   A $\frac{1}{6}H$.
   B H.
   C $6H$.
   D $12H$.

4. The mass of air in a container of volume 640 cm³ is 0.8 g. What is the density of air in kg m⁻³?
   A 1.25 kg m⁻³
   B 800 kg m⁻³
   C 1.25 × 10⁻³ kg m⁻³
   D 8.00 × 10³ kg m⁻³

5. When 500 cm³ of water is mixed with 500 cm³ of alcohol, the volume of the mixture is 918 cm³. What is the density of the mixture? (Density of water = 1.0 g cm⁻³; density of alcohol = 0.80 g cm⁻³)
   A 0.90 g cm⁻³
   B 0.92 g cm⁻³
   C 0.95 g cm⁻³
   D 0.98 g cm⁻³

6. When 2.0 cm³ of a liquid vaporised, the volume of the vapour is 2400 cm³. What is the ratio of the density of the liquid to the density of the vapour?
   A $\frac{1}{1200}$
   B $\frac{1}{2400}$
   C 240
   D 1200

7. A steel ball bearing of radius 5 mm is of weight W. What is the weight of a steel ball bearing of radius 10 mm?
   A $2W$
   B $4W$
   C $8W$
   D $16W$

8. The acceleration of free fall on Planet X is 2.0 m s⁻². The acceleration of free fall on Planet Y is 5.0 m s⁻². The mass of an object on Planet X is 20 kg. Which statement about the object is correct?
   A Its weight on Planet X is 10 N.
   B Its mass on Planet Y is 20 kg.
   C Its weight on Planet Y is 20 N.
   D Its inertia on Planet Y is greater.

9. A piece of wood floats with $\frac{1}{4}$ of its volume above the surface of water. If the density of water is 1.0 g cm⁻³, the density of the wood is
   A 0.25 g cm⁻³.
   B 0.67 g cm⁻³.
   C 0.75 g cm⁻³.
   D 1.25 g cm⁻³.

10. A cylinder is placed on a balance as shown in the figure. Water is poured into the cylinder and the reading m of the balance is recorded for different height h of water in the cylinder.

    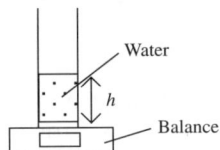

    Which graph shows correctly the variation of the balance reading m with the height h?

    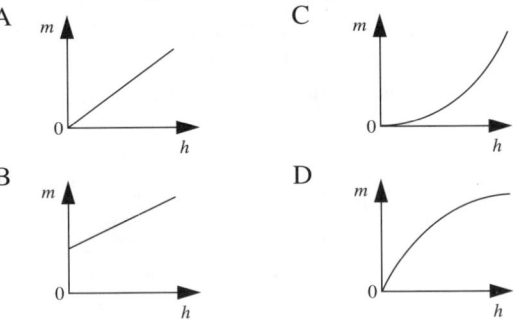

Structured Questions

Section A

1. When 1.0 cm³ of water turns into vapour, the volume is 1600 cm³. Determine the density of water vapour.
   (Density of water = 1.0 g cm⁻³)

2. 500 cm³ of brine of density 1.20 g cm⁻³ is mixed with 1000 cm³ of water. (Density of water = 1.0 g cm⁻³)
   (a) Calculate the density of the mixture. State one assumption you made in your calculation.
   (b) Would you expect the density of the mixture to be greater or less than the answer in 2(a)? Explain your answer.

3. Identical wooden cubes are placed in three different liquids A, B and C as shown in the figure below.

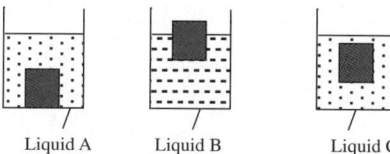

Compare the density of the wood with the densities of the liquids A, B and C. Explain your answer.

4. The figure shows the steps taken by a student to determine the density of a piece of cork.

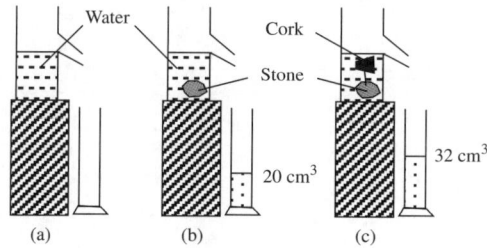

A stone is placed in the displacement can and the water displaced is collected in a measuring cylinder (Figure (b)). The piece of cork is tied to the stone and lowered into the displacement can. The volume of water displaced is as shown in figure (c). The mass of the piece of cork is 9.2 g.
   (a) Calculate
      (i) the volume of the piece of cork,
      (ii) the density of cork.
   (b) What is the purpose of the piece of stone?

Section B

1. An alloy is made of one part by mass of aluminum and two parts of copper. The densities of aluminum and copper are 2.7 g cm⁻³ and 8.9 g cm⁻³ respectively.
   (a) Calculate the mass of (i) aluminum and (ii) copper in a piece of the alloy of mass 12.0 g.
   (b) What is the volume of (i) aluminum and (ii) copper in the piece of alloy?

2. Figure 1(a) shows two simple pendulums P and Q hanging from the roof of a vehicle when the vehicle is at rest. The bob of P is a solid lead sphere and that of Q is a hollow aluminum sphere. Both the spheres are of the same size.

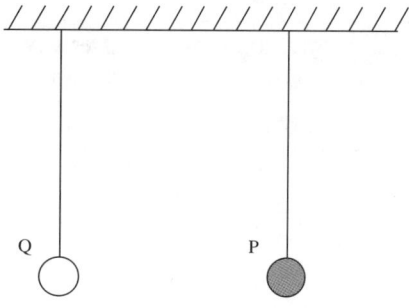

Figure 1(a)

(a) In figure 1(b), draw the positions of the pendulums when the vehicle accelerates uniformly in the direction shown. Show clearly the difference in the positions of the pendulums. Explain for the difference.

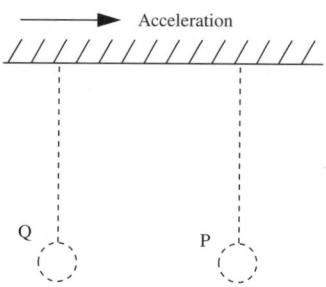

Figure 1(b)

(b) In figure 1(c), draw the positions of the pendulums when the vehicle decelerates uniformly.

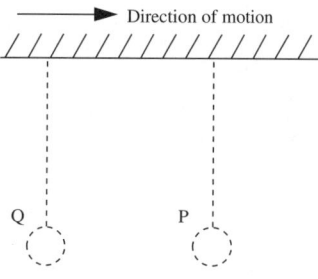

Figure 1(c)

Data-based Question

3. The purity of gold used in jewellery is measured in *carat*. Pure gold is 24 carat gold. 22 carat gold has 22 out of 24 parts by mass of gold and 5.5% of silver and 2.8% of copper.
   (a) Complete the table for a piece of 22 carat gold jewellery of mass 20 g.
   (b) Hence calculate the density of 22 carat gold.

Metal	Density ($g\ cm^{-3}$)	Percentage by mass	Mass (g)	Volume (cm^3)
Gold	19.3			
Silver	10.5	5.5%		
Copper	8.90	2.8%		

CHAPTER 5
Turning Effect of Forces

5.1 Moments

1. The turning effect of a force about a point is known as its **moment** about that point.

> Moment of a force = force × perpendicular distance from the line of action of the force to the pivot
> = Fd

2. The unit for moment of a force is newton metre (N m).

Example

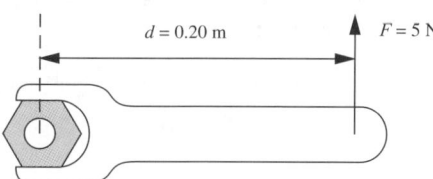

A spanner of length 0.20 m is used to loosen a nut. If the force applied is 5 N,
moment of the force = Fd
   = (5 N)(0.20 m)
   = 1.0 N m

It is easier to loosen a nut using a longer spanner because the same force generates a greater turning effect or moment.

Example

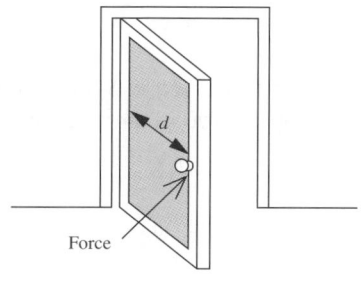

It is easier to close a heavy door by applying a force as far away as possible from the hinges so that d is larger. Thus the moment Fd is greater.

Example

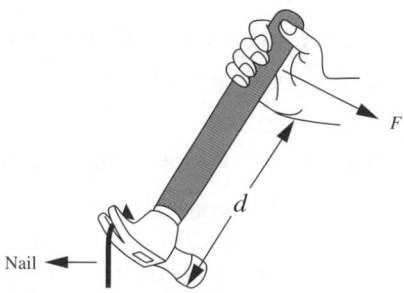

You just require a small force to pull out a nail when you use a hammer with a long handle. Again the principle of generating a large moment with a large value of d, the distance of the force from the pivot is large, even though the force is small.

Principle of moments
When a body is in equilibrium, the sum of clockwise moments is equal to the sum of anticlockwise moments about the same point.

Example

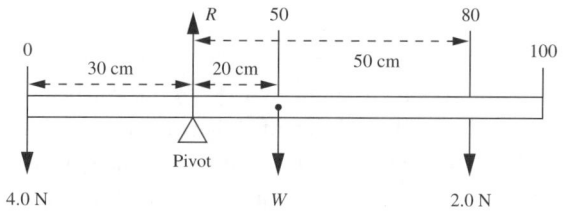

A uniform metre rule is pivoted at the 30.0 cm mark. A 4.0 N load is hung at the zero mark. To balance the metre rule horizontally a load of 2.0 N is hung at the 80.0 cm mark. Calculate
(a) the weight W of the metre rule;
(b) the normal reaction R at the pivot.

Solution

(a) Taking the moments about the pivot,

sum of clockwise = sum of anticlockwise
moments   moments

$W(20 \text{ cm}) + (2 \text{ N})(50 \text{ cm}) = (4.0 \text{ N})(30 \text{ cm})$

$W = 1.0 \text{ N}$

(b) Since the metre rule is in equilibrium, we can conclude,

sum of upward forces = sum of downward forces

$R = (4.0 + W + 2.0) \text{ N}$
$= (4.0 + 1.0 + 2.0) \text{ N}$
$= 7.0 \text{ N}$

Problem Solving Technique

In the above example, there are two unknowns: R and W.

To solve for R and W, apply two principles:

1. Principle of moments.
   Moments are taken about the pivot in order to obtain an equation that does not involve R. Hence the value of W can be found.
2. Equating sum of forces in one direction (upwards) with sum of forces in the opposite direction (downwards).

Example

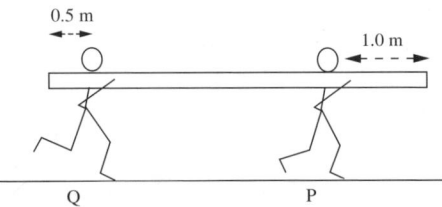

Two workers P and Q carry a uniform beam of weight 1200 N and length 4.0 m on their shoulders. P is 1.0 m from one end of the beam and Q is 0.5 m from the other end. What is the force on each of their shoulders respectively?

Solution

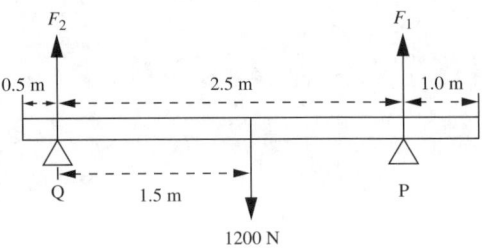

The force on P's and Q's shoulders equal the normal reaction F_1 and F_2 respectively.

Taking moments about Q,

sum of clockwise = sum of anticlockwise
moments   moments

$(1200 \text{ N})(1.5 \text{ m}) = F_1(2.5 \text{ m})$

$F_1 = 720 \text{ N}$

$F_1 + F_2 = 1200 \text{ N}$

$F_2 = 1200 \text{ N} - 720 \text{ N}$
$= 480 \text{ N}$

Self Evaluation 5.1

1. A metre rule of weight 5 N is pivoted at one end P. The rule is raised to a horizontal position and then released.

   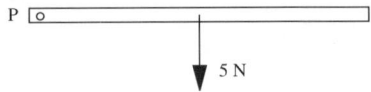

   What is the moment produced by the weight of the rule when the rule is horizontal?

2. A non-uniform rod AB of length $3L$ is placed on supports at the ends of the rod. The centre of gravity of the rod is at a distance of L from one end.

   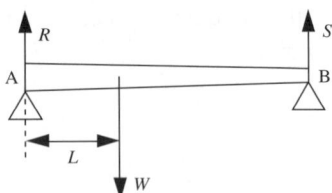

   Find the forces R and S that the supports exert on the rod in terms of W.

3. A uniform rod of length 2.0 m and weight 8.0 N is pivoted at O and a load of 3.0 N is placed at one end of the rod.

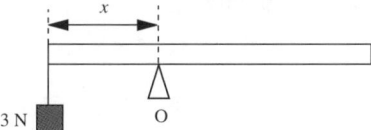

If the rod is in equilibrium, calculate
(a) the distance x from O;
(b) the reaction at the pivot.

4. A diver of weight 500 N stands at the end of a diving board which is 2.4 m long as shown in the figure.

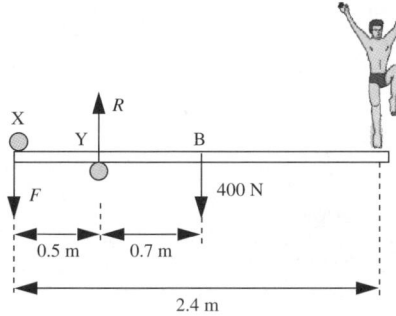

The weight of the diving board is 400 N. Calculate
(a) the force F on the board at X;
(b) the reaction R at Y.

5.2 Centre of Gravity

1. The centre of gravity (C.G.) of an object is the point where the whole weight of the object acts or seems to act.
2. The centre of gravity of some common shapes are as shown below.

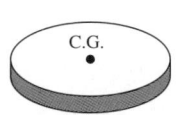

(a) Circular disc C.G. at centre of circle

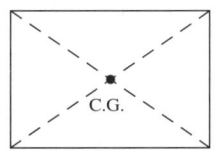

(b) A rectangular laminar

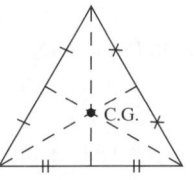

(c) A triangular laminar

Self Evaluation 5.2

1. Mark with a cross and label it C, the centre of gravity of the uniform lamina in various shapes shown below.

(a) Circular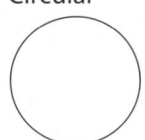

(b) Eclipse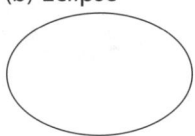

(c) Rectangle

(d) Triangle

2. The figure shows a uniform lamina. Its centre of gravity is marked C. Two holes A and B are made on the lamina.

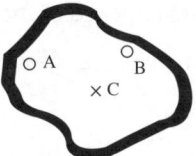

Draw diagrams to show the orientation of the lamina when it is freely suspended from a pin stuck
(a) through the hole A;
(b) through the hole B.

5.3 Stability

1. **Stability** of an object is the ability of the object to return to its original position when slightly displaced.
2. An object is more stable if:
   – its centre of gravity is lower;
   – its base area is large.

Example
(a) A Formula One racing car is more stable than a family saloon because the racing car has a low centre of gravity and a wide base.
(b) A double-decker bus is less stable because its centre of gravity is high. Passengers are not allowed to stand on the upper deck as this would raise the position of the centre of gravity.

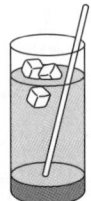

(c) A wine glass has big base to increase its stability.

(d) A punch glass has a thick glass bottom so that its centre of gravity is lowered.

Self Evaluation 5.3

1. Four identical soft drink cans are as shown below.

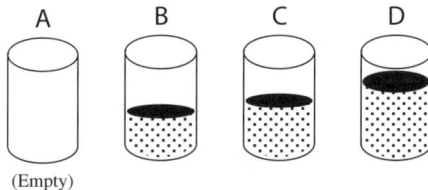

If they are knocked at the top accidentally, which is the most unlikely to topple over?

2. Explain why passengers are not allowed to stand on the upper deck of a double-decker bus.

REVISION EXERCISE 5

Multiple Choice Questions

1. A force of 12 N is required to be applied at the end of the spanner to loosen a nut.

   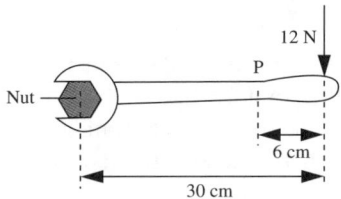

   What is the force required at P that is 6 cm from the end of the spanner to loosen the nut?
   A 12 N C 30 N
   B 15 N D 60 N

2. A uniform rod of length 30.0 cm and weight 6.0 N is pivoted at O.

   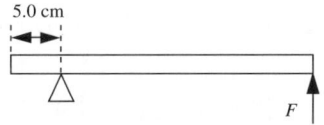

   The force F required to keep the rod horizontal is
   A 2.4 N. C 18 N.
   B 7.2 N. D 36 N.

3. A half-metre rule is pivoted at the 20 cm mark. To keep the rule in equilibrium a mass of 50 g is suspended from the 0 mark.

   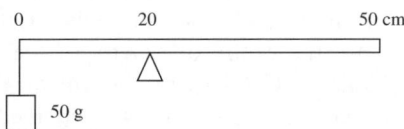

   What is the mass of the rule?
   A 33 g C 125 g
   B 100 g D 200 g

4. A load of 9.0 N is placed on a light rod which is suspended from two newton meters P and Q as shown in the figure. The length of the rod is 36.0 cm.

   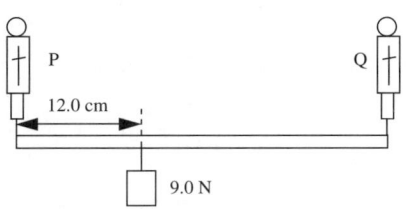

   The readings of the newton meters are
	Reading of P	Reading of Q
A	3.0 N	6.0 N
B	4.5 N	4.5 N
C	6.0 N	3.0 N
D	9.0 N	9.0 N

5. It is easier to loosen a screw using a screw driver
   A which is long.
   B which is short.
   C which has a thin handle.
   D which has a thick handle.

6. Three identical bricks are stacked on top of each other. Which arrangement is unstable?

   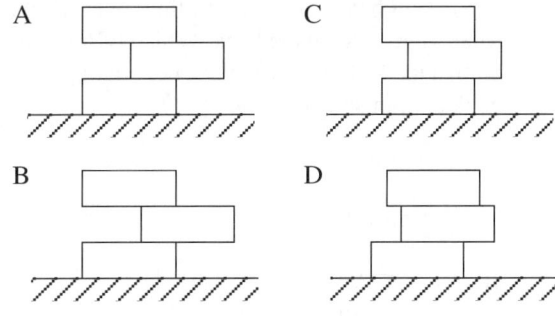

7. A uniform lamina is freely suspended from a pin through a hole O. The laminar is in equilibrium in

   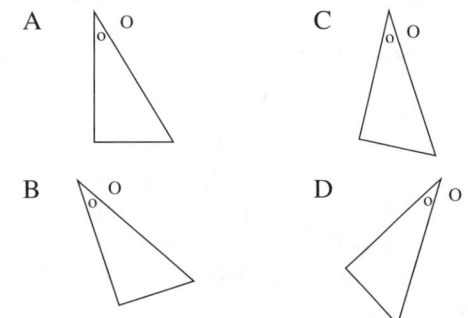

8. The centre of gravity of a spherical glass bowl filled with water is most likely at the point

   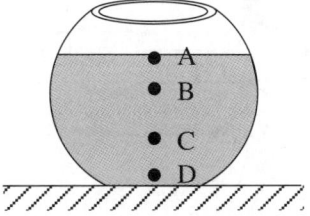

9. A metre rule is pivoted at the 50 cm mark. A force of 5.0 N acts at the 20 cm mark in the direction as shown.

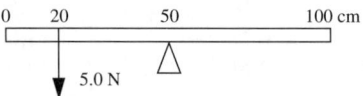

Which force would prevent the rule from turning?
A   A force of 15.0 N downwards at the 60 cm mark
B   A force of 10.0 N upwards at the 65 cm mark
C   A force of 5.0 N downwards at the 70 cm mark
D   A force of 3.0 N upwards at the 100 cm mark

10. The figures below show the outlines of four vehicles when viewed from the back. Which of the vehicles is most likely to overturn when negotiating a curved track at high speed?

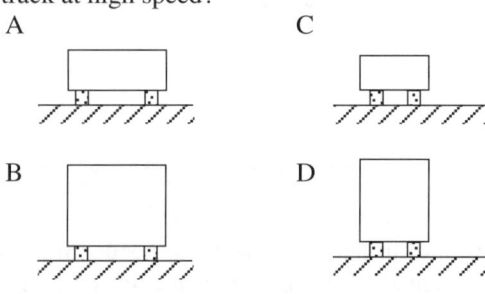

Structured Questions

Section A

1. Figure 1(a) shows how John carrying a heavy beam over his shoulder. The centre of gravity C of the beam is directly above his shoulder. Figure 1(b) shows how the beam is carried by Tom. The centre of gravity C of the beam is behind Tom's shoulder.
   (a) Mark clearly the forces exerted by John and Tom on the beam.
   (b) Use your diagram to explain whose method is better.

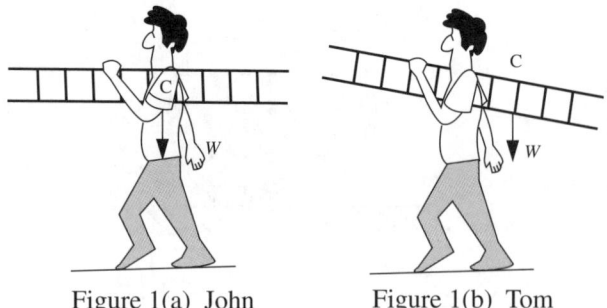

Figure 1(a) John   Figure 1(b) Tom

2. A uniform rod of length 0.80 m is freely pivoted about its centre of gravity C. Forces of 7 N and 5 N act at the ends of the rod as shown in the figure.

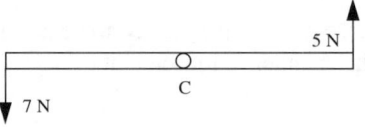

(a) Find the sum of the moments of the forces about the point C.
(b) Is the rod in equilibrium?
(c) What is the effect of the forces on the rod?

3. Figure 2(a) shows a uniform square lamina of sides 10 cm. Figure 2(b) shows a lamina in the shape of an isosceles triangle of base 10 cm and height 15 cm.

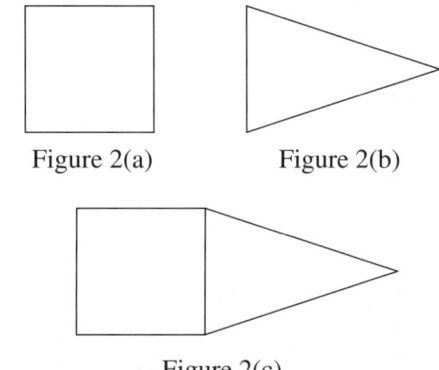

Figure 2(a)   Figure 2(b)

Figure 2(c)

(a) Draw suitable lines to locate the centre of gravity of the lamina in figures 2(a) and 2(b). Label the centre of gravity as O and P in figures 2(a) and 2(b) respectively.
(b) In Figure 2(c), mark the points O and P and mark the centre of gravity of the combined lamina as G. Give a reason why the position of the centre of gravity of the combined lamina is at the point you marked as G.

4. Figure 3(a) shows the rest position of a uniform sheet of metal when it is freely pivoted about P. Its centre of gravity is at C.

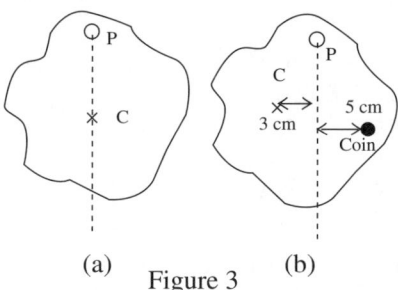

Figure 3

(a) On figure 3(a), indicate with an arrow the line of action of the weight of the sheet.
(b) Figure 3(b) shows the rest position of the sheet when a coin of mass 15 g is stuck to the sheet.
   (i) Calculate the mass of the sheet.
   (ii) Mark with a cross the likely position of the centre of gravity of the sheet and coin. Label the cross G.

5. The figure shows a lorry used to carry heavy loads. Identify and explain *two* features of the lorry that contribute to its stability.

Section B

1. Figures 4(a), 4(b) and 4(c) show three different ways of carrying a load of weight *W* by two workers using a rigid pole.

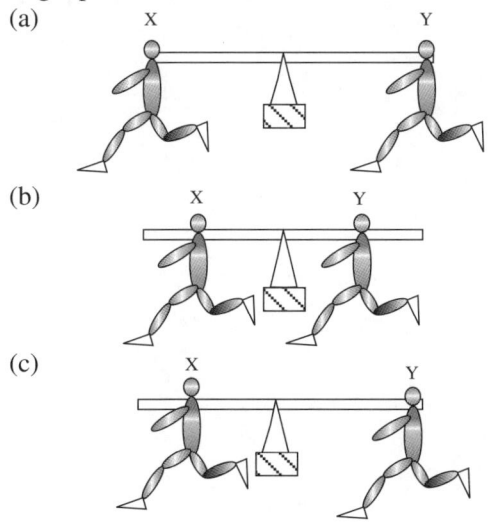

Figure 4

In figures 4(a) and 4(b), the load is at equal distance from X and Y. In figure 4(c) the load is closer to X.
(a) In figure 4(a), compare the forces on X and Y due to the load.
(b) From the perspective of the forces on each of the workers, is there any difference between the forces in figure 4(b) compared to those in figure 4(a)?
(c) In figure 4(c), compare the forces on X and Y due to the load.

2. (a) Figure 5(a) shows an aluminum lamp pole fixed to a concrete block on the ground.

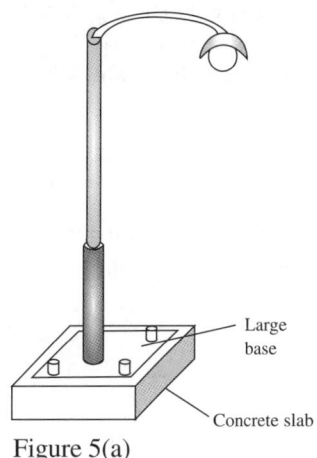

Figure 5(a)

Explain why
(i) the pole has a large base;
(ii) the pole is fixed to a concrete slab.
(b) Figure 5(b) shows a toy that returns to its rest position when displaced.

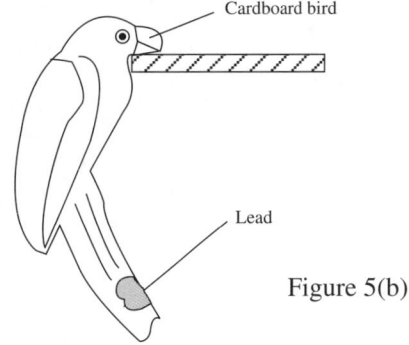

Figure 5(b)

The toy is made of cardboard with a piece of lead stuck in the position shown.
(i) Explain the purpose of a piece of lead in the position shown.
(ii) In figure 5(b), mark with a cross the centre of gravity of the toy and label it G.
(iii) Explain why the toy returns to its rest position when slightly displaced.

Data-based Question

3. The figure shows a balance designed by a student for measuring mass. A fixed mass of 200 g is hung on the zero mark of a half-metre rule and the rule is pivoted at the 10 cm mark. A light pan hangs on the right arm of the balance.

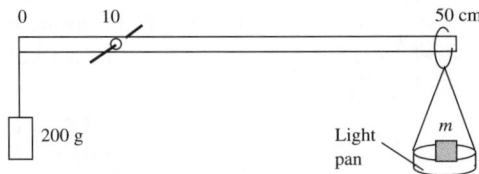

(a) What is the mass m in the pan that would make the half-metre rule balance when the pan is at the 50 cm mark?

(b) Different masses are then placed on the pan and the distance of the pan from the pivot is adjusted until the rule is balanced. On the figure of the half-metre rule shown below, mark accurately the positions of the pan when the mass of 50 g, 80 g, 100 g and 400 g are placed in it such that the rule is balanced. Label the markings as "50 g, 80 g, 100 g and 400 g".

```
   0    10    20    30    40    50 m
  ┌──────────────────────────────────┐
  │     ○                            │
  └──────────────────────────────────┘
```

(c) Using the same half-metre rule and pan, suggest two modifications to the design of the balance which would enable it to measure mass less than 50 g.

CHAPTER 6
Pressure

6.1 Pressure

1. **Pressure** is the normal force acting per unit area.

   Pressure $p = \dfrac{\text{force}}{\text{area}}$

   $$p = \dfrac{F}{A}$$

2. The SI unit for pressure is the pascal (Pa) or $N\,m^{-2}$.

Example
What is the pressure on the floor when a lady of mass 42 kg
(a) is standing barefoot on the floor. The total surface area of her feet on the floor is $200\,cm^2$.
(b) is standing in high heeled. The total surface area of the area of contact between the floor and the shoes is $50\,cm^2$.
(Acceleration of free fall = $10\,m\,s^{-2}$)

Solution
(a) Force on the floor is
   F = weight of lady
   = $(42\,kg)(10\,m\,s^{-2})$
   = 420 N

   Pressure $p = \dfrac{F}{A}$ $\quad 1\,cm^2 = (10^{-2}\,m)^2$
   $= \dfrac{420\,N}{200 \times 10^{-4}\,m^2}$
   $= 2.1 \times 10^4\,N\,m^{-2}$

(b) Pressure $p = \dfrac{420\,N}{50 \times 10^{-4}\,m^2}$
   $= 8.4 \times 10^4\,N\,m^{-2}$

3. Since pressure = $\dfrac{\text{force}}{\text{area}}$, the pressure exerted on a surface can be increased by:
   – increasing the force;
   – decreasing the area.

   This principle is used to hammer a nail into a piece of wood.

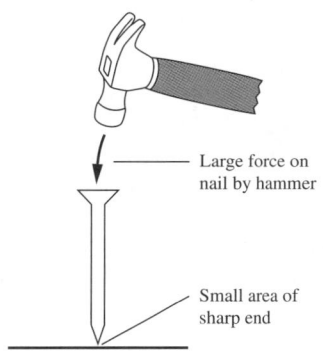

4. On the other hand, the pressure exerted on a surface can be decreased by:
   – decreasing the force;
   – increasing the surface area.

5. This principle is used in:
   (a) the construction of skyscrapers. The area of reinforced concrete foundation of a skyscraper is larger than the floor area of the ground floor.
   (b) lorries that carry heavy loads. They have many wheels. Thus, the area of contact with the road is increased. This reduces the pressure on the road due to each wheel.

Transmission of Pressure

6. Pressure is transmitted with equal magnitude in all directions through an incompressible liquid.
7. This principle is illustrated using a flask with holes around it.

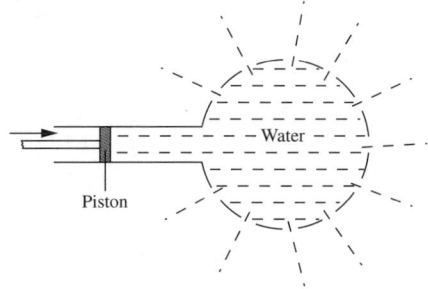

8. When the piston is pushed into the flask, water shoots out with equal force in all directions.
9. An application of this principle is in the **hydraulic system** such as the hydraulic press.

Hydraulic Press

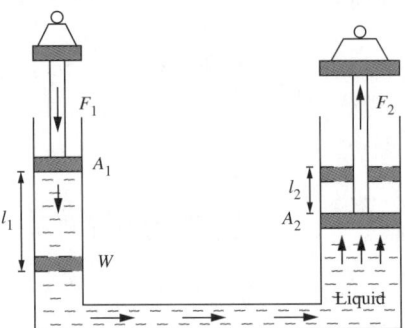

10. When a force F_1 pushes the small piston of cross-sectional area A_1, the pressure produced is

$$p = \frac{F_1}{A_1}$$

11. This pressure is transmitted through the liquid to the larger piston.
12. The force on the larger piston of cross-sectional area A_2 produced by the transmitted pressure is

$$F_2 = pA_2$$
$$= F_1 \left(\frac{A_2}{A_1}\right)$$
$$> F_1 \qquad (\because A_2 > A_1)$$

13. If the small piston moves through a distance of ℓ_1, the volume of liquid transferred from the small cylinder to the large cylinder is $A_1\ell_1$.
    If ℓ_2 is the distance moved by the large piston, then
$$A_2\ell_2 = A_1\ell_1$$
$$\ell_2 = \ell_1 \left(\frac{A_1}{A_2}\right)$$
$$< \ell_1$$

14. Another hydraulic system is the hydraulic lift which is used in workshops.

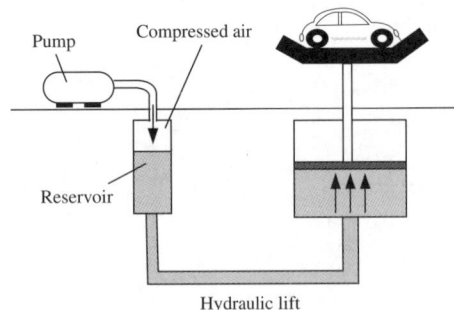

Hydraulic lift

15. The pressure on the liquid surface in the reservoir is increased by pumping air into the reservoir.
16. The pressure is transmitted to the larger cylinder and the car is lifted.
17. To lower the car, the compressed air in the reservoir is released.

Self Evaluation 6.1

1. A brick measures 30 cm × 10 cm × 6 cm and weighs 24 N is placed on the table. Calculate the maximum pressure and the minimum pressure that can be exerted by the brick on the table.

2. Alice of mass 42 kg wears high heel shoes to work. The surface area of the sole of the shoe is 8.0 cm².
   (a) Find the pressure she exerts on the floor.
   (b) Explain why Alice finds it difficult to walk on soft ground with her high heel shoes.

3. Explain the two features of the thumbtack shown in the figure using the concept of pressure.

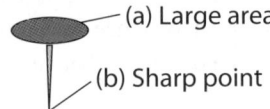

4. The figure below shows a hydraulic system.

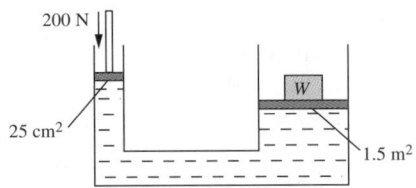

Calculate
(a) the load W that can be raised by a force of 200 N applied to the piston of cross-sectional area 25 cm².
(b) the ratio of the distance x moved by the piston to the height y the load is raised.

6.2 Pressure Difference

1. The figure shows a column of liquid of height h in a container of cross-sectional area A.

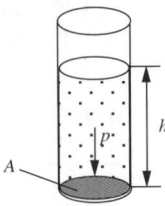

2. The pressure due to the weight of the column of liquid of density ρ and height h is given by

$$\text{Pressure } p = \frac{\text{weight of liquid column}}{\text{area of the base}}$$
$$= \frac{Ah\rho g}{A}$$

$$p = h\rho g$$

**Pressure due to a column of liquid
= height of column of liquid
× density of the liquid
× gravitational field strength**

3. Hence the pressure difference between two points in a liquid distance h apart is given by

$$\text{pressure difference } \Delta p = p_2 - p_1$$
$$= h\rho g$$

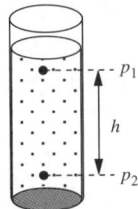

4. The pressure in a liquid acts in all directions with the same magnitude.

Example

The Challenger Deep in the Mariana Trench, Pacific Ocean, is the deepest point in the world at 11.03 km.
(a) What is the pressure due to the sea water at the bottom of the trench?
(b) What is the force on the external walls of a submarine area 25 m² at the bottom of the trench?
(Density of sea water = 1100 kg m⁻³, $g = 10\,\text{m s}^{-2}$)

Solution
(a) Pressure
$p = h\rho g$
$= (11.03 \times 10^3\,\text{m})(1100\,\text{kg m}^{-3})(10\,\text{m s}^{-2})$
$= 1.21 \times 10^8\,\text{Pa}$

(b) Force on the external walls of the submarine is
$F = pA$
$= (1.21 \times 10^8\,\text{Pa})(25\,\text{m}^2)$
$= 3.0 \times 10^9\,\text{N}$

> Note that when substituting the values of h, ρ and g in the equation $p = h\rho g$, h must be in m, ρ in kg m⁻³ and g in m s⁻².

5.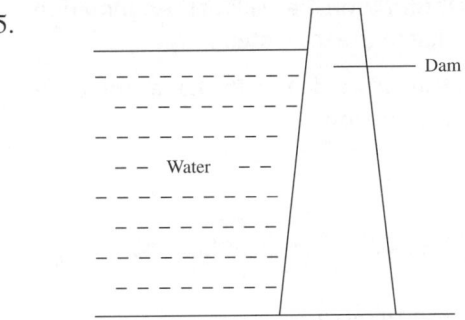

The base of a dam is much thicker than the top to withstand the higher pressure. The principle of pressure due to a liquid column is used in the public water supply. The reservoir is situated on the top of a hill. Because of the height, the pressure of water in the pipes is able to bring water to most houses.

Self Evaluation 6.2

1. Brine, of density 1200 kg m⁻³, is poured to a height of 8.0 cm in a cylinder. Kerosene, of density 780 kg m⁻³, is then poured on top of the brine until the kerosene column is 12.0 cm high.

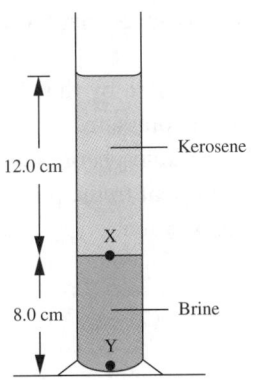

Calculate
(a) the pressure at the point X due to the column of kerosene.
(b) the pressure due to the column of brine of height 8.0 cm.
(c) the total pressure at the point Y due to the brine and kerosene.

2. A submarine of total surface area 264 m² is at a depth of 250 m below the water surface. If the density of sea water is 1.2 g cm⁻³, calculate
(a) the pressure due to water at a depth of 250 m.
(b) the force on the walls of the submarine due to the sea water.

3. Explain why a dam is thicker at the base than at the top.

6.3 Pressure Measurement

Atmospheric Pressure

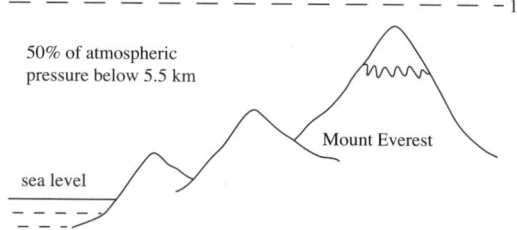

1. The Earth's atmosphere is made up of a layer of air that extends more than 40 km above Earth's surface.
2. The pressure exerted by this layer of air is called the atmospheric pressure.
3. At sea level, the atmospheric pressure is 1.03×10^5 Pa which is equivalent to the pressure due to a 10 m high column of water.

4. The atmospheric pressure can be measured using a **mercury barometer** as shown in the figure.

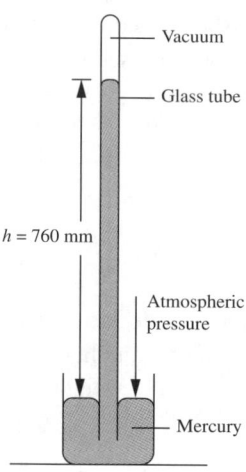

Mercury barometer

The atmospheric pressure at sea level is able to support a column of mercury 760 mm high. The equation $p = h\rho g$ can be used to show that this quantity (760 mm of mercury) is the atmospheric pressure in Pa.

$p = h\rho g$
$= (0.760 \text{ m})(13\ 600 \text{ kg m}^{-3})(10 \text{ m s}^{-2})$
$= 1.03 \times 10^5$ Pa

5. The existence of atmospheric pressure is demonstrated by the following experiments.
(a) The column of water in the test-tube is supported by atmospheric pressure.

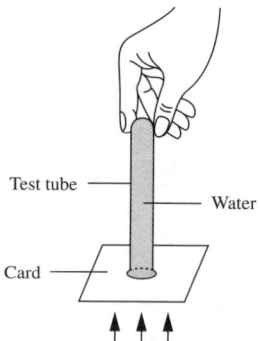

(b) (i) The aluminium can is heated to expel the air.

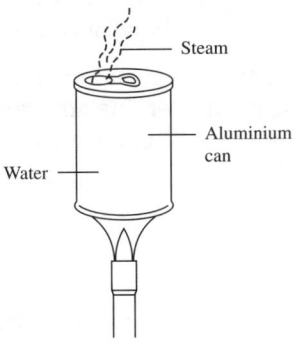

(ii) The can is then inverted into a trough of cold water. The steam in the can condenses and atmospheric pressure crushes the can.

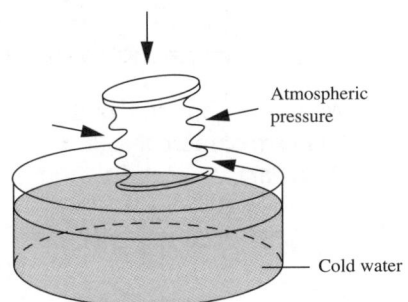

6. Applications of atmospheric pressure include the following examples.
   (a) When the air in the straw is sucked out, pressure in the straw decreases. The atmospheric pressure forces water into the straw.

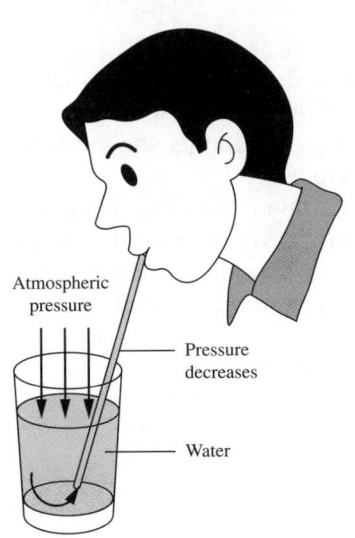

(b) When the piston of the syringe is withdrawn, pressure in the syringe decreases. The atmospheric pressure forces the water into the syringe.

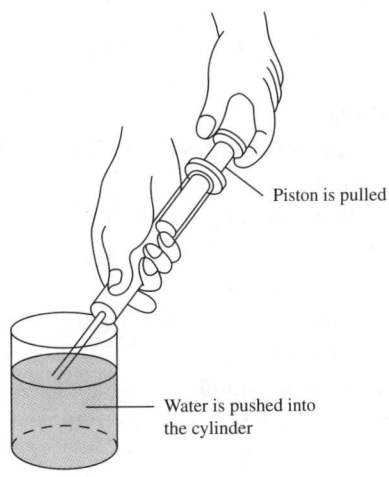

Manometer

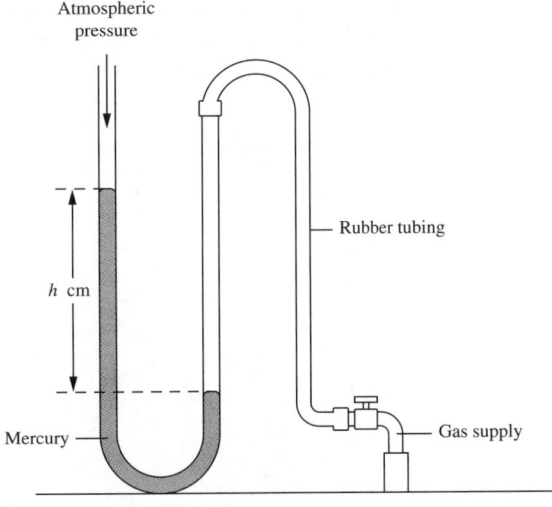

7. A manometer is used to measure pressure difference.
8. It consists of a U-tube containing mercury (to measure high pressure differences) or water (to measure small pressure differences).
9. The figure above shows a manometer used to measure the difference between the pressure of a gas supply and the atmospheric pressure.

10. The pressure of the gas supply p is balanced by the weight of the column of mercury (of height h being the difference in the mercury levels in the two limbs of the manometer) and the atmospheric pressure p_{atm} that is on the left side of the U-tube.

$$p = p_{atm} + h\rho_{Hg}g$$

Example

If atmospheric pressure = 1.03×10^5 Pa and $h = 50$ cm,
pressure of gas supply – atmospheric pressure
= pressure due to 50 cm of mercury
= $h\rho g$
= $(0.50 \text{ m})(13.6 \times 10^3 \text{ kg m}^{-3})(10 \text{ m s}^{-2})$
= 6.8×10^4 Pa
Pressure of gas supply
= atmospheric pressure + 6.8×10^4 Pa
= $(10.3 \times 10^4 + 6.8 \times 10^4)$ Pa
= 1.71×10^5 Pa

Self Evaluation 6.3

1. The figure below shows a mercury barometer P and another tube Q which has a little air trapped in it.

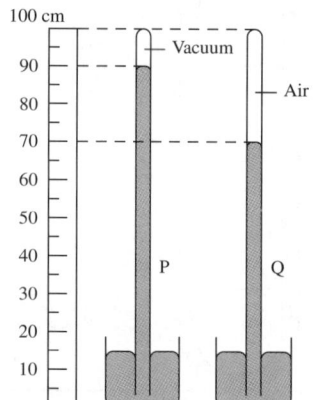

(a) What is the atmospheric pressure, in cm mercury?
(b) What is the pressure of the air in tube Q, in cm mercury?
(c) The tube Q is then pushed downwards so that the lower end is deeper in the bowl of mercury.
    (i) How does the length of the air column in the tube change?
    (ii) Explain why the difference in the mercury levels between tube Q and the bowl decreases.

2. A mercury manometer is connected to a gas cylinder. The atmospheric pressure is equal to 76 cm of mercury.

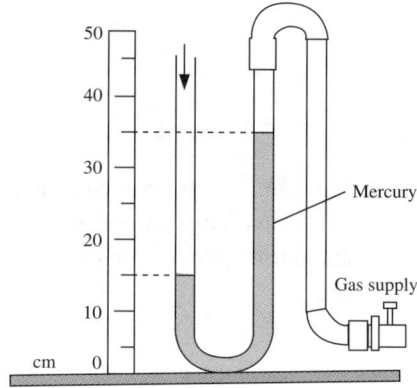

What is the pressure of the gas cylinder
(a) in cm of mercury;
(b) in Pa?

3.

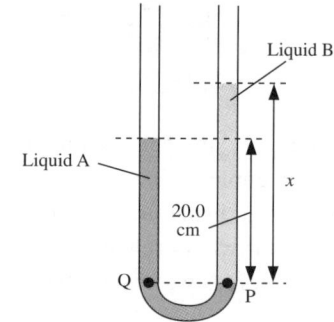

Two liquids A and B of density 1.0 g cm^{-3} and 0.80 g cm^{-3} respectively, are poured into an U-tube as shown in the figure above.
(a) Compare the pressure at the points P and Q, which are at the same level.
(b) Calculate the pressure at the point Q due to the column of liquid A.
(c) Hence calculate the height x of the liquid B above the point P.

REVISION EXERCISE 6

Multiple Choice Questions

1. The mass of a car is 1800 kg. What is the pressure on the road if the surface area of the tyres in contact with the road is 600 cm²?
   A 3.0 N cm⁻²   C 30 N cm⁻²
   B 3.3 N cm⁻²   D 33 N cm⁻²

2. Two concrete blocks P and Q have dimensions as shown in the figures.

   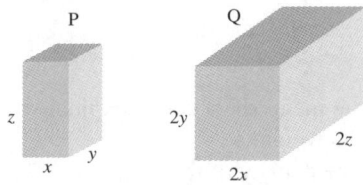

   Standing on one of its faces as shown, the pressure exerted by block P is p.
   What is the pressure exerted by block Q when it stands on the face as shown in the figure?

   A $\left(\dfrac{x}{2z}\right)p$ C $\left(\dfrac{x}{y}\right)p$

   B $\left(\dfrac{z}{x}\right)p$ D $\left(\dfrac{2y}{z}\right)p$

3. Which of the following unit is equivalent to the pascal (Pa)?
   A N cm⁻²   C N m
   B N m⁻²   D N m²

4. Liquids of different densities are poured into identical cylinders to different heights as shown in the diagrams. In which diagram is the pressure on the base of the cylinder the largest?

   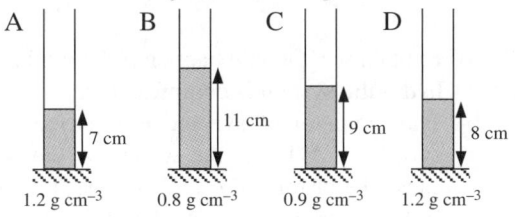

5. Equal masses of the same liquid are poured into four containers of different shapes. In which container is the pressure on the base the greatest?

   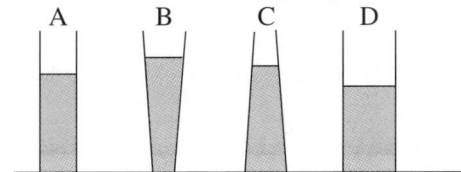

6. Which graph shows correctly the variation of the pressure p below the surface of water as the depth of water h increases?

   A 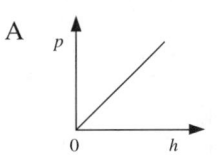   C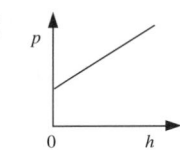

   B 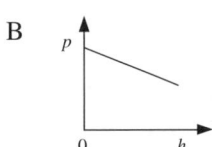   D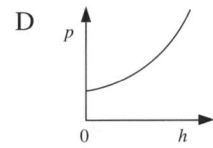

7. If the density of air decreases as the height h above the surface of the Earth increases, which graph best shows how the atmospheric pressure p_{at} changes with height h?

   A 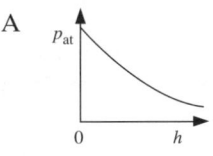   C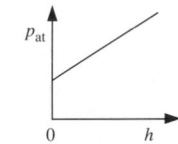

   B 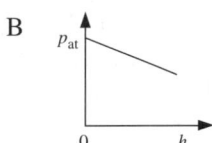 D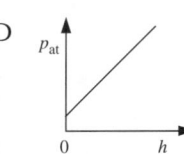

8. The figure shows a syringe filled with an incompressible liquid. The diameter of the piston is 1.0 cm and the diameter of the nozzle is 0.2 cm. The nozzle is closed with a finger.

   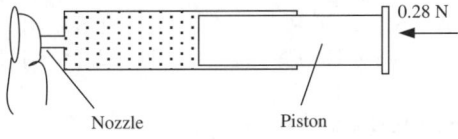

   The piston is pushed with a force of 0.28 N. What is the pressure exerted by the liquid on the finger?
   A 0.36 N cm⁻²   C 8.9 N cm⁻²
   B 5.6 N cm⁻²   D 45 N cm⁻²

9. The atmospheric pressure is 76 cm of mercury. A mercury barometer set up by a student is as shown in the figure below.

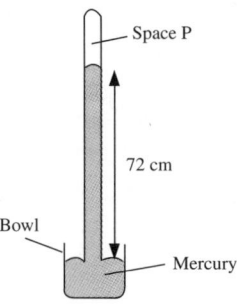

The possible fault in the setup is that
A   some air get into the space P.
B   the length of the barometer tube is insufficient.
C   there is not enough mercury in the bowl.
D   the temperature of the surrounding is high.

10. A manometer is connected to a gas cylinder. The atmospheric pressure is equivalent to 75 cm of mercury.

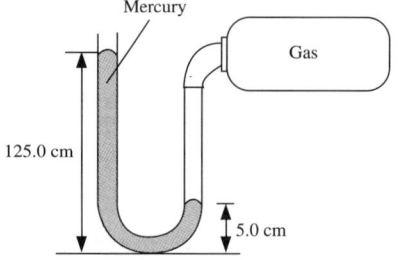

What is the pressure of the gas in the cylinder in Pa? (Density of mercury = 13 600 kg m^{-3}, $g = 10$ N kg^{-1})
A 6.1×10^4 Pa   C 1.6×10^5 Pa
B 6.8×10^4 Pa   D 2.7×10^5 Pa

Structured Questions

Section A

1. Heavy table sometimes make marks on the floor on which its legs stand. The figure below shows the design of two heavy tables P and Q with legs made of stainless steel.

 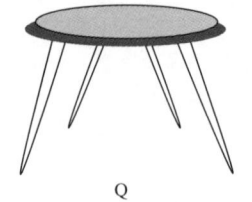

(a) Discuss which table is most likely to make marks on the floor.
(b) Explain which table is more unlikely to topple over.

2. A red-hot metal sheet is placed on a horizontal surface to cool.

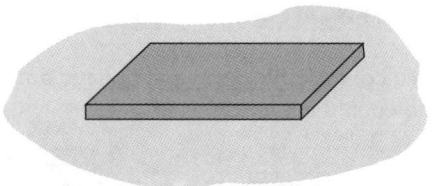

As the metal sheet cools, explain what happens to
(a) its weight.
(b) the density of the metal.
(c) the surface area of the sheet in contact with the horizontal surface.
(d) the pressure on the horizontal surface.

3. The figure shows a hydraulic system which consists of two syringes A and B connected by a tube filled with an incompressible liquid

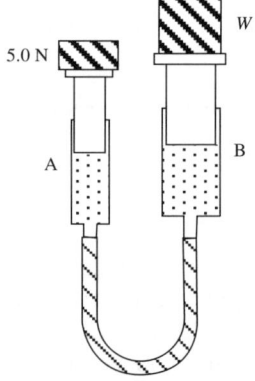

(a) Explain what would happen if the liquid in the hydraulic system is compressible.
(b) The diameter of syringe B is twice that of syringe A. What is the weight W that would cause the pistons of A and B to be stationary?
(c) If the piston of A is pushed into the syringe by a distance of 2.0 cm, through what distance would the load W be raised?

4. The figure below shows a mercury barometer.

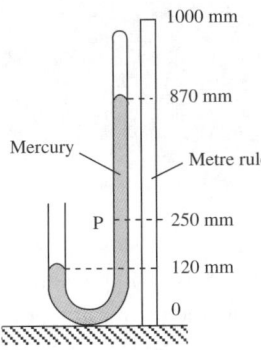

(a) Deduce from the figure the atmospheric pressure as recorded by the barometer in $N\,m^{-2}$.
(b) What is the pressure at the point P? Give your answer in $N\,m^{-2}$.
(Density of mercury = 13 600 kg m^{-3}, g = 10 N kg^{-1})

Section B

1. The figure shows a hydraulic system used to raise a car in a workshop.

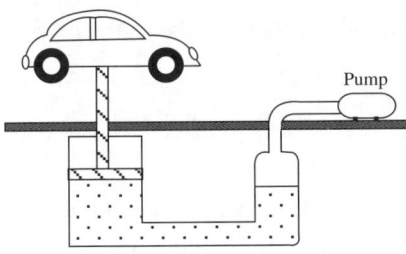

A pump is used to increase the pressure of the air in the reservoir.
(a) State the principle used in the hydraulic system shown in the figure.
(b) State an important property of the liquid used in the system.
(c) Explain how the car can be raised
(d) What is the force required to raise a car of mass 1200 kg at a constant speed?
(e) The cross-sectional area of the reservoir is 500 times the cross-sectional area of the cylinder. Calculate the force on the liquid surface in the reservoir.

2. The figure shows an air-bag which is connected to a water manometer. The top surface of the air-bag has an area of 25 cm^2.

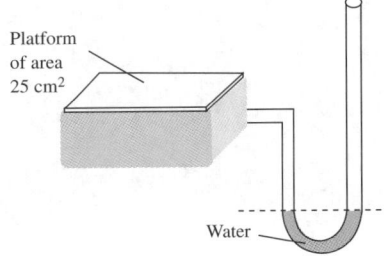

(a) Compare the pressure of the air in the bag with the atmospheric pressure. Give a reason for your answer.
(b) A load of weight 5 N is then placed on the platform. Calculate
   (i) the increased pressure on the air in the bag;
   (ii) the difference in height of the water levels in the manometer.
(c) How would the answer to (b) (ii) be affected
   (i) if the manometer tube has twice the diameter?
   (ii) if the manometer contains a liquid of higher density?
   Explain your answers.
(Density of water = 1000 kg m^{-3}, g = 10 N kg^{-1})

Data-based question

3.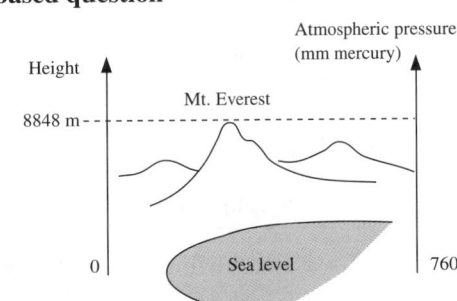

The atmospheric pressure is due to the weight of the air above the surface of the Earth. The atmospheric pressure at sea level is 760 mm of mercury. The density of mercury is 13 600 kg m^{-3}.
(a) Calculate the atmospheric pressure at sea level in Pa.
(b) Assuming that the density of air is constant and is 1.1 kg m^{-3}, estimate the height of the Earth's atmosphere.
(c) Calculate the atmospheric pressure in mm of mercury, on top of Mt. Everest which is of height 8488 m.
(d) Discuss whether you would expect the actual height of the Earth's atmosphere to be higher or lower than the answer to (b) above.

CHAPTER 7
Energy, Work and Power

7.1 Energy Conversion and Conservation

1. **Energy** is the capacity to do work and is measured in joule (J).
2. Mechanical energy can be in the form of:
   (i) kinetic energy – energy of a body by virtue of its motion;
   (ii) elastic potential energy – energy stored in an elastic body that is stretched or compressed;
   (iii) gravitational potential energy – energy stored in a body due to its position in a gravitational field.

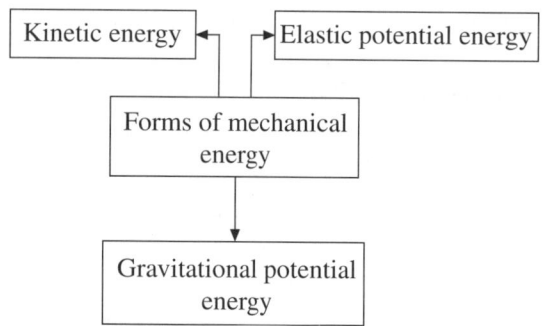

3. A body of mass m moving with velocity v has **kinetic energy** given by $\frac{1}{2}mv^2$.

Example
A ball of mass 300 g moving with a velocity of $4.0\,\text{m s}^{-1}$ has kinetic energy
$$E_k = \frac{1}{2}mv^2$$
$$= \frac{1}{2}(0.300\,\text{kg})(4.0\,\text{m s}^{-1})^2$$
$$= 2.4\,\text{J}$$

4. **Gravitational potential energy** is the energy possessed by a body due to its position relative to some reference point such as the ground. A body of mass m at a height h above the ground has gravitational potential energy given by mgh where g is the *acceleration of free fall*.

Example
A diver of mass 60 kg standing on a diving board 15 m above the swimming pool has gravitational potential energy
$$E_p = mgh$$
$$= (60\,\text{kg})(10\,\text{m s}^{-2})(15\,\text{m})$$
$$= 9000\,\text{J}$$

5. Besides mechanical energy, there are **chemical potential energy** stored in the molecular bonds. This energy is released in a chemical reaction.

> *Problem Solving Technique*
> Note that in all calculations using the equations such as $E_k = \frac{1}{2}mv^2$ or $E_p = mgh$, m must be in kg, v in m s^{-1}, g in m s^{-2} and h in m.

6. **Thermal energy** is the energy related to temperature. The higher the temperature of a substance, the greater is its thermal energy.
7. Energy can be converted from one form to another.
8. **Principle of conservation of energy** states that energy can neither be created nor destroyed but can be converted from one form to another. The total energy is always constant.
9. Examples of energy conversion and conservation:
   (a) Gravitational potential energy to kinetic energy

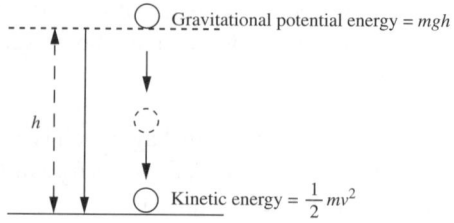

A ball of mass m at a height h has gravitational potential energy defined by mgh. As the ball falls to the ground, its gravitational potential energy decreases but its kinetic energy increases. The total energy of the system remains constant. When the ball reaches the ground, all of its gravitational potential energy mgh is converted into kinetic energy.

From principle of conservation of energy, we have

gain in kinetic energy = loss in gravitational potential energy

$$\frac{1}{2}mv^2 = mgh$$

(b) Kinetic energy to gravitational potential energy

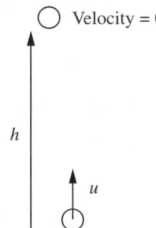

When a ball of mass m is thrown vertically upwards with a velocity u, it possesses kinetic energy defined by $\frac{1}{2}mu^2$. As the ball rises, its kinetic energy is converted into gravitational potential energy. At the highest point, the ball stops momentarily. Thus we can conclude

gain in gravitational potential energy = loss in kinetic energy

$$mgh = \frac{1}{2}mu^2$$

Example
A brick drops from a height of 20 m. What is its speed when it hits the ground?

Solution
From the principle of conservation of energy, we have:

gain in kinetic energy = loss in gravitational potential energy

$$\frac{1}{2}mv^2 = mgh$$
$$v = \sqrt{2gh}$$
$$= \sqrt{2(10 \text{ m s}^{-2})(20 \text{ m})}$$
$$= 20 \text{ m s}^{-1}$$

Example
A ball is thrown vertically upwards with an initial velocity of 20 m s^{-1}.
(a) What is its speed after rising 15 m?
(b) What is the maximum height attained?

Solution
(a) From principle of conservation of energy, we have

loss in kinetic energy = gain in gravitational potential energy

$$\frac{1}{2}mu^2 - \frac{1}{2}mv^2 = mgh$$
$$v^2 = u^2 - 2gh$$
$$= (20 \text{ m s}^{-1})^2$$
$$- 2(10 \text{ m s}^{-2})(15 \text{ m})$$
$$v = 10 \text{ m s}^{-1}$$

(b) Let H be the maximum height attained.
From principle of conservation of energy, we have

gain in gravitational potential energy = loss in kinetic energy

$$mgH = \frac{1}{2}mu^2$$
$$H = \frac{u^2}{2g}$$
$$= \frac{(20 \text{ m s}^{-1})^2}{2(10 \text{ m s}^{-2})}$$
$$= 20 \text{ m}$$

Self Evaluation 7.1

1. A ball of mass 0.36 kg is released from rest from a height of 2.0 m. (Neglect air resistance).
   (a) What is its initial gravitational potential energy?
   (b) What is its gravitational potential energy after falling through a height of 1.5 m?
   (c) What is its kinetic energy after falling 1.5 m?
   (d) Calculate its speed after falling 1.5 m.

2. A block of mass 2.4 kg slides down an inclined plane from rest as shown in the figure.

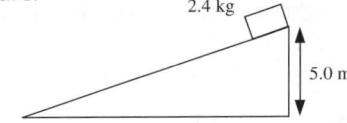

(a) What is its initial gravitational potential energy?
(b) When the block reaches the bottom of the inclined plane, its speed is 8.0 m s⁻¹. What is the kinetic energy of the block at the bottom of the inclined plane?
(c) Use the principle of conservation of energy to account for any difference in the answers to (a) and (b).

3.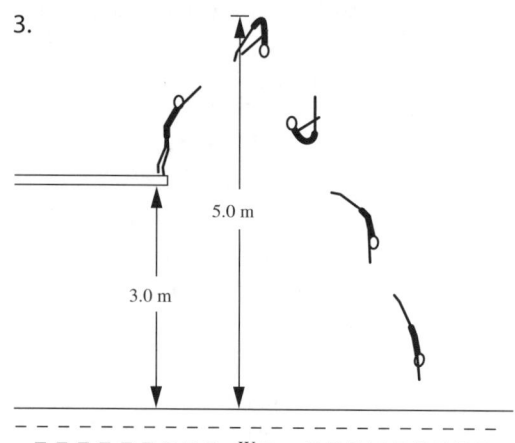

A swimmer of mass 30 kg jumps off a diving board and reaches a maximum height of 5.0 m from the water surface.
(a) What is the gain in gravitational potential energy when the swimmer reaches the highest point?
(b) At what speed does the swimmer hit the water surface?

4.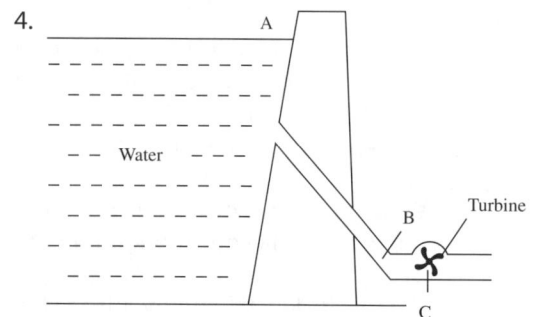

The diagram shows water behind a high dam.
(a) What is the form of energy of the water at (i) A and (ii) B?
(b) Describe the energy transformation at C.

7.2 Work

1. When the application of a force produces motion, **work** is said to be done.

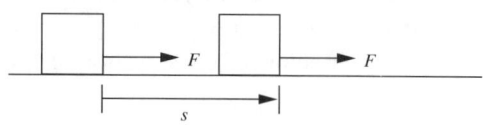

2. Work done by a force is
   W = Force × displacement in the direction of the force
   = Fs

3. Since the force is in newton (N) and the displacement in metre (m), then the unit for work done is newton-metre (N m). This unit is given the name of joule (J).

Example
Find the work done when a force of 50 N moves an object through a distance of (a) 2.0 m, (b) 40 cm and (c) 2.0 km.

Solution
(a) Work done = Fs
  = (50 N)(2.0 m)
  = 100 J
(b) Work done = (50 N)(0.40 m) *(40 cm = 0.40 m)*
  = 20 J
(c) Work done = (50 N)(2000 m) *(2.0 km = 2000 m)*
  = 1.0×10^5 J

4.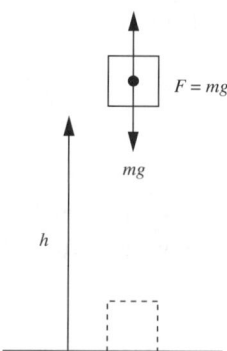

The weight of an object of mass m is mg. To raise the object of mass m, a force $F = mg$ is required. Work done to raise the mass m through a vertical height h is
$$W = Fs$$
$$= mgh$$

Example
(a) Work done to raise a mass of 5 kg through a height of 2.5 m is
$$W = mgh$$
$$= (5 \text{ kg})(10 \text{ m s}^{-2})(2.5 \text{ m})$$
$$= 125 \text{ J}$$
(b) Work done to raise a mass of 20 g through a height of 30 cm is
$$W = mgh$$
$$= (0.020 \text{ kg})(10 \text{ m s}^{-2})(0.30 \text{ m})$$
$$= 0.06 \text{ J}$$

5. The work done on a body can increase:
   - the kinetic energy of the body;
   - the potential energy of the body.

Problem Solving Technique
When applying the equation, $W = Fs$, s is the displacement in the direction of the force F. If s and F are in opposite directions, the work done is negative. This means that work is done against the force F.

Example
A force of 10 N pushes a 4 kg mass across a smooth floor. What is the velocity of the mass after being pushed through 20 m?

Solution
Gain in kinetic energy = work done by the force
$$\frac{1}{2}mv^2 = Fs$$
$$v^2 = \frac{2Fs}{m}$$
$$v^2 = \frac{2(10 \text{ N})(20 \text{ m})}{(4 \text{ kg})}$$
$$v = 10 \text{ m s}^{-1}$$

Example
A car of mass 1500 kg was travelling at a speed of 20 m s^{-1} when the brakes were applied. After travelling through 400 m, the speed of the car became 5 m s^{-1}. What is the retarding force on the car?

Solution
work done by retarding force = loss in kinetic energy
$$Fs = \frac{1}{2}mu^2 - \frac{1}{2}mv^2$$
$$F = \frac{m(u^2 - v^2)}{2s}$$
$$= \frac{(1500 \text{ kg})[(20 \text{ m s}^{-1})^2 - (5 \text{ m s}^{-1})^2]}{2(400 \text{ m})}$$
$$= 703 \text{ N}$$

Self Evaluation 7.2

1. When a force F moves an object through a distance s in the direction of F, the work done is W. Complete the table below.

	Force F	Distance s	Work done W
(a)	8.0 N	25 cm	
(b)		5.0 m	100 J
(c)	5.0 N		0.20 J

2. The total mass of a cyclist and a bicycle is 80 kg. The cyclist is travelling at 16 m s^{-1} on a level road before he stops pedalling. The cyclist travels a further distance of 120 m before stopping. Calculate the total retarding force on the cyclist.

3. A trolley of mass 2.0 kg is moving at 1.5 m s^{-1} on a smooth horizontal floor. A constant force of 2.8 N pushes a trolley through a distance of 5.0 m. Calculate the final speed of the trolley when the force is removed.

7.3 Power

Power is the rate of doing work.
$$\text{Power } P = \frac{\text{work done}}{\text{time taken}}$$

Units for power: watt (W) $\equiv$ J s^{-1}
kilowatt (kW) $\equiv$ 1000 W
Megawatt (MW) $\equiv$ 1 000 000 W

Example
A boy of mass 40 kg takes 15 s to run up a flight of stairs of height 10 m. What is his average power? ($g = 10\,\text{m s}^{-2}$)

Solution

$$\text{Power} = \frac{\text{work done}}{\text{time taken}}$$
$$= \frac{mgh}{t}$$
$$= \frac{(40\text{ kg})(10\text{ m s}^{-2})(10\text{ m})}{(15\text{ s})}$$
$$= 267\text{ W}$$

Example
A 15 kW pump is used to pump water to the top of a building, which is 100 m high. What is the maximum mass of water that can be pumped to the top of the building in each second?

Solution

$$\text{Power} = \frac{\text{work done}}{\text{time taken}}$$
$$P = \frac{mgh}{t}$$

Mass of water per second is

$$\frac{m}{t} = \frac{P}{gh}$$
$$= \frac{(15\,000\text{ W})}{(10\text{ m s}^{-2})(100\text{ m})}$$
$$= 15\text{ kg s}^{-1}$$

Example
A car requires 360 kW of power to travel at a constant speed of 24 m s^{-1}. What is the total resistance to the car's motion?

Solution

$$\text{Power } P = \frac{\text{work done}}{\text{time taken}}$$
$$P = \frac{Fs}{t} \qquad (\tfrac{s}{t} = v)$$
$$= Fv$$

Total resistance is

$$F = \frac{P}{v}$$
$$= \frac{360\,000\text{ W}}{24\text{ m s}^{-1}}$$
$$= 15\,000\text{ N}$$

Self Evaluation 7.3

1. A student of mass 40 kg takes 20 s to run up a flight of stairs of height 7.0 m. Calculate the minimum power of the student.

2. A car travelling at 20 m s^{-1} encounters a resistive force of 500 N. What is the power of the car?

3. The output power of an electric pump is 2 kW. Calculate the time taken to pump 200 kg of water through a vertical height of 15 m.

REVISION EXERCISE 7

Multiple Choice Questions

1. The figure shows a simple pendulum hanging from the point O. A horizontal needle N is clamped below O.

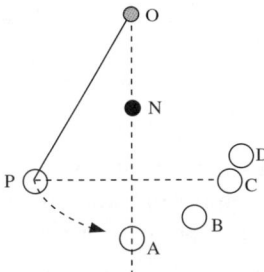

   The pendulum bob is released from the point P. Which of the points marked A, B, C or D would the bob swing to before swinging back? (Neglect air resistance.)

2. A trolley is released from rest from the top of a smooth inclined plane. It moves down the incline and comes to a stop when it compresses a helical spring.

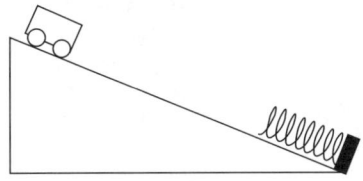

   Which of the following describes the energy conversion correctly?
   A Gravitational potential energy → kinetic energy → elastic potential energy
   B Kinetic energy → Gravitational potential energy → elastic potential energy
   C Elastic potential energy → kinetic energy → Gravitational potential energy
   D Gravitational potential energy → elastic potential energy → kinetic energy

3. A ball is kicked into the air and it follows the path shown in the figure.

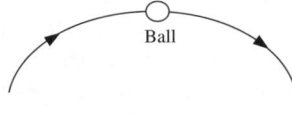

   When the ball is at the highest point, it has
   A gravitational potential energy only.
   B kinetic energy only.
   C gravitational potential energy and kinetic energy only.
   D gravitational potential energy and kinetic energy and elastic potential energy.

4. The kinetic energy of a body of mass m moving with a velocity v is K. What is the kinetic energy of a body of mass $2m$ and moving with a velocity $2v$?
   A K B $2K$ C $4K$ D $8K$

5.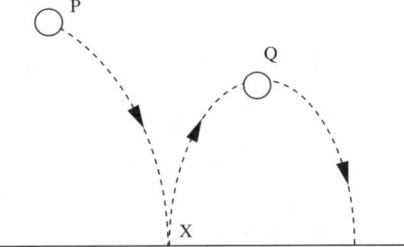

   A ball dropped from P bounces to Q before dropping again. Which one of the following is true?
   A Energy is not conserved.
   B When the ball reaches the ground at X, its kinetic energy equals its gravitational potential energy.
   C When the ball hits the ground at X, part of its energy is elastic potential energy.
   D From X to Q, its kinetic energy increases.

6. A stone of mass 0.50 kg is projected vertically upwards with an initial velocity of 4.0 m s^{-1}. What is its kinetic energy when it reaches a height of 0.5 m?
   A 0 J   B 1.5 J   C 2.5 J   D 4.0 J

7. A force of 6.4 N pushes on a trolley of mass 2.5 kg which was initially at rest on a smooth horizontal surface. What is the speed of the trolley after it moves through a distance of 8.0 m?
   A 3.1 m s^{-1} C 20.5 m s^{-1}
   B 6.4 m s^{-1} D 25.6 m s^{-1}

8. An electric motor has an output power of 50 W. What is the minimum time taken for it to lift a load of weight 20 N through a height of 12.0 m?
   A 3.0 s   C 30.0 s
   B 4.8 s   D 48.0 s

9. The power of a car engine is 20 kW when it is travelling at 20 m s^{-1}. If the total resistive force is 150 N, what is the rate at which thermal energy is dissipated from the engine?
   A 3 kW   C 15 kW
   B 4 kW   D 17 kW

10. A stone drops from a building of height H. Which graph shows correctly the variation of the gravitational potential energy (PE) of the stone with the height h of the stone above the ground?

   A 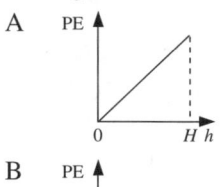   C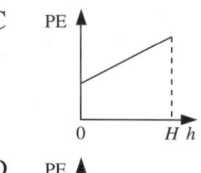

   B 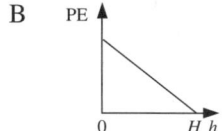   D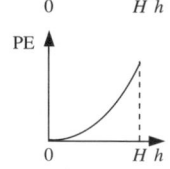

Structured Questions

Section A

1. A worker pushes a box on the floor with a force of 450 N through a distance of 5.8 m. The frictional force between the box and the floor is 240 N.
   (a) How much work is done by the worker?
   (b) What is the work done against frictional force?
   (c) What is the gain in kinetic energy of the box?

2. A player kicked a ball of mass 0.40 kg into the air and the ball rises to a maximum height of 12.0 m. The speed of the ball at the highest point is 8.0 m s^{-1}.

   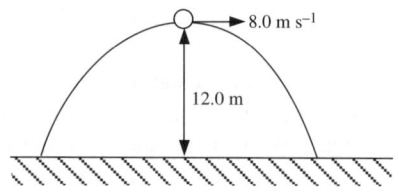

   (a) Neglecting air resistance, calculate the kinetic energy and the potential energy of the ball at the highest point.
   (b) Find the speed of the ball when it leaves the ground.
   (c) Describe briefly the transformation of energy of the ball during its flight.

3. The figure shows a hydroelectric power station.

   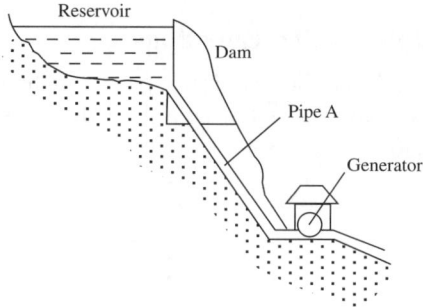

   (a) What form of energy does the water in the reservoir has due to its height?
   (b) Describe the transformation of energy of the water
      (i) as it moves through the pipe A;
      (ii) when it flows through the generator.
   (c) Explain why only a fraction of the energy of the water in the reservoir is transformed into electricity.

4. The figure shows a pile-driver used to drive a pile into the ground.

   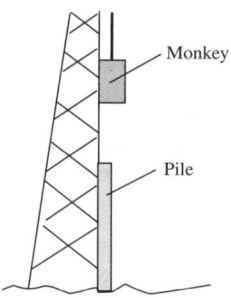

   The monkey, which is a heavy metal block is raised and released from rest to strike the pile.
   (a) If you want to estimate the power developed in lifting the monkey through a height of 4.0 m, what two other quantities you would have to measure?
   (b) Calculate the speed of the monkey after falling through a height of 4.0 m.
   (c) When the monkey hits the pile, it moves together with the pile and finally comes to rest.
      (i) What forms of energy the monkey loses?
      (ii) State two forms of energy into which the 'lost' energy is transformed to.
   (d) A student noticed that the length of the pile driven into the ground keeps decreasing after each successive strike by the monkey. What can be deduced about the resistive force experienced by the pile?

5. A car was travelling at 20 m s^{-1} when it crashed into a wall. The car came to rest in 0.15 s. A passenger who was strapped with a safety belt moved forwards a distance of 0.20 m against the force exerted by the safety belt.
   (a) Calculate
       (i) the kinetic energy of the passenger before the crash if his mass is 56 kg;
       (ii) the average force exerted by the safety belt on the passenger.
   (b) State what happens to the kinetic energy of the car.

Section B

1. The figure shows a child sand-boarding down a sand dune from a height H.

   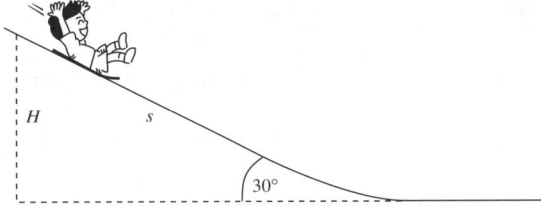

   (a) The total mass of the child and board is 35 kg. The potential energy of the child and board at a height H is 8750 J and the kinetic energy is zero. Calculate the value of the height H.
   (b) At the bottom of the sand dune, the total kinetic energy of the child and board is 7000 J. Calculate the speed of the child and board.
   (c) From the answers to (a) and (b), determine the work done against friction between the board and the sand.
   (d) From the data shown in the figure, determine the distance s.
   (e) Calculate the average frictional force between the board and the sand.
   (f) Suggest a method of reducing the friction between the board and the sand.

2. (a) Below are three sources of energy: waves, coal and wind.
       (i) Classify each of them as renewable or non-renewable energy source.
       (ii) State one environmental problem created by the use of each of these energy sources.
   (b) The figure shows a wind turbine used to produce electricity.

   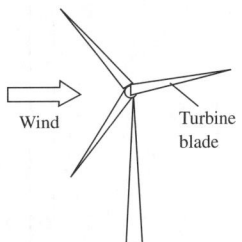

   Complete the block diagram below to show the energy transformations.

   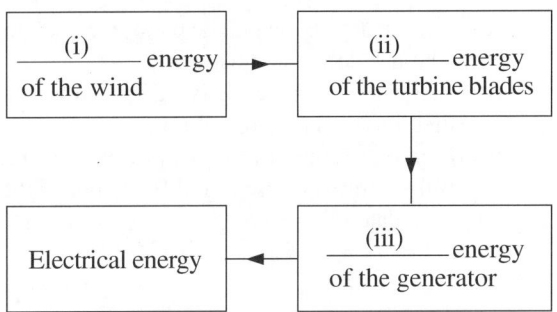

   (c) 10 000 m^3 of air travelling at 8.0 m s^{-1} hits the turbine blades every second. The density of air is 1.2 kg m^{-3}. Calculate
       (i) the mass of air incident on the turbine blades in 1.0 s.
       (ii) the kinetic energy of this mass of air.
       (iii) the input power to the turbine of the generator.
       (iv) Use the following equation to calculate the electrical power generated by the wind turbine, if its efficiency is 60%.
       Efficiency
       $$= \frac{\text{electric power generated}}{\text{input power}} \times 100\%$$
       (v) Explain why the generation of electricity using the wind turbine is not 100% efficient.

Data-based Question

3. The picture shows three persons in a wall-climbing competition 60 s after the start. John, Tommy and Ben are at 4.5 m, 3.9 m and 3.5 m from the ground respectively.

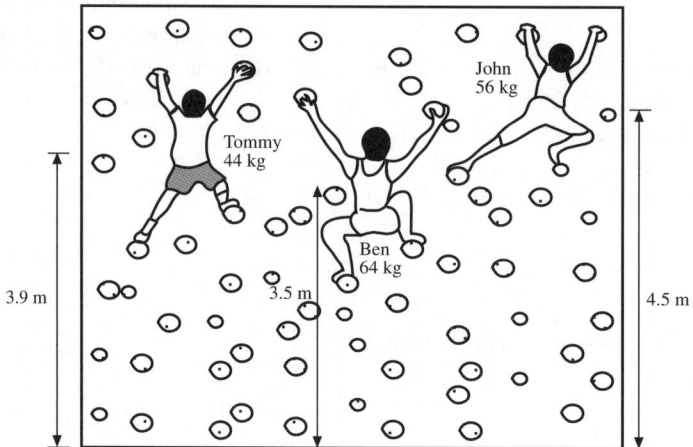

(a) Use the data shown in the picture, calculate the work done by each of the climbers in 60 s. Hence determine who has done the most work.
(b) Calculate the power delivered by each climber. Hence deduce who delivered the greatest power during the first 60 s of the competition.
(c) Explain whether the actual power delivered by each climbers is greater than the answer in (b).
(d) If the climbers were to fall from the height mentioned, who would hit the ground with the greatest speed? Calculate this speed.

CHAPTER 8
Kinetic Model of Matter

8.1 States of Matter

1. All materials are made up of matter. Any substance that has mass and volume is matter.
2. There are three states of matter: solid, liquid and gas.
3. Table 1 shows the different properties of the three states of matter.

Solid	Liquid	Gas
Has a fixed shape	Take the shape of its container	No fixed shape
Has a fixed volume	Has a fixed volume	Same volume as its container
Has surfaces all round	Has a definite surface at the top (except for a liquid droplet)	No surface
Does not flow	Can flow	Can flow easily
Highly uncompressible	Not compressible	Highly compressible

Table 1

Self Evaluation 8.1

1. Ice, water and steam are three different states of water. Which of the states
   (a) has a definite shape?
   (b) can flow easily?
   (c) spread rapidly?
   (d) is most easily compressed?

8.2 Brownian Motion

1. Brownian motion is the continuous haphazard motion of particles, such as, that of smoke particles in a smoke cell.

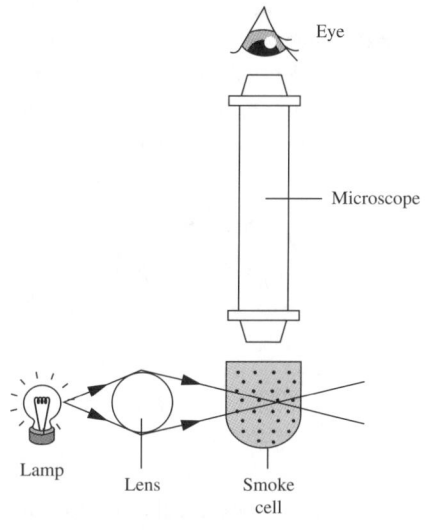

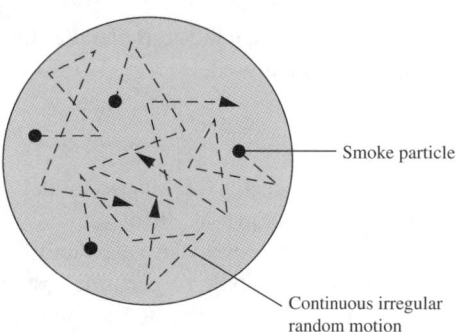

2. The random motion of the smoke particles is due to the unbalanced forces acting on the smoke particles when air molecules collide with them. (See figure below).

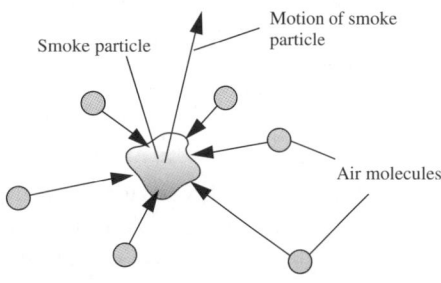

3. From the observations made in Brownian motion, the kinetic model of matter was proposed.

4. Inferences from observations made in Brownian motion:
   (a) Random motion of smoke particles.

   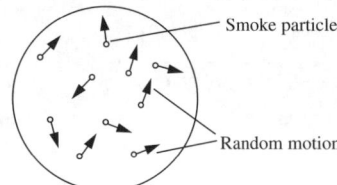

   Inference:
   (i) At any instant, different air molecules are moving with different velocities.
   (b) Irregular motion of a smoke particle.

   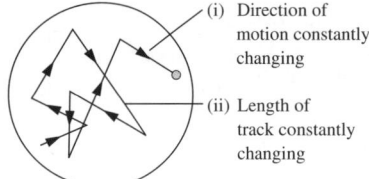

   Inference:
   (i) Air molecules collide into each other.
   (ii) Separation between air molecules is large and not constant.
5. At higher temperatures, the motion of the smoke particles is observed to be more vigorous. This leads to the conclusion that the air molecules move faster at higher temperature.

Diffusion

6. Another evidence for the kinetic model of matter is the process known as diffusion.
7. Diffusion occurs rapidly in gases and liquids.
8. The scent from a bottle of perfume opened at one end of a room can be detected at the other end of the room within a few seconds.
9. Evidently, the perfume molecules have moved rapidly across the room.

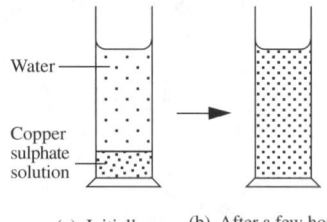

(a) Initially (b) After a few hours

10. Initially the water layer floats on top of the copper(II) suphate solution. After a few hours, the solution becomes homogeneous pale blue colour because the copper(II) sulphate solution at the bottom and the water on top diffuses into each other. This provides evidence of liquid molecules moving from one region to another.

Self Evaluation 8.2

1.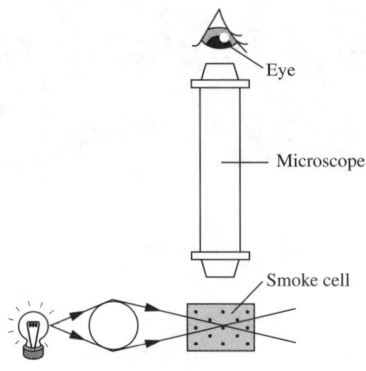

   Figure 1(a)

   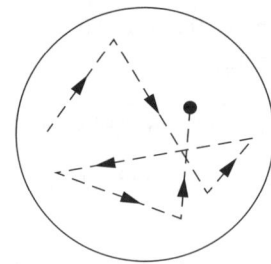

   Figure 1(b)

   What evidence does this experiment provide about air molecules?
   A They can be seen through the microscope.
   B They are in constant random motion.
   C They move when hit by smoke particles.
   D They emit light when they collide with smoke particles.

2. Brownian motion of dust particles in the air is caused by
   A convection current in the air.
   B random collisions between dust particles.
   C dust particles falling towards the ground.
   D random collisions of air molecules with the dust particles.

3. (a) What is Brownian motion?
   (b) What causes Brownian motion?
   (c) What conclusions can be drawn from Brownian motion?

8.3 Kinetic Model

1. The kinetic model of matter states the following postulates.
   - Matter is made up of a large number of particles such as atoms and molecules.
   - The particles are in constant motion.
   - The particles attract and repel each other.
   - The particles have kinetic energy and potential energy.
2. Table 2 shows the various aspects of solid, liquid and gas from the kinetic model perspective.

Aspect	Solid	Liquid	Gas
	Atoms in a solid	Molecules in a liquid	Molecules in a Gas
1. Arrangement of particles	Atoms are arranged close together in a regular pattern	Molecules are close together but not arranged in a regular pattern	Molecules are far apart
2. Motion of particles	Atoms vibrate about their individual mean positions	Molecules move about in a random manner	Molecules move randomly at high speeds colliding elastically into each other and the walls of the container
3. Forces between particles.	Strong attractive and repulsive forces between atoms	Weaker attractive and repulsive forces compared to forces between atoms in a solid	Intermolecular forces are negligible except during collisions
4. Energy of particles	Atoms have kinetic energy and potential energy	Higher kinetic and potential energy	Zero potential energy and very high kinetic energy

Table 2

3. The kinetic model can be used to explain the various characteristics of solids, liquids and gases.

Solids

4. Crystals structure

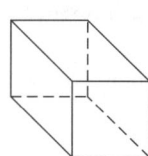
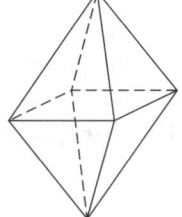

The well defined shape and smooth surface of a crystal provides evidence that molecules in solids are arranged in regular manner and in fixed positions.

5. The fact that it is extremely difficult to compress a solid proves that strong repulsive forces exist between atoms in a solid.
6. On the other hand, it is extremely difficult to extend the length of a metal rod. This proves that strong attractive forces exist between atoms in a solid.

Liquids

7. Liquid is able to flow and takes the shape of its container. This shows that the attractive forces between liquid molecules are weaker compared to the solid molecules.
8. Due to the repulsive force between molecules, the amount that a liquid can be compressed is negligible.
9. The higher density of liquids compared to gases implies that liquid molecules are closer to each other.
10. When a liquid is heated, the molecules vibrate and move about more vigorously. Thus, the liquid expands but only slightly.

Gases

11. A gas is able to completely fills its container. This shows that the forces between gas molecules are negligible.
12. The forces between gas molecules are negligible because of the large separation between gas molecules compared to the size of the molecules.
13. The large separation between molecules also makes a gas easily compressible.

Effect of Heat

14. Particles in a solid possess:
    - kinetic energy due to their constant vibrations about their mean position;
    - potential energy due to the forces between them.
15. When a solid is heated:
    - the kinetic energy of the particles increases. The particles vibrate more vigorously and the amplitude of vibration increases, so the temperature of the solid increases.
    - the potential energy of the particles increases as the separation between them increases.
16. When a liquid is heated, the kinetic energy and potential energy of the particles will increase.
17. When a gas is heated, the kinetic energy of the gas molecules increases and this increases the speed of the gas molecules.

Pressure of a Gas

18. The volume, pressure and temperature of a gas describe the physical condition of a gas.
19. Changes in the condition of a gas can be explained using the kinetic model.
20. The pressure of a gas is due to the elastic collisions of the gas molecules with the walls of the container.
21. When a gas molecule collides with the wall of a container, a force is exerted on the wall.
22. The magnitude of this force increases if:
    - the speed of the molecule is greater;
    - more molecules collide with the wall per unit time.
23. The pressure on the wall is the normal force per unit area on it.
24. When a fixed mass of gas at constant volume is heated, both its temperature and pressure increase because:
    - the kinetic energy of gas molecules increases. Hence the speed of the gas molecules increases.
    - the rate of collision of the gas molecules with the walls of the container increases.
    - the gas molecules knock harder on the walls.
25. When a fixed mass of gas is heated at constant pressure, both its temperature and volume increase.
26. As shown in figure 2(a), the initial pressure on the piston due to the collision of the gas molecules equals the external pressure.

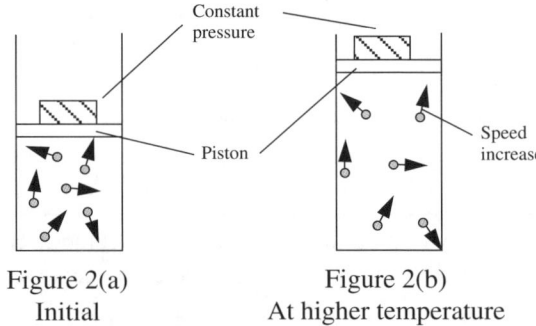

Figure 2(a)　　　　　　Figure 2(b)
Initial　　　　　　　At higher temperature

27. According to the kinetic model, when the temperature of the gas increases at constant pressure:
    - the kinetic energy of the gas molecules increases.
    - the force on the piston due to the collisions of the air molecules increases.
    - the piston is pushed out until the pressure on the piston equals the external pressure which is constant.

    Hence the volume of the gas increases.

28. When a fixed mass of gas is compressed at constant temperature, its pressure would increase.

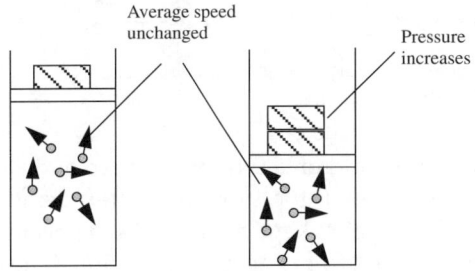

(a) Initial   (b) At higher pressure

29. When the volume of the gas is reduced:
    - the area of the walls of the container decreases.
    - the number of gas molecules per unit volume increases.
    - the rate of collision of gas molecules with unit area of the walls of the container increases. Hence the pressure increases.
30. For a fixed mass of gas at constant temperature, when the pressure of the gas is doubled, the volume is halved. Conversely when the pressure is halved, the volume is doubled.

Example

A kinetic model of a gas is shown in the figure. The gas molecules are represented by the marbles in a tray which is "agitated" on a horizontal table.

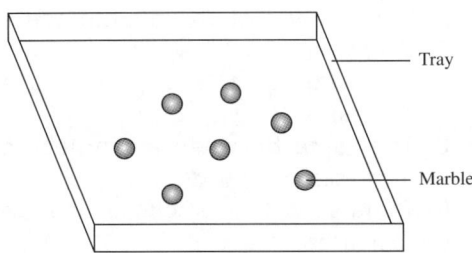

(a) Compare the size of the gas molecules with the distance between gas molecules.
(b) (i) Mark with arrows to show the directions of motion of the gas molecules at a particular instant.
    (ii) Describe what happens to the gas molecules during the motion.
(c) To demonstrate the motion of the gas molecules at a higher temperature, the tray is "agitated" more vigorously. Describe the change in the motion of the gas molecules.
(d) Hence explain the increase in pressure of a gas at constant volume when the temperature increases.

Solution

(a) The size of the gas molecules is very small compared to the distance between them.
(b) (i)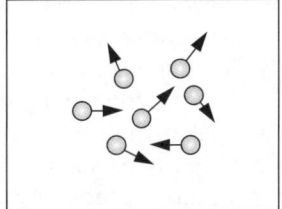

   (ii) The gas molecules collide with each other and with the walls of the container.
(c) The gas molecules move faster and collide more frequently and with greater force with the walls of the container.
(d) The pressure increases because:
    - the speed of gas molecules increases.
    - the collision of gas molecules with the walls is more frequent.
    - pressure = $\dfrac{\text{force}}{\text{area}}$, so when the force increases, the pressure increases.

Self Evaluation 8.3

1. Which one of the following statements about liquid molecules is correct?
   A They move freely at great speeds.
   B They vibrate about their respective mean positions.
   C They are in constant random translation motion.
   D They are arranged regularly in planes.

2. A liquid of the same volume as a solid expands faster when heated. Which one of the following deductions is correct?
   A The liquid molecules are bigger.
   B The liquid molecules expand faster.
   C The forces between liquid molecules are weaker than those between the molecules in the solid.
   D The liquid molecules collide more frequently with each other.

3. Some air in a sealed container is heated. Which one of the following increases?
   A The force of attraction between air molecules.
   B The force on the walls of the container produced by collisions of the air molecules.
   C The average distance between air molecules.
   D The number of air molecules per unit volume.

4. In which states of matter is the force of attraction between the molecules the greatest and in which state is the speed of the molecules the greatest?

	Greatest force of attraction	Greatest speed
A	Solid	Solid
B	Solid	Gas
C	Liquid	Solid
D	Liquid	Gas

5. Which of the following comparisons between molecules in water and molecules in steam is correct?
   A Size of molecules in water is larger.
   B Mass of molecules in water is larger.
   C Distance between molecules in water is larger.
   D Force between molecules in water is larger.

6.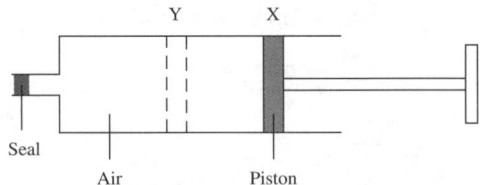

   The outlet of a syringe is sealed and air is trapped in the syringe. The temperature of the air is kept constant. As the piston is pushed from X to Y, the pressure of the air increases because
   A the rate of collision of the air molecules with the piston increases.
   B the rate of collision among air molecules increases.
   C the air molecules are moving faster.
   D the forces between air molecules increases.

7. Air in a closed container is heated. Which of the following increases?
   A Size of the air molecules.
   B Mean separation between air molecules.
   C Mean speed of the gas molecules.
   D Number of gas molecules.

8. Air is trapped in a cylinder fitted with a movable piston. When the cylinder is placed in a beaker of cold water the piston moves into the cylinder. Which statement is correct?
   A The speeds of the air molecules decrease.
   B The size of the air molecules decreases.
   C The force between air molecules increases.
   D The rate of collision among air molecules increases.

REVISION EXERCISE 8

Multiple Choice Questions

1. Which of the following provides evidence that atoms in a solid are arranged in an orderly manner?
   A Brownian motion
   B Diffusion
   C Structure of a crystal
   D A stretched rubber

2. Which of the following describes correctly motion of a copper atom in a piece of copper?
   A Vibration about a mean position
   B Free random motion at great speeds
   C Random motion
   D Rotation and linear motion

3. What is observed in Brownian motion?
   A Gas molecules are moving.
   B Gas molecules collide with each other.
   C Gas molecules collide with smoke particles.
   D Motion of dust particles in air.

4. Which of the following arranges in correct increasing order the kinetic energy of molecules in ice, water and steam?
   A Steam, water, ice
   B Ice, water, steam
   C Water, ice, steam
   D Steam, ice, water

5. An air cell is observed under a microscope. When the temperature increases, the specks of light move faster because
   A the air molecules expand.
   B the average distance between air molecules increases.
   C faster air molecules collide with the dust particles.
   D the dust particles burn brighter at higher temperature.

6. A beaker is pushed into water in a tank slowly. Which of the following increases as the depth of the beaker below the water surface increases?

   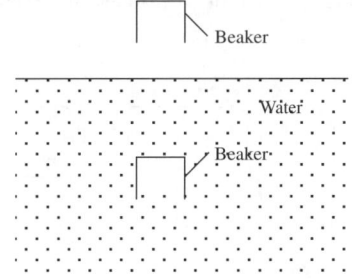

   A Speed of air molecules in the beaker.
   B Number of molecules per unit volume.
   C Separation between air molecules in the beaker.
   D Volume of the air molecules in the beaker.

7. The volume of a fixed mass of gas is increased at constant temperature. The physical quantity that remains unchanged is
   A density of the gas.
   B mean separation between gas molecules.
   C pressure of the gas.
   D mean speed of gas molecules.

8. As an air bubble rises from the bottom of a pond,
   A its volume increases and the pressure in the bubble decreases.
   B its volume increases and the pressure in the bubble increases.
   C its volume decreases and the pressure in the bubble decreases
   D its volume decreases and the pressure in the bubble increases.

9. Air is trapped in a glass tube by a thread of mercury. The figure below shows the glass tube in three different positions.

   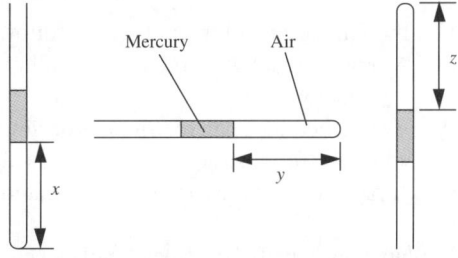

   Which of the following compares the lengths of the air column x, y and z correctly?
   A $x > y > z$ C $y > x > z$
   B $x > z > y$ D $z > y > x$

10. A soap bubble is inside a cylinder fitted with a piston. When the piston is moved into the cylinder, what happens to the pressure of the air in the cylinder and to the volume of the soap bubble?

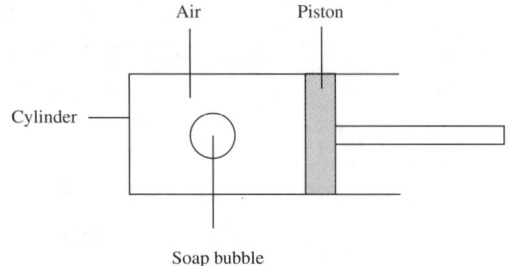

	Pressure of the air	Volume of bubble
A	Increases	Increases
B	Increases	Decreases
C	Decreases	Increases
D	Decreases	Decreases

Structured Questions

Section A

1. (a) In the space provided illustrate the arrangement of molecules in the solid state, liquid state and gaseous state. You may use small circles to represent the molecules.

    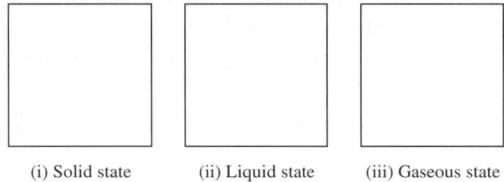

    (i) Solid state   (ii) Liquid state   (iii) Gaseous state

    (b) Explain in terms of forces between the molecules, why
    (i) a solid has a definite shape;
    (ii) a liquid takes the shape of the container;
    (iii) a gas has no definite shape.

2. Use the kinetic model to explain the followings.
    (a) A large force only produces a small extension in a steel wire.
    (b) A stretched wire can return to its original length when the force stretching it is released.
    (c) A piece of metal expands when heated.

3. Explain why a dented ping pong ball can be restored to its original shape by placing it in hot water.

4. (a) Explain the kinetic theory as applied to a gas.
    (b) Use the kinetic theory to explain
    (i) how a gas exerts a pressure;
    (ii) how the pressure of a fixed mass of gas at constant volume changes when the gas is heated.

5. The figure shows a balloon in a cylinder that is fitted with a movable piston.

    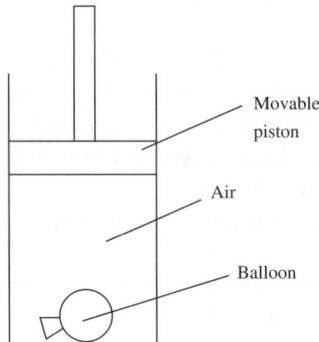

    Discuss and explain what happens to the volume of the balloon
    (a) when the piston is pushed into the cylinder;
    (b) when the piston is pulled upwards.

6. Figure 3(a) shows a cylinder fitted with a piston connected to a mercury manometer. The atmospheric pressure is 75.0 cm of mercury. The volume of the air inside the cylinder is 50.0 cm^3.

    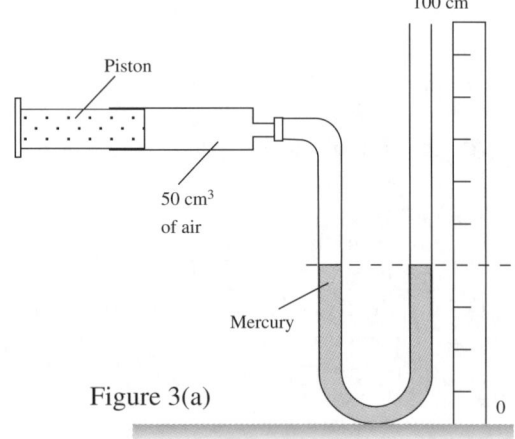

    Figure 3(a)

    (a) What is the pressure of the air in the cylinder?
    (b) When the piston is moved, the mercury levels in the manometer change to as shown in figure 3(b).

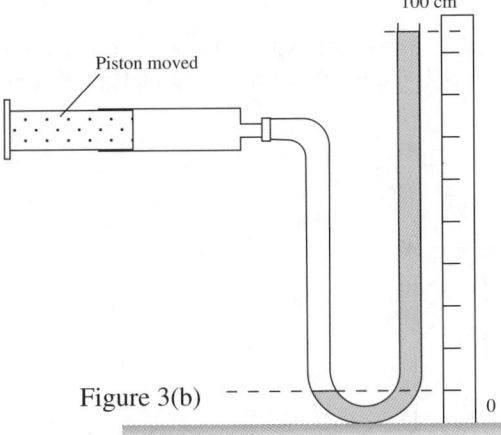

Figure 3(b)

(i) What is the pressure of the air in the cylinder?
(ii) Calculate the volume of the air in the cylinder.

Section B

1. (a) Figure 4(a) shows a dust particle in the air moving with a velocity represented both in magnitude and direction by an arrow.

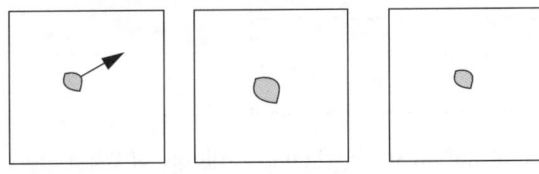

Figure 4(a)   Figure 4(b)   Figure 4(c)

What cause the dust particle to move?
(b) Figure 4(b) shows another dust particle which is bigger and under the same conditions as the dust particle in 4(a). Mark in figure 4(b) an arrow to represent the speed of this dust particle. Explain for any difference in the speed.
(c) Figure 4(c) shows the same dust particle as in 4(a) but the air around it is at a higher temperature. State and explain any difference in the motion of this dust particle compared to the dust particle in 4(a).
(d) What is the name given to the motion of the dust particles described above?
(e) State two inferences about the motion of air molecules from the observation mentioned in 4(a).

2. (a) Air is pumped into the tyres of a car. Explain, in terms of the kinetic theory,
    (i) why the pressure increases as more air is pumped into the tyre;
    (ii) why the pressure in the tyres increases after the car had travelled a long distance.
(b) The figure shows air trapping in a syringe fitted with a piston. The nozzle of the syringe is sealed.

Compare the pressure of the air in the syringe with the atmospheric pressure.
(c) The piston is pushed into the syringe until the volume of the trapped air is halved. Explain the change(s), if any, to
    (i) the number of air molecules in the syringe;
    (ii) the density of the air inside the syringe;
    (iii) the mean speed of the air molecules in the syringe at constant temperature;
    (iv) the pressure inside the syringe.

Data-based question

3. The figure shows a cylinder of cross-sectional area 1.0×10^{-4} m^2 fitting with a piston. The volume of air at atmospheric pressure, 1.0×10^5 Pa, trapped in the cylinder is 100 cm^3. When a weight of 10.0 N is placed on the piston, the volume of the trapped air becomes 50 cm^3.

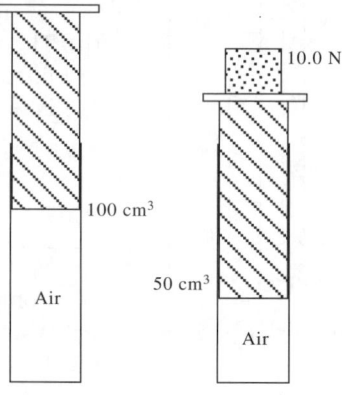

(a) Calculate
   (i) the pressure on the piston due to the weight of 10.0 N;
   (ii) the pressure of the trapped air when the weight of 10.0 N is on the piston.

(b) The table below shows the volume V of the trapped air and its pressure P for different weight on the piston. The first two sets of readings had been filled.

Weight (N)	0	2.5	10.0	15.0	20.0
p ($\times 10^5$ Pa)	1.0	1.25			
V (cm^3)	100	80	50		

   (i) Use the answer to (a)(ii) above to fill in the value of the pressure when the volume of the trapped air is 50 cm^3.
   (ii) Use the same method as in (a) above to calculate the pressure when the weight on the piston is 15.0 N and 20.0 N. Write your answers in the above table.
   (iii) Use the answer for the relationship between pressure and volume of the trapped air to complete the above table.

CHAPTER 9
Transfer of Thermal Energy

1. Thermal energy or heat is the form of energy that is transferred from a region of higher temperature to a region of lower temperature.
2. The three main methods of heat transfer are:
   - conduction;
   - convection;
   - radiation.

9.1 Conduction

1. **Conduction** is the main mode of heat transfer in solids.
2. In conduction, heat is transferred from one atom to another by the vibration of atoms.
3. Heat is also transferred by the movement of free electrons from the hot end to the cool end, thus metals are good conductors of heat.
4. Liquids and gases are poor conductors of heat.
   (a)

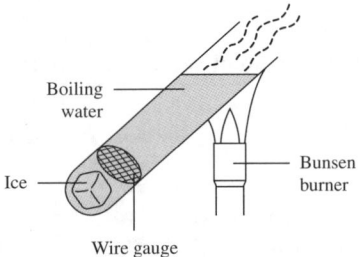

   As shown in the figure, water at the top of the test tube boils, but the ice at the bottom remains. This shows that water is a poor conductor of heat.
   (b)

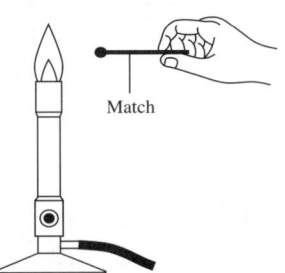

   A match stick held 3 or 4 cm from a Bunsen flame does not ignite. So air is a poor conductor of heat.

5. Pockets of air trapped in materials such as wool, fibre, glass, and expanded polystyrene reduce heat transfer by conduction.
   (a) Wool is used as winter clothings.
   (b) Fibre glass wool is used as insulation in roofs, between double-walls of buildings and in gas ovens.
   (c) Expanded polystyrene is used in walls of refrigerators.
6. Good conductors of heat such as copper, aluminium, and steel are used for making cooking utensils.

Self Evaluation 9.1

1.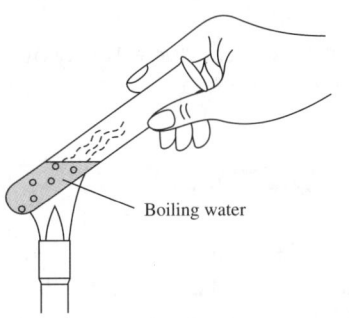

   A person can still hold on the test tube when the water in it is boiling (see the figure) because
   A glass is a poor conductor of heat.
   B glass is a poor radiator of heat.
   C water is a poor conductor of heat.
   D water is a poor radiator of heat.

2. In which of the following is most of the heat transferred by conduction?
   A The boiling of water in an electric kettle
   B The baking of bread in an oven
   C The deep frying of chicken in oil
   D The heating of a soldering iron

3. Spoons of different materials are used to stir a hot drink. Which of the following spoons will heat up the fastest?
   A Plastic spoon
   B Steel spoon
   C Glass spoon
   D Wooden spoon

4.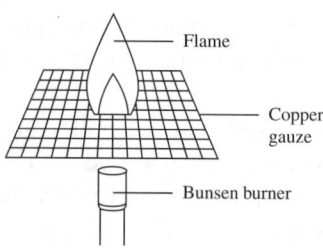

When a Bunsen burner is lighted above copper gauze, there is no flame above the gauze because
A heat is radiated from the copper gauze.
B there is no gas below the gauze.
C convection current is created below the gauze.
D heat is conducted away by the gauze.

9.2 Convection

1. **Convection** is the main mode of heat transfer in fluids – liquids and gases. It involves the movement of the hotter fluids from the hot region to the cool region.
2. The figure below shows how convection current is set up when water in a beaker is heated.

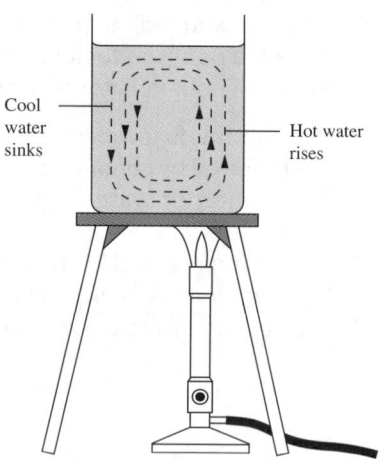

Convection current in water

Water at the bottom that is heated expands. Its density decreases and the warm water rises.
3. The cool water at the top being denser moves down and gets heated in turn. As a result, convection current is set up with the less dense warm fluids carrying thermal energy upwards.
4. (a) The heating element of an electric kettle is located at the bottom so that a convection current can be set up in the water.
   (b) The radiator that heats up a room in the winter is located in the lower portion of the room for the same reason.
   (c)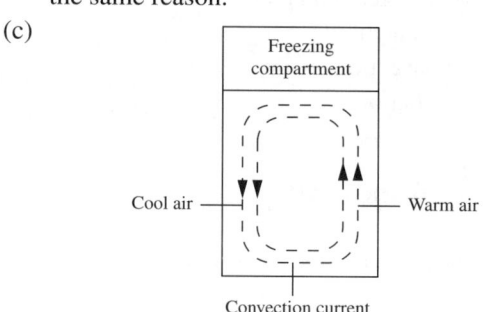

The freezing compartment of a refrigerator is located at the top such that the air cooled by the freezing compartment being denser moves down and the warm air moves up. Soon the entire space in the refrigerator is cooled.
5. Sea breezes and land breezes are due to convection currents.

Formation of sea breeze during the day

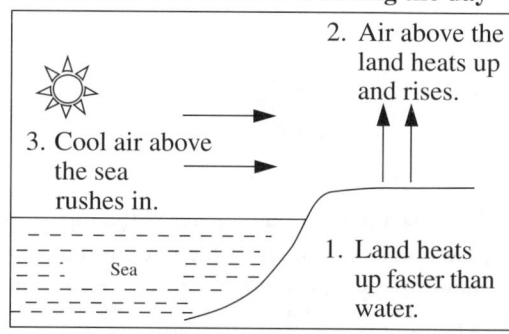

Formation of land breeze during the night

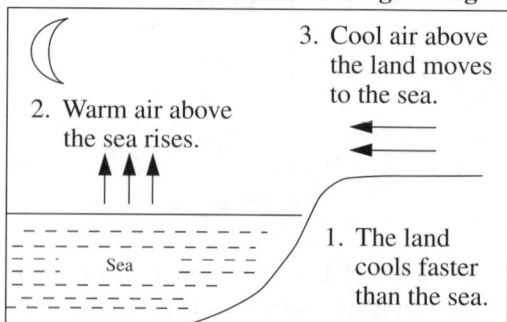

Self Evaluation 9.2

1. Four identical thermometers – A, B, C and D – are placed at an equal distance from a lighted 100 W bulb.

   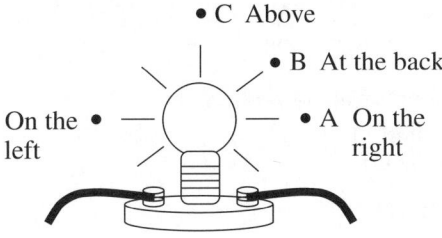

   Which thermometers gives the highest reading?

2.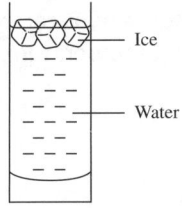

   Water in a glass is cooled by some pieces of ice floating on the water surface. The main process by which water at the bottom of the glass gets cooled is
   A   conduction.   C   radiation.
   B   convection.   D   freezing.

3. When convection current is set up in a room, which one of the following does not happen?
   A   Air expands when heated.
   B   Density of hot air increases.
   C   Hot air rises to the top.
   D   Cool air moves down.

4.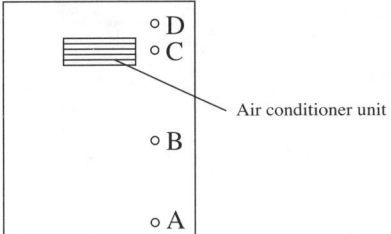

   A room is cooled by an air conditioner unit as shown. At which of the points A, B, C or D is the temperature lowest?

9.3   Radiation

1. **Radiation** is the method of heat transfer that does not require a material medium.
2. Heat is transferred by infra red waves. For example, heat from the Sun is transferred by radiation to the Earth.
3. The rate of heat transfer by radiation from a hot body is affected by:
   (a) the colour and texture of the surface of the body.
       A dull black surface is the best radiator of heat whereas a shiny smooth surface is the worst radiator of heat.
   (b) surface temperature of the body.
       The rate of radiation increases as the temperature increases.
   (c) surface area of the body.
       The rate of radiation increases as the surface area increases.
4. If the temperature of an object is *higher* than that of its surroundings, it is a net **emitter of radiation**.
5. If the temperature of an object is *lower* than that of its surroundings, it is a net **absorber of radiation**.
6. **A rough dull black surface is both a good emitter and a good absorber.**
7. **A smooth polished surface is both a poor emitter and a poor absorber.**
8. (a) The inner surface of an electric or gas oven is rough and painted dull black so that it is a good emitter of radiated heat.
   (b) The coils of a solar heater are painted dull black so that it is a good absorber of radiated heat.
   (c) Space suits of astronauts are shiny so as not to absorb much radiated heat.
   (d) Water is kept warm longer in a shiny chrome kettle compared to water in a kettle blackened with soot because the shiny chrome is a poor emitter of heat.

Self Evaluation 9.3

1. Four cars of the same model but painted with different colours are parked under the hot sun with the windows closed. After an hour, the temperature inside which car will be the highest?
   A White car
   B Black car
   C Red car
   D Yellow car

2. People sitting round an open fire feel warm because heat is transferred mainly by
   A conduction.
   B convection.
   C radiation.
   D freezing.

3. Thermal energy is transferred from the Sun to the Earth by
   A conduction.
   B convection.
   C radiation.
   D convection and radiation.

4. Figure 1(a) shows two cans P and Q. Each can contains the same volume of water initially at 90 °C. Figure 1(b) shows the same cans containing water initially at 0 °C. The temperature of the room is 30 °C.

   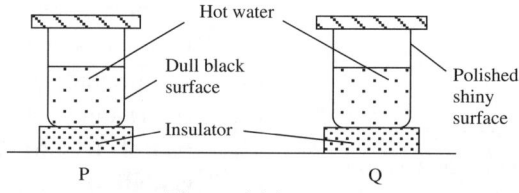
   Figure 1(a)

   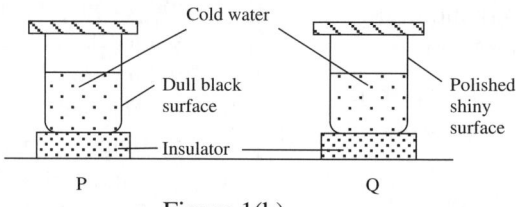
   Figure 1(b)

   After five minutes, water in which containers will be at a higher temperature?

	Figure 1(a)	Figure 1(b)
A	P	Q
B	P	P
C	Q	Q
D	Q	P

REVISION EXERCISE 9

Multiple Choice Questions

1. The materials in increasing order of thermal conduction are
   A copper, aluminum, iron.
   B copper, iron, aluminum.
   C aluminum, copper, iron.
   D iron, aluminum, copper.

2. The figure shows a coil of copper wire above a candle flame.

   The candle flame is extinguished when the coil of copper wire is lowered into the candle flame because
   A no air enters the coil.
   B the coil conducts heat away.
   C copper is not burnt by the flame.
   D hot air moves upwards.

3. Which methods of transfer of thermal energy does not require a material medium?
   A Conduction
   B Convection
   C Radiation
   D Convection and conduction

4. The heating element of an electric kettle is positioned at the bottom because
   A hot water rises.
   B heat is conducted to the top.
   C the temperature of water is higher at the bottom.
   D the thermal energy is radiated from the bottom.

5. The figure shows a double-wall glass window.

   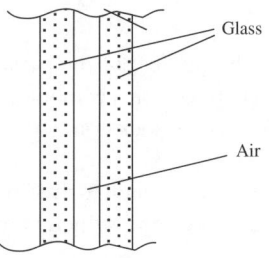

   A double-wall window can
   A reduce the intensity of light.
   B prevent the window from breaking.
   C reduce the rate of heat flow through the window.
   D increase conduction of heat through the window.

6. An astronaut who performs space walk outside the spacecraft should wear a suit which has a
   A dull black surface.
   B highly reflective surface.
   C red-coloured surface.
   D white surface.

7. A thick woollen jacket keeps a person warm because
   A the air is trapped in the wool.
   B the wool is warm.
   C the wool heats up easily.
   D the air flow through the wool easily.

8. Thermal energy is transferred through the movement of the material in the medium in
   A conduction.
   B convection.
   C radiation.
   D conduction and convection.

9. The vacuum between the walls of a thermo flask prevents heat transfer by
   A conduction.
   B convection.
   C radiation.
   D conduction and convection.

10. Which of the following coloured clothes will absorb the least amount of thermal energy from the surroundings?
    A White   C Grey
    B Black   D Red

Structured Questions

Section A

1. Explain why the feet of the person feel cold when he stands barefoot on a cement floor but do not feel cold if he has his socks on.

2. The figure shows hot drink in a cup made of expanded polystyrene which is white in colour.

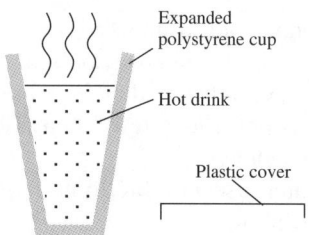

   (a) Explain how the cup keeps the drink warm longer.
   (b) If a plastic cover is provided, explain how the cover keeps the drink warm even longer.

3. The figure shows a filament lamp with a plastic cover hanging from the ceiling.

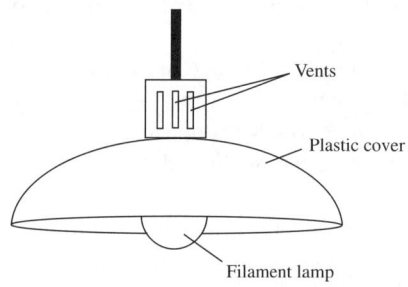

   (a) Explain the purpose of the vents in the plastic cover. What would happen if a cover with no vents is used?
   (b) Why does the lamp become hot five minutes after it is switched on?
   (c) Explain why a person who sits directly below the filament lamp feels warm.

4.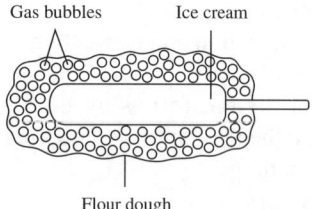

The figure shows a "fried ice cream". A slab of ice cream is dipped in dough mixed with bicarbonate of soda and deep fried in hot oil.

   (a) Explain why the ice cream does not melt in the hot oil.
   (b) Explain the method of heat transfer in the hot oil.

5. Use the kinetic model of matter to explain
   (a) why copper is a good thermal conductor;
   (b) why air is a poor conductor of heat.

Section B

1. Explain the following design of a passenger plane in terms of conduction, convection and radiation of heat.
   (a) The external surface of the plane is highly reflective.
   (b) A layer of insulating fibre is between the external wall and the passenger cabin.
   (c) Double-wall glass windows.

2. Two copper cans are filled with water initially at 90°C. One can is lagged with felt and the other can is not lagged.

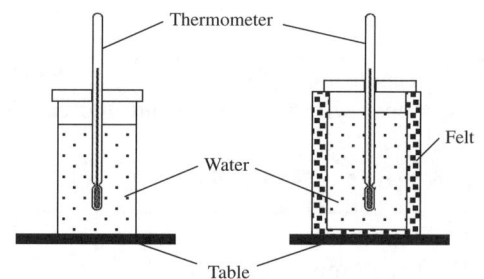

The graph below shows the change in the temperature with time for water in the can which is not lagged.

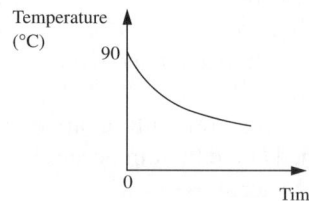

   (a) (i) State the three methods of transfer of thermal energy.
       (ii) Explain the roles of these three methods for the heat lost from the can that is not lagged.
   (b) Copy the graph shown above and on the same axes sketch a graph to show how the temperature of water in the lagged can changes with time. Explain the difference in the two curves.

Data-based Question

3. The figure shows two kettles placing on identical hot metal plates to boil the water.

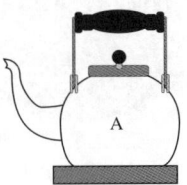
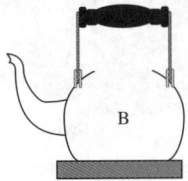

Copper kettle with highly polished exterior

Open aluminum kettle with exterior covered with soot

(a) State the process by which thermal energy from the hot plate is transferred
   (i) through the base of the kettles;
   (ii) throughout the water.
(b) Discuss how the following factors determine water in which of the kettles will reach boiling point more rapidly.
   (i) Nature of exterior surface
   (ii) Type of metal
   (iii) Kettle with or without cover
(c) After the water in each kettle had boiled, the kettles were removed from the hot plate and allowed to cool.
   Discuss whether water in A or B will be at a lower temperature after five minutes.

CHAPTER 10
Temperature and Thermal Properties of Matter

10.1 Temperature

1. **Temperature** is the degree of hotness of an object.
2. Temperature can be measured by a thermometer.
3. To define a temperature scale, we need
   - a thermometric property
   - two fixed points
   - a numerical scale
4. A **thermometric property** is a physical quantity that increases or decreases with increasing temperature.
5. Examples of thermometric properties:
   (a) The volume of a fixed mass of liquid in a glass bulb — used in a mercury-in-glass thermometer.
   (b) The resistance of a length of platinum wire — used in a resistance thermometer.
   (c) The pressure of a fixed mass of gas at constant volume — used in a gas thermometer.
   (d) The voltage of a thermocouple — used in a thermocouple thermometer.
6. Two temperatures that are easily and accurately reproducible are selected as **fixed points**. The fixed points are used as reference temperatures.
7. In the Celsius (°C) scale of temperature the two fixed points are:
   (a) the **lower fixed point** — the temperature of pure melting ice. It is fixed as 0 °C.
   (b) the **upper fixed point** — the temperature of steam from pure water, boiling under standard atmospheric pressure. It is fixed as 100 °C.
8. In the Celsius (°C) scale of temperature, the temperature interval between the lower fixed point (ice point) and the upper fixed point (steam point) in divided into 100 equal divisions. Each division is 1 °C.
9. Temperature θ °C can be converted into kelvin (K), the SI unit for temperature using the relationship
$$\theta\,°C = (\theta + 273)\,K$$

Example:
(a) $0\,°C = (0 + 273)\,K = 273\,K$
(b) $100\,°C = (100 + 273)\,K = 373\,K$
(c) $-50\,°C = (-50 + 273)\,K = 223\,K$

Mercury-in-glass Thermometer

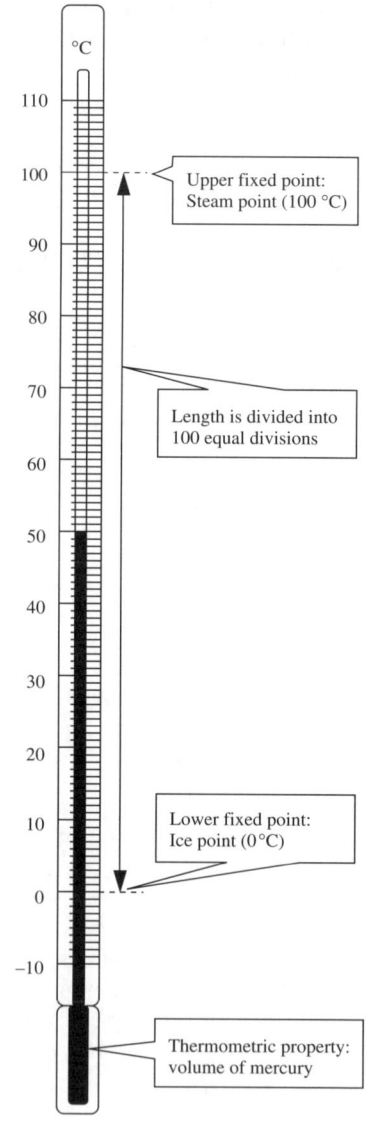

10. **To calibrate a mercury-in-glass thermometer.**
    (a) Lower fixed point: Place the bulb of the thermometer in pure melting ice. When the mercury meniscus is steady, mark its position as 0 °C.

    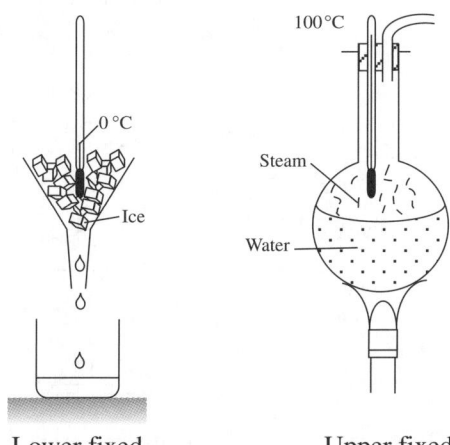

    Lower fixed point, 0 °C   Upper fixed point, 100 °C

    (b) Upper fixed point: Place the bulb of the thermometer in steam from pure water boiling at standard atmospheric pressure. When the mercury meniscus is steady, mark its position as 100 °C.
    (c) Divide the distance between the 0 °C mark and the 100 °C mark into 100 equal divisions. Each division is 1 °C.

11. A thermometer is more sensitive if it can detect a small change in temperature. The sensitivity of a mercury-in-glass thermometer is increased by
    – using a narrower capillary tube;
    – using a bigger mercury bulb.

12. Mercury can be used in thermometers to measure temperature between its freezing point, –39 °C, and its boiling point, 357 °C. The range of a normal laboratory mercury-in-glass thermometer is –10 °C to 110 °C.

13. Mercury expands quite *linearly* with increase in temperature — for the same increase in temperature the length of the mercury thread increases by the same amount.

14. The responsiveness of a mercury-in-glass thermometer increases if the time taken for the thermometer to respond to changes in temperature is shorter.

15. This happens if the glass wall of the thermometer bulb and the glass stem is thinner.

Problem Solving Technique

In solving problems involving the Celsius (Centigrade) scale of temperature, write two expressions that show the change of temperature is proportional to the corresponding change in the values of the thermometric property.

(change of temperature) $\propto$ (change in thermometric property)

$(100 - 0)\,°C \propto (14.5 - 2.5)\,cm$ (1)
$(\theta - 0)\,°C \propto (6.1 - 2.5)\,cm$ (2)

Then use $\frac{(2)}{(1)}$ to solve for the unknown.

Example:
The lengths of the mercury thread in a mercury-in-glass thermometer are as follows:
At the ice point = 2.5 cm
At the steam point = 14.5 cm
At room temperature, θ = 6.1 cm

(a) What is the room temperature?
(b) What is the length of the mercury thread at 72 °C?

Solution

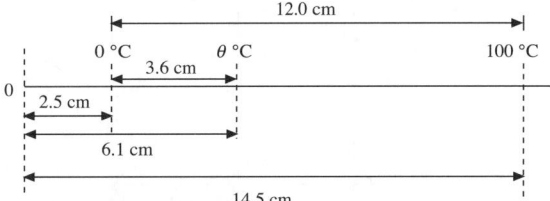

(a) Difference in temperature
$(100 - 0)\,°C \propto (14.5 - 2.5)\,cm$
$100\,°C \propto 12.0\,cm$ (1)
Difference in temperature
$(\theta - 0)\,°C \propto (6.1 - 2.5)\,cm$
$\theta\,°C \propto 3.6\,cm$ (2)
$\frac{(2)}{(1)} : \frac{\theta}{100\,°C} = \frac{3.6\,cm}{12.0\,cm}$
$\Rightarrow \theta = \left(\frac{3.6\,cm}{12.0\,cm}\right)(100\,°C)$
$= 30\,°C$

(b)

```
        |◄——— 12.0 cm ———►|
    0°C            72°C   100°C
0 |2.5 cm|                  |
  |------|       l          |
         |--- (l – 2.5) cm -|
```

From (a) 100 °C ∝ 12.0 cm

72 °C ∝ (l − 2.5) cm   (3)

$\dfrac{(3)}{(1)} = \dfrac{72}{100} = \dfrac{l-2.5}{12.0}$

$\Rightarrow l - 2.5 \text{ cm} = \left(\dfrac{72\,°C}{100\,°C}\right)(12 \text{ cm})$

$l = 11.14 \text{ cm}$

Self Evaluation 10.1

1. Which one of the following is NOT suitable as a thermometric property?
   A Volume of a fixed mass of liquid
   B Resistance of a piece of wire
   C Pressure of a fixed mass of gas at constant volume
   D Friction between the surfaces

2. The figure shows the length of the mercury thread column in a thermometer at 0 °C, 100 °C and x °C.

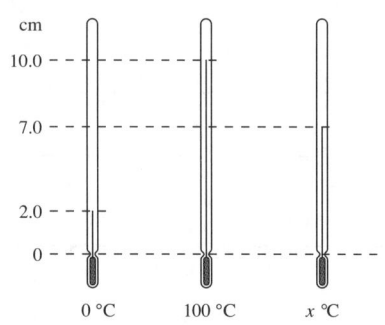

   What is the value of x?
   A 37.5
   B 50.0
   C 62.5
   D 70.0

3. To fix the upper fixed point of a thermometer on the centigrade (Celsius) scale, the bulb of the thermometer is place in
   A boiling water.
   B melting ice.
   C steam at standard atmospheric pressure.
   D melting pure naphthalene.

10.2 Thermocouple Thermometer

1. The figure shows a simple **thermocouple thermometer**.

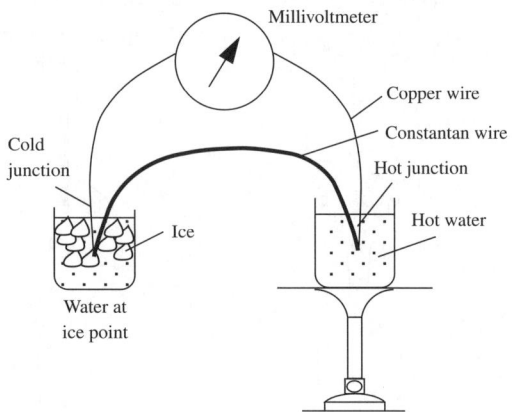

2. The thermocouple thermometer consists of a copper wire and a constantan wire joined together at the ends. A millivoltmeter is connected to the copper wire.

3. One end of the thermocouple thermometer, known as the cold junction, is placed in melting ice at 0 °C (ice point). The other end, known as the hot junction, is placed in the object whose temperature is to be measured, example hot water.

4. The thermometric property used in the thermocouple thermometer is the variation of the voltage generated between the cold and the hot junctions of the thermocouple as the temperature difference between the two junctions increases.

5. A millivoltmeter is used to measure the voltage generated. The scale of the millivoltmeter is calibrated in °C so that the temperature can be read directly.

6. **Advantages of the thermocouple thermometer**
   - It is able to measure temperature over a wide range, from −250 °C to 1000 °C. Thus it can be used as a standard thermometer for measuring high temperatures.
   - It is very sensitive — able to detect small changes in temperature and able to response fast.

Example

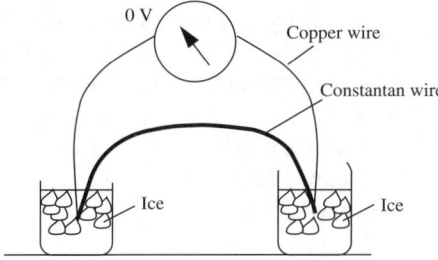
Figure (a)

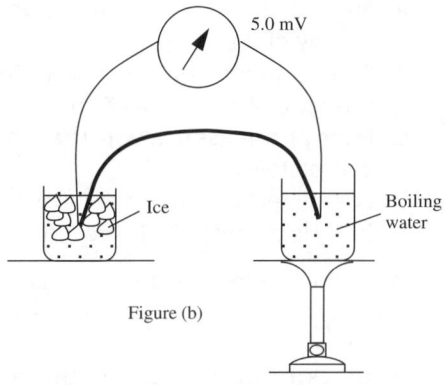
Figure (b)

The above figure shows how a thermocouple thermometer is calibrated. When both the junctions are at the ice point as shown in figure (a), the voltage generated is 0 V.
One junction is then placed in boiling water at 100 °C (steam point), the voltage generated is 5.0 mV.
(a) On the scale of the millivoltmeter shown below, mark as accurately as possible the values 0 °C, 20 °C, 40 °C, 60 °C, 80 °C and 100 °C

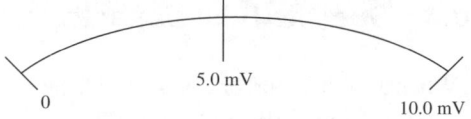

(b) With the cold junction at the ice point and the hot junction in a liquid, the voltage generated is 3.6 mV. What is the temperature of the liquid?
(c) What is the voltage generated when the temperature of the hot junction is at 180 °C?

Solution

(a)

Note: 0 mV corresponds to 0 °C and
5.0 mV corresponds to 100 °C.
Then divide the length of the arc between the 0 °C and 100 °C mark into 5 equal parts.
Each part represents a temperature interval of 20 °C.

(b) $(5.0 - 0)$ mV $\propto (100 - 0)$ °C (4)
$(3.6 - 0)$ mV $\propto (\theta - 0)$ °C (5)

$$\frac{(5)}{(4)} : \frac{\theta}{100\,°C} = \frac{3.6\,\text{mV}}{5.0\,\text{mV}}$$
$$\Rightarrow \theta = 72\,°C$$

(c) $(5.0 - 0)$ mV $\propto (100 - 0)$ °C (4)
$(x - 0)$ mV $\propto (180 - 0)$ °C (6)

$$\frac{(6)}{(4)} : \frac{x}{5.0\,\text{mV}} = \frac{180\,°C}{100\,°C}$$
$$\Rightarrow x = 9.0\,\text{mV}$$

Self Evaluation 10.2

1. The thermometric property used in the thermocouple thermometer is
   A the resistance of a thermocouple.
   B the voltage of a thermocouple.
   C the temperature of a thermocouple.
   D the volume of a thermocouple.

2. Which of the following is NOT an advantage of the thermocouple thermometer?
   A Can be used to measure high temperatures
   B Can be used to measure low temperatures
   C Is sensitive to rapid changes in temperature
   D Suitable for normal use

3. When the hot junction of a thermocouple thermometer is at steam point, the voltage generated is 12 mV. When the hot junction is in a boiling liquid, the voltage generated is 10 mV. What is the boiling point of the liquid?
   A 83 °C   C 100 °C
   B 90 °C   D 120 °C

10.3 Internal Energy

1. According to the kinetic model of matter,
   - solids, liquids and gases are made up of atoms in constant motion.
   - atoms in solids and liquids attract and repel each other. Force between gas molecules is negligible.
2. Since atoms are in constant motion, they possess kinetic energy. Because of the forces between atoms, atoms have potential energy.
3. The **random thermal energy** of a body is the **total kinetic energy the molecules in the body**.
4. The internal energy of a body is the **sum of the kinetic energy and potential energy of the atoms** in the body.
5. When a body is heated, its temperature increases.
   (a) Solid
      (i) The potential energy of the atoms increases because the separation between atoms increases.
      (ii) The kinetic energy of the atoms increases because the atoms vibrate faster and with larger amplitudes.
   (b) Liquid
      (i) The potential energy of the atoms increases because the separation between atoms increases.
      (ii) The kinetic energy of the liquid molecules increases because the molecules move faster.
   (c) Gas
      (i) The potential energy of atoms is zero and is unaffected by change in temperature.
      (ii) The kinetic energy of the atoms increases as they move faster at higher temperatures. Hence the **internal energy** of a body **increases as the temperature increases**.

Self Evaluation 10.3

1. Which of the following arrangements is in the correct order of increasing internal energy of the same mass of water, ice and steam?
   A Water, ice, steam
   B Steam, water, ice
   C Ice, water, steam
   D Ice, steam, water

2. Which of the following describes correctly the internal energy of a body?
   A Sum of kinetic energy and potential energy of the body.
   B Sum of kinetic energy and potential energy of atoms in the body.
   C Energy released when the body is completely burnt.
   D Energy released when the mass of the body is completely destroyed.

3. When the temperature increases, the internal energy of a solid changes because
   A the kinetic energy of the atoms increases but the potential energy decreases.
   B the kinetic energy of the atoms decreases but the potential energy increases.
   C both the kinetic energy and potential energy of the atoms decrease.
   D both the kinetic energy and potential energy of the atoms increase.

10.4 Specific Heat Capacity

1. When a solid, liquid or gas is heated, thermal energy is transferred to the molecules. The kinetic energy and potential energy of the molecules increases.
2. Thus, the **internal energy** of the solid, liquid, or gas increases.
3. The **heat capacity** C of an object is the amount of thermal energy required to raise the temperature of the object by $1\,°C$ or $1\,K$. The unit for heat capacity is $J\,°C^{-1}$ or $J\,K^{-1}$.
4. The **specific heat capacity** c of a material is the amount of thermal energy required to raise the temperature of 1 kg of the material by $1\,°C$ or $1\,K$. The unit for specific heat capacity c is $J\,kg^{-1}\,°C^{-1}$ or $J\,kg^{-1}\,K^{-1}$.

5. The table below shows the specific heat capacity of some common materials.

Material	Specific heat capacity ($J\ kg^{-1}\ °C^{-1}$)
Water	4 200
Aluminium	880
Copper	390
Steel	460
Ethanol	2 500
Glass	650

6. Water has a high specific heat capacity which makes it useful as a cooling as well as a heating agent.
7. Water is used in the radiator of a car engine. Water is able to absorb a lot of heat before its temperature rises by 1 °C. Hence, it can act as an effective cooling agent.
8. Because water has a high specific heat capacity, a hot water bottle is used to keep a patient warm. For every 1 °C drop in temperature of the hot water in the bottle, 4200 J of heat is given off by 1 kg of water. Hence the hot water bottle is able to keep the patient warm for a long time.
9. Metals such as copper and steel have low specific heat capacities and are suitable for making cooking utensils. Very little thermal energy is required to heat up the cooking utensils such as pots and frying pans.
10. When the temperature of a material of mass m rises by θ °C, the heat Q absorbed is

$$Q = mc\theta$$

11. When its temperature drops by θ °C, the heat Q lost is

$$Q = mc\theta$$

Problem Solving Technique
When apply the equation, $Q = mc\theta$, θ is the **change in temperature** and is equal to the higher temperature minus the lower temperature.

Example
The heat capacity of a block of metal is 600 $J\ °C^{-1}$.
(a) What is the heat required to raise its temperature
  (i) by 5 °C;   (ii) from 30 °C to 50 °C?
(b) If the initial temperature of the metal block is 100 °C, what is its final temperature after it loses 2400 J of heat?

Solution
(a) (i) Heat capacity = 600 $J\ °C^{-1}$
     When the temperature rises by 5 °C,
     heat required = (600 $J\ °C^{-1}$)(5 °C)
                   = 3000 J
   (ii) Increase in temperature = (50 – 30) °C
                                = 20 °C
     Heat required = (600 $J\ °C^{-1}$)(20 °C)
                   = 12 000 J

(b) As heat loss is 2400 J, drop in temperature
    $$= \frac{2400\ J}{600\ J\ °C^{-1}}$$
    = 4 °C
    Hence the final temperature = (100 – 4) °C
                                = 96 °C

Example
Calculate the total heat required to raise the temperature of 2.0 kg of water in an aluminium kettle of mass 0.50 kg from 30 °C to 100 °C.
(Specific heat capacity of water and aluminium is 4200 $J\ kg^{-1}\ °C^{-1}$ and 880 $J\ kg^{-1}\ °C^{-1}$ respectively.)

Solution
Using $Q = mc\theta$
Heat gained by water
= (2.0 kg)(4200 $J\ kg^{-1}\ °C^{-1}$)(100 °C – 30 °C)
= 588 000 J
Heat gained by kettle
= (0.5 kg)(880 $J\ kg^{-1}\ °C^{-1}$)(100 °C – 30 °C)
= 30 800 J
Total heat gained = 618 800 J

Example
A copper block of mass 400 g is heated using a Bunsen burner. It is then transferred into 200 g of water initially at 30 °C. The final temperature of the mixture is 50 °C. What is the initial temperature of the copper block?

(*Specific heat capacity of copper and water is 390 J kg^{-1} °C^{-1} and 4200 J kg^{-1} °C^{-1} respectively.*)

Solution
Let x be the initial temperature of copper block.
Heat gained by water = heat loss by copper
(0.200 kg)(4200 J kg^{-1} °C^{-1})(50 °C − 30 °C) = (0.400 kg)(390 J kg^{-1} °C^{-1})(x − 50 °C)
$x = 158$ °C

Example
A 50 W immersion heater is used to heat a beaker containing 300 g of ethanol. The mass of the beaker is 60 g and the initial temperature of the ethanol is 30 °C. What is the final temperature of the ethanol after the immersion heater has been switched on for 10 minutes?
(*Specific heat capacity of ethanol and glass is 2500 J kg^{-1} °C^{-1} and 650 J kg^{-1} °C^{-1} respectively.*)

Solution
Heat supply by immersion heater = heat gained by ethanol and beaker
(50 W)(10 × 60 s)
= [(0.300 kg)(2500 J kg^{-1} °C^{-1}) + (0.060 kg)(650 J kg^{-1} °C^{-1})](x − 30 °C)
$x = 68$ °C

Self Evaluation 10.4

1. The mass of a piece of copper is 600 g and its specific heat capacity is 0.400 J g^{-1} °C^{-1}.
   (a) What is the heat capacity of the piece of copper?
   (b) The initial temperature of the piece of copper is 28 °C. If 1200 J of heat is absorbed by the copper piece, what is its final temperature?
   (c) Calculate the heat dissipated by the piece of copper when its temperature drops from 100 °C to 30 °C.

2. An electric heater of power 2.0 kW is used to heat 1.50 kg of water initially at a temperature of 30 °C in an aluminum container of mass 0.40 kg. The specific heat capacity of water and aluminum is 4.20 J g^{-1} °C^{-1} and 0.90 J g^{-1} °C^{-1} respectively.

   (a) Calculate the heat required to raise the temperature of
   (i) the water and
   (ii) the container to 100 °C.
   (b) What is the time required to boil the water in the container?

10.5 Melting, Boiling and Evaporation

Melting/Solidification

1. When a solid melts, it changes from the solid to the liquid state at a certain temperature known as its **melting point**.
2. Heat is absorbed, but the temperature of the substance *remains unchanged*. The heat absorbed is known as **latent heat of fusion**.
3. During **solidification** (or freezing), a liquid changes into a solid. Latent heat of fusion is **released** but the temperature remains unchanged.
4. For a pure substance, both melting point and solidification (or freezing) point are the same. For example, pure ice melts at 0 °C and pure water freezes at 0 °C.
5. The reason why the temperature of the ice remains constant when it melts is as follow.
   – When ice melts, the thermal energy supplied (latent heat of fusion) causes the internal energy, kinetic energy and potential energy of the water molecules to increase. Since the temperature is constant 0 °C, the kinetic energy remains unchanged. The potential energy changes due to the change in the separation between molecules.
   – Energy is required to change the strong bonds between molecules in ice to the weaker bonds between molecules in water.
   – There is very small change in volume. Hence work done against atmospheric pressure is negligible.
6. **Factors Affecting the Melting Point of Water**
   (a) Addition of impurities, such as salts, lowers the melting point of water to below 0 °C.
   Hence, antifreeze is added to the water in the cooling system of a car to prevent it from freezing in the winter and salt is added to ice as freezing mixture to obtain temperatures below 0 °C.

(b) Increase in pressure reduces the melting point of ice.

Boiling/Condensation

7. **Boiling** is the process in which a liquid changes to gas at a **constant temperature** which is known as the **boiling point** of the liquid.
8. When a liquid boils thermal energy is transferred to the liquid without a change in temperature.
9. The heat required by a liquid to change to vapour at its boiling point is known as the **latent heat of vaporisation**.
10. Conversely, **condensation is the process** when a vapour changes into liquid. During condensation heat is lost by the vapour at constant temperature.
11. Pure water boils at 100 °C at atmospheric pressure of 1.03×10^5 Pa.
12. The boiling point of water is increased above 100 °C when impurities, such as salt, are dissolved in it. The boiling point of a vegetable soup which contains dissolved substances is greater than 100 °C.

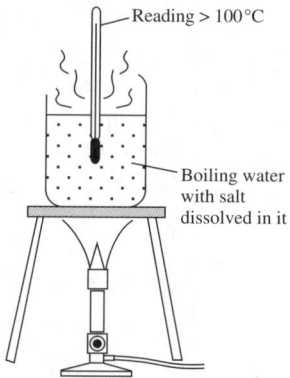

13. When the external pressure is increased, the boiling point of water is above 100 °C.

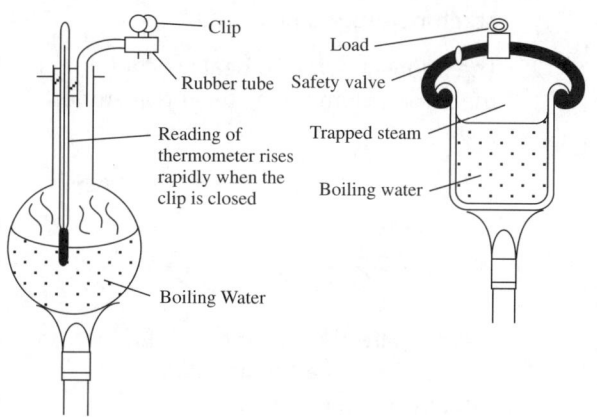

(a) In the pressure cooker, steam trapped in the cooker increases the pressure above the water. This causes the water to boil at above 100 °C. The higher boiling point of water enables food to be cooked in a shorter time.
(b) Autoclaves are used in hospitals to sterilise surgical instruments. Steam trapped in the autoclave causes the pressure in the autoclave to rise. Thus, water in it boils at a higher temperature.
14. Water boils below 100 °C when the pressure above the water is reduced.
15. At high altitude where the atmospheric pressure is lower than that at sea-level, water boils at temperatures below 100 °C. Thus, coffee or tea can taste bland.

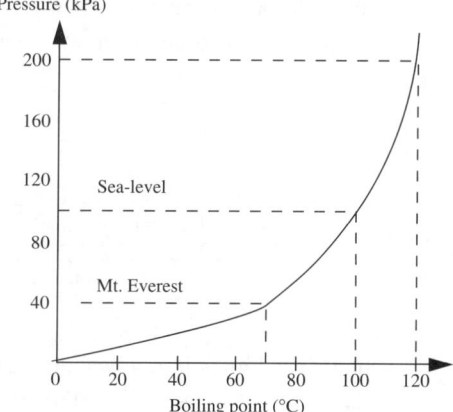

16. The graph above shows the variation of the boiling point of water with external pressure. On top of Mount Everest, water boils at 70 °C.
17. Applications of boiling under reduced pressure
    (a) Freeze dry is used to preserve food such as coffee powder, garlic and vegetables. The food is placed in a container and the pressure is slowly reduced to increase the rate of evaporation and to lower the boiling point of water. As the pressure in the container is further reduced, boiling and freezing can occur simultaneously.
    (b) Fractional distillation of petroleum at low pressure prevents the hydrocarbon from cracking and the heavier products of distillation can be obtained at lower temperature.
    (c) Refining of cane sugar a low pressure saves fuel costs.

(d) Evaporated milk is produced by boiling milk under reduced pressure at low temperature so that the vitamins in the milk are not destroyed by heat.

Evaporation

18. Evaporation is the process in which a liquid changes to vapour at temperatures below the boiling point of the liquid.
19. During evaporation, liquid molecules that have high kinetic energy escape from the liquid surface. The molecules that remain in the liquid have less kinetic energy. Hence the temperature of the liquid drops.
20. Evaporation produces cooling effect.
    (a) A hand rubbed with ethanol feels cool because ethanol evaporates rapidly. Heat required for evaporation is absorbed from the hand.
    (b)
    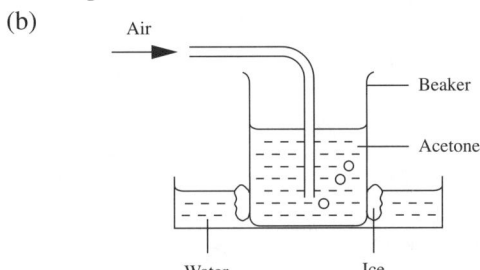
    When air is blown into a beaker of acetone, a layer of ice is formed outside the beaker. Heat which is required for the acetone to evaporate is absorbed from the water.
21. Applications of cooling by evaporation.
    (a) When sweating occurs, heat is absorbed from the body. This cools down the body.
    (b) In the refrigerator, the evaporation of *freon* under low pressure in the cooling coils absorbs heat from the surrounding. When the freon condenses under high pressure in the condenser coils outside the refrigerator, latent heat of evaporation is given off.
22. The rate of evaporation *increases* if
    − the surface area of the liquid increases.
      A bigger surface means there are more molecules on the surface and thus more molecules are able to escape — the rate of evaporation increases.
    − the temperature of the liquid increases.
      At higher temperature, the kinetic energy of the liquid molecules increases. More liquid molecules are able to escape from the liquid.
    − the humidity of the surrounding air decreases.
      If the humidity is high, there is a lot of water vapour above the liquid. Liquid molecules that escape from the liquid can collide with the water molecules and return to the liquid. The reverse occurs when the humidity is low.
    − there is a breeze.
      A breeze would blow away any liquid molecules that evaporate. When the space above the liquid surface is clear of vapour, subsequent liquid molecules that escape from the liquid would not be knocked back into the liquid.
23. Boiling and evaporation differ with respect to the following aspects.

Aspects	Boiling	Evaporation
Temperature	At a fixed temperature	At all temperatures below the boiling point
Place	Throughout the whole liquid	Only at the liquid surface
Rate	Fast	Slower
Visual	Bubbles can be seen	No bubbles

Self Evaluation 10.5

1. State two situations when water will boil at temperatures above 100 °C.
2. The figure shows two beakers containing the same volume of water and acetone.

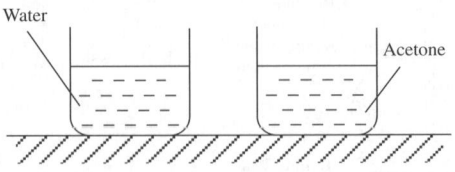

(a) Compare the volume of liquid left in each beaker after one hour.
(b) Explain your answer.

3. Air is bubbled into a beaker of acetone. A thermometer is used to measure the temperature of the acetone.

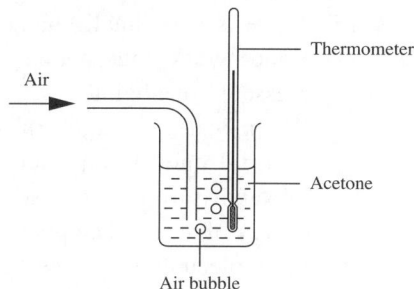

(a) Why does the rate of evaporation of acetone increase when air is blown into it?
(b) Describe and explain how the reading of the thermometer changes.

10.6 Specific Latent Heat

1. The **latent heat** L of a substance is the thermal energy transferred when the substance changes from one state to another at constant temperature.
   The unit for latent heat is the joules (J).
2. The **specific latent heat** l of a substance is the thermal energy transferred when a **unit mass** of the substance changes from one state to another at constant temperature. The unit for specific latent heat is J g^{-1} or J kg^{-1}.
3. The specific latent heat of fusion l of ice is 3.34×10^5 J kg^{-1}, which means that to melt 1 kg of ice, 3.34×10^5 J of heat is required.
4. The heat required to melt a mass m of a solid of specific latent heat of fusion l is

$$Q = ml$$

5. Conversely, when a mass m of a liquid freeze at its freezing point, the heat loss

$$Q = ml$$

6. In molecular terms, the latent heat of fusion supplied to melt a solid is used to increase the separation between the molecules.

7. Work is done against the attractive force between the molecules. Hence the internal energy of the substance increases.
8. The specific latent heat of vaporisation of water l is 2260 J g^{-1} means that 2260 J of heat is required to change 1 g of water to steam at 100 °C.
9. Conversely, when 1 g of steam at 100 °C condenses, 2260 J of heat is liberated.
10. Because of the high value of the specific latent heat of steam, it can be used for heating purpose. For example, in a hot drink dispenser machine, steam is passed into the drink to make the drink hot.

Example
Calculate the heat required to melt the following masses of ice at 0 °C.
(a) 4.0 kg   (b) 200 g
(Latent heat of fusion of ice = 3.34×10^5 J kg^{-1})

Solution
(a) Heat required
$Q = ml$
$= (4.0 \text{ kg})(3.34 \times 10^5 \text{ J kg}^{-1})$
$= 1.34 \times 10^6$ J
(b) Heat required
$Q = ml$
$= (0.200 \text{ kg})(3.34 \times 10^5 \text{ J kg}^{-1})$
$= 6.68 \times 10^4$ J

Example
The freezer compartment of a refrigerator removes heat at a rate of 2000 W. 500 g of water at 30 °C is placed in the freezer. How long does the water take to freeze?
(Specific latent heat of fusion of ice
= 3.34×10^5 J kg^{-1}, specific heat capacity of water
= 4200 J kg^{-1} °C^{-1})

Solution
Heat removed by freezer = heat lost by water when its temperature drops from 30 °C to 0 °C + heat lost by water when it freezes.

$$Pt = mc\theta + ml$$

Time taken t
$$= \frac{(0.500 \text{ kg})(4200 \text{ J kg}^{-1} °\text{C}^{-1})(30\,°\text{C} - 0\,°\text{C}) + (0.500 \text{ kg})(3.34 \times 10^5 \text{ J kg}^{-1})}{2000 \text{ W}}$$
$= 115$ s

Heating Curve

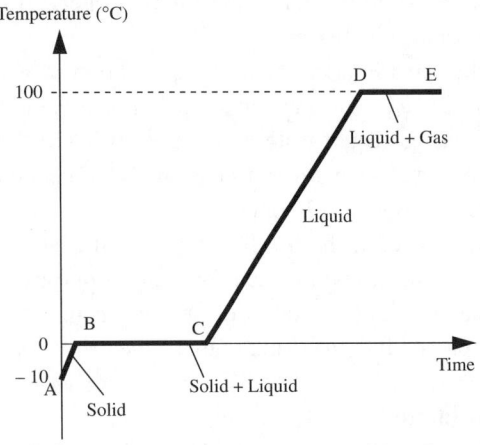

11. The figure above is the graph showing the variation of temperature with time for a certain quantity of water. Initially it is in the solid state (ice) at $-10\,°C$. It is then heated at a constant rate.

12. Along AB, it is in the solid state. The heat absorbed can be calculated using
    heat gained = mass × specific heat capacity of ice
    × increase in temperature
    $= mc\theta$

13. From B to C, melting occurs and the water is in both solid (ice) and liquid state.
    Heat required to melt the ice
    = mass of ice × specific latent heat of fusion
    $= ml$

14. At C, all the ice has melted. The heat supplied causes the temperature of water to rise until it starts to boil at D.
    Heat gained = mass of water
    × specific heat capacity of water
    × increase in temperature
    $Q = mc'\theta'$

15. Along DE, the water boils. Its boiling point is $100\,°C$. Water changes to steam.
    Heat required to evaporate water = mass of water × specific latent heat of vaporisation
    $Q = mL$

16. Explanation in molecular terms
    (a) (i) When ice melts, the thermal energy supplied (latent heat of fusion) increases the internal energy of the water – kinetic energy and potential energy of water molecules.
    (ii) Energy is required to change the strong bonds between molecules in ice to the weaker bonds between molecules in water.
    (iii) There is very small change in volume. Hence work done against atmospheric pressure is negligible.
    (b) (i) When water changes into steam, the thermal energy supplied (latent heat of vaporisation) increases the internal energy of steam. The potential energy of the molecules increases because of the increase in separation between molecules. The kinetic energy of the molecules also increases because molecules in steam are moving faster than water molecules.
    (ii) More energy is required to **break** the bonds between the water molecules. The bonding between molecules in steam is negligible.
    (iii) Energy is also required to do work against the atmospheric pressure. There is a large increase in volume when water turns into steam, 1 cm³ of water turns into 1600 cm³ of steam.

Example

Calculate the time taken by a 1 kW immersion heater to change 2.0 kg of ice, initially at $-10\,°C$, completely into steam at $100\,°C$.
(Specific heat of ice $c = 2100$ J kg^{-1} °C^{-1}; specific heat of water $c' = 4200$ J kg^{-1} °C^{-1}; specific latent heat of fusion of ice $l = 3.34 \times 10^5$ J kg^{-1}; specific latent heat of vaporisation of water $L = 2.26 \times 10^6$ J kg^{-1})

Solution

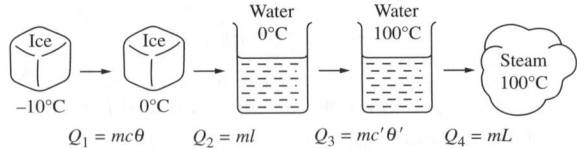

The ice at $-10\,°C$ changes to steam at $100\,°C$ in four stages as shown in the figure above.
Heat required to heat ice from $-10\,°C$ to $0\,°C$
$Q_1 = mc\theta$
$= (2.0 \text{ kg})(2100 \text{ J kg}^{-1}\text{°C}^{-1})(0\,°C - (-10\,°C))$
$= 42\,000$ J

Heat required to melt ice at 0 °C
$Q_2 = ml$
$= (2.0 \text{ kg})(3.34 \times 10^5 \text{ J kg}^{-1})$
$= 668\,000 \text{ J}$

Heat required to heat water from 0 °C to 100 °C
$Q_3 = mc'\theta'$
$= (2.0 \text{ kg})(4200 \text{ J kg}^{-1}\,°\text{C}^{-1})(100\,°\text{C} - 0\,°\text{C})$
$= 840\,000 \text{ J}$

Heat required to change water to steam at 100 °C
$Q_4 = mL$
$= (2.0 \text{ kg})(2.26 \times 10^6 \text{ J kg}^{-1})$
$= 4.52 \times 10^6 \text{ J}$

Total heat required $= 4.2 \times 10^4 \text{ J} + 6.68 \times 10^5 \text{ J}$
$+ 8.4 \times 10^5 \text{ J} + 4.52 \times 10^6 \text{ J}$
$= 6.07 \times 10^6 \text{ J}$

Time taken $= \dfrac{\text{heat required}}{\text{power}}$
$= \dfrac{6.07 \times 10^6 \text{ J}}{1000 \text{ W}}$
$= 6.07 \times 10^3 \text{ s}$

Cooling Curve

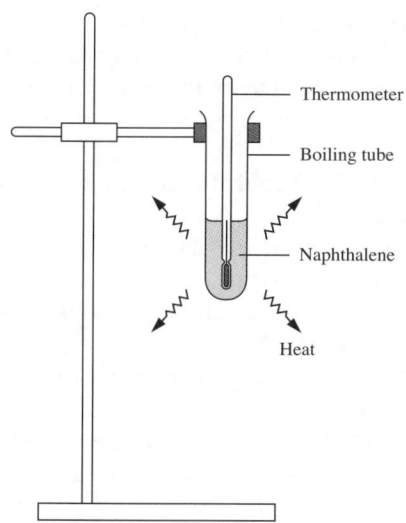

17. When some molten naphthalene is allowed to cool, its cooling curve is as shown below.

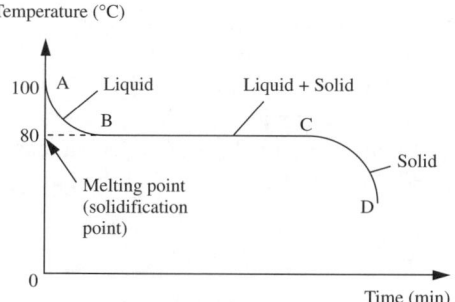

18. Along BC, although heat is continuously lost, the temperature of naphthalene remains at 80 °C, which is its solidification point (or melting point). Latent heat of fusion is dissipated.

Self Evaluation 10.6

1. An immersion heater of power 50 W is used to heat 40 kg of a liquid. The initial temperature of the liquid is 28 °C. After 5.0 minutes, the temperature of the liquid becomes 40 °C.
   (a) Calculate the specific heat capacity of the liquid.
   (b) Further heating of the liquid causes its temperature to increase to 80 °C where the temperature of the liquid remains constant.
      (i) Explain why the temperature of the liquid remains constant at 80 °C even though heat is continuously supplied.
      (ii) Explain what happens to the heat supplied.

2. (a) A gas burner raises the temperature of 0.5 kg of water from 25 °C to 70 °C in 60 seconds. Assuming that the specific heat capacity of water is 4200 J kg^{-1} °C^{-1}, calculate the average rate of heat transferred to the water.
   (b) The same gas burner is used to melt 0.5 kg ice at 0 °C. If the specific latent heat of fusion of ice is 3.34×10^5 J kg^{-1}, calculate the time required to melt the ice.

3. A plastic cup contains 50 g of ice at 0 °C. 50 g of water at 30 °C is poured into the cup. The heat capacity of the cup is negligible.
   (a) Calculate
      (i) the heat lost by the water when its temperature drop from 30 °C to 0 °C.
      (ii) the mass of ice that melts to bring the temperature of the water to 0 °C.
   (b) Describe how the temperature of the water in the cup varies with time.
   (Specific heat capacity of water = 4200 J kg^{-1} °C^{-1};
   specific latent heat of fusion of ice = 3.34×10^5 J kg^{-1})

REVISION EXERCISE 10

Multiple Choice Questions

1. In the centigrade scale of temperature, the lower fixed point is the ice point. What is the ice point in K?
   A 0
   B 100
   C 273
   D 373

2. A piece of copper of heat capacity 25 J K^{-1} is heated and its temperature increases from 30 °C to 85 °C. What is the increase in internal energy of the copper piece?
   A 750 J
   B 1375 J
   C 2125 J
   D 2875 J

3. Which of the following has the most internal energy?
   A 100 g of ice
   B 100 g of water at room temperature
   C 100 g of boiling water
   D 100 g of steam at 100 °C

4. On top of Mount Everest, water boils at a temperature
   A less than 100 °C because the atmospheric pressure is lower than at sea level.
   B less than 100 °C because the temperature is lower than at sea level.
   C more than 100 °C because the temperature is lower than at sea level
   D more than 100 °C because the air is less dense.

5. When the temperature of a block of metal of mass 800 g drops from 60 °C to 55 °C, it loses 2400 J of thermal energy. What is the specific heat capacity of the metal?
   A 0.60 J g^{-1} °C^{-1}
   B 1.70 J g^{-1} °C^{-1}
   C 40 J g^{-1} °C^{-1}
   D 50 J g^{-1} °C^{-1}

6. A piece of lead is heated at a constant rate until all of it melts. Which graph shows correctly how the temperature θ changes with time t?

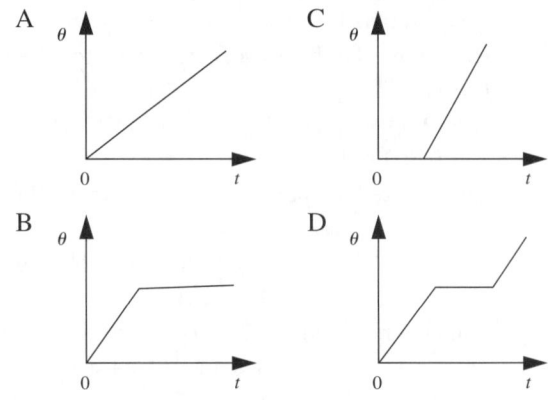

7. When water boils, the molecules
   A expand.
   B gain thermal energy.
   C increase in number.
   D break up into atoms.

8. The rate of evaporation of a liquid decreases when
   A the humidity of the air increases.
   B the surface area of the liquid increases.
   C the temperature of the liquid increases.
   D the room temperature increases.

9. The hand feels cold after it is rubbed with ethanol because
   A the temperature of the ethanol is lower than the body temperature.
   B ethanol on the skin prevents the loss of heat from the body.
   C thermal energy is transferred from ethanol to the body
   D when ethanol evaporates, heat is absorbed from the body.

10. Which of the following involves the largest amount of transfer of thermal energy? (Specific heat capacity of water = 4.2 J g^{-1} °C^{-1}; specific latent heat of fusion of ice = 334 J g^{-1} °C^{-1}; specific latent heat of vaporisation of water = 2 260 J g^{-1} °C^{-1})
    A 2 g of water turns into steam.
    B 100 g of water cools from 100 °C to 90 °C.
    C 50 g of ice melts at 0 °C.
    D Temperature of 20 g of water increases from 30 °C to 50 °C.

Structured Questions

Section A

1. Define (a) the lower fixed point and
   (b) the upper fixed point
   of the centigrade scale of temperature.

2. (a) What constitute the internal energy of a cube of copper at room temperature?
   (b) How does the internal energy of the copper cube change when it melts?

3. The figure below is the cooling curve of a substance initially in the liquid state.

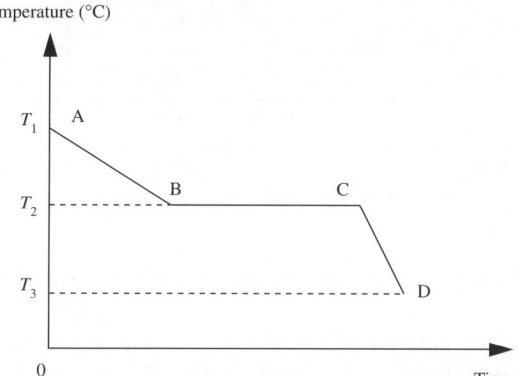

   (a) Along which section of the curve is the substance in
       (i) the solid state;
       (ii) the liquid state?
   (b) What is the temperature at which the liquid solidifies? Explain the reason for your answer.
   (c) Which has the greater value, the heat capacity of the substance in the solid state or its heat capacity in the liquid state? Why?

4. Use the kinetic model of matter to explain the following phenomena.
   (a) Why does the temperature of the solid increase when the solid is heated?
   (b) When the solid melts, its temperature does not increase even though the solid is heated. Why?
   (c) Why does the boiling point of water increases when the external pressure increases?

5. An immersion heater of 250 W is used to heat a liquid in a plastic container of negligible heat capacity. The variation of the temperature of the liquid with time is as shown in the figure. After 600 s, all the liquid has evaporated.

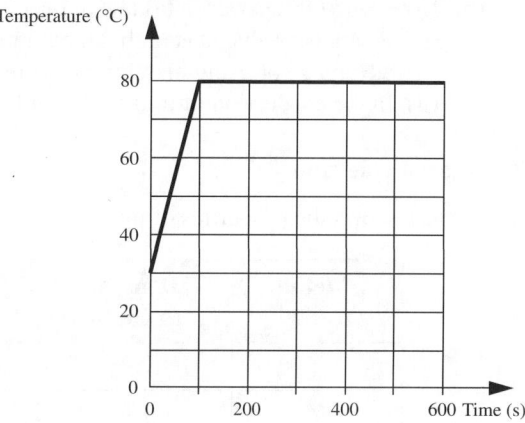

   (a) What is the rate of increase in temperature for the first 100 s?
   (b) What is the boiling point of the liquid?
   (c) Calculate
       (i) the heat capacity of the liquid;
       (ii) the latent heat of vaporisation of the liquid.

Section B

1. The figure shows a thermocouple thermometer. Junction A of the thermocouple is in melting ice.

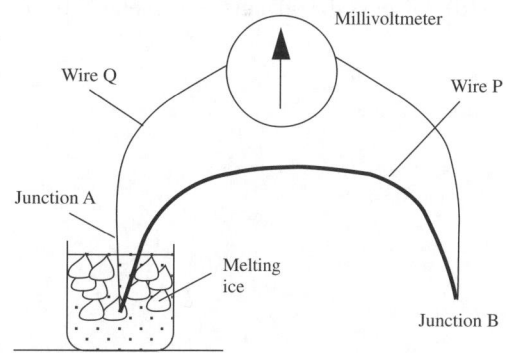

   (a) Suggest suitable metals for the wire P and the wire Q.
   (b) What would be the millivoltmeter reading when junction B is placed in another beaker containing melting ice? Give a reason for your answer.
   (c) When junction B is placed in steam from water boiling in a beaker, the millivoltmeter reads 25 mV. What is the temperature of the junction B when the millivoltmeter reads 7.5 mV?

(d) Explain whether the thermocouple thermometer is suitable to measure the following temperatures.
   (i) Temperature in an electric oven
   (ii) Rapid changing temperature in a diesel engine

2. (a) State how the boiling point of water is affected by the external pressure.
   (b) How can your answer to (a) above be applied to explain the following observations?
      (i) Steam is produced at high temperature in boilers for turning turbines of power generators. What is the advantage of using high temperature steam?
      (ii) In the production of evaporated milk, the boiling point of the milk must be lower than 100 °C.

Data-based Question

3. Table 1 shows the properties of three metals X, Y and Z.

Metal	Density (g cm^{-3})	Specific heat capacity (J g^{-1} °C^{-1})	Melting point (°C)
X	2.7	0.90	700
Y	1.8	0.15	1800
Z	8.0	0.40	1600

Table 1

Three cooking pots of the same shape are made from the same volume of 800 cm^3 of each of the metals X, Y and Z.
(a) Which pot is the heaviest? Show how you arrive at your answer.
(b) Each pot contains equal volume of water and is heated by a hot plate that supplies thermal energy at the same rate. Water in which of the pots will be the first to boil?
(c) After the water in each of the pots had boiled, the pots are removed from the hot plate and allowed to cool. Heat is lost from the pots at the same rate. After five minutes, water in which pot will be at the highest temperature?
(d) Discuss the advantage of metal Y over the other two metals.

CHAPTER 11

General Wave Properties

11.1 Wave Motion

1. A wave is a means of transfer of energy through vibrations.

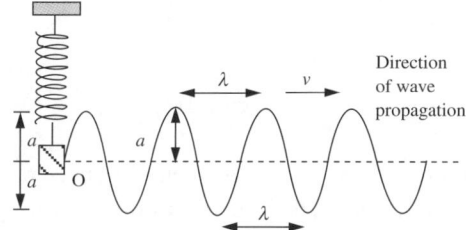

2. The above figure shows a load hanging from the end of a spring. One end of a string is attached to the load. When the load vibrates up and down about its mean position O with an amplitude a, the string is set into vibration.
3. A wave is set up in the string and energy is transferred by the vibrations along the string.
4. The string acts as a medium for the wave motion.

11.2 Wave Terms

1. The **amplitude** a of a wave is the maximum displacement of a particle of the medium from the undisturbed position.
2. If the load vibrates with a frequency f, each particle vibrates with the same frequency. The **frequency** of a wave is the number of complete vibrations per second of a particle of the medium. The unit for frequency is the hertz (Hz).
3. The time taken for a complete vibration is known as the **period** T.

$$\text{Period } T = \frac{1}{f}$$

4. The distance between successive crests or successive troughs is known as the **wavelength** λ.

5. The **speed** of a wave is the distance travelled per second by a wave pulse along the direction of the waves.

Speed of wave = frequency × wavelength
$$v = f\lambda$$

6. A **wavefront** is a surface in which all the particles on it vibrate in phase. The figure below shows (a) plane wavefronts and (b) circular wavefronts from a point source. The direction of the wave motion is perpendicular to the wavefronts.

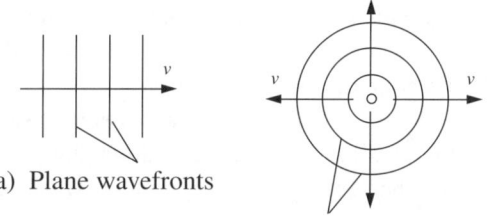

(a) Plane wavefronts

(b) Circular wavefronts

Self Evaluation 11.1

1. One end of a rope is moved up and down 5 times per second through a distance of 10 cm. The wave generated is as shown in the figure.

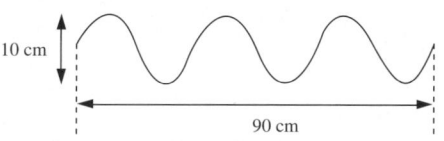

What is (a) the frequency;
(b) the amplitude;
(c) the wavelength and
(d) the speed of the wave?

11.3 Longitudinal and Transverse Waves

1. The type of waves travelling along the string is known as **transverse waves**. In a transverse wave, the direction of vibration is **perpendicular** to the direction of wave motion.
2. Other examples of transverse waves are water waves and light waves.
3. If one end of a slinky spring is repeatedly pushed and pulled, energy is transferred along the spring in the form of **longitudinal waves**.

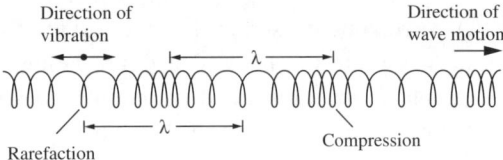

4. In a **longitudinal wave**, the direction of vibrations is **parallel** to the direction of wave motion. A series of compressions and rarefactions travel along the direction of wave propagation.
5. The wavelength λ is the distance between successive compressions or successive rarefactions.
6. Another example of longitudinal wave is sound waves.

Example

A transverse wave is set up when one end of a rope is moving up and down at a rate of 4 times per second. The speed of the wave along the rope is 0.25 m s^{-1}.
Calculate
(a) the period of vibration and
(b) the wavelength.

Solution
(a) Frequency $f = 4.0$ Hz
$$\text{Period } T = \frac{1}{f}$$
$$= \frac{1}{4.0 \text{ s}^{-1}}$$
$$= 0.25 \text{ s}$$
(b) Speed $v = f\lambda$
$$\text{Wavelength } \lambda = \frac{v}{f}$$
$$= \frac{0.25 \text{ m s}^{-1}}{4.0 \text{ s}^{-1}}$$
$$= 0.0625 \text{ m}$$

Example

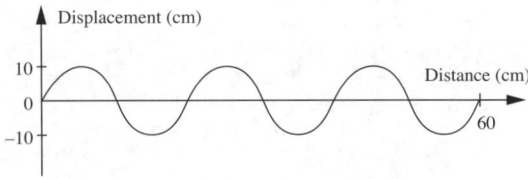

Figure 1(a)

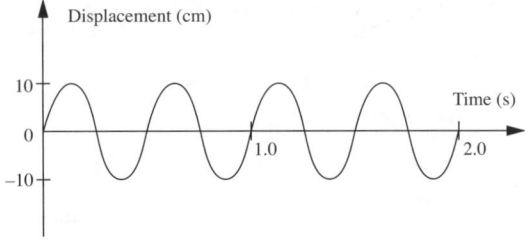

Figure 1(b)

Figure 1(a) is the displacement-distance graph and figure 1(b) is the displacement-time graph of a wave travelling along a slinky spring.
(a) What is the wavelength?
(b) Calculate
 (i) the period,
 (ii) the frequency and
 (iii) the velocity of the wave.

Solution
(a) From figure 1(a), 60 cm = 3λ
$$\text{Wavelength } \lambda = \frac{60 \text{ cm}}{3}$$
$$= 20 \text{ cm}$$

(b) (i) From figure 1(b), 2.0 s = $4T$
$$\text{Period } T = \frac{2.0 \text{ s}}{4}$$
$$= 0.50 \text{ s}$$
(ii) Frequency $f = \frac{1}{T}$
$$= \frac{1}{0.50 \text{ s}}$$
$$= 2.0 \text{ Hz}$$
(iii) Velocity $v = f\lambda$
$$= (2.0 \text{ s}^{-1})(20 \text{ cm})$$
$$= 40 \text{ cm s}^{-1}$$

Water Waves

7.

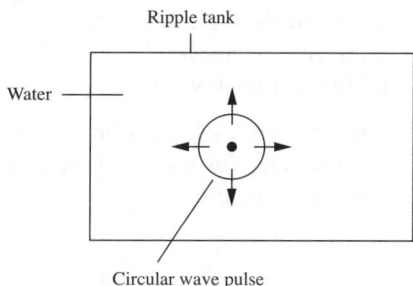

When a drop of water falls into a ripple tank, a circular wavefront is produced. The wavefront is the line that joins all the peaks of a wave.

8. As the wavefront moves outwards, the radius of the circle increases. The circular shape of the wave front shows that the water waves travel at a constant speed in all directions.

9. As the wavefront travels outwards, energy is transferred along the direction of wave motion without the transfer of matter.

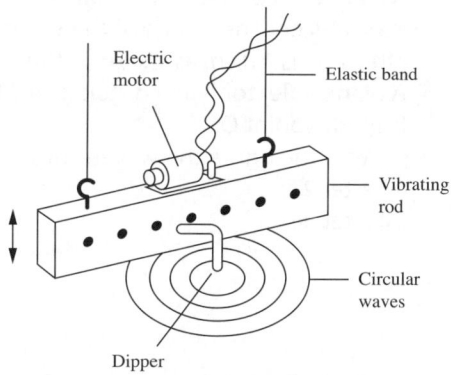

10. Continous circular waves are produced in a ripple tank using a vibrating rod with a dipper that touches the water surface. The frequency of the wave can be increased by increasing the speed of rotation of the electric motor.

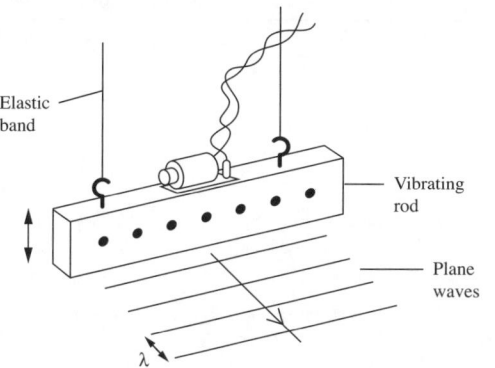

11. Continous straight waves are produced when the straight vibrating rod touches the water surface.

12. Reflection of water waves

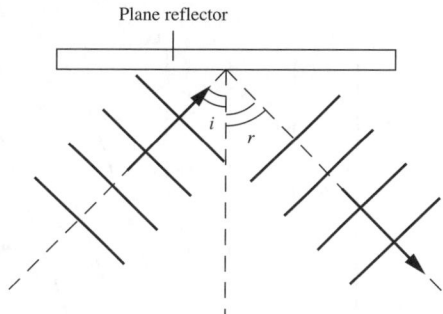

Angle of incidence = angle of reflection
$$i = r$$

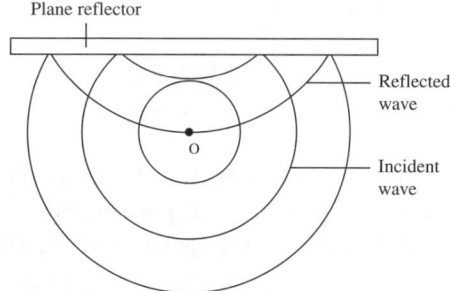

Circular waves reflected from a plane reflector seems to come from I, the image of O in the reflector.

13. **Refraction of waves** is the change in the velocity of waves when moving from one medium into another.

14. Refraction of water waves can be seen when water waves travel from deep water to shallow water or vice versa.

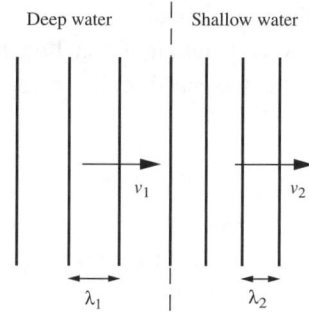

The wavelength and velocity of the waves decrease when they travel from deep water to shallow water.

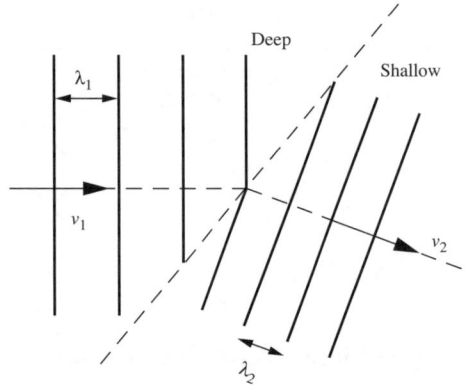

The direction of the water waves deflects closer to the normal when moving from the deep water to shallow water.

$\lambda_2 < \lambda_1$
$v_2 < v_1$,

where λ_1 and v_1 are the wavelength and velocity of the water wave in the deep water respectively and λ_2 and v_2 are the wavelength and velocity of the water wave in the shallow water respectively.

15. The frequency of the water waves does not change when the waves move from the deep water to the shallow water or vice versa.

Example
(a) Water waves are generated by a vibrator that vibrates at a frequency of 5 Hz in a ripple tank. The wavelength of the wave is 12 cm. Calculate the speed of the water waves.
(b) The water waves then move to a shallow region in the ripple tank.
The wavelength in the shallow region is 8 cm. What is the speed of the waves in the shallow region?

Solution
(a) Speed $v = f\lambda$
$= (5 \text{ s}^{-1})(12 \text{ cm})$
$= 60 \text{ cm s}^{-1}$
(b) In the shallow region, $f = 5$ Hz
$v = f\lambda$
$= (5 \text{ s}^{-1})(8 \text{ cm})$
$= 40 \text{ cm s}^{-1}$

Self Evaluation 11.2

1. Give **two** examples each for
   (a) transverse wave;
   (b) longitudinal wave

2. The frequency of the vibrator in a ripple tank is 25 Hz. The planes of the wavefronts are shown below.

   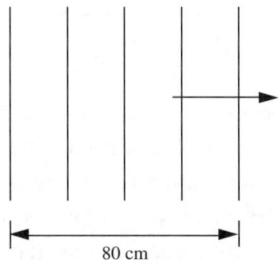

   (a) What is the wavelength?
   (b) Calculate the speed of the wave.
   (c) What is the distance travelled by the wavefront in 0.5 s?

3. When a drop of water falls onto the water surface at O, a circular wavefront is produced. The radius of the wavefront after 1.0 s is 1.0 cm as shown in the figure. A plane reflector is at a distance of 2.0 cm from the point O.
   Draw in the figure the wavefront
   (a) after 2 s;
   (b) after 3 s.

   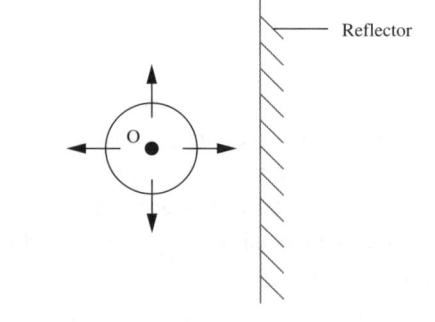

REVISION EXERCISE 11

Multiple Choice Questions

1. Examples of transverse and longitudinal waves are _____ and _____ respectively.

	Transverse	Longitudinal
A	water	sound
B	light	water
C	sound	light
D	water	light

2. A transverse wave moves along a rope in the direction shown in the figure.

   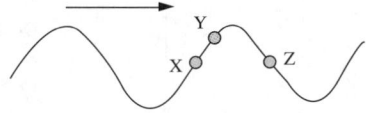

   The points X, Y and Z are moving in the directions shown in

   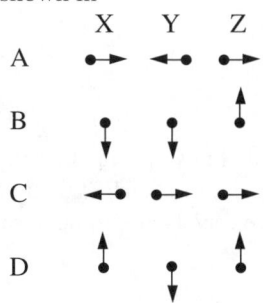

3. The figure shows a wave travelling along a rope.

   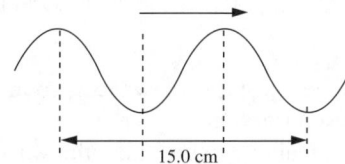

   What is the wavelength of the wave?
   A   5.0 cm
   B   10.0 cm
   C   15.0 cm
   D   20.0 cm

4.

   The figure represents an instantaneous picture of a wave travelling along a rope. The frequency of the wave is 2.0 Hz. Which one of the following represents the instantaneous picture of the wave 1.0 s later?

   A

   B

   C

   D

5. The figure shows a wave moving along a rope. The amplitude is equal to the distance marked.

   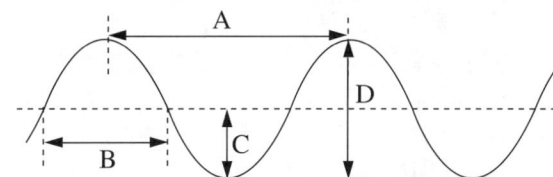

6. The figure shows the displacement-time graph of a wave motion.

   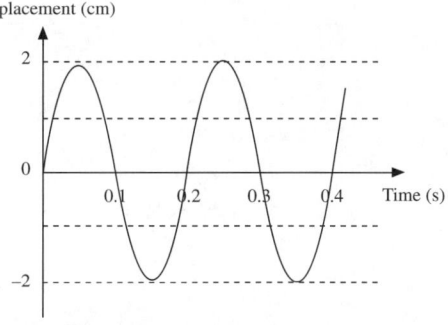

   What is the frequency of the wave motion?
   A   2.0 Hz   C   4.0 Hz
   B   5.0 Hz   D   10.0 Hz

7. The displacement-distance graph of a wave motion is as shown below.

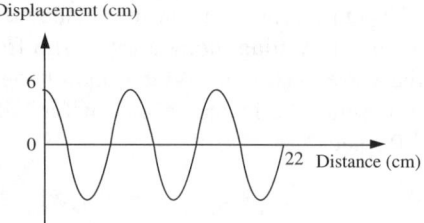

If the frequency of the wave is 30 Hz, what is the speed of the wave?
A 90 cm s^{-1}
B 120 cm s^{-1}
C 132 cm s^{-1}
D 240 cm s^{-1}

8. The figure shows parallel water waves travelling in a ripple tank. The wavefront at X travels to Y in 5.0 s. What is the frequency of the wave?

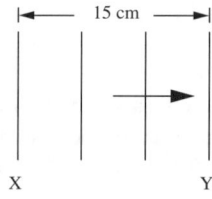

A 0.6 Hz
B 3.0 Hz
C 15 Hz
D 75 Hz

9. The figure shows a ripple from the point O in a ripple tank. In which direction is the speed of the ripple greatest?

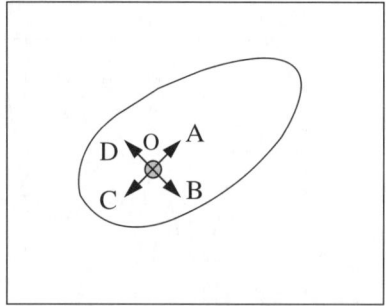

10. A circular ripple is produced at the point P in front of a straight reflector. Which one of the following shows the reflected wave?

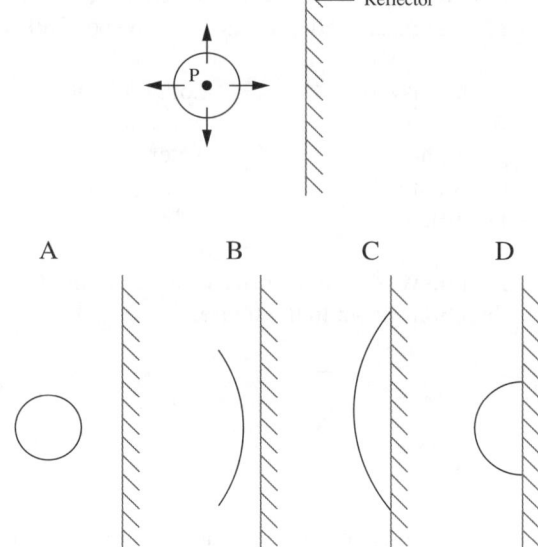

Structured Questions

Section A

1. One end of a sketched slinky spring is repeatedly pushed and pulled so as to make 10 vibrations in 5.0 seconds. The wave travels along the spring as shown in the figure.

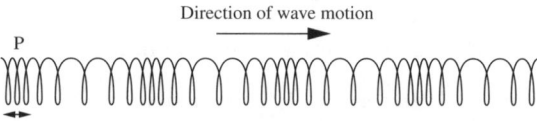

(a) Name the type of waves produced. Give a reason for your answer.
(b) In the above figure show the wavelength λ of the wave.
(c) What is the frequency of the wave?
(d) If the wavelength is 6.0 cm, what is the speed of the waves?

2.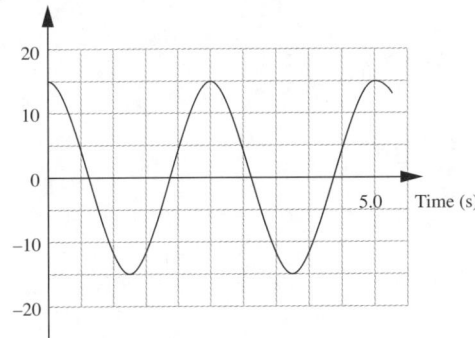

The graph above shows the variation of the displacement of a ripple tank vibrator with time.
(a) Determine
  (i) the amplitude of vibration.
  (ii) the period of vibration.
  (iii) the frequency of the vibration.
(b) If the speed of the waves produced is 28.0 mm s^{-1}, what is the wavelength of the waves?

3. A transverse wave in a string has amplitude of 4.0 cm and a wavelength of 6.0 cm.
(a) On the grid provided draw a full scale diagram for the displacement-distance graph of the wave. Each division of the grid represents 2.0 cm.

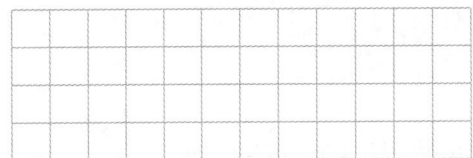

(b) Describe the motion of each particle on the string when the transverse wave travels along it.

4. The displacement-time graph of a wave is shown below.

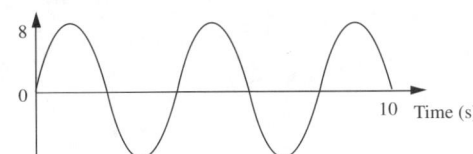

(a) What is
  (i) the amplitude;
  (ii) the period and;
  (iii) the frequency of the wave?
(b) Another wave travelling in the same medium with the same speed has twice the amplitude and frequency. Draw the displacement-time graph for this wave.

5. The figure shows the direction of a wave propagating in a medium. P is a particle in the medium in the path of the wave.

(a) With the aid of diagrams, describe how the particle P moves when the wave is
  (i) a transverse wave;
  (ii) a longitudinal wave.
(b) Describe and explain changes in the motion of the particle P if the frequency and amplitude of the transverse wave in the medium is doubled.

Section B

1. The figure shows plane wavefronts moving from the region P to the region Q in a ripple tank. The amplitudes of the wave in both the regions P and Q are the same.

(a) What is meant by a *wavefront*?
(b) Draw a diagram to show the cross-section of the water in the ripple tank when the wave travels from P to Q.
Show in your diagram the water in which region is deeper.
(c) Make measurements in the figure above to determine the wavelengths of the wave in regions (i) P and (ii) Q.
(d) The frequency of the wave is 8.0 Hz. Calculate the speed of the wave in (i) region P and (ii) region Q.
(e) Name the phenomenon of the wave demonstrated in the figure above.

2. The figure shows a stretched slinky spring.

   (a) Describe how the end P of the spring should be moved to produce
       (i) a longitudinal wave;
       (ii) a transverse wave along the spring.
       Draw a sketch for each of the wave in (i) and (ii).
   (b) A longitudinal wave of wavelength 20 cm and travelling at a speed of 120 cm s^{-1} is set up along the slinky spring.
       (i) What is the frequency of the wave?
       (ii) What is its period?
   (c) Draw (i) the displacement-distance graph and (ii) the displacement-time graph for the wave. Mark suitable values on both axes of the graphs.

Data-based Question

3. The figure shows waves approaching a headland.

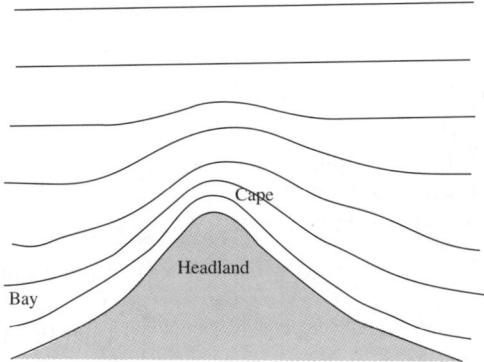

   What can be inferred from the following features of the waves? Give your reasons.
   (a) Waves far from the land are **far apart** and almost **parallel**.
   (b) Separation between the waves is smaller at the cape.
   (c) The sea is rough at the cape.
   (d) The sea is calm at the bay.

CHAPTER 12

Light

12.1 Reflection of Light

1. **Laws of reflection of light**

   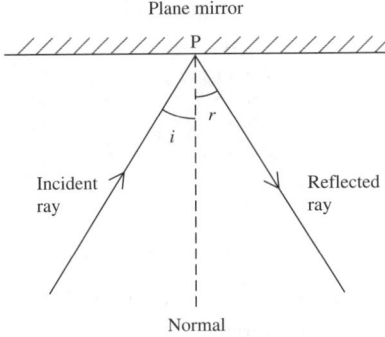

   i is the angle of incidence and r is the angle of reflection.

   (a) At the point of incidence P, the incident ray, the normal to the plane mirror and the reflected ray all lie in the same plane.
   (b) The angle of incidence i is equal to the angle of reflection r.

2. Characteristics of image formed by a plane mirror.

   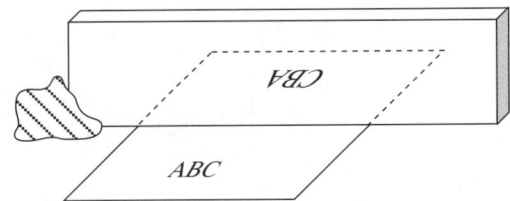

   (a) It is the same size as the object.
   (b) It is formed at the same distance from the mirror, but behind it, as the object is in front of the mirror.
   (c) It is virtual, i.e. it cannot be formed on a screen.
   (d) It is laterally inverted.

3. The ray diagram shows the formation of image by a plane mirror.

   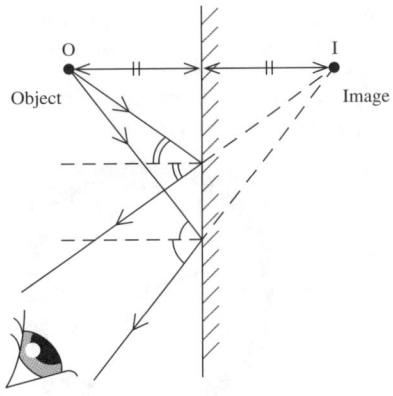

Example

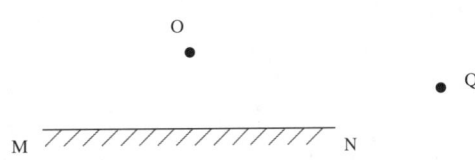

An object O is placed in front of a plane mirror MN.
(a) Mark the position of the image on the diagram.
(b) When the eye is at P, it can see the image in the mirror. Draw a ray from O to the eye at P.
(c) When the eye is at Q, can it see the image in the mirror?

Solution

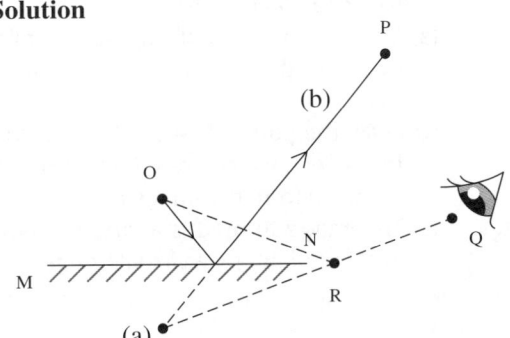

115

(c) The eye at Q cannot see the image in the mirror. For the image to be seen in the mirror, the length of the mirror needs to be extended at least to the point R.

Self Evaluation 12.1

1. An optician's chart is placed 25 cm behind a patient and a plane mirror is 175 cm in front of him. What is the distance of the image from the patient's eyes?
   A 200 cm   C 375 cm
   B 300 cm   D 400 cm

2. The figure shows the image of a wall clock in a plane mirror.

   The time shown is
   A 9:25   C 3:25
   B 3:35   D 2:35

3.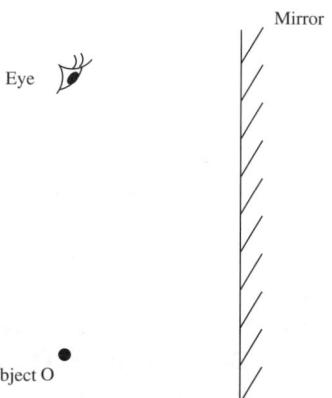

   The figure shows an object O and the eye in front of a plane mirror.
   (a) Mark the position of the image of the object in the mirror. Label the image as I.
   (b) Draw the paths of two light rays from the object, which are reflected by the mirror to form the image I.
   (c) The image formed is a virtual image. What is meant by a virtual image?

4. (a) A student stands 2.0 m in front of a plane mirror.
      (i) What is the distance between the student and his image in the mirror?
      (ii) If the student is 1.2 m tall, how tall is his image?
   (b) The T-shirt worn by the student has the number 18 printed on it and he stands beside the mirror as shown.

   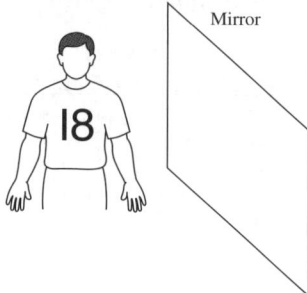

   Draw the image of the number as seen in the mirror.

12.2 Refraction of Light

1. **Refraction** of light is the bending of a ray of light as it travels from one medium into another.
2. Refraction of light occurs due to the change in the speed of light as it travels from one medium to another.

   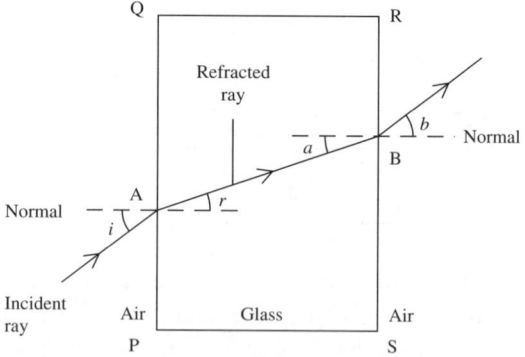

3. At A, light travels from a less dense medium (air) to a denser medium (glass), its speed decreases and it is *refracted towards the normal*.

> angle of refraction < angle of incidence
> in glass   in air
> $r < i$

4. At B, light travels from a denser medium (glass) to a less dense medium (air), it is *refracted away from the normal*.

> angle of refraction > angle of incidence
> in air   in glass
> $b > a$

5. As the sides PQ and SR of the glass block are parallel, the ray emerging from the glass block at B is *parallel* to the incident ray at A.

$$\angle a = \angle r \qquad \angle b = \angle i$$

Laws of refraction of light

6. (a)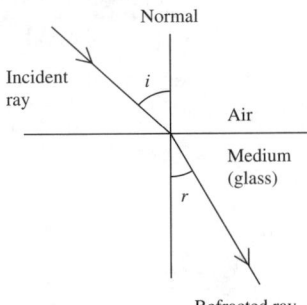

   At the point of incidence, the incident ray and the refracted ray are on the *opposite sides of the normal to the surface* and all three lie in the same plane.

   (b) The ratio

   $$\frac{\sin i}{\sin r} = \text{constant} \qquad (Snell's\ law)$$

   i is the angle incidence and
   r is the angle of refraction.
   If i is the angle of incidence in air and r is the angle of refraction in the medium (e.g. glass), then

   $$\frac{\sin (\text{angle in air})}{\sin (\text{angle in median})} = n,$$

   where n is known as the **refractive index** of the medium.

Medium	Refractive index n
Water	1.33
Glass	1.50
Diamond	2.40

Example
The refractive index of glass is 1.50.
(a) A ray of light is incident on a glass block at an angle of 45°. What is the angle of refraction in glass?
(b) A ray of light emerging from a glass block is incident on the glass surface at an angle of 30°. Calculate the angle of refraction in air.

Solution
(a)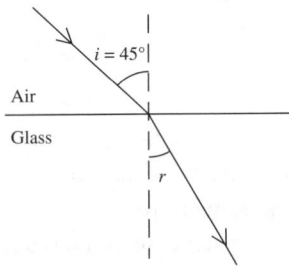

Refractive index of glass is
$$n = \frac{\sin (\text{angle in air})}{\sin (\text{angle in glass})}$$
$$1.50 = \frac{\sin 45°}{\sin r}$$
$$\sin r = \frac{0.7071}{1.50}$$
$$r = 28.13°$$

(b)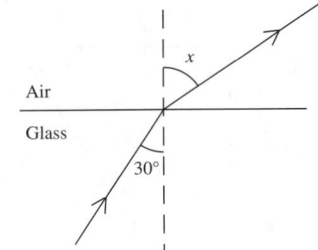

Refractive index of glass is
$$n = \frac{\sin (\text{angle in air})}{\sin (\text{angle in glass})}$$
$$1.50 = \frac{\sin x}{\sin 30°}$$
$$\sin x = (1.50)(0.500)$$
$$x = 48.59°$$

7. **Refractive index** of a medium is also equal to the *ratio of the speed of light in vacuum to that in the medium.*

> Refractive index n is
> $$n = \frac{\text{speed of light in vacuum}}{\text{speed of light in the medium}}$$
> $$n = \frac{c}{v}$$

The speed of light in vacuum c is 3.00×10^8 m s^{-1}.

Example

The refractive index n of water is 1.33.

From the refractive index $n = \dfrac{c}{v}$

Speed of light in water $v = \dfrac{c}{n}$
$$= \frac{3.00 \times 10^8 \text{ m s}^{-1}}{1.33}$$
$$= 2.26 \times 10^8 \text{ m s}^{-1}$$

8. Phenomena due to the refraction of light.
   (a) A swimming pool appears shallower when one views from above.
   (b) A person standing in the water in a swimming pool appears shorter.
   (c) A straw in a glass of water appears bent.
9. The above phenomena can be explained using the ray diagram below.

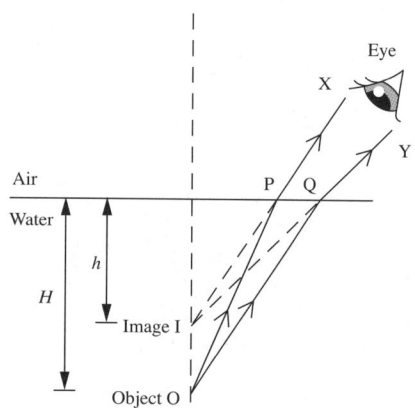

Rays OP and OQ from an object O in the water are refracted away from the normal along PX and QY.
The rays PX and QY that enter the eye seems to come from I.

Hence I is the image of O as seen by the eye. I is closer to the water surface. The apparent depth h is less than the real depth H.

Refractive index n is
$$n = \frac{\text{real depth}}{\text{apparent depth}}$$
$$= \frac{H}{h}$$

Note that this relationship is only true for light travelling from a less dense medium to a denser medium, example air to water.

When light travels from the denser medium to the less dense medium, the apparent image distance in the less dense medium is **greater** than the real image distance. (See the next example).
Then

> Refractive index n is
> $$n = \frac{\text{apparent depth}}{\text{real depth}}$$

Always remember that the larger distance should be the numerator.

Example

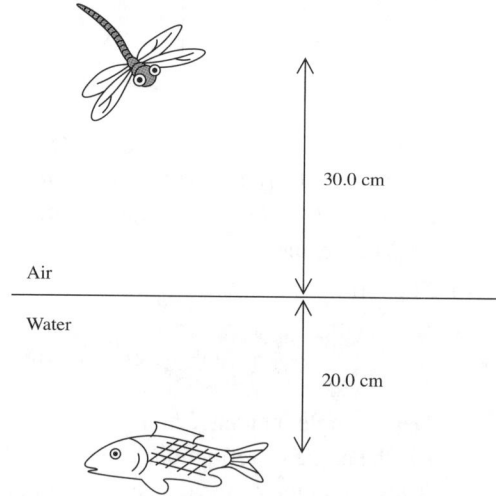

A dragonfly is 30.0 cm above the water surface in a lake. A fish which is 20.0 cm below the water surface sees the dragonfly. The refractive index of water is $\dfrac{4}{3}$.

(a) What is the apparent depth of the fish as seen by the dragonfly?
(b) What is the apparent height of the dragonfly from the water surface as seen by the fish?

Solution

(a) Refractive index of water is

$$n = \frac{\text{actual depth}}{\text{apparent depth}} = \frac{H}{h}$$

Apparent depth of fish $h = \frac{H}{n}$

$$= \frac{20.0 \text{ cm}}{4/3}$$

$$= 15.0 \text{ cm}$$

(b) Since the fish is in the denser medium (water), the apparent height of the dragonfly is greater than the real height.

$$\text{Refractive index} = \frac{\text{apparent height}}{\text{real height}}$$

Apparent height $= \left(\frac{4}{3}\right)(30.0 \text{ cm})$

$$= 40.0 \text{ cm}$$

Total Internal Reflection

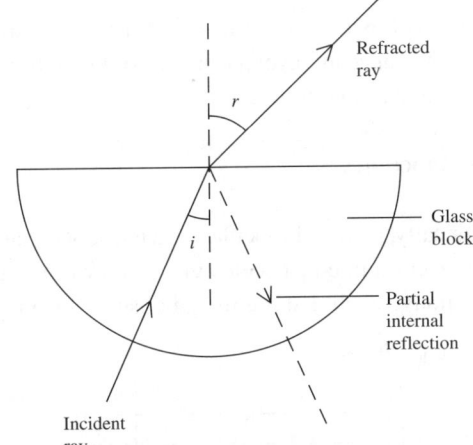

10. When a ray of light is incident in a glass block at a small angle i, it is refracted into air.
11. The angle of refraction r in air is larger than the angle of incidence i in glass.
12. Part of the incident ray is reflected. This is called **partial internal reflection**.

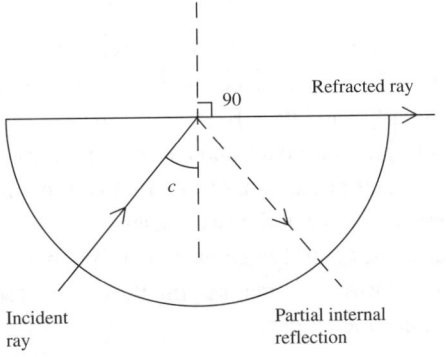

13. As the angle of incidence i in the glass increases, the angle of refraction r in the air also increases.
14. The largest angle of refraction in air is 90°. When the refracted ray is parallel to the glass surface, partial internal reflection still occurs.
15. The maximum angle of incidence c for light to be refracted into air is known as the **critical angle** of glass.
16. We know that refractive index is

$$n = \frac{\sin(\text{angle in air})}{\sin(\text{angle in glass})}$$

$$= \frac{\sin 90°}{\sin c}$$

$$n = \frac{1}{\sin c}$$

17. When the angle of incidence in glass is greater than the critical angle c, all the light is reflected back. No light is refracted into the air. **Total internal reflection** occurs.

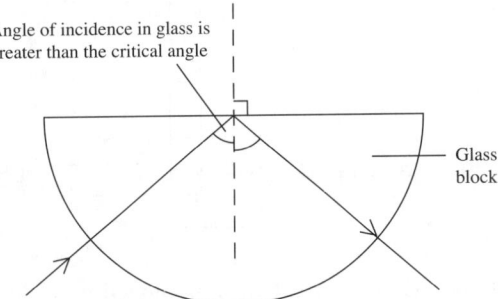

Total internal reflection

18. The two conditions necessary for total internal reflection are
    - light must travel from a denser medium towards a less dense medium such as light passes from glass to air;
    - the angle of incidence must be greater than the critical angle.

Example
The refractive index of glass, water and diamond is 1.50, 1.33 and 2.42 respectively. Calculate the critical angle of (a) glass, (b) water, and (c) diamond.

Solution

(a) Refractive index $n = \frac{1}{\sin c}$

$$\sin c = \frac{1}{n}$$

$$= \frac{1}{1.50}$$

$$c = 42°$$

(b) $\sin c = \dfrac{1}{1.33}$
$c = 49°$

(c) $\sin c = \dfrac{1}{2.42}$
$c = 24°$

Applications of Total Internal Reflection and Refraction

Periscope

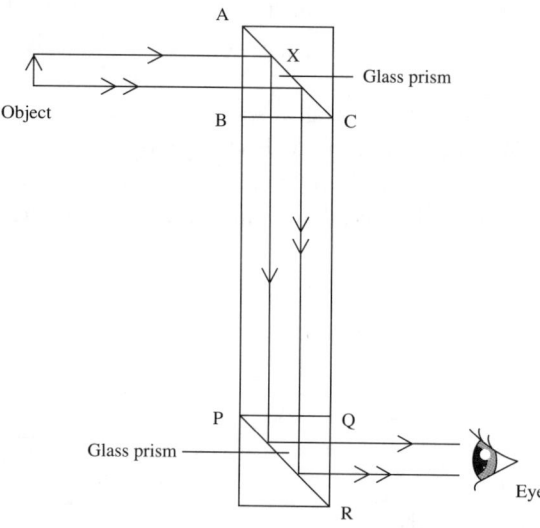

19. A periscope uses two right-angled isosceles glass prisms.
20. At the point X, the angle of incidence in glass is 45° which is greater than the critical angle of glass (42°).
21. Hence total internal reflection occurs at X and the ray is deflected through 90°.
22. Total internal reflection again occurs at the surface PR of the right-angled isosceles glass prism PQR.
23. Periscopes that use glass prisms produce sharper images. Periscopes that use mirrors produce multiple images.

Fibre Optics

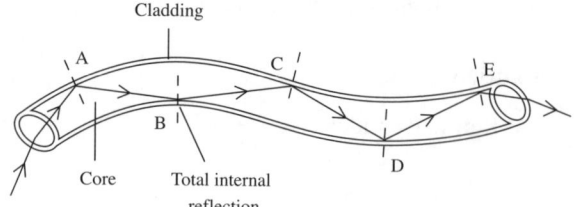

24. Fibre optics has a relatively high refractive index cylindrical inner core that carries light and a relatively low refractive index outer concentric shell known as cladding.
25. Total internal reflection occurs at A, B, C, D, etc. because the refractive index of the core is greater than the refractive index of the cladding and the angles of incidence in the core-cladding boundary is greater than the critical angle. Hence light is transmitted from one end to the other.
26. An endoscope, which consists of a light pipe, is used by doctors to observe the internal organs and the foetus. The light pipe consists of a number of optical fibres to transmit light.
27. Optical fibres are also used for telecommunication to replace copper wires.
28. The advantages of using fibre optics is that:
    – it can transmit more data;
    – it is relatively immune to external electrical interference;
    – it is flexible, hence it does not break easily;
    – the data can travel more than 10 km without the need to reamplify.

Prism binoculars

29. Basically, a prism binoculars is a telescope that uses two right-angled isosceles glass prisms to reinvert the image such that the image observed is upright.

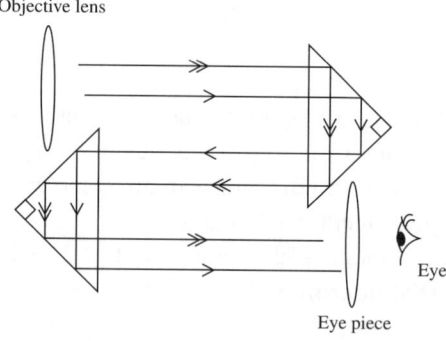

30. The two prisms are placed between the objective lens and the eye piece to reinvert the image both vertically and laterally.
31. Total internal reflection occurs in both prisms.
32. The total optical path of the light is three times the distance between the two lenses.
33. Hence the magnifying power of the prism binoculars is three times the magnifying power of a telescope of the same length.

34. Total internal reflection in prisms is also used in single-lens-reflex (SLR) cameras to reinvert the image both vertically and laterally.

Fish-eye-view

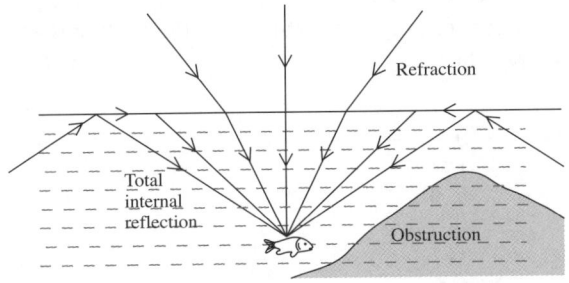

35. The figure above shows that a fish is able to see objects above the water and inside the water.
36. Light from above the water is refracted into the water.
37. Total internal reflection enables the fish to see objects on the other side of an obstruction.

Mirage Effect

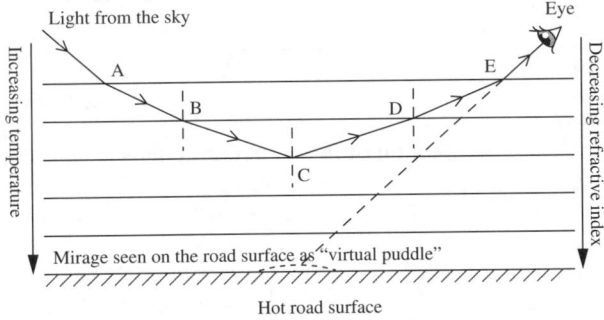

38. On a hot day, mirage can be seen on the surface of a straight highway. A mirage appears as a shiny surface that looks like water on the road.
39. The figure above shows the formation of a mirage.
40. The layer of air closer to the hot road surface is hotter and thus less dense than that above which results in having a lower refractive index.
41. Light from the sky is gradually refracted away from the normal at A and B as it approaches the hot road. However, the eye does not realise the bending of light rays and interprets the light as if it were reflected from the ground.
42. Total internal reflection occurs at C when the angle of incidence is greater than the critical angle.
43. The reflected light is then gradually refracted towards the normal and finally enters the observer's eye.
44. The light appears to come from a puddle on the road, which is actually an image of the bluish sky, i.e. the image.

Self Evaluation 12.2

1.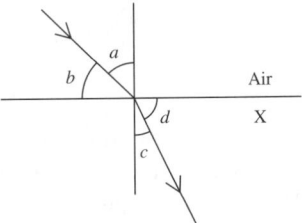

   A ray of light travels from air into a medium X. The refractive index of X is equal to

   A $\dfrac{c}{a}$ C $\dfrac{\sin a}{\sin c}$

   B $\dfrac{d}{b}$ D $\dfrac{\sin a}{\cos b}$

2. A ray of light is incident at an angle of 40° with the normal in a glass as shown in the figure. The refractive index of glass is 1.50.

   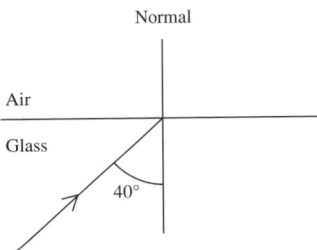

   The angle that the emerging ray makes with the normal is

   A 25.4°   C 60.0°
   B 40.0°   D 74.6°

3. A pin O is fixed at one end of a glass block. A student observes the pin O from the other end. In which position will the image of the pin appear?

   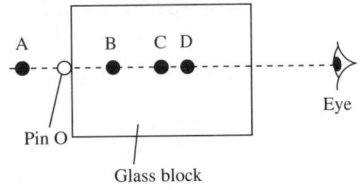

4.

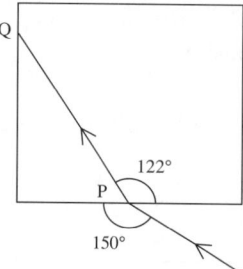

A ray of light passes through a rectangular glass block as shown in the figure.
(a) What is the angle of incidence at the point P?
(b) What is the angle of refraction at the point P?
(c) Calculate the refractive index of the glass.
(d) Complete the path of the light ray at the point Q.

5. (a) Complete the following figure to show the path of the light ray as it passes through the glass block.
   (i)
   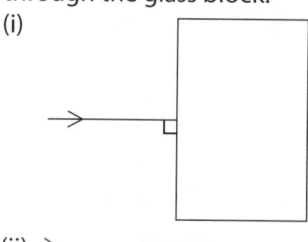

   (ii)
   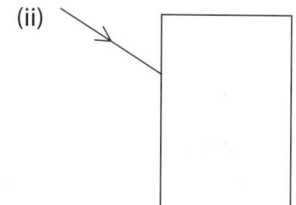

   (iii)
   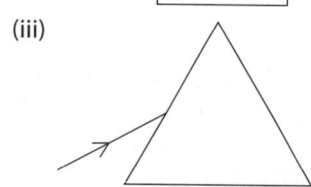

(b) How does the speed of light change as the light ray passes from the air to the glass as shown in (a)(ii) above?

12.3 Thin Lenses

1. There are two types of thin lenses:
   – converging lens
   – diverging lens
2. A converging lens is thicker in the middle than at the edge.

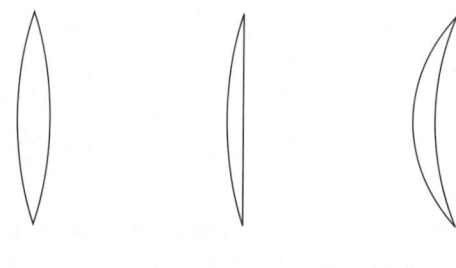

Double convex   Plano convex   Positive meniscus

3. A thin converging lens converges parallel beams of light passing through it.

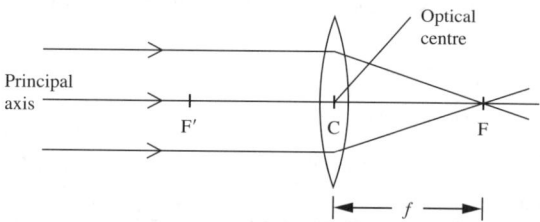

Action of thin converging lens

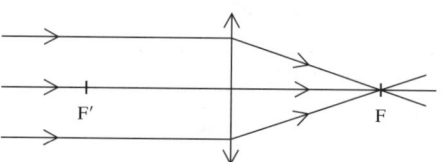

Simplified ray diagram

4. The converging lens converges parallel rays of light by refracting the rays to pass through a single point F.
5. The **optical centre** C of a converging lens is the point at the centre of the lens, through which the ray passes without being deviated.
6. The line that passes through the optical centre C and is perpendicular to the lens is known as the **principal axis**.
7. Rays parallel to the principal axis are brought to a focus at the **focal point** F which lies on the principal axis.
8. The **focal length** of the converging lens is the distance from the optical centre C of the lens to the focal point F.

9. Rays parallel to the principal axis incident on the other side of the thin converging lens are brought to a focus at the point F′. Hence a converging lens has two **principal foci** F and F′ — one on each side of the lens.
10. The distance from the optical centre C to the principal focus F′ is equal to that from C to F, which is its focal length f.
11. The power of a converging lens is equal to the reciprocal of its focal length in metres.

$$\text{Power of a lens} = \frac{1}{f} \quad (f \text{ in metres})$$

The unit for the power of a lens is the diopter (D).

Examples

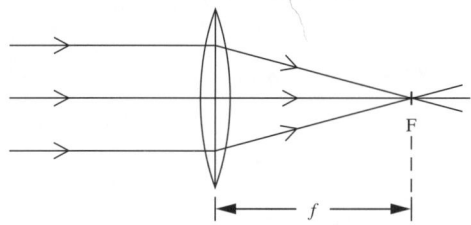

$f = 20$ cm $= 0.2$ m
Power of lens $= \dfrac{1}{0.20 \text{ m}}$
$= +5.0$ D

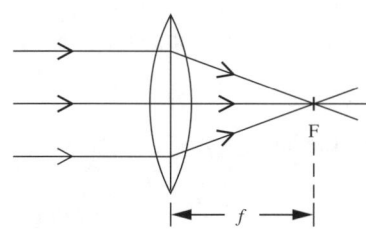

$f = 10$ cm $= 0.10$ m
Power of lens $= \dfrac{1}{0.10 \text{ m}}$
$= +10.0$ D

For lenses of the same material, a lens with a *shorter* focal length is *thicker* and the *power* of the lens is *greater* compared to a thinner lens.

Thin Diverging Lens

12. A diverging lens is thicker at the edge than at the middle.

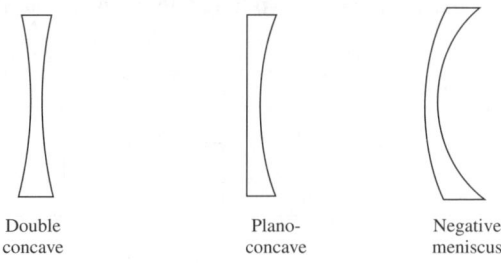

Double concave   Plano-concave   Negative meniscus

Diverging lenses

13. Rays parallel to the principal axis of a diverging lens **diverge** from a point F, known as the **focal point** of the diverging lens.

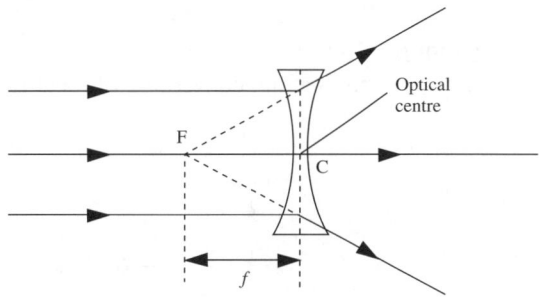

Rays parallel to the principal axis diverge from the focal point F

14. The focal length f of a diverging lens is the distance between the optical centre and the focal point of the lens. The focal length of a diverging lens has a negative value.
15. Lenses of glasses worn by a short-sighted person are diverging lenses (negative meniscus).

Example
The power of the glasses worn by a student is -0.250 D. What is the focal length of the lenses?

Solution
Power of the lens $= -0.250$ D $= \dfrac{1}{f}$

Focal length $f = -\dfrac{1}{0.250 \text{ m}}$
$= -4.00$ m

Ray Diagram for a Converging Lens

16. A ray diagram, drawn accurately, may be used to illustrate the formation of images, of an object, by a thin converging lens.
17. Two rays are drawn to locate the position of the image.

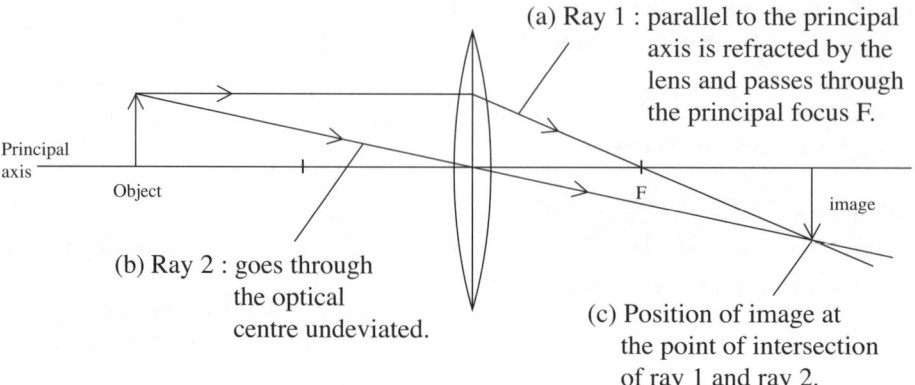

(a) Ray 1 : parallel to the principal axis is refracted by the lens and passes through the principal focus F.

(b) Ray 2 : goes through the optical centre undeviated.

(c) Position of image at the point of intersection of ray 1 and ray 2.

Example

The figure shows a thin converging of focal length f.

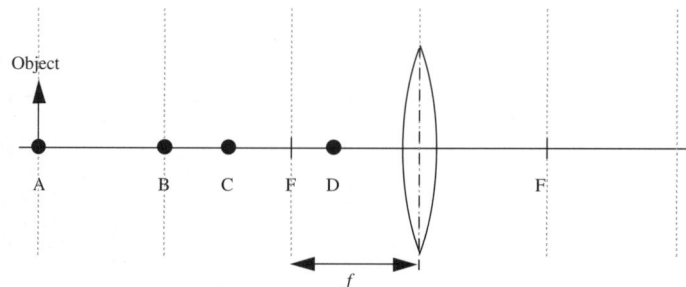

Draw ray diagrams to illustrate the formation of the image by the lens when the object distance is
(a) at A, which is at a distance of $3f$ from the lens.
(b) at B, which is at a distance of $2f$ from the lens.
(c) at C, which is at a distance greater than f but less than $2f$ from the lens.
(d) at D, which is at a distance less than f from the lens.
Describe the characteristics of the image formed.

Solution

(a) Object at A, object's distance > $2f$

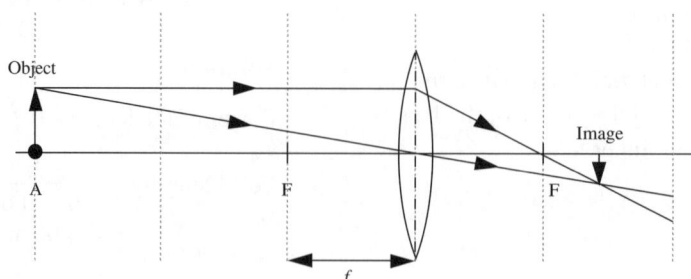

Image is real, inverted and diminished.

(b) Object at B, object's distance = $2f$

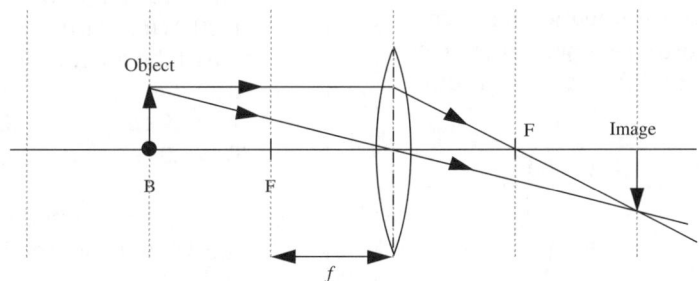

Image is real, inverted and of the same size as the object.

(c) Object at C, $f <$ object's distance $< 2f$

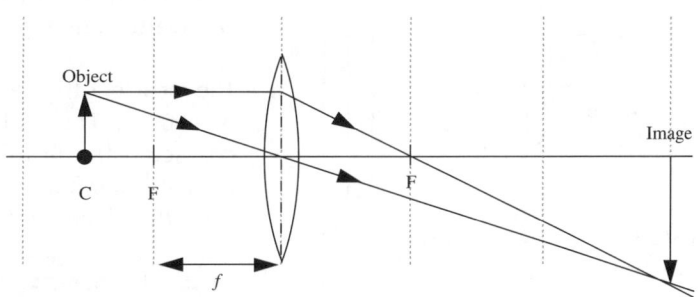

Image is real, inverted and magnified.

(d) Object at D, object's distance $< f$

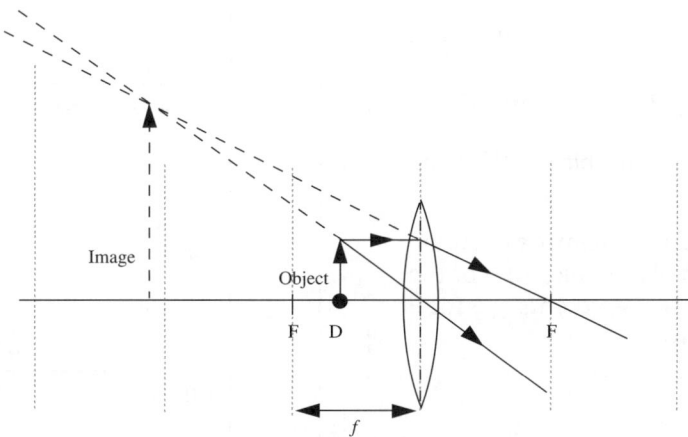

Image is virtual, upright and magnified.

Notes
- Virtual rays and virtual images are drawn using broken lines.
- A real image is one that is formed when actual rays of light are brought to a focus.
- A real image can be formed on a screen.
- A real image is inverted.
- A virtual image cannot be formed on a screen.
- A virtual image is upright.

Self Evaluation 12.3

1. Which one of the following diagrams shows the effect of a converging lens when a parallel beam of light passes through it?

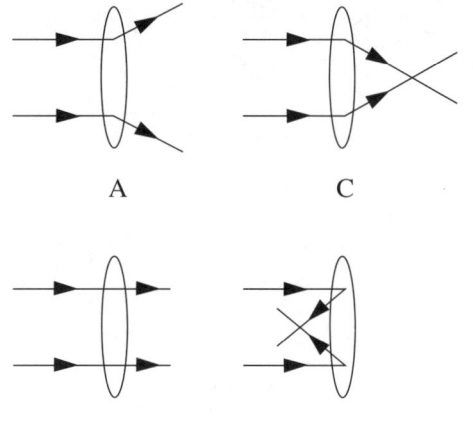

2. The focal length of a thin converging lens is 10.0 cm. An object is placed at a distance of 20.0 cm from the lens. The image formed by the lens is
   A virtual, upright and of the same size as the object.
   B real, inverted and smaller than the object.
   C real, inverted and of the same size as the object.
   D virtual, upright and bigger than the object.

3. The figure shows how the image is formed by a magnifying glass. Which one of the following distances represents the focal length of the lens?

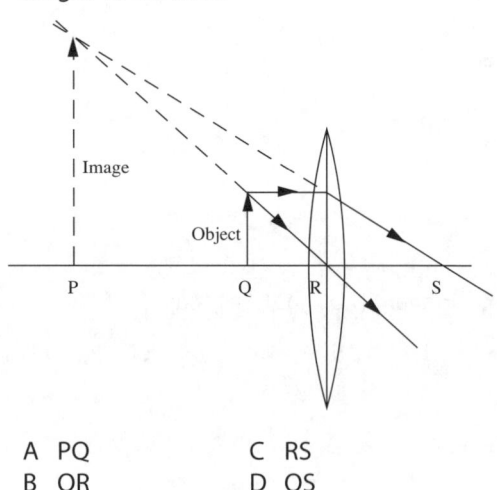

   A PQ
   B QR
   C RS
   D QS

4. The focal length of a thin converging lens is 20.0 cm. A virtual image is formed by the lens if the object's distance is at _____ from the lens.
   A 10.0 cm
   B 25.0 cm
   C 30.0 cm
   D 40.0 cm

5. The glasses of a student's pair of spectacles are diverging lenses. The image formed by the lenses is
   A upright and bigger than the object.
   B upright and smaller than the object.
   C inverted and smaller than the object.
   D inverted and bigger than the object.

6. The focal length of a thin converging lens is 30.0 cm. The table below shows the characteristics of the images formed by the lens for different object's distances. Fill in the blanks in the table.

Object's distance	Characteristics of image
(a)	Image is formed at the principal focus and it is real and inverted
(b) 60.0 cm	
(c)	Image is real, inverted and magnified
(d) 20.0 cm	
(e) 80.0 cm	

REVISION EXERCISE 12

Multiple Choice Questions

1. A student is 4.0 m from a plane mirror. He then walks 1.0 m towards the mirror. What is the distance between the student and his image in the mirror?
   A   2.0 m
   B   3.0 m
   C   4.0 m
   D   6.0 m

2. A girl of height 1.6 m stands at a distance of 2.4 m from a vertical plane mirror. What is the minimum length of the mirror for the girl to see the full image of herself in the mirror?
   A   0.67 m
   B   0.80 m
   C   1.20 m
   D   1.5 m

3. Which diagram shows correctly the path of a ray entering from water into glass?

   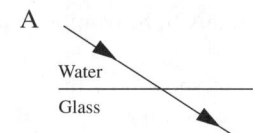
   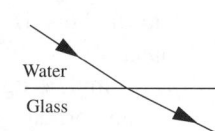
   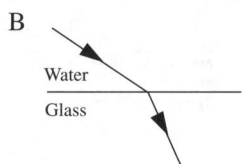
   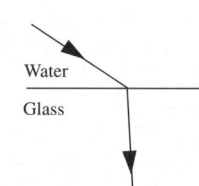

4. The refractive index of glass is 1.48. A ray is incident on a semi-circular glass block at the point O, the path of the ray after the point O is

   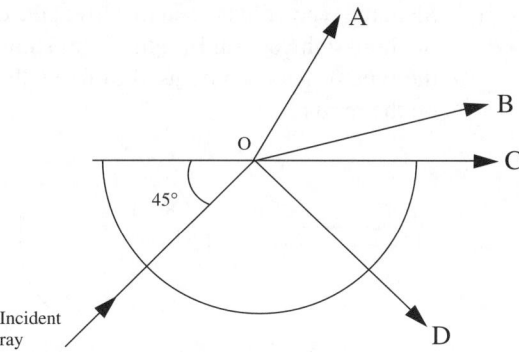

5. The optical fibre used in an endoscope uses the principle of
   A   total internal reflection of light.
   B   linear propagation of light.
   C   reflection of light.
   D   refraction of light.

6. Which diagram shows correctly the path of a ray through a 60° prism?

   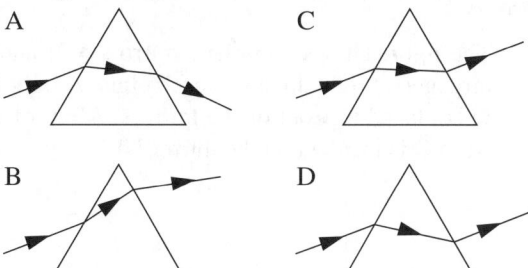

7. The power of a lens is −2.0 D. What is the type of lens and what is its focal length f?
   A   Converging lens, $f = 2.0$ m
   B   Converging lens, $f = 50$ cm
   C   Diverging lens, $f = 2.0$ m
   D   Diverging lens, $f = 50$ cm

8. A lens forms an image that is upright and larger than the object. What is the type of lens? Is the image real or virtual?
   A   Converging lens and the image is real.
   B   Converging lens and the image is virtual.
   C   Diverging lens and the image is real.
   D   Diverging lens and the image is virtual.

9. An object of height 5.0 cm is placed 20.0 cm from a diverging lens of focal length 10.0 cm. The characteristics of the image are
   A   upright and larger than the object.
   B   inverted and smaller than the object.
   C   upright and smaller than the object.
   D   inverted and larger than the object.

10. An object is placed 20 cm from a converging lens and a real image is formed, 20 cm from the lens. The object is now moved so that it is 18 cm from the lens. Which of the following is correct?
    A   The new image is bigger and its distance from the lens is less than 20 cm.
    B   The new image is bigger and its distance from the lens is greater than 20 cm.
    C   The new image is smaller and its distance from the lens is less than 20 cm.
    D   The new image is smaller and its distance from the lens is greater than 20 cm.

Structured Questions

Section A

1. The figure shows two plane mirrors MN and NP arranged at right angles to each other. A light bulb O is placed in front of the mirrors. A ray of light from O is incident on the mirror NP.

   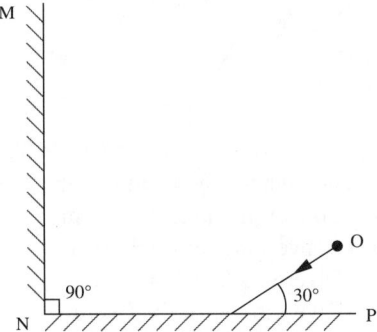

   (a) Mark accurately, with a '×', the position of the image formed by
   - (i) the mirror NP;
   - (ii) the mirror MN.

   (b) (i) Complete the path of the light ray from O until it is reflected from the mirror MN. Show the values of all the angles between the ray and the mirrors.

   (ii) Hence show the possible position of a third image of the bulb O due to the reflection of light from the two mirrors.

2. The figure shows a ray incident normally at the point P which is on the hypotenuse face of the glass prism. The refractive index of the glass is 1.60.

   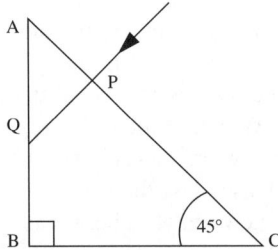

   (a) Calculate the critical angle for the glass.
   (b) What is the angle of incidence at the point (i) P and (ii) Q?
   (c) State and explain what happens to the ray at point Q.
   (d) Draw the subsequent path of the ray until it emerges from the prism.

3. The figure shows a ray that is incident at an angle of 50° from the normal on one side of a thick glass plate of refractive index 1.55. Part of the ray is reflected and the rest refracted.

   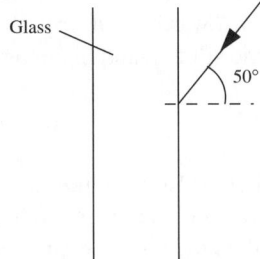

   (a) Draw the reflected part of the ray.
   (b) Calculate the critical angle for the glass.
   (c) Draw the refracted part of the ray until it emerges from the glass plate.

4. A normal eye is able to focus light from a distant object.
   (a) Complete figure 1(a) to show how the lens of the normal eye focuses the rays.

   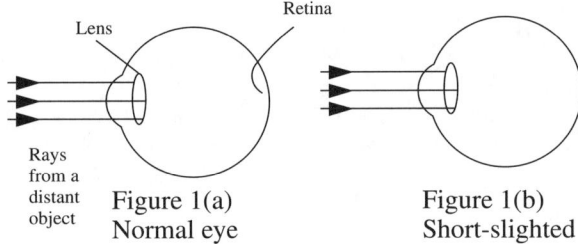

   Figure 1(a) Normal eye   Figure 1(b) Short-sighted

   (b) Complete figure 1(b) to show how the eye of a short-sighted person focuses the rays.
   (c) State the type of lens used to correct the defect of short-sightedness. In figure 1(c) show how the type of lens can be used to focus the rays on the retina.

   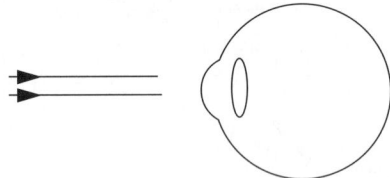

   Figure 1(c)

5. The figure shows an object PQ near a thin converging lens. F and F' are the principal foci of the lens.

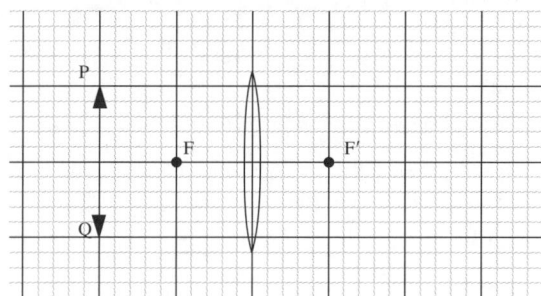

(a) (i) Draw rays to find the positions of the images of the points P and Q.
   (ii) State three characteristics of the image of the object PQ.
(b) The converging lens is then replaced by a diverging lens as shown below.

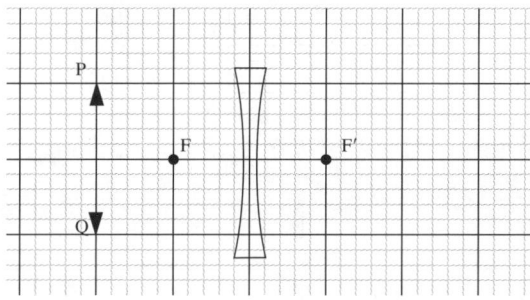

State three characteristics of the image formed by the diverging lens.

Section B

1. The figure shows two parallel rays incident on a spherical water droplet. The broken lines are normal to the points of incidence. The refractive index of water is 1.33.
   (a) Ray 1 is along the diameter of the sphere.
      (i) What is the angle of incidence of ray 1 at the surface of the droplet?
      (ii) Draw the path of ray 1 through the droplet.
   (b) Ray 2 is at an angle of incidence of 30° to the surface of the droplet. It is refracted into the droplet as shown.
      (i) Calculate the angle of refraction of ray 2 inside the water droplet.
      (ii) Show on the figure the path of ray 2 when it emerges from the water droplet.

(c) Calculate the critical angle of water.

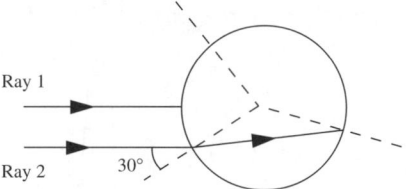

2. The figure shows a ray of light travelling from air into a liquid L and through a piece of glass.

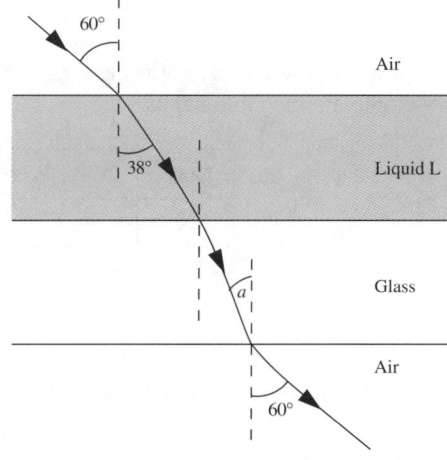

(a) Calculate the refractive index of liquid L.
(b) Which has a higher refractive index, liquid L or the glass? Explain your answer.
(c) If the refractive index of the glass is 1.52, calculate the angle a.
(d) The figure below shows the glass above the liquid L. A ray is incident at an angle of 60° from the normal. Complete the path of the ray until it emerges from liquid L.

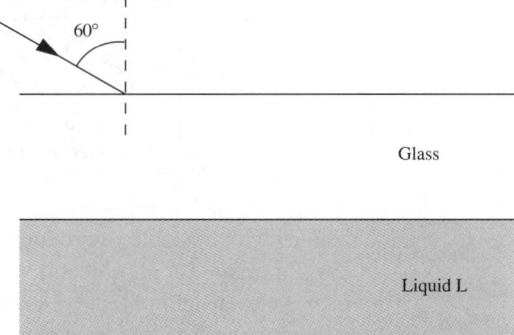

129

Data-based Question

3. The figure shows three lenses L, M and N that are drawn to scale.

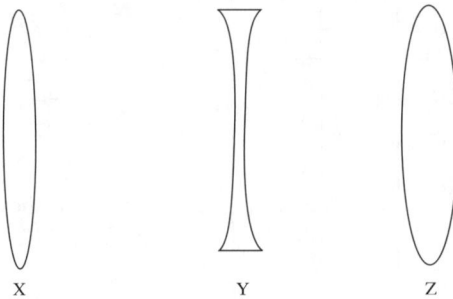

The power of the lenses, not necessary in order, is +5 D, +10 D and −5 D.

(a) Complete the table below.

Lens	Power (D)	Focal length (cm)
X		
Y		
Z		

(b) In the table below name the lens which is most suitable for the purpose shown.

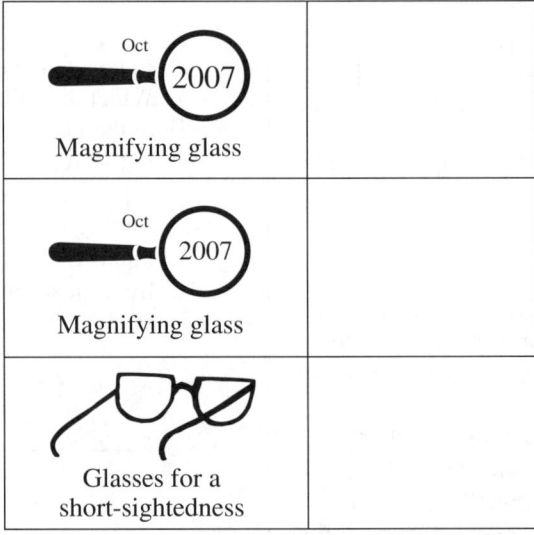

(c) Name the lens which is able to produce
   (i) an upright image for all object distances.
   (ii) an image of a distant object on a screen placed 20 cm behind the lens.
   (iii) a real and magnified images when the object is 15 cm away from the lens.
   (iv) a virtual and magnified image when the object is 18 cm away from the lens.

CHAPTER 13
Electromagnetic Spectrum

13.1 Properties of Electromagnetic Waves

1. The table below shows the main components of the electromagnetic spectrum.

Typical wavelength	Component	Typical source
10^{-14} m	Gamma-rays	Radioactive materials
10^{-10} m	X-rays	X-ray tube
10^{-8} m	Ultra-violet (UV)	Mercury vapour lamp
4×10^{-7} m – 7×10^{-7} m	Visible light	Electric bulb
10^{-5} m	Infra-red (IR)	Hot objects
10^{-2} m	Microwaves	Electrical transmitters
10 m	Radio waves	Electrical transmitters

2. Common properties.
   (a) They travel at the speed of 3×10^8 m s^{-1} in vacuum.
   (b) They are in the form of transverse waves.
   (c) They exhibit wave properties such as reflection, refraction, diffraction and interference.
   (d) They obey the relationship speed, v = frequency × wavelength

   $$v = f\lambda$$

Self Evaluation 13.1

1. The figure shows the electromagnetic spectrum.

Electromagnetic Spectrum
Radio waves
A
B
Visible light
C
X-rays
D

Name the type of radiations labelled A, B, C and D.

2. Which type of electromagnetic radiation:
   (a) has the longest wavelength?
   (b) has the highest frequency?
   (c) is not visible but can be detected by your body?
   (d) is emitted by unstable nucleus?

3. (a) Give a typical wavelength of the:
      (i) red light;
      (ii) violet light.
   (b) When light travels from air to glass, violet light is refracted more than red light. Which of them has the greater speed
      (i) in vacuum;
      (ii) in glass?

4. Microwaves have a wavelength of 3 cm. What is the frequency of these microwaves?

13.2 Applications of Electromagnetic Waves

Radio Waves

1. Radio waves have the longest wavelength among the electromagnetic waves; from a few centimetres to several hundred metres.
2. Radio waves are produced by electric currents oscillating in an electrical circuit containing a coil and capacitor.
3. They are used in radio and television communication.
4. Radio waves act as carrier waves for audio signals (sound) and video signals (pictures). The advantages are that radio waves travel at a speed of 3.0×10^8 m s^{-1} and can travel through vacuum.
5. The process of combining audio or video signals with radio waves is known as **modulation**.
6. Two types of modulations are used:
   - amplitude modulation (AM) and
   - frequency modulation (FM).
7. The modulated radio waves are beamed from the aerial of a transmitting station. The modulated radio waves are received by the aerial of the radio or television receiver.
8. The audio (sound) or video (picture) signals are then separated from the radio wave by a **demodulator**.
9. Radio waves used for radio transmission are long wave (LW), medium wave (MW) and short wave (SW).
10. Television transmission uses very high frequency (VHF) or ultra high frequency (UHF) radio waves.

Microwaves

11. Microwaves are radio waves with very short wavelengths in the range of a few centimetres.
12. They are used for satellite television transmission and transmission of telephone signals.
13. The advantages of microwaves for telecommunication are:
    - microwave can penetrate the ionosphere, a layer of charged particles around the Earth. Short wave (SW) radio waves are reflected by the ionosphere.
    - more data can be carried by microwaves.
    - length of aerial for transmission is short.
    - microwaves are suitable for communication between satellites and their earth stations.
14. **Radars** use short pulses of microwave which are reflected by objects, such as an airplane. The reflected waves give information about the object such as its location and its speed.
15. Microwaves are also used in speed traps.
16. Microwaves generated by klystron tubes, are used in microwave ovens. The frequency of the microwaves used is 2.45 Ghz which is also the frequency of vibration of water molecules.
17. Microwaves generated in the oven causes the water molecules to vibrate vigorously due to the effect of resonance. As a result, heat is produced.

Infra-red Waves

18. Infra-red waves are electromagnetic waves just beyond the red end of the visible spectrum.
19. All objects with temperature greater than 0 K emit infra-red waves. The higher the object's temperature, the shorter is the wavelength of the infra-red waves produced.
20. Infra-red photography is used:
    - to take pictures in the dark using film which is sensitive to infra-red radiations;
    - in thermography to detect pathological tissue growths, such as the growth of cancer cells.
21. In astronomy, infra-red waves are used to observe cosmic objects that are not hot enough to glow in the visible light region.
22. Infra-red radiation plays an important role in the **greenhouse effect**. Infra-red radiation emitted by objects on the Earth are trapped by water vapour, ozone and carbon dioxide. As the amount of carbon dioxide in the atmosphere increases due to the burning of fossil fuels, more infra-red radiation are trapped and the temperature of the Earth increases.
23. Infra-red waves are used in household electrical appliances such as television remote controls and intruder alarms.
24. A beam of infra-red is produced by the light emitting diodes (LEDs) inside the television remote control unit. A detector on the television set receives the signal and carries out the instruction.
25. In the intruder alarm, a LED emits a beam of infra-red across the doorway to a receiver. An intruder that enters the door, blocks off the beam and this in turn sets off the alarm.

Visible Light

26. The wavelengths of visible light varies from 4×10^{-7} m (violet) to 7×10^{-7} m (red).
27. Light of any particular wavelength (one colour) is known as monochromatic light.
28. Laser (**l**ight **a**mplification by **s**imulated **e**mission of **r**adiation) is an example of monochromatic light.
29. A beam of laser has very high intensity and does not diverge over a large distance.
30. Laser is used:
    - in eye surgery, such as Laser-Assisted *In Situ* Keratomileusis (LASIK), for correcting myopia. Laser is also used for cauterising or sealing blood vessels.
    - for precision cutting of metals in industries.
    - in precision surveying. During the construction of a sky scrapper, a beam of laser is used as a plumb line.
    - in telecommunications. Laser transmitted along optical fibres is used in telephone communications.
    - in holography. Laser is used in the production of three-dimensional images.

Ultra-violet Radiation

31. **Ultra-violet (UV) radiation** is the electromagnetic radiation beyond the violet end of the visible light. The wavelengths range from 10^{-8} m to 10^{-7} m.
32. The main source of ultra-violet radiation is the Sun. Ultra-violet radiation causes suntan, skin cancer and cateract.
33. Most of the ultra-violet radiations from the Sun is absorbed by the ozone layer in the Earth's stratosphere.
34. The use of freons in aerosol cans and as refrigerants has resulted in the depletion of the ozone layer.
35. In sun beds, ultra-violet radiation from a sun lamp is used to treat patients suffering from jaundice. The ultra-violet radiation simulates the production of vitamin D in the body.
36. In fluorescent lamps, which are widely used in home and schools, ultra-violet radiation is produced by mercury vapour in the lamp. The chemical coated on the fluorescent tube absorbs the ultra-violet radiation and emits visible light. It fluoresces when the ultra-violet radiation falls on it.
37. Ultra-violet radiation is used in banks to view the watermarks on the currency notes and 'invisible' signatures in bank passbooks.
38. Ultra-violet radiation can kill bacteria and virus. Thus, it is used to sterilise surgical instruments.
39. Ultra-violet lamps are used to reduce spoilage of fresh food, such as meat and fish, by eliminating bacteria. Ultra-violet radiation is also used to kill bacteria in clams and fresh oysters.

X-rays

40. X-rays have wavelength of 10^{-13} m to 10^{-8} m.
41. They are produced in X-ray tubes where high speed electrons collide with a metal target.
42. X-rays have strong penetrating power. Matters of higher density absorbs more X-rays than those of lower density.
43. X-rays can damage tissues.
44. In hospital, X-rays are used:
    - in X-ray photography. X-rays penetrate the soft tissues easily and are absorbed more by the bones. Hence the bones will show up in the less exposed part of the photographic film.
    - for killing cancerous cells.
45. In industries, X-rays are used:
    - to detect flaws in the welding of metal pipes used to carry natural petroleum gas;
    - to detect metallic objects inside the airline passenger's baggage;
    - for the analysis of crystal strutures. Distance between atomic planes in a crystal can be measured using X-rays diffraction.

Gamma Rays

46. Gamma rays have the shortest wavelengths, from 10^{-10} m to 10^{-14} m.
47. Gamma rays are emitted during radioactive decay of unstable nuclei.
48. They have very high penetrating power, only stopped by lead of thickness of a few centimetres.
49. Gamma rays are used:
    - to kill cancerous cells;
    - to sterilise hospital equipment, such as syringe and gauze;
    - to irradiate food such as fruits and meat so that they stay fresh longer. Gamma rays can kill any bacteria, virus or bugs in the food.

> **Self Evaluation 13.2**
>
> 1. Name the type of electromagnetic radiations used in
>   (a) television remote control;
>   (b) satellite television;
>   (c) sunbeds;
>   (d) endoscope;
>   (e) speed trap.
> 2. (a) State two applications of ultra-violet radiations.
>   (b) Give two harmful effects of ultra-violet radiations.
> 3. (a) How are X-rays and gamma rays produced?
>   (b) State a physical difference between X-rays and gamma-rays.
>   (c) What is the characteristic that is common to both X-rays and gamma rays?
> 4. What are the types of electromagnetic radiations emitted by
>   (a) a candle flame;
>   (b) a fluorescent lamp?

5. The ionising radiation have sufficient energy to ionise atoms and molecules inside the body to form ions. As a result, DNA chains may be damaged and it may lead to cell mutation which may result in cancer.
6. The two main concerns of ionising radiations are:
   – carcinogenesis – causes cancer;
   – genetic (hereditary) effects caused by the mutation in the sperm or egg cell.

> **Self Evaluation 13.3**
>
> 1. Name the types of the electromagnetic radiations that
>   (a) cause ionisation;
>   (b) do not cause ionisation.

13.3 Effects of Electromagnetic Radiations on Cells and Tissue

1. Human beings are living in a sea of electromagnetic radiations. Human body is not transparent to electromagnetic radiations and can absorb some of the electromagnetic radiations when the body is exposed to them. Excessive exposure to the radiations may cause heating, ionisation and damage to cells and tissue.
2. Heating is the main effect of non-ionising electromagnetic radiations such as microwaves, infra-red, visible light and ultra-violet.
3. The effects of exposure to ultra-violet radiations include tanning, sunburn, formation of vitamin-D, skin cancer (melanoma) and cataract of the eye.
4. The ionising radiations are X-rays and gamma-rays. These radiations have high penetration power. The somatic effects of these radiations are deep-sited burns and damage to cells and tissue.

REVISION EXERCISE 13

Multiple Choice Questions

1. In the spectrum of visible light, which colour has the shortest wavelength and which colour has the longest wavelength?

	Shortest wavelength	Longest wavelength
A	Red	Violet
B	Violet	Red
C	Green	Red
D	Violet	Green

2. Which of the following is a typical wavelength of visible light?
   A 5 nm C 500 nm
   B 50 nm D 50 μm

3. Which of the following groups of electromagnetic radiations is arranged in the increasing order of frequency?
   A Light, infra-red, X-ray
   B X-ray, infra-red, light
   C Infra-red, light, X-ray
   D Infra-red, X-ray, light

4. All electromagnetic waves have the same
   A frequency.
   B wavelength.
   C energy in vacuum.
   D speed in vacuum.

5. Which type of electromagnetic waves is used in the mobile phone communication?
   A Microwaves C Infra-red
   B Ultra-violet D Gamma ray

6. The diagram shows different regions of the electromagnetic spectrum.

   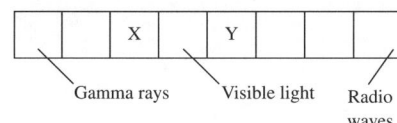

   What are the types of electromagnetic radiations labelled X and Y?

	X	Y
A	Ultra-violet	Infra-red
B	Microwaves	X-ray
C	X-ray	Microwaves
D	Infra-red	Ultra-violet

7. A radio station transmits radio waves at a frequency of 100 MHz. The speed of radio waves is 3.0×10^8 m s^{-1}. What is the wavelength of the radio waves?
   A 0.30 m C 30.0 m
   B 3.00 m D 300 m

8. Which of the following electromagnetic waves produces ionisation?
   A Radio waves C Visible light
   B Infra-red D X-rays

9. Besides light which of the following is also emitted by the mercury vapour lamp?
   A Microwaves C X-rays
   B Radio waves D Ultra-violet

10. What type of electromagnetic waves is emitted by a human body?
    A Visible light
    B Infra-red
    C Ultra-violet radiation
    D Microwaves

Structured Questions

Section A

1. Infrared, ultra-violet, microwaves and X-rays are electromagnetic waves. Name the type of wave given in the preceding sentence that
   (a) can penetrate steel of a few mm thick;
   (b) is used in sunbeds;
   (c) is used in telecommunication;
   (d) causes the temperature of the Earth to rise.

2. Explain how X-rays
   (a) cause damage to tissues.
   (b) are used to produce X-ray photograph of dislocated elbow.

3. (a) State one use of the heating effect of microwaves.
   (b) Microwaves are also used in telecommunication. What are the advantages of using microwaves for telecommunication?

4. (a) What is the frequency of red light of wavelength 700 nm?
   (b) The refractive index of glass is 1.50, what is the
       (i) frequency;
       (ii) speed;
       (iii) wavelength
       of the red light in the glass?

5. (a) Explain why a person's ear feels warm after using a cell phone over a long period.
   (b) A person who sunbaths in a room with glass walls does not have a good tan compared to another person who sunbaths on the balcony. Explain why.

6. The closest star is at a distance of 4×10^{16} m away. How long does the light from the star take to reach us?

7. (a) A laser pointer emits a radiation of wavelength 500 nm. Identify the type of electromagnetic radiation that has a wavelength of 500 nm.
   (b) The power of the laser pointer is 5 mW and the power of a filament lamp is 60 W. Explain the danger of shining a laser pointer into the eyes compared to shining a torch light into the eyes.

8. (a) What differentiates one type of electromagnetic radiation from another?
   (b) Give three reasons why sound wave is not an electromagnetic wave.

Section B

1. (a) Complete the table below by giving a typical wavelength for each of the electromagnetic waves.

Type of electro-magnetic waves	Wavelength
(i) Visible light	
(ii) Infra-red	
(iii) Ultra-violet	

   (b) State three common characteristics of these types of electromagnetic waves.
   (c) State two uses for each of the following electromagnetic waves
   (i) visible light;
   (ii) infra-red;
   (iii) ultra-violet.

2. (a) What is the source of gamma rays?
   (b) What are the properties of gamma rays that made it hazardous to health? Why?
   (c) State two negative effects of gamma rays.
   (d) State two uses of gamma rays.
   (e) Give two precautions when using gamma rays.

3. The table below shows four types of electromagnetic radiations.

Types	Frequency	Wavelength
Microwaves	1×10^{10} Hz	(iii)
(i) P	(iv)	5×10^{-7} m
(ii) Q	(v)	3×10^{-8} m
X-rays	1×10^{18} Hz	(vi)

   (a) (i) What is the speed of the electromagnetic radiations in vacuum?
       (ii) Do the various types of electromagnetic radiations travel with the same speed in glass?
   (b) From the data provided in the table, fill in the blanks marked (i) to (vi).
   (c) State the source(s) of microwave and X-ray.
   (d) Give one hazard of over exposure to
       (i) ultra-violet radiation,
       (ii) X-rays.

CHAPTER 14
Sound

14.1 Sound Waves

1. Sound is produced by vibrating objects such as strings (piano and guitar), air columns (flutes and trumpets) and membrane (drum).

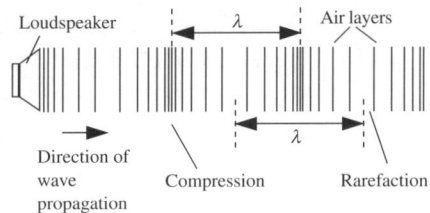

2. The above figure shows how sound waves are produced by the vibrating cone of a loudspeaker.
3. Vibration of the cone of the loudspeaker causes the air layer in front of it to vibrate. This in turn causes the next air layer to vibrate and so on.
4. As a result of the vibration, a series of alternating higher pressure regions called **compressions** and lower pressure regions called **rarefactions** are produced. As the vibrations continue, the disturbances propagate outwards.
5. Since the vibrations of the air layers are parallel to the direction of wave propagation, sound wave is a longitudinal wave.
6. Energy from the vibrating cone is propagated through the air by the vibrations of air layers.
7. The **wavelength** λ equals the distance between successive compressions or successive rarefactions.
8. The **frequency** f of the wave equals the frequency of vibration of the cone of the loudspeaker and is also equal to the frequency of vibrations of the air layers.
9. The speed of sound wave is

$$v = \text{frequency} \times \text{wavelength}$$
$$= f\lambda$$

Example
The frequency of the sound from a vibrating guitar string is 650 Hz. If the speed of sound in the air is 330 m s^{-1}, what is the wavelength?

Solution
$$v = f\lambda$$
$$330 \text{ m s}^{-1} = (650 \text{ Hz})(\lambda)$$
$$\lambda = 0.51 \text{ m}$$

Self Evaluation 14.1

1. A sound wave travels in air.
   (a) Describe the motion of an air molecule relative to the direction of propagation of the sound wave.
   (b) Draw a diagram to show the instantaneous positions of the layers of air along the direction of propagation of the sound wave. Label a compression and a rarefaction.

2. The displacement-distance graph of a sound wave in air is shown in the figure below.

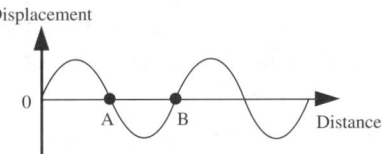

   (a) Show on the figure a distance which equals the wavelength of the sound wave.
   (b) Discuss which of the points A or B is
       (i) a compression,
       (ii) a rarefaction.

3. (a) A loudspeaker emits a sound wave of frequency 600 Hz. If the speed of sound in the air is 330 m s^{-1}, calculate the wavelength of the sound wave.
   (b) What is the distance between
       (i) successive compressions;
       (ii) successive rarefactions;
       (iii) a compression and the nearest rarefaction?

14.2 Speed of Sound

1. Sound requires a medium for its transmission. This is demonstrated by the experiment shown in the figure below.

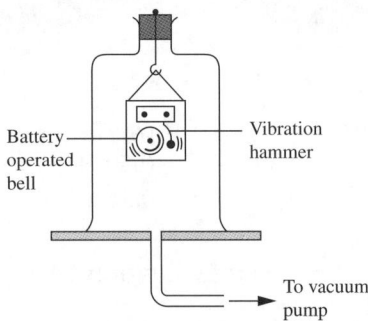

2. A battery operated bell is switched on. When the air inside the bell jar is slowly withdrawn, the sound of the ringing bell decreases until eventually no sound is heard, although the hammer is still vibrating. This shows that sound cannot travel through a vacuum.
3. Speed of sound in air   : 330 m s^{-1}
   Speed of sound in water : 1400 m s^{-1}
   Speed of sound in steel : 5000 m s^{-1}
4. The audible frequency range for a normal human is 20 Hz to 20 kHz.
5. Animals, such as dogs, dolphins and whales are able to hear sounds of frequencies higher than 20 kHz.
6. Direct determination of the speed of sound in air.

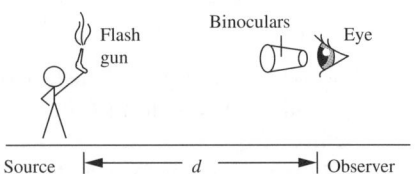

If d is distance between source and observer and t is time interval between seeing the flash and hearing the sound by the observer, then the speed of sound in the air is $v = \dfrac{d}{t}$.

Example

In an experiment to determine the speed of sound, a student stands 150 m from a wall and claps two pieces of wood together.

(a) When he claps once, what is the time interval t between the sound of the clap and its echo heard by the student, in terms of v the speed of sound?

(b) When he claps at a certain regular rate, he no longer hears the echo.
Explain why and calculate the speed of sound if he claps at 67 times per minute.

Solution

(a) Distance travelled by the sound to and back from the wall = 2(150 m)
Hence $vt = 300$ m
Time interval between the clap and its echo is
$t = \dfrac{300 \text{ m}}{v}$.

(b) The student does not hear the echo because the echoes and the sound of the claps overlap exactly. The time interval between successive claps = time interval between a clap and its echo

$$\dfrac{60}{67} = \dfrac{300}{v}$$

Speed of sound is

$$v = \left(\dfrac{67}{60 \text{ s}}\right)(300 \text{ m})$$
$$= 335 \text{ m s}^{-1}$$

Self Evaluation 14.2

1. The time keeper in a 100 m race in a school sport starts the stopwatch after hearing the shot from the starter's pistol. Will the time recorded be more or less than the correct time and by how much?

2. The speeds of sound in air, water and steel, not necessary in the same order, are 6000 m s^{-1}, 300 m s^{-1} and 1500 m s^{-1}. What are the speeds of sound in (a) air, (b) water and (c) steel? Explain how you derive the answers.

3. An observer hears the sound of the thunder 2.2 s after seeing the flash of the lightning. The speed of sound in the air is 340 m s^{-1}. What is the distance of the lightning from the observer?

14.3 Echo

1. Echo is produced by the reflection of sound.
2. Echo may be used for determining distance – **echolocation**. Echolocation used the time lapse

between the emission of sound and the reception of the echo for determining distances.
3. Bats, whales and dolphins produce sound continuously. Bats are able to navigate in the dark by listening to the echo. Whales and dolphins use echolocation to locate their preys.
4. Echolocation is used to determine the depth of an ocean.
5. Echolocation is used in seismic survey to locate oil underground.

Example

A pulse of ultrasound is transmitted from a boat to the bottom of an ocean. The time between transmission and reception of the reflected ultrasound is 2.8 s. What is the depth of the ocean? (Speed of ultrasound in water = 1500 m s^{-1})

Solution

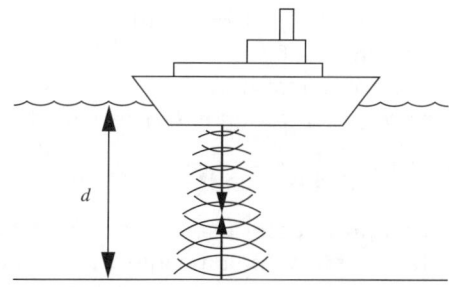

Let d be the depth of the ocean. Total distance travelled by ultrasound from the boat to the ocean bed and back is $2d$.

$$2d = \text{speed} \times \text{time}$$

$$\therefore \text{Depth of ocean } d = \frac{(1500 \text{ m s}^{-1})(2.8 \text{ s})}{2}$$

$$= 2100 \text{ m}$$

Self Evaluation 14.3

1. A student stands between two walls as shown in the figure and claps his hands once.

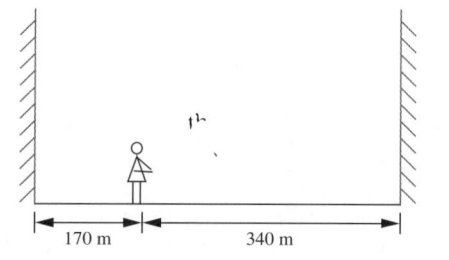

(a) How long after the clap will he hear
   (i) the first echo;
   (ii) the second echo?
(b) What is the time interval between the two echoes?

2. A person A standing near a wall of a quadrangle gives a clap.

(a) Draw the path of the sound wave that returns to A after reflection from the four walls.
(b) Explain why a series of echoes of decreasing loudness could be heard.

14.4 Ultrasound

1. Sound waves of frequency above 20 kHz are known as **ultrasound**.
2. Although ultrasound is undetected by human, it can be detected by animals like dogs, bats and whales.
3. In medicine, ultrasound is used for:
   – pre-natal scanning. A real-time image of the fetus is produced using pulse-echo technique.
   – examination of organs such as liver, heart, kidney and breast.
4. Advantages of using of ultrasound in medicine:
   (a) over X-rays.
   Ultrasound does not produce any adverse effects. X-rays can damage cells and has carcinogenesis and genetic (hereditary) effects.
   (b) over audible sound waves.
   Ultrasound has a shorter wavelength, so there is less diffraction and the wave will spread less. Hence ultrasound can be used to detect smaller objects and produce sharper images.
5. In industries, ultrasound is used:
   – in quality control by applying pulse-echo technique. It used to detect the level of liquid, powder or any material in a container. A pulse of ultrasound is transmitted from a sensor fixed at a height. If the level of the content in

the container is lower than normal, the time between transmission and reception of the ultrasound pulse is increased. The container is rejected.

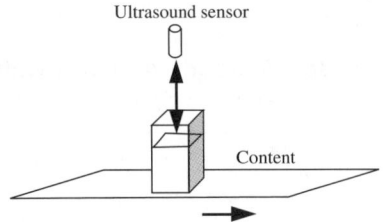

- to determine the depth of an ocean, locate shoal of fish and sunken vessel using sonar or pulse-echo technique.
- to remove old paint from aircrafts.
- in sensors that are used to prevent collision of a reversing vehicle.
- to study the degree of hardening of cement-based material by measuring the time taken for a pulse to travel through the material.

Example

Sonar is used to determine the depth h of oil-bearing rock below the Earth's surface. An explosive is detonated at the point P. The detector placed at Q records the first pulse 0.5 s after the explosion and the second pulse 0.3 s later.

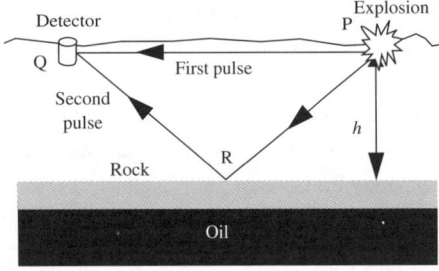

The speed of sonar in the ground is 1800 m s^{-1}.
Calculate
(a) (i) the distance between P and Q;
(ii) the total distance travelled by the second pulse detected by the detector.
(b) What is the depth h?

Solution
(a) (i) Distance PQ = (0.5 s)(1800 m s^{-1})
= 900 m

(ii) Distance travelled
= (0.5 s + 0.3 s)(1800 m s^{-1})
= 1440 m

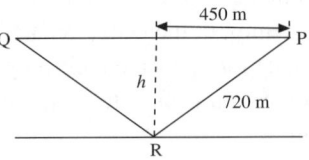

(b) $h^2 = (720 \text{ m})^2 - (450 \text{ m})^2$
$h = 562$ m

Self Evaluation 14.4

1. A survey ship sends an ultrasound pulse from the surface to the ocean floor. The echo is received 6.0 s after the transmission. If the speed of sound in sea water is 1500 m s^{-1}, calculate the depth of the ocean.

2. In medicine, ultrasound is used for scanning the fetus.
   (a) What is ultrasound?
   (b) Why is ultrasound used instead of
      (i) X-ray or;
      (ii) audible sound?

3. A fishing vessel uses sonar to detect shoals of fish. The time interval between transmission and reception of the pulse of ultrasound is 0.60 s.
   If the speed of ultrasound in water is 1500 m s^{-1}, what is the distance of the shoal of fish from the fishing vessel?

REVISION EXERCISE 14

Multiple Choice Questions

1. The figure shows a sound wave travelling in air in the direction shown. P and Q are two air molecules separated by a distance of one wavelength along the direction of propagation of the wave.

   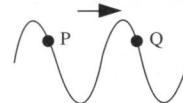

   Which of the following correctly shows the instantaneous directions of motion of P and Q?

   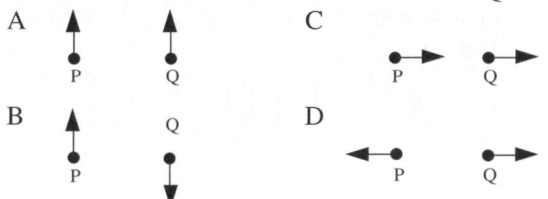

2. The speed of sound in air is 340 m s^{-1}. When a sound wave travels in air, the distance between successive compressions is 0.68 m. What is the frequency of the sound wave?
   A 231 Hz C 500 Hz
   B 250 Hz D 1000 Hz

3. The figure shows the displacement-distance graph of a sound wave in air.

   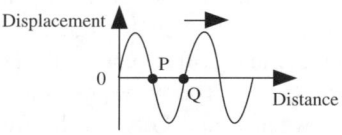

   A compression or rarefaction is at the point P and the point Q
   A P: compression   Q: rarefaction
   B P: rarefaction   Q: compression
   C P: compression   Q: compression
   D P: rarefaction   Q: rarefaction

4. The displacement-distance graph of a sound wave is shown in the figure. Which point has the maximum pressure?

   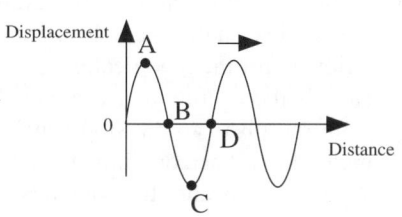

5. When sound travels from air into water, how do the speed and the wavelength change?

	Speed	Wavelength
A	Decreases	Decreases
B	Decreases	Increases
C	Increases	Increases
D	Increases	Decreases

6. When the tension in the string of a guitar is increased, but other factors remain unchanged, the sound produced
   A is louder.
   B has higher pitch.
   C has longer wavelength.
   D travels faster.

7. The displacement-time graph of two notes P and Q are shown below.

   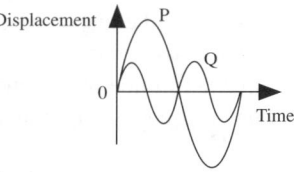

   Which note is louder and which note has a higher pitch?

	Louder	Higher pitch
A	P	P
B	P	Q
C	Q	P
D	Q	Q

8. Two persons X and Y are at a distance of 100 m from a high wall.

   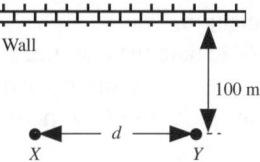

   When X gives a clap, the time interval between the two sounds heard by Y is 0.2 s. If the speed of sound is 340 m s^{-1}, what is the distance d between X and Y?
   A 68 m   C 130 m
   B 136 m   D 260 m

9. Which of the following is a typical frequency of ultrasound?
   A 10 Hz   C 1×10^4 Hz
   B 1000 Hz   D 1×10^5 Hz

10. Which of the following is the advantage of using ultrasound over X-ray for the purpose of medical scanning?
  A Ultrasound has shorter wavelength.
  B Ultrasound is more penetrating.
  C Ultrasound is less harmful.
  D Ultrasound produces sharper images.

Structured Questions

Section A

1. The displacement-time graph of a sound wave is shown below.

   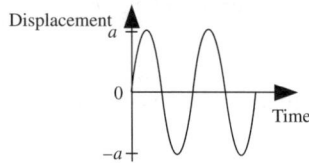

   Draw on the figure the displacement-time graph of another sound wave which has
   (a) the same amplitude but of higher pitch;
   (b) the same frequency but louder.

2. A sound wave of frequency 100 Hz travels in the air in the direction shown in the figure. P and Q are two air particles in the path of the wave.

   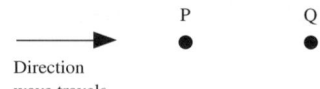

   (a) In the above figure, draw arrows to show the motion of the particle P as the sound wave passes.
   (b) The speed of sound is 340 m s^{-1}. The distance between the particles P and Q is half a wavelength.
      (i) Calculate the distance between P and Q.
      (ii) State one similarity and one difference in the motions of the particles P and Q.

3. A loudspeaker is connected to an audio frequency generator. The frequency of the audio frequency generator is slowly increased and sound from the loudspeaker is first detected by an observer when the frequency is 20 Hz. The observer could not hear sound of frequency higher than 20 kHz. The speed of sound in air is 340 m s^{-1}.
   (a) Calculate the shortest and the longest wavelength of the sound detected by the observer.
   (b) Explain how the pitch of the sound heard by the observer varies as the frequency increases from 20 Hz to 20 kHz.

4. Explain the following.
   (a) A doctor can hear the heartbeats of a patient clearly using a stethoscope.
   (b) Astronauts on a space-walk outside the spacecraft talk to each other using radio waves.
   (c) There is a time lapse between seeing the lightning and hearing the thunder.

5. State three differences between sound waves and light waves.

Section B

1. Figure 1(a) shows the instantaneous positions of the layers of air between P and Q in front of a loudspeaker emitting sound of frequency 1000 Hz.

   Figure 1

   (a) Describe the motion of a layer of air in front of the loudspeaker.
   (b) Mark the following on figure 1(a).
      (i) A compression region.
      (ii) A rarefaction region.
      (iii) One wavelength λ.
   (c) State how the motion of the air layer would change if the sound from the loudspeaker is louder and of frequency 500 Hz.
   (d) In figure 1(b) draw the positions of the air layers between P and Q when the frequency of the sound is 500 Hz.

2. In an experiment to determine the speed of sound in air, a person at one end of a field fires a pistol. A second person at the other end starts a stop-watch on seeing the puff of smoke from the pistol and stops the watch on hearing the shot. The time recorded is 1.20 s and the distance between the two persons is 390 m.
   (a) Calculate the speed of sound.
   (b) Suggest a modification to the experiment that would give a more accurate result. Explain the rationale for the modification.
   (c) How is the result affected by a wind blowing from the pistol to the stop-watch? Suggest a method to reduce or eliminate the effect.
   (d) What would be the effect of tall buildings close to the field?

3. In echolocation, ultrasound is used to locate shoals of fish in the sea. A pulse of ultrasound from the ship is reflected by the shoal.

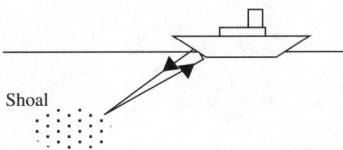

(a) What is meant by ultrasound?
(b) The frequency of the ultrasound is 50 kHz and its speed in water is 1500 m s^{-1}. Calculate the wavelength of the ultrasound.
(c) The figure shows the trace on the screen of a cathode-ray oscilloscope (c.r.o.) of the transmitted pulse and the reflected pulse. The time base of the c.r.o. is 0.10 s per division.

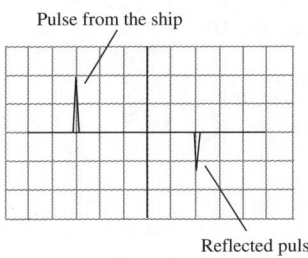

  (i) Explain why the amplitude of the reflected pulse is lower.
  (ii) What is the time interval between the transmitted pulse and the reflected pulse?
  (iii) Calculate the distance of the shoal from the ship.
(d) Assuming that the shoal does not move as the ship moves closer to it, state two changes to the trace observed on the screen.
(e) State one advantage of ultrasound over audible sound for the purpose of locating shoals of fish.

CHAPTER 15
Static Electricity

15.1 Laws of Electrostatics

Electric Charges

1. An object is positively charged if there are more positive charges than negative charges on the object.
2. An object is negatively charged if there are more negative charges than positive charges on the object.
3. If there are equal positive and negative charges on an object, the object is neutral.
4. An object can be charged by friction.
   (a) When a polythene strip is rubbed with a piece of dry cloth, electrons are transferred from the cloth to the polythene strip. The polythene strip gets negatively charged and the cloth which loses electrons becomes positively charged.
   (b) When a acetate strip is rubbed with a piece of dry cloth, electrons are transferred from the acetate strip to the cloth. The acetate strip becomes positively charged and the cloth negatively charged.
5. Electric charge is measured in coulomb (C).
6. **Laws of electrostatics**

   Like charges repel and unlike charges attract.

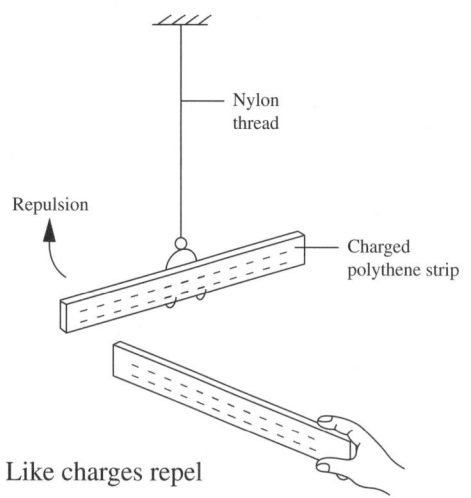

Like charges repel

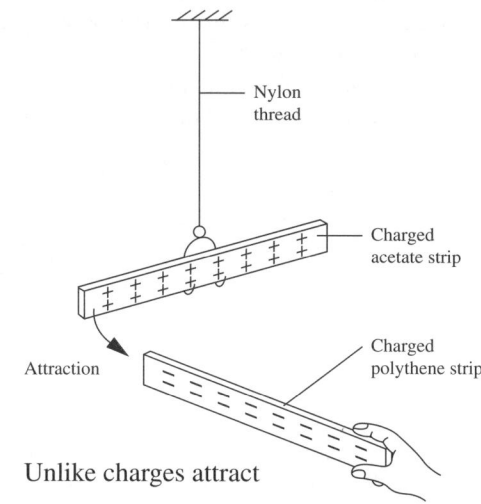

Unlike charges attract

7. Charge does not flow in **electrical insulation** such as polythene, acetate, glass, wood and rubber.
8. Electrical conductors allow charge to flow through them. Metals are good electrical conductors.

Self Evaluation 15.1

1. A polythene rod is rubbed with a piece of dry cloth. The polythene rod is charged negatively because
   A it gains electrons and the cloth gains protons.
   B it loses proton and the cloth loses protons.
   C it gains the electrons that are lost by the cloth.
   D it loses protons to the cloth.

2. A positively charged conductor becomes neutral when touched by someone because
   A negative charges from the ground flows to the conductor.
   B positive charges flow from the conductor to the ground.

C negative charges flow from the conductor to the ground.
D positive charges from the ground flow to the conductor.

3. Two light spheres X and Y of equal mass are suspended from nylon threads of the same length. The charge on sphere X is +2 C and the charge on sphere Y is +3 C. Which of the following shows the equilibrium position of the spheres?

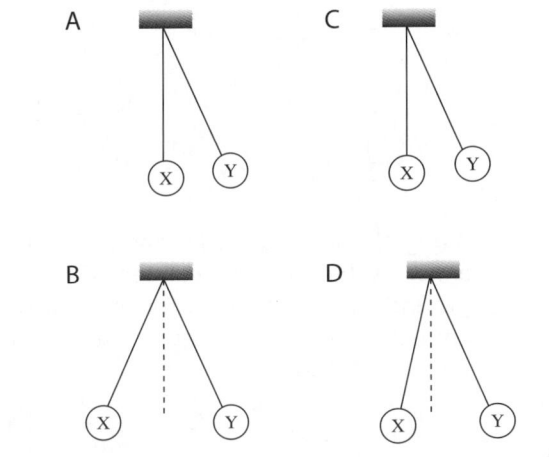

15.2 Principles of Electrostatics

Charging by Induction

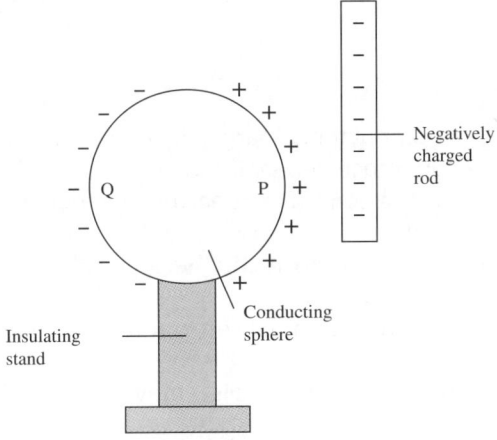

1. When a negatively charged rod is held near an uncharged insulated conducting sphere, electrons are repelled from the side P to the side Q.

2. The side P is now positively charged and the side Q is negatively charged.
3. The charges induced on the sides P and Q are temporary. When the negatively charged rod is removed, the positive and negative charges would recombine and the conducting sphere remains neutral.
4. A conductor can be charged by induction.

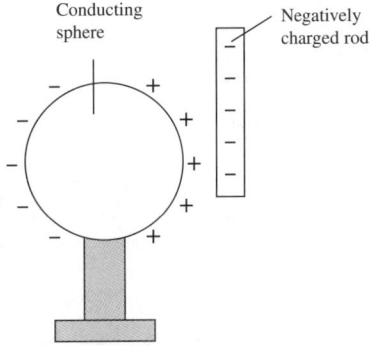

(a) Hold the negatively charged rod near to the conducting sphere.

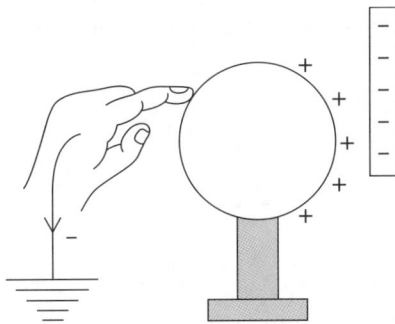

(b) Touch the conducting sphere to earth it. Electrons flow to the Earth.

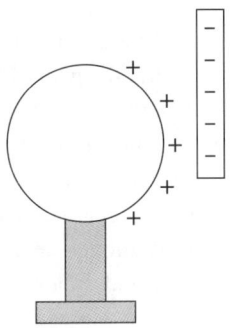

(c) Remove the finger.

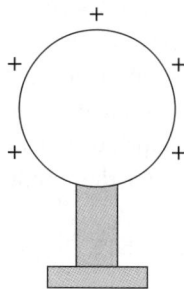

(d) Remove charged rod.

Example

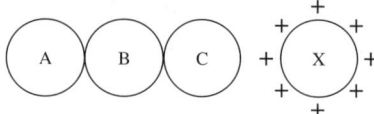

Three insulated conducting spheres A, B and C are in contact with each other. Another sphere X which is positively charged is placed close to the sphere C. Sphere A is then moved away, followed by sphere B. Finally the charged sphere X is removed. State the charge on each sphere after separation.

Solution

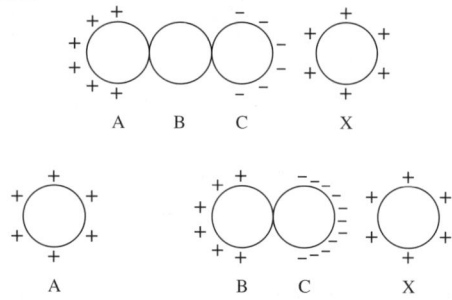

Initially, because of electrostatic induction, sphere A gets positively charged, sphere B remains neutral and sphere C gets negatively charged.

When sphere A is moved away, it remains positively charged. Positive charge is now induced on sphere B and sphere C remains charged negatively.

When sphere B is moved away, sphere B remains positively charged and sphere C remains negatively charged.

Self Evaluation 15.2

1. A positively charged rod is held close to a metal sphere on an insulating stand. Which of the figures correctly shows the charge distribution on the metal sphere?

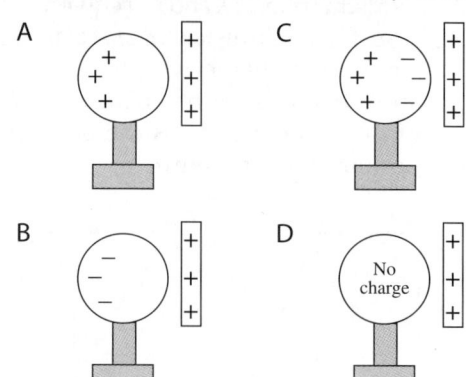

2. A negatively charged rod is held close to a metal sphere which is connected to the ground by a wire. Which of the figures correctly shows the charge distribution on the metal sphere?

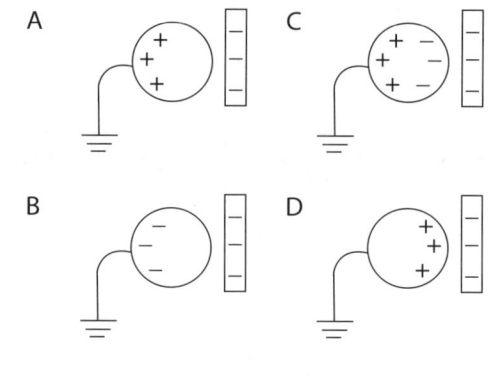

3. A conductor is charged by induction. The four processes are listed below.
   I   The conductor is earthed by touching it.
   II A charged rod is held close to the conductor.
   III The hand is removed from the conductor.
   IV The charged rod is removed.

   Which is the correct order of charging the conductor by induction?
   A I, II, III, IV   C II, I, III, IV
   B I, II, IV, III   D II, I, IV, III

15.3 Electric Field

1. An **electric field** is the region in which an electric charge experiences a force.
2. The electric field of an isolated point charge is shown below.

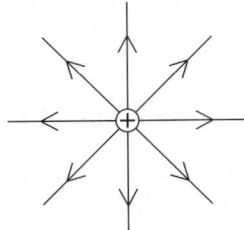

A positive charge

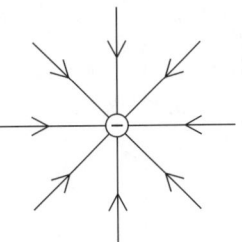

A negative charge

3. A line of force in an electric field is the path along which a free positive charge would move. The direction of the field line give the direction of the force on a free positive charge.
4. The direction of the electric field points *away* from a positive charge and *towards* a negative charge.
5. Electric field lines, which are close together denote a stronger electric field.

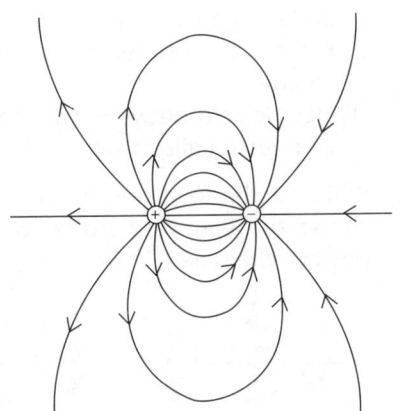

Two unlike charges

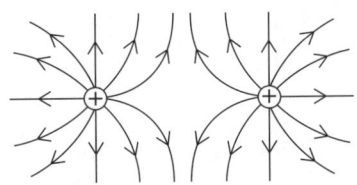

Two like charges

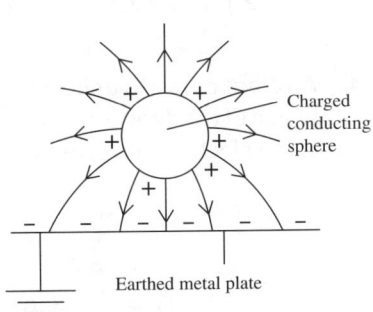

Earthed metal plate

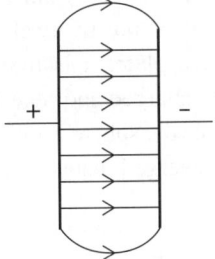

Two conducting plates

6.

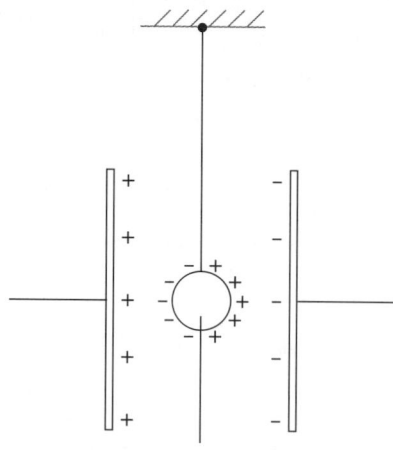

Light, conducting sphere

When a light conducting sphere is hung from a nylon thread in the electric field between two oppositely charged parallel metal plates, positive charge is induced on the side facing the negative plate and negative charge is induced on the other side of the sphere.

7.

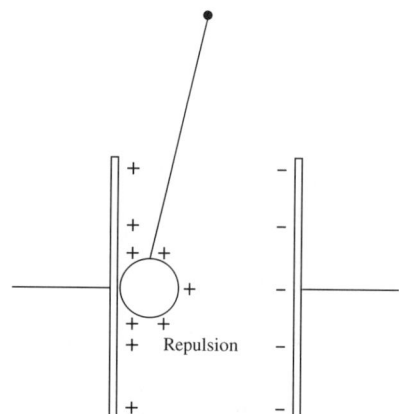

If the conducting sphere touches the positive plate, it is charged positively. Like charge repel and the sphere is pushed away from the positive plate to the negative plate. When the positively charged sphere touches the negative plate, it is first discharged and then negatively charged and repelled from the negative plate. Hence the sphere oscillates between the two oppositely charged plates.

8.

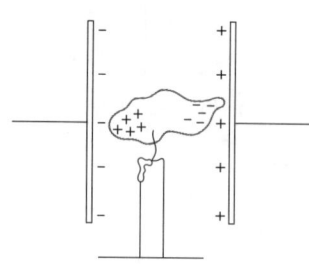

A candle flame placed in the electric field between two oppositely charged plates is distorted as shown in the figure above.

A flame contains both positive and negative charges. The positive charges are attracted to the negative plate and the negative charges to the positive plate.

Self Evaluation 15.3

1. The figure shows four points in the electric field produced by two point charges $+Q$ and $-Q$. At which of the points is the electric field strongest?

2. Which of the following electric fields is uniform?
   A Electric field of a positive charge.
   B Electric field between a positive charge and a negative charge.
   C Electric field between two positive charges.
   D Electric field between two oppositely charged parallel plates.

3. Which of the following figures correctly shows the electric field between two positive charges?

   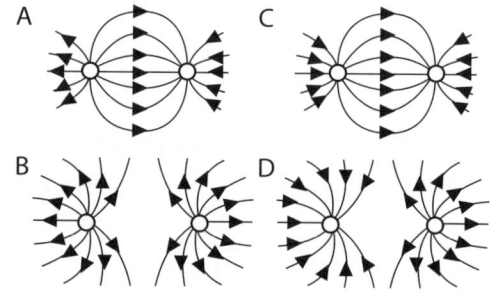

4. An electron is in a uniform electric field. In which of the directions shown in the figure is the electron accelerated?

   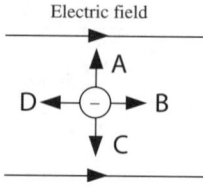

148

5. The figure shows a charged light conducting sphere oscillating in the electric field between two oppositely charged parallel metal plates.

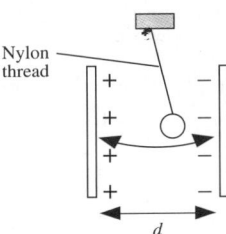

Which of the following statements correctly describes the change in the motion of the sphere when the distance d between the plates is reduced?
A The frequency of the oscillation increases.
B The amplitude of the oscillation increases.
C The sphere sticks to the positive plate.
D The sphere stops oscillating.

6. The figure shows the electric field between two point charges, Q_1 on the left and Q_2 on the right.

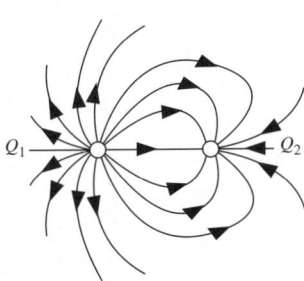

From the pattern of the electric field, it can be deduced that
A Q_1 is negative, Q_2 is positive and magnitude of Q_1 is greater.
B Q_1 is negative, Q_2 is positive and magnitude of Q_1 is smaller.
C Q_1 is positive, Q_2 is negative and magnitude of Q_1 is greater.
D Q_1 is positive, Q_2 is negative and magnitude of Q_1 is smaller.

15.4 Hazards due to and Applications of Electrostatic Charging

Hazards Due to Electrostatic Charging

1. **Petrol tankers**
   (a) As the tanker travels, friction between the tanker and the air, can build up sufficient electric charge to cause a spark.
   (b) The spark will cause the petrol vapour to explode.
   (c) To prevent this from occurring, a metal chain hung from the lorry to the ground enables the charge to escape to the earth.

2. **Aeroplane**
   (a) Charges build up due to friction when a plane flies through the air.
   (b) The plane tyres are made of special conducting rubber to allow the charge to flow to the ground when the plane lands.

3. **Operating Theatre**
   (a) In operating theatres, gases used to anaesthetize patients are highly flammable.
   (b) Charges that build up due to the movement of blankets and clothes can cause a spark.
   (c) To prevent this from happening, anaesthetic machines and trolleys are linked to the ground by metal chains. Doctors and nurses wear anti-static clothing and conducting shoes.

4. **Electronic factory**
   (a) In an air-conditioned factory, electric charges easily build up due to friction caused by the movements of workers.
   (b) The charge build-up can damage the integrated circuits (IC).
   (c) As a precaution, all workers that handle electronic components, such as ICs, are linked to the ground by a metal chain.

5. **Lightning**
   (a) When clouds drift through the air, friction between two clouds or between the clouds and the surrounding air causes a charge build-up in them.
   (b) When sufficient charge builds up in a cloud, a strong electric field is produced between two charged clouds or between a charged cloud and the ground.

(c) The air is ionised and a lightning occurs.
(d) During a lightning, a large quantity of charge flows in a short time. This can cause damage to life and property.
(e) A lightning conductor reduces the chances of lightning striking a building.
(f) A lightning conductor consists of sharp metal spikes placed on top of a building, connected by copper strips to a metal plate in the ground.
(g) A thundercloud which carries negative charges induces positive charges on the sharp metal spikes.
(h) This cause the air molecules to ionise. The electrons produced are attracted to the positively charged spikes and the positive ions to the negatively charged thundercloud which gets discharged. Thus, a lightning fails to occur.

Applications of Electrostatic Charging

6. **Photocopier**
   (a) A photocopier uses a drum coated with selenium which is a photoconductor thus becomes a good conductor when exposed to light and a poor conductor in the dark.

   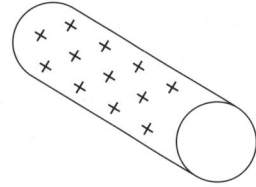

   (b) The photoconductive drum is positively charged.

   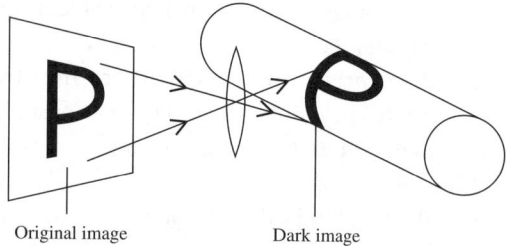

   Original image   Dark image

   (c) Light reflected off the original is focused on the drum. All areas of the photoconductive drum is exposed to light except the dark image. Electrons produced in the bright area neutralise the positive charge. The dark image remains positively charged.

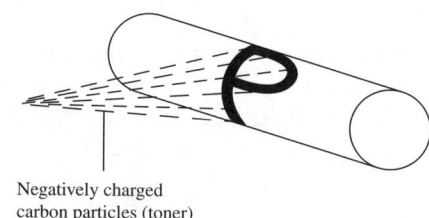

Negatively charged carbon particles (toner)

(d) Negatively charged carbon particles (toner) are attracted to the positively charged dark image.

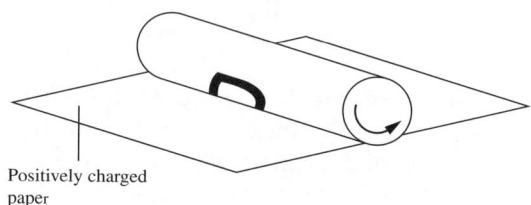

Positively charged paper

(e) The toner is transferred to a positively charged paper.
(f) Heat is used to fix the toner onto the paper.

7. **Electrostatic Precipitator**

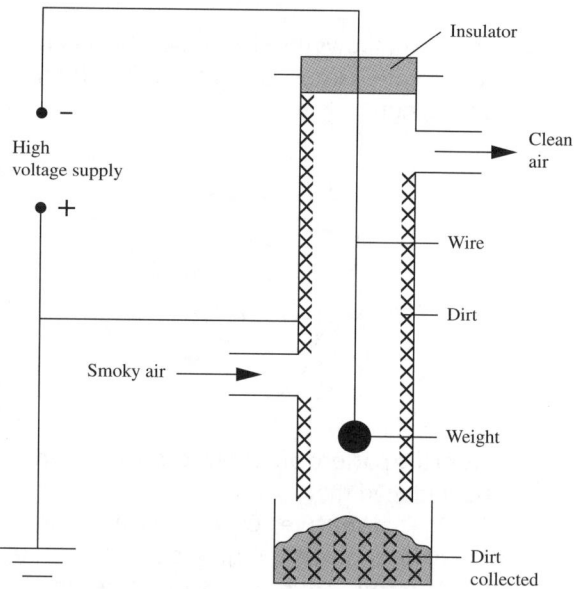

(a) An electrostatic precipitator is used to remove dust and smoke particles from the chimneys of factories.
(b) A high voltage is maintained between the wire that runs down the centre of the duct and its walls.
(c) The electric field between the wire and the walls ionises the air.

(d) The negatively charged dust particles are attracted to the walls.

(e) The duct is periodically shaken and the dust particles are collected at the bottom. The chimney is periodically cleaned.

8. **Electrostatic Spray Painting**
   (a) The car body is earthed.
   (b) A high voltage is applied between the car body and the nozzle of the spray gun.
   (c) As paint droplets emerge from the nozzle, they are charged and attracted to the car body.
   (d) Advantages of electrostatic spray painting:
      – it gives a more uniform coat of paint;
      – it reduce paint loss.

9. **Ink-jet Printer**

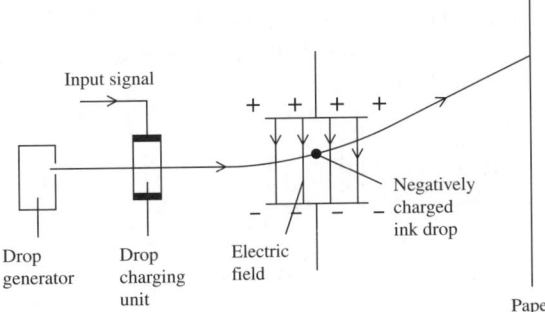

   (a) Drops of ink pass through the drop charging unit.
   (b) The charge on each ink drop is controlled by the input signal from the computer.
   (c) The negatively charged ink drop is deflected by the electric field between the two oppositely charged parallel metal plates.
   (d) The position that the ink drop lands on, is determined by the charge it carries.

Self Evaluation 15.4

1. The figure shows electrostatic spraying used to paint a metal plate. The nozzle of the spray gun is connected to the positive terminal of the voltage supply. The negative terminal of the voltage supply is connected to the metal plate. The paint droplets are positively charged as they emerge from the nozzle.

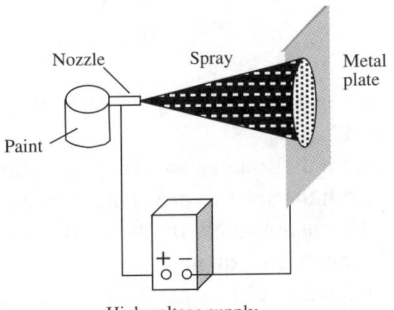

   (a) Explain why the paint droplets spread out as they emerge from the nozzle.
   (b) Why are the droplets attracted to the metal plate?
   (c) State one advantage of electrostatic spray painting.

REVISION EXERCISE 15

Multiple Choice Questions

1. Two charged spheres X and Y hang from nylon threads of the same length from the point P. They are in equilibrium as shown in the figure.

   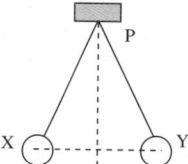

   Which of the following statements is certainly correct?
   A   Both the spheres are charged positively.
   B   Both the spheres are charged negatively.
   C   The magnitudes of the charges on the both spheres are equal.
   D   Both the spheres have the same weight.

2. The distance between two positive charges of 2 C and 3 C is fixed. The electrostatic forces on the charges are F_1 and F_2.

   Which of the following comparisons between the magnitudes of the forces F_1 and F_2 is correct?
   A $F_1 = F_2$ C $3F_1 = 2F_2$
   B $2F_1 = 3F_2$ D $4F_1 = 9F_2$

3. Which of the diagrams correctly shows the forces F_1 and F_2 between two point charges?

   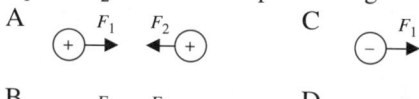

4. When conducting sphere P on an insulating stand is brought near a positively charged light sphere Q hanging from a nylon thread, the sphere Q is attracted to P. Which of the following conclusions about the sphere P is correct?
   A   Sphere P is neutral.
   B   Sphere P is charged positively.
   C   Sphere P is charged negatively.
   D   Sphere P is either negatively charged or neutral.

5. Three uncharged conducting spheres X, Y and Z initially are arranged so that they touch each other. A positively charged sphere P is then brought close to sphere X as shown in the figure.

   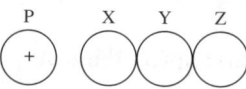

   What are the types of charge induced, if any, on the spheres X, Y and Z?

	X	Y	Z
A	Negative	Neutral	Negative
B	Negative	Neutral	Positive
C	Positive	Neutral	Negative
D	Positive	Negative	Negative

6. A negatively charged rod is held close to a metallic sphere P which is initially not charged (Figure 1(a)). Next, the sphere P is connected to the Earth by touching it (Figure 1(b)). The hand is then removed (Figure 1(c)).

   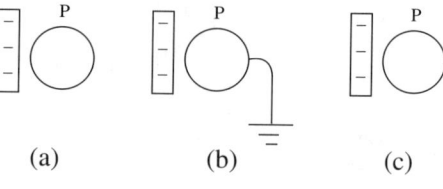

   Figure 1

   What are the types of charge, if any, on the sphere P in figure (a), (b) and (c)?

	(a)	(b)	(c)
A	No charge	positive	positive
B	Positive	no charge	positive
C	Negative	no charge	positive
D	No charge	negative	negative

7. P is a point in the electric field produced by an isolated negative charge $-Q$. Which is the direction of the electric field at the point P?

   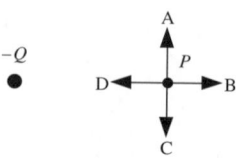

8. Which of the following electric fields is uniform?

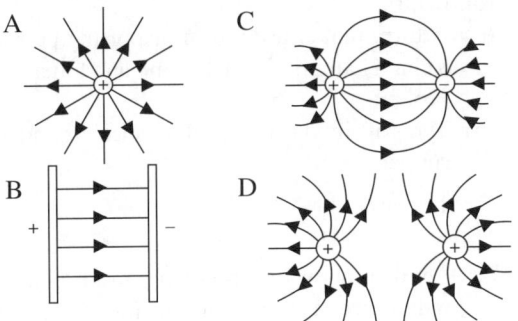

9. A negatively charged ink droplet is injected into the electric field between two oppositely charged plates. Which of the figures shows correctly the path of the ink droplet in the electric field?

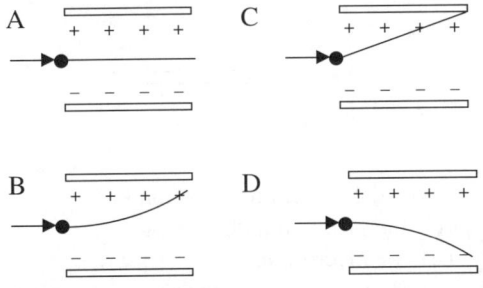

10. A negatively charged oil drop stays stationary in the electric field between two oppositely charged parallel plates as shown in the figure.

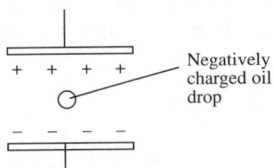

What happens to the oil drop when the two plates are moved closer to each other?
A   The oil drop moves downwards.
B   The oil drop moves upwards.
C   The oil drop moves towards the left.
D   The oil drop moves towards the right.

Structured Questions

Section A

1. A strip of plastic is rubbed with a piece of dry cloth and then hung over an insulating rod as shown in the figure.

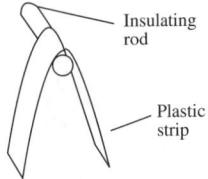

   (i) What happens to the plastic strip when it is rubbed with a dry cloth?
   (ii) Why do the ends of the strip diverge?
   (iii) Explain briefly how you can test whether the charge on the strip is positive or negative.

2. (a) A piece of polythene is used to rub a metal on an insulating stand.
      (i) Explain in terms of electron flow why the polythene is negatively charged.
      (ii) Is the metal charged?
   (b) The charged polythene piece is placed on the table and a metal disc is placed on top of it as shown in figure 2(a). Draw the charge distribution on the metal disc in figure 2(a).

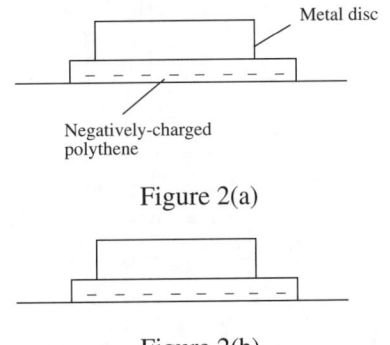

   (c) The metal disc is then touched with the hand. The hand is then removed. Draw in figure 2(b) the final charge distribution on the metal disc.

3. (a) Draw the electric field pattern around
      (i) a positive charge;
      (ii) a negative charge.
   (b) What is the difference between the two electric fields? Explain.

4. (a) Figure 3(a) shows a pair of metal plates P and Q on the insulating stands and both P and Q are connected to a high voltage supply.

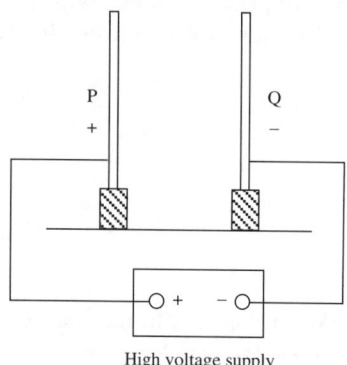

Figure 3(a)

   (i) Draw the electric field pattern between the plates. Show clearly the direction of the electric field.
   (ii) The electric field between the plates is a *uniform electric field*. What is meant by a *uniform electric field*?

   (b) A charged light conducting sphere hanging from a nylon thread is placed in the electric field between the plates as shown in figure 3(b).

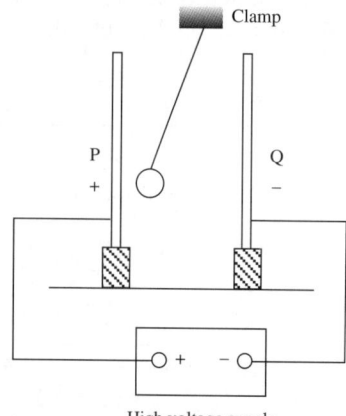

Figure 3(b)

   (i) What is the charge on the sphere?
   (ii) Why is the nylon thread not vertical?
   (iii) When the clamp is slowly moved horizontally towards the plate Q but not touching Q, the inclination of the thread stays constant. What conclusion can be made about the electric force on the sphere and the electric field?

5. Use the principles of electrostatics to explain the following.
   (a) A lorry tanker used for transporting petrol has a chain hanging from the tank and touching the ground.
   (b) Tyres of airplanes are made of special conducting rubber.

Section B

1. (a) Figure 4 shows a proton p and an electron e which are free to move in the electric field between the two oppositely charged parallel plates.

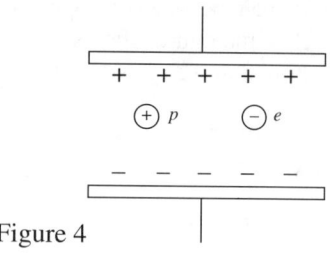

Figure 4

   Show the direction of motion of
   (i) the proton p and;
   (ii) the electron e.

   (b) In an "ink-jet" printer, the electric field between two oppositely charged parallel plates is used to deflect charged ink droplets. Figure 5 shows three identical ink droplets injected into the electric field with the same speed. The droplet P is charged positively, droplet Q is charged negatively and droplet R is not charged.

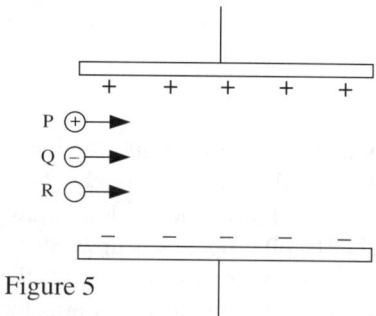

Figure 5

   Sketch the paths of the three droplets P, Q and R in the electric field in figure 5.

   (c) Figure 6 shows two ink droplets X and Y, both carrying the same amount of positive charges. The mass of droplet X is twice that of droplet Y. Both droplets start from rest at the left plate and move along the straight lines in the electric field between two parallel charged plates.

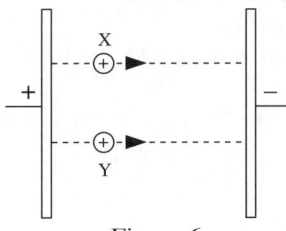

Figure 6

Discuss which one of the droplets takes a shorter time to reach the negative plate?

2. (a) An uncharged light conducting sphere hanging from a nylon thread is placed between two oppositely charged parallel metal plates as shown in figure 7.

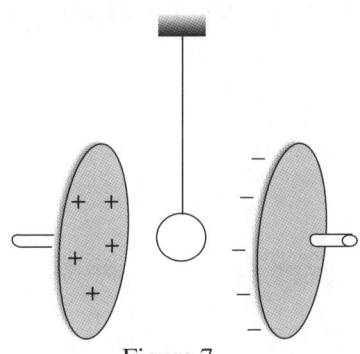

Figure 7

Draw the distribution of charges on the conducting sphere.

(b) The ball is displaced to touch the positive plates and then released.
  (i) Describe and explain what happens to the sphere after touching the positive plate.
  (ii) What happens to the charge on the plates during the subsequent motion of the sphere?
  (iii) Why does the sphere stop eventually?
  (iv) Explain the changes to the motion of the sphere if the separation between the charged plates is reduced.

3. Figure 8 shows a dust precipitator installed in a cement factory to reduce the emission of dust into the atmosphere.

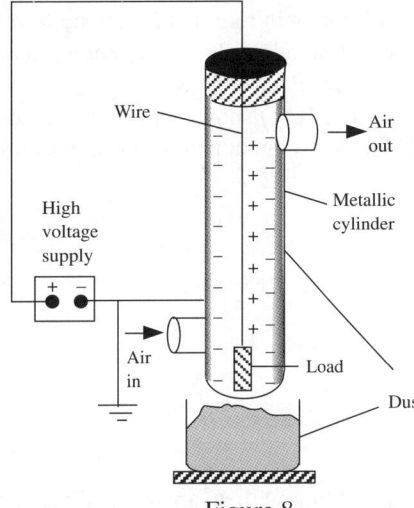

Figure 8

An electric field is set up between the central wire which is at a positive electric potential and the metallic cylinder which is at a negative electric potential.

(a) In figure 9, draw the electric field lines between the central wire and the metallic cylinder.

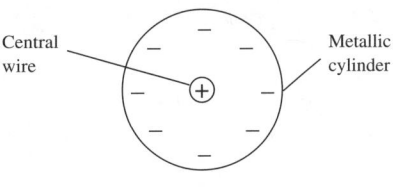

Figure 9

(b) What happens to the air molecules in the electric field?
(c) What causes the dust particle to be charged?
(d) What happens to the dust particles that are charged?

4. (a) An electron P is injected into the uniform electric field shown in the figure 10(a).

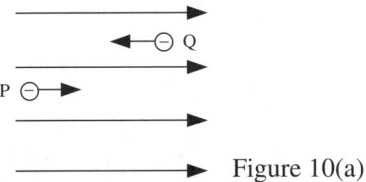

Figure 10(a)

(i) Mark on the diagram with an arrow labelled F the direction of the electric force on the electron P.

(ii) Hence explain how the speed of the electron P varies in the electric field.
(iii) Draw in figure 10(a) the path of the electron P in the electric field.
(iv) If another electron Q enters the electric field from the right, how would its speed vary as it moves in the electric field?

(b) Figure 10(b) shows an electron entering a uniform electric field with a velocity v in the direction shown. The subsequent path of the electron is shown.

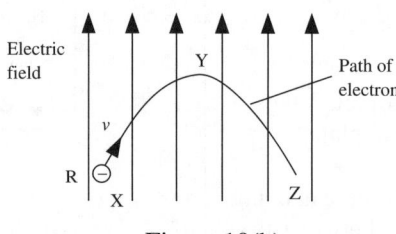

Figure 10(b)

(i) Mark with an arrow the direction of the electric force on the electron when it is at the point X.
(ii) Describe and explain how the speed of the electron varies from X to Y and from Y to Z.

CHAPTER 16
Current of Electricity and D.C. Circuits

16.1 Conventional Current and Electron Flow

1. An electric current is a flow of electric charge. In an electric circuit the current is due to the flow of free electrons.
2. The figure below shows a battery and a lamp are connected in a circuit. Electrons flow from the negative terminal of the battery but the conventional direction of the current I is from the positive terminal of the battery. Hence the directions of the current and electron flow are opposite.

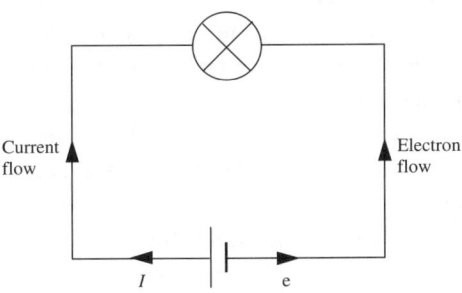

3. Current is the rate of flow of charge.

$$\text{Current} = \frac{\text{charge}}{\text{time}}$$

$$I = \frac{Q}{t}$$

4. The unit for current is the ampere (A) where

$$1 \text{ ampere} = \frac{1 \text{ coulomb}}{1 \text{ second}}$$

$$1 \text{ A} = 1 \text{ C s}^{-1}$$

5. The electric charge Q that flows in a time interval t is given by

$$\text{Charge} = \text{current} \times \text{time}$$
$$Q = It$$

Example
When the lightning strikes, 100 C of charge flows in 0.02 s. What is the current?

Solution
Current $I = \dfrac{Q}{t}$

$= \dfrac{100 \text{ C}}{0.02 \text{ s}}$

$= 5000$ A

Example
How much charge flows through an electric bulb when a current of 0.5 A flows for an hour?

Solution
Charge = current × time
$= (0.5 \text{ A})(3600 \text{ s})$
$= 1800$ C

Self Evaluation 16.1

1. A current of 2.0 A is supplied to a lamp. How much charge flows through the lamp (i) in 20 s and (ii) 10 minutes?
2. Eight coulombs of charge flows through a flash bulb in 2.0 s. What is the mean current?

16.2 Electromotive Force

1. The **electromotive force** (e.m.f.) of a source of electricity, for example a battery, is the total work done per coulomb of electricity by the source in driving the charge round a complete circuit.
2. The e.m.f. of a source is measured in volts (V) which is joules per coulomb (J C^{-1}).
3. The e.m.f. of a dry cell is 1.5 V means that the work done by the dry cell to drive a charge of 1 C around the circuit is 1.5 J.

4.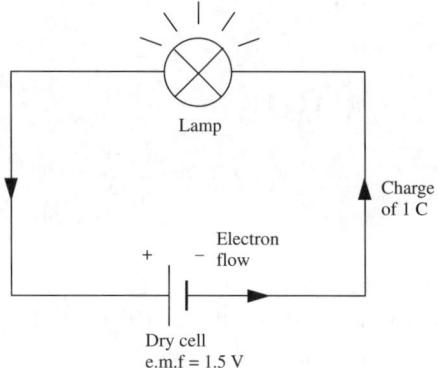

In the figure, the work done by the source is to drive the free electrons through the wires, the lamp and the cell.

5. The energy is dissipated in the form of heat in the connecting wires and cells, and light and heat from the lamp.

6. A battery consists of a number of cells in series.
   (a) When three dry cells are connected in series, their e.m.f. add.

   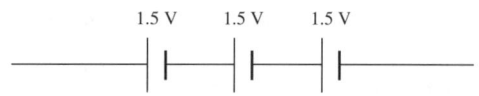

   Effective e.m.f. = (3)(1.5 V)
   = 4.5 V

   (b) When the three cells are connected in parallel, the effective e.m.f. is 1.5 V.

   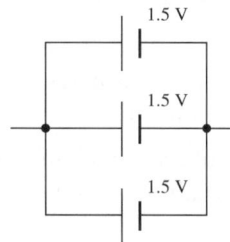

Self Evaluation 16.2

1. A dry cell of e.m.f 1.5 V is connected in a circuit. Calculate the work done by the dry cell to drive the following charge round the circuit.
   (a) 5.0 C   (b) 20 mC

2. A portable radio uses four dry cells of e.m.f. 1.5 V each in series. What is the effective e.m.f. of the battery?

16.3 Potential Difference

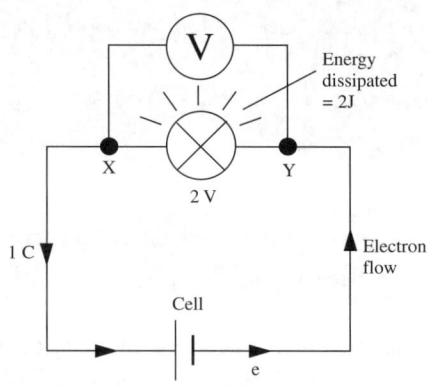

1. The **potential difference** V across a circuit component, for example a bulb in the above figure, is the work done to drive a charge of 1 C through the component.

2. The unit for potential difference is the volt (V) which is joules per coulomb ($J\ C^{-1}$).

3. In the above figure, if the potential difference across the lamp is 2 V, then the energy dissipated from the lamp when 1 C of charge flows through it is 2 joules.

4. The work done in driving the charge through the lamp is dissipated in the form of heat and light in the bulb.

5. To measure the potential difference between two points X and Y, a voltmeter is connected across the two points as shown in the above figure.

6. From the definition of potential difference,

$$\text{potential difference} = \frac{\text{work done}}{\text{charge}}$$

$$V = \frac{W}{Q}$$

Energy dissipated = work done
= QV ($Q = It$)
= IVt

Example
When a charge of 5.0 C flows through a bulb, 10 J of energy in the form of light and heat is dissipated. What is the potential difference across the bulb?

Solution

Potential difference = $\dfrac{\text{energy dissipated}}{\text{charge}}$

$= \dfrac{10 \text{ J}}{5.0 \text{ C}}$

$= 2.0 \text{ V}$

Example

When a bulb is connected to a battery, the current in the bulb is 0.5 A and the potential difference across it is 1.5 V.
(a) How much charge flows through the bulb in 5.0 minutes?
(b) What is the energy dissipated from the bulb in 5.0 minutes?

Solution

(a) Charge $Q = It$
$= (0.5 \text{ A})(300 \text{ s})$
$= 150 \text{ C}$

(b) Energy dissipated $= QV$
$= (150 \text{ C})(1.5 \text{ V})$
$= 225 \text{ J}$

Self Evaluation 16.3

1. A battery of e.m.f. 3.0 V is connected to a lamp as shown in the figure.

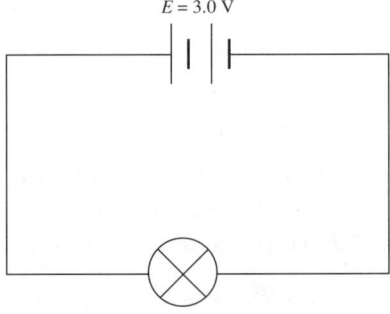

$E = 3.0 \text{ V}$

When 4.0 C of charge flows through the lamp, the energy dissipated from the lamp is 10.0 J.
(a) What is the potential difference across the lamp?
(b) What is the work done by the battery to drive the charge of 4.0 C round the circuit?
(c) Account for the difference in the work done by the battery and the energy dissipated from the lamp.

2. In the circuit shown, the reading of the ammeter is 0.50 A and the reading of the voltmeter is 2.5 V.

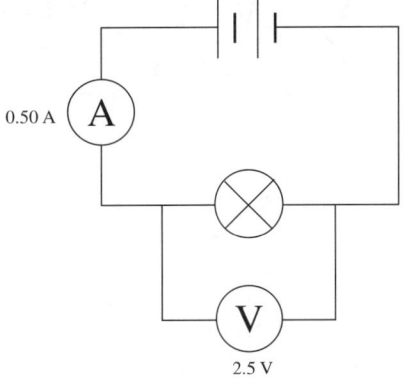

0.50 A

2.5 V

Calculate
(a) the charge that flows in the circuit in 15 s.
(b) the energy dissipated in the lamp in 15 s.

16.4 Resistance

1. The resistance R of a conductor is the ratio of the potential difference V across it and the current I that flows through it.

$$R = \dfrac{V}{I}$$

Hence potential difference across a conductor of resistance R can be given by

$$V = IR.$$

2. Resistance is measured in ohm (Ω).
3. To determine the resistance R of a conductor, a voltmeter is connected across the conductor to measure the potential difference V and an ammeter is connected in series with the conductor to measure the current I.

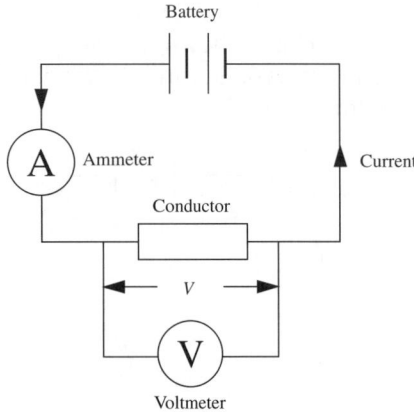

Resistance $R = \dfrac{V}{I}$

Example

In an experiment to determine the resistance of a conductor, the voltmeter reading is 6.4 V and the ammeter reading is 0.40 A. Calculate the resistance of the conductor.

Solution

Resistance $R = \dfrac{V}{I}$

$= \dfrac{6.4 \text{ V}}{0.40 \text{ A}}$

$= 16\ \Omega$

4. The resistance R of a piece of wire is:
   – directly proportional to its length l;
   – inversely proportional to its cross-sectional area A and;
   – dependent on the material of the wire.

   $$\text{Resistance } R = \dfrac{\rho l}{A}$$

   where ρ is the resistivity of the wire material.

Example

A piece of constantan wire of length 2.0 m has a resistance of 10.0 Ω.
What is the resistance of another piece of constantan wire
(a) of the same thickness but of length 0.40 m?
(b) of half the cross-sectional area and of length 0.80 m?

Solution

Resistance $R = \dfrac{\rho l}{A}$

When $l = 2.0$ m, $R = 10.0\ \Omega$

$10.0\ \Omega = \dfrac{\rho(2.0 \text{ m})}{A}$

$\Rightarrow\ \rho = 5.0A\ \Omega\ \text{m}$

(a) When $l = 0.40$ m,

$R_1 = \dfrac{\rho(0.40 \text{ m})}{A}$

$= \dfrac{(5.0A\ \Omega\ \text{m})(0.40 \text{ m})}{A}$

$R_1 = 2.0\ \Omega$

(b) When $l_2 = 0.80$ m, $A_2 = \dfrac{A}{2}$

$R_2 = \dfrac{\rho(0.80 \text{ m})}{\dfrac{A}{2}}$

$= \dfrac{(5.0A\ \Omega\ \text{m})(0.80 \text{ m})}{\dfrac{A}{2}}$

$R_2 = 8\ \Omega$

5. Resistors in **series**

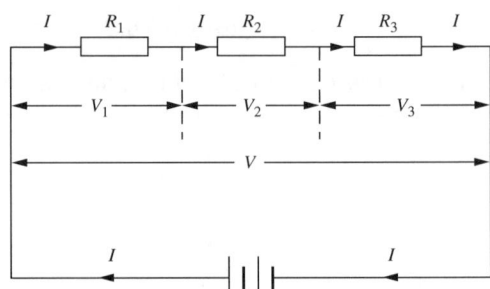

When resistors are connected in series, the same current I passes through all the resistors. Thus the potential difference across each resistor is

$$V_1 = IR_1,\ \ V_2 = IR_2,\ \ V_3 = IR_3.$$

The total potential difference across the resistors equals the sum of the potential difference across each resistor.

$$\begin{aligned}V &= V_1 + V_2 + V_3 \\ &= IR_1 + IR_2 + IR_3 \\ &= I(R_1 + R_2 + R_3)\end{aligned}$$

Therefore the effective resistance of 3 resistors in series is

$$R_{\text{eff}} = \dfrac{V}{I} = R_1 + R_2 + R_3$$

6. Resistors that are connected **in series** can act as a potential divider. The potential difference applied across the resistors is divided among the resistors in proportion to the resistances.

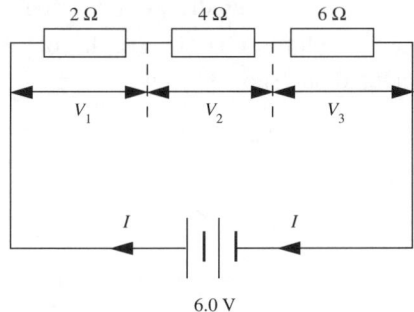

The effective resistance R is
$$R = (2\,\Omega + 4\,\Omega + 6\,\Omega) = 12\,\Omega$$
$$V_1 = \left(\frac{2\,\Omega}{12\,\Omega}\right)(6.0\text{ V}) = 1.0\text{ V}$$
$$V_2 = \left(\frac{4\,\Omega}{12\,\Omega}\right)(6.0\text{ V}) = 2.0\text{ V}$$
$$V_3 = \left(\frac{6\,\Omega}{12\,\Omega}\right)(6.0\text{ V}) = 3.0\text{ V}$$

The current in the circuit is
$$I = \frac{V}{R} = \frac{6.0\text{ A}}{12\,\Omega} = 0.50\text{ A}$$

7. Resistors in **parallel**

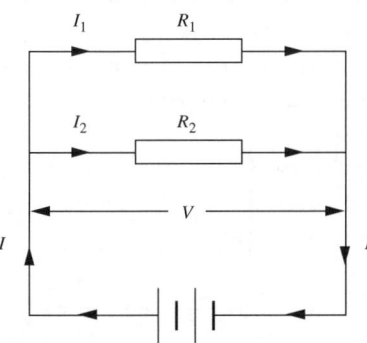

When resistors are connected in **parallel**, the potential difference V across all the resistors are the same.

While the current in each of the resistors is
$$I_1 = \frac{V}{R_1},\ I_2 = \frac{V}{R_2}$$

Thus the total current I through the set equals the sum of the currents through individual resistors.

$$I = I_1 + I_2$$
$$= \frac{V}{R_1} + \frac{V}{R_2}$$
$$\frac{I}{V} = \frac{1}{R_1} + \frac{1}{R_2}$$

Hence the effective resistance R is given by
$$\frac{I}{V} = \frac{1}{R} = \frac{1}{R_1} + \frac{1}{R_2}$$
$$\Rightarrow \frac{1}{R} = \frac{R_2 + R_1}{R_1 R_2}$$

Equivalent resistance R is
$$R = \frac{R_1 R_2}{R_1 + R_2}$$
$$V = I_1 R_1 = I_2 R_2 = IR$$
$$= I\left(\frac{R_1 R_2}{R_1 + R_2}\right)$$

Therefore $I_1 = \left(\dfrac{R_2}{R_1 + R_2}\right)I$

$I_2 = \left(\dfrac{R_1}{R_1 + R_2}\right)I$

8.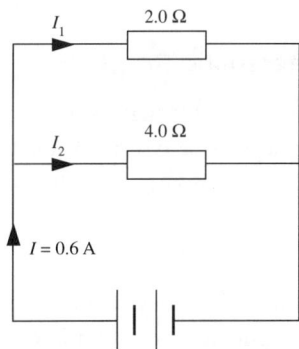

In the above circuit,
$$I_1 = \left(\frac{R_2}{R_1 + R_2}\right)I = \left(\frac{4\,\Omega}{2\,\Omega + 4\,\Omega}\right)(0.6\text{ A})$$
$$= 0.4\text{ A}$$
$$I_2 = \left(\frac{R_1}{R_1 + R_2}\right)I = \left(\frac{2\,\Omega}{2\,\Omega + 4\,\Omega}\right)(0.6\text{ A})$$
$$= 0.2\text{ A}$$

Example
Resistors of 6 Ω and a 12 Ω are connected in parallel to a 6 V battery.
(a) What is the effective resistance?
(b) What is the current from the battery?
(c) What is the current in each of the resistor?

Solution

(a) $\dfrac{1}{R} = \dfrac{1}{R_1} + \dfrac{1}{R_2}$

$= \dfrac{1}{6\,\Omega} + \dfrac{1}{12\,\Omega}$

$R = 4.0\,\Omega$

(b) Current from the battery is

$I = \dfrac{V}{R} = \dfrac{6.0\text{ V}}{4.0\,\Omega}$

$= 1.50\text{ A}$

(c) Current I_1 through the 6 Ω resistor is

$I_1 = \dfrac{V}{R_1}$

$= \dfrac{6.0\text{ V}}{6.0\,\Omega}$

$= 1.0\text{ A}$

Current I_2 through the 12 Ω resistor is

$I_2 = \dfrac{V}{R_2}$

$= \dfrac{6.0\text{ V}}{12.0\,\Omega}$

$= 0.50\text{ A}$

I-V Characteristic Graph

9. **Ohm's Law** states that the current I in a metallic conductor is directly proportional to the potential difference V across it, if the temperature remains constant.

$$I \propto V$$

10. A conductor that obeys Ohm's law is known as an ohmic conductor. Non-ohmic conductors do **not** obey Ohm's law.

11. To determine experimentally whether a conductor obeys Ohm's law, different potential differences are applied across the conductor and the corresponding current is measured. A graph of current I against potential difference V is then plotted. This is known as the *I-V* characteristic graph.

12. The *I-V* **characteristic graphs** of an ohmic conductor is a straight line through the origin. An example of an ohmic conductor is a constantan wire at constant temperature.

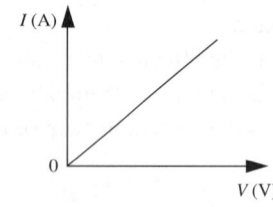

I-V characteristic graph of an ohmic conductor

Resistance R of the conductor is

$R = \dfrac{V}{I}$

$= \dfrac{1}{\text{gradient of the graph}}$

13. The *I-V* characteristic graphs of non-ohmic conductor are shown below.

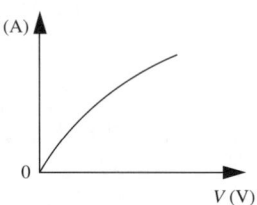

I-V characteristic graph of a filament lamp

(a) Gradient of the graph decreases as the potential difference increases implies that resistance of the lamp increases as current increases.

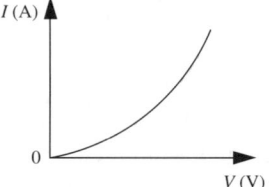

I-V characteristic graph of a thermistor

(b) Resistance of the thermistor decreases as the current increases.

14. The resistance of a metallic conductor increases with increasing temperature.

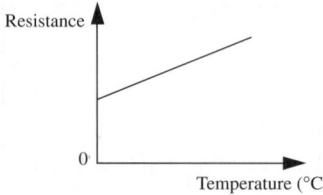

15. The resistance of the filament of a bulb is the lowest when it is cold before it is switched on. At the instant the bulb is switched on the current through the bulb is the highest. Hence the filament is most likely to fuse.

16. As the temperature of the filament increases, its resistance increases and the current decreases.

Semiconductor diode

17. A diode is an electric component used as a rectifier to convert alternating current (a.c.) to direct current (d.c.).
18. The circuit symbol of a semiconductor diode is shown in the figure below.

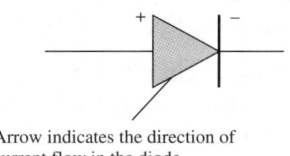

Arrow indicates the direction of current flow in the diode

19. The *I-V* characteristic graph of a semiconductor diode is shown below.

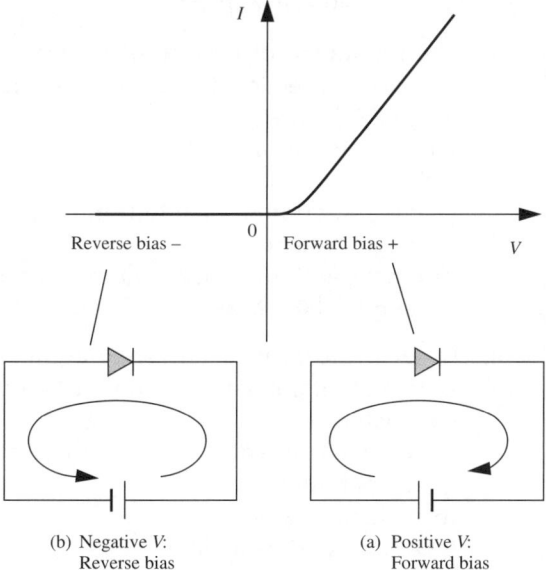

(b) Negative *V*: Reverse bias
(a) Positive *V*: Forward bias

20. (a) For positive values of *V*, the diode is said to be forward biased. Beyond a small potential difference *V* of 0.7 V, the current *I* would increase when the potential difference *V* across the diode increases.
    (b) For negative values of *V*, the diode is said to be reverse biased. The current through the diode is negligible.
21. The action of the diode may be summarised as follows.
    (a) When in forward bias, current flows through the diode. Its resistance is negligible.
    (b) When in reverse bias, no current flows through the diode and its resistance is infinity.
22. Since the diode only allow current to flow in one direction only, it can be used as a rectifier.
23. Half-wave rectification
    Half-wave rectification is obtained by connecting a diode in series with an a.c. supply and a load of resistance *R* as shown.

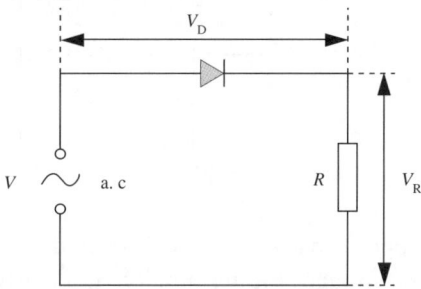

Figure 1(b) and 1(c) show the variation of voltage with time across the load V_R and the diode V_D respectively when an a.c. voltage *V* is applied to them.

Since the rectified voltage across the load V_R is half of the supply voltage *V*, the rectification is known as half-wave rectification.

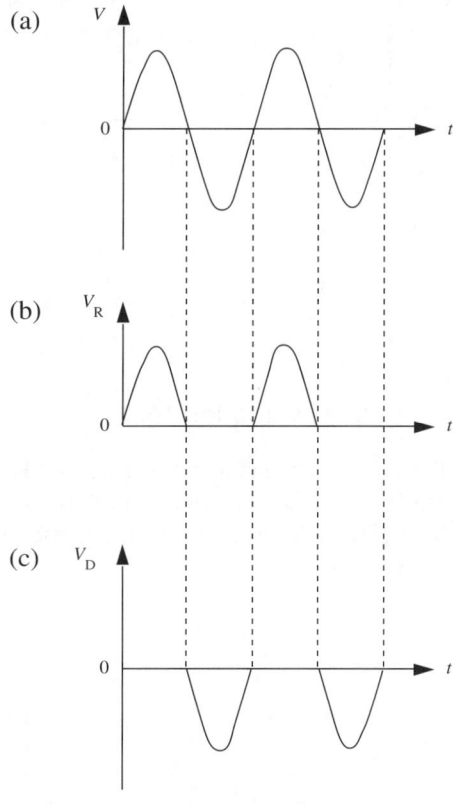

Figure 1

163

24. Full-wave rectification is achieved using four diodes as shown in the figure.

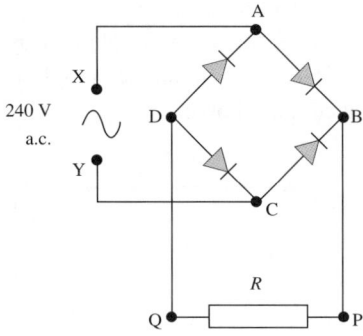

Suppose that for the positive half cycle of the a.c. voltage, the terminal X is positive and Y negative. Then the current would flows in the loop XABPQDCY. During the negative half cycle, the current would flow in the loop YCBPQDAX.

25. In both the positive and negative half cycles of the a.c. voltage, the current would flow in the same direction P to Q across the load of resistance R. The voltage-time graph for the potential difference V_R across the load is as shown.

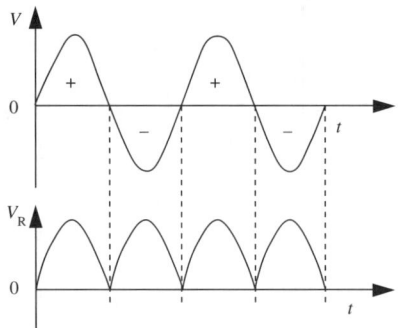

Self Evaluation 16.4

1. Three resistors of resistances R_1, R_2 and R_3 are connected in series with a 6.0 V battery of negligible internal resistance as shown in the figure.

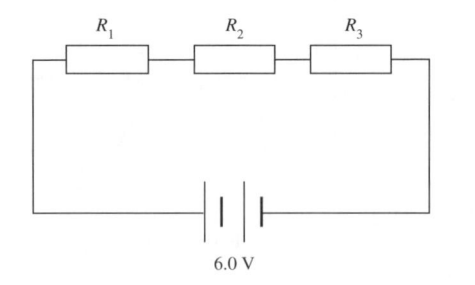

(a) The current in the resistor of resistance R_1 is 0.60 A and the potential difference across it is 1.8 V. What is the value of the resistance R_1?
(b) The resistance R_2 is 6.0 Ω. What is the potential difference across the 6.0 Ω resistor?
(c) Calculate the resistance R_3.

2. (a) Draw a circuit showing three 6.0 Ω resistors connected in parallel to a 12.0 V battery.
(b) Calculate
  (i) the current through each resistor.
  (ii) the total current.
  (iii) the effective resistance of the three resistors in parallel.

3. The resistance of a piece of nichrome wire of cross-sectional area 1.00 mm² and length 50.0 cm is 2.8 Ω.
What is the resistance of another piece of nichrome wire of
(a) cross-sectional area 1.00 mm² and length 1.00 m?
(b) cross-sectional area 2.00 mm² and length 1.00 m?

4. Draw the graph of current I against potential difference V for the following conductors.
(a) A constantan wire at constant temperature
(b) A filament lamp
(c) A semiconductor diode

16.5 Potential Divider circuit

1. A potential divider is used to obtain a fraction of the voltage from a source of e.m.f.
2. A rheostat or a variable carbon resistor is usually used as a variable potential divider.

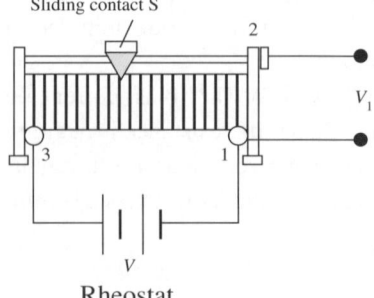

Rheostat

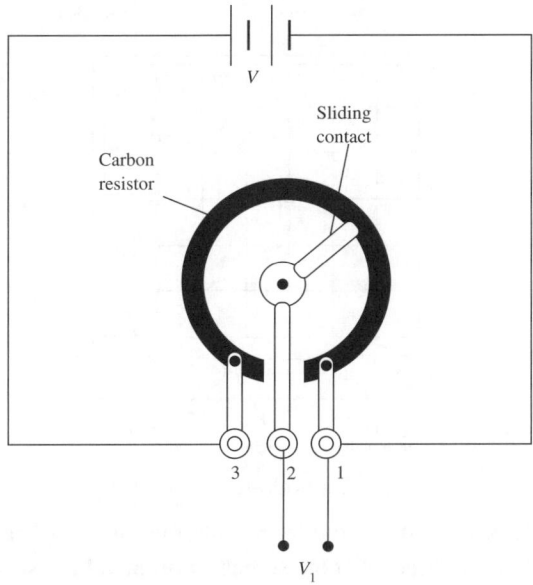

3. The circuit diagram of a variable potential divider is shown below.

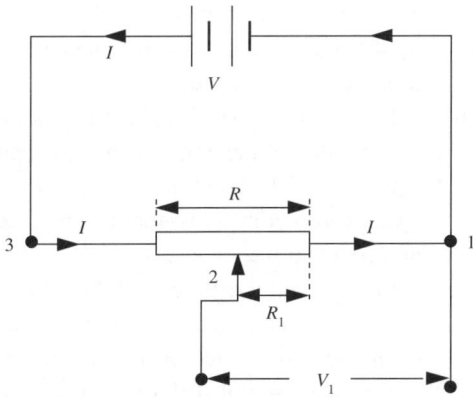

4. If V is the voltage supply, R is the resistance between terminals 1 and 3, R_1 is the resistance between terminals 1 and 2 and I is the current in the resistor, then $V = IR$ and $V_1 = IR_1$

$$\frac{V_1}{V} = \frac{IR_1}{IR}$$

$$V_1 = \left(\frac{R_1}{R}\right)V$$

(a) If the sliding contact 2 is $\frac{1}{4}$-way from terminal 1, then

$$V_1 = \left(\frac{1}{4}\right)V$$

(b) If the sliding contact 2 is at the mid-point, then

$$V_1 = \left(\frac{1}{2}\right)V$$

Hence when the sliding contact moves from right to left, the potential difference V_1 increases.

Transducer

5. A transducer is a device that changes non-electrical energy to electrical energy. Examples of transducers are **thermistor** and **light-dependent resistor (LDR)**.

Thermistor   LDR

6. A thermistor is a semiconductor resistor. Its resistance decreases with increasing temperature.
7. A light-dependent resistor (LDR) is a resistor whose resistance depends on the intensity of light incident on it. In the dark it has a high resistance. When the intensity of light on it increases, the resistance decreases.
8. Figure 2 below shows how the LDR is used as a transducer to switch on the lamp (a) when daylight begins and (b) when the day begins to get dark.

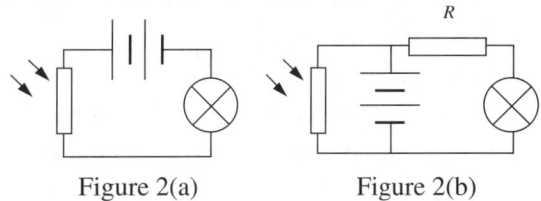

Figure 2(a)   Figure 2(b)

9. In figure 2(a), in the dark the resistance of the LDR is high compared to the resistance of the lamp. So the potential difference across the lamp would be very low and it would not light up.
10. When daylight begins, the intensity of light on the LDR increases and the resistance of the LDR drops to a low value. The potential difference across the lamp increases and it lights up.
11. In figure 2(b), during the day, light falls on the LDR and the resistance of the LDR is lower than the combined resistance of the lamp and resistor R. The current in the lamp is small and it does not light up.
12. In the dark the resistance of the LDR is high compared to the combined resistance of the lamp and resistor R. The current in the lamp increases and it lights up.

13. The figure below shows how a thermistor can be used as an input transducer in a potential divider.
14. In the circuit, the thermistor is used to measure the temperature in an oven.

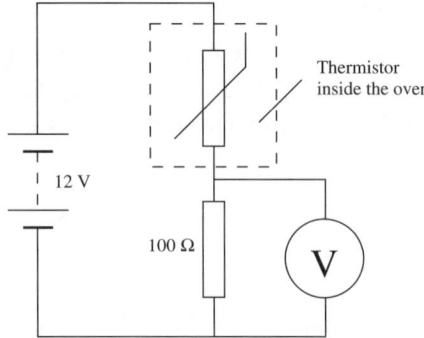

15. At room temperature, the resistance of the thermistor is 1000 Ω.

    The voltmeter's reading is $\left(\dfrac{100\ \Omega}{1000\ \Omega + 100\ \Omega}\right)(12\ V)$
    $= 1.1\ V$

16. As the temperature in the oven increases, the resistance of the thermistor decreases. Hence the potential difference across the thermistor decreases and that across the 100 Ω resistor increases.
17. Suppose that the resistance of the thermistor at 200 °C is 10 Ω, then the voltmeter's reading is
    $\left(\dfrac{100\ \Omega}{100\ \Omega + 10\ \Omega}\right)(12\ V) = 11\ V$
18. The scale of the voltmeter can be calibrated in °C to give the temperature in the oven directly.

16.6 Cathode-Ray Oscilloscope (c.r.o)

1. The figure shows a cathode-ray oscilloscope which can be used to:
   - display waveforms (graph of voltage against time);
   - measure potential differences;
   - measure short time interval.

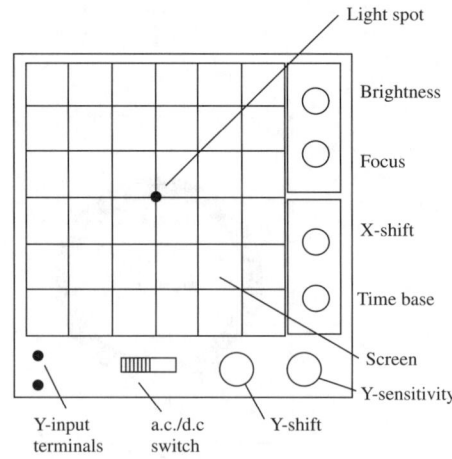

Cathode-ray oscilloscope

2. (a) In the cathode-ray tube an electron beam is directed at the screen, forming a light spot.
   (b) The electron beam is deflected in the vertical direction by the electric field between two parallel plates.
   (c) The strength of the electric field is determined by the potential difference connected to the Y-input terminals of the c.r.o.
   (d) When the time base of the c.r.o. is switched on, an internal generated voltage is applied to a pair of parallel plates to cause the light spot to sweep repeatedly across the screen horizontally at a constant frequency.
   (e) With a potential difference V being connected to the Y-input terminals and the time base being switched on, a waveform that represents the graph of potential difference V against time would be shown on the screen of the c.r.o.

Display Waveforms

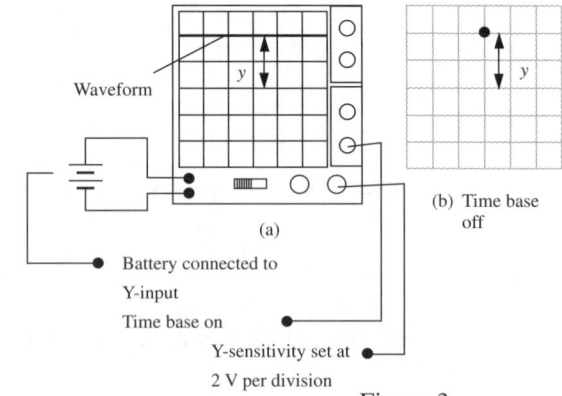

Figure 3

3. Figure 3(a) shows the waveform or graph of V against time t for the e.m.f. of a battery.

(a) The horizontal line for the waveform shows that the e.m.f. of the battery is constant.
(b) The line is at a distance y (2 divisions) above the centre of the screen. Suppose the Y-sensitivity is set at 2 V per division, then the e.m.f. of the battery is (2×2) V = 4 V.
(c) When the time base is switched off, the trace on the screen is just a light spot displaced by 2 divisions from the centre of the screen vertically as shown in figure 3(b).

4. Waveform of an a.c. voltage

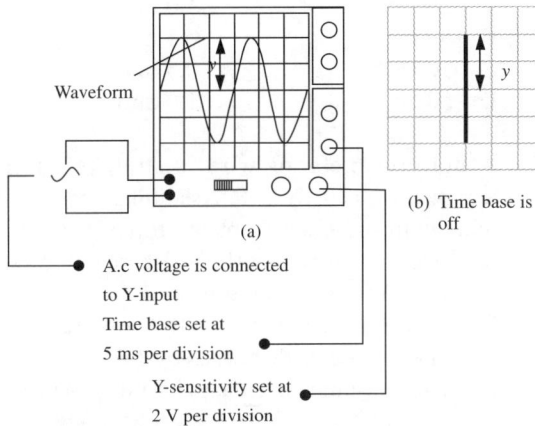

From the waveform on the screen, the following deductions can be made.
(a) The graph of the potential difference V against time is a sine curve.
(b) The peak voltage V_0 is 4.0 V and the r.m.s. voltage $V_{r.m.s}$ is given by
$$V_{r.m.s.} = \frac{V_0}{\sqrt{2}} = \frac{4.0 \text{ V}}{\sqrt{2}} = 2.83 \text{ V}$$
(c) The period of the a.c. voltage input is
$T = (4 \text{ div})(5 \text{ ms div}^{-1}) = 20 \text{ ms}$
Hence the frequency is
$$f = \frac{1}{T}$$
$$= \frac{1}{20 \times 10^{-3}} \text{ Hz}$$
$$= 50 \text{ Hz}$$
If the waveform has **two complete cycles** of the a.c. voltage as shown in the figure, then the frequency of the a.c. voltage is **twice** that of the time base.
(d) When the timebase is switched off, the trace is a vertical line. The length of the line represents $2V_0$.

5. The figure below shows the waveform of the half-wave rectified output voltage obtained using a semiconductor diode.

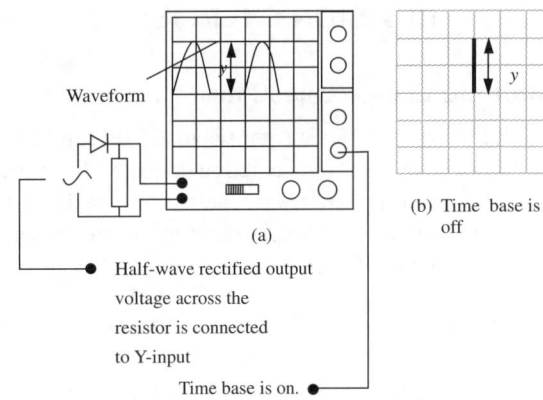

6. Measure short time interval
(a) The c.r.o. can be used to measure short time interval such as that between the emission of sound from a source and the reception of the echo.
(b) The pulse of sound from a whistle and its echo can be detected by a microphone that is connected to the Y-input of the c.r.o.
(c) The timebase control is adjusted until two peaks are seen on the screen of the c.r.o.

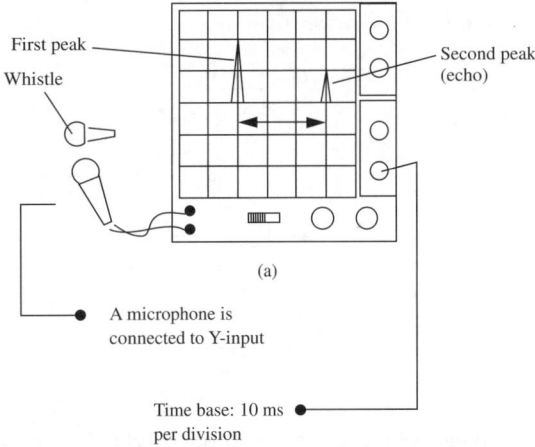

(d) From the above figure, the time interval t between the sound pulse and its echo is
$t = 3$ divisions on the time base
$= (3 \text{ div}) (10 \text{ m s div}^{-1})$
$= 30 \text{ ms}$
If the distance D of the wall from the whistle and the microphone is 4.8 m, the speed of sound v is
$$v = \frac{2D}{t}$$
$$= \frac{2(4.8 \text{ m})}{30 \times 10^{-3} \text{ s}}$$
$$= 320 \text{ m s}^{-1}$$

REVISION EXERCISE 16

Multiple Choice Questions

1. Two resistors P and Q of resistance 5.0 Ω and 10.0 Ω respectively are connected in series with a battery. The potential difference across the resistor P is 3.0 V. What is the total potential difference across the resistors P and Q?
   A 1.5 V C 6.0 V
   B 3.0 V D 9.0 V

2. Two resistors of resistances R_1 and R_2 are connected in parallel to a battery of negligible internal resistance. If $R_1 < R_2$, which of the following statements is correct?
   A The same current flows in both the resistors.
   B The potential difference across R_1 is smaller than that across R_2.
   C The effective resistance is less than R_1.
   D The e.m.f. of the battery equals the sum of the potential differences across R_1 and R_2.

3. A 1 Ω resistor and a 3 Ω resistor are connected in parallel as shown below. The currents in the resistors are I_1 and I_3 respectively.

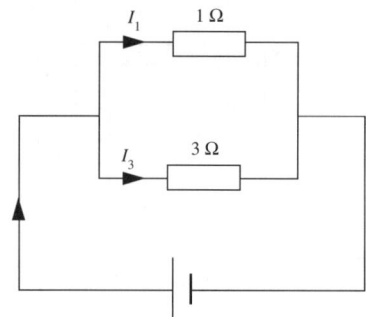

   Which of the following correctly relates the currents I_1 and I_3?
   A $I_1 = 3I_3$ C $3I_1 = I_3$
   B $I_1 = 4I_3$ D $4I_1 = I_3$

4. Three resistors X, Y and Z of resistances 2 Ω, 6 Ω and 8 Ω are connected in series to a battery of e.m.f. 8.0 V and negligible internal resistance. The potential differences across the resistors are V_x, V_y and V_z. What are the values of V_x, V_y and V_z?

	V_x	V_y	V_z
A	1.0 V	3.0 V	4.0 V
B	3.0 V	4.0 V	1.0 V
C	3.0 V	1.0 V	4.0 V
D	4.0 V	3.0 V	1.0 V

5. Four pieces of wires of different materials are of the same length and diameter. Which wire has the lowest resistance?
   A Copper wire
   B Tungsten wire
   C Steel wire
   D Constantan wire

6. Which of the following pieces of constantan wire has the highest resistance?

	Length	Diameter
A	50 cm	1.0 mm
B	50 cm	0.5 mm
C	100 cm	0.5 mm
D	50 cm	1.0 mm

7. A uniform piece of wire is stretched until its length increases by 1%. Assuming that the wire thins uniformly, which of the following correctly describes the change in the resistance of the wire?
   A The resistance increases by 1%.
   B The resistance increases by more than 1%.
   C The resistance decreases by 1%.
   D The resistance decreases by more than 1%.

8. The graph of current I against potential difference V for a conductor is shown below.

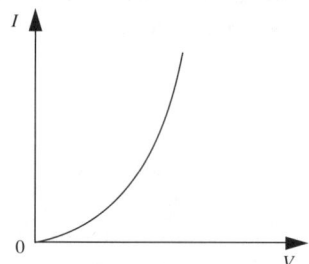

   Which of the following deductions from the graph is correct?
   A The conductor is an ohmic conductor.
   B The resistance of the conductor decreases as the potential difference increases.
   C The resistance of the conductor is zero when no current flows in it.
   D The resistance of the conductor increases when the temperature increases.

9. Which of the following graphs is the *I-V* characteristic curve of a semiconductor diode?

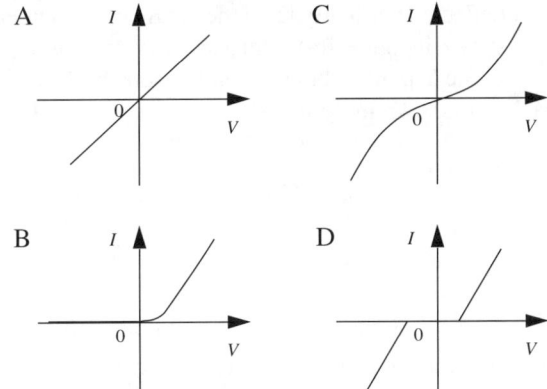

10. In which of the following circuits is the lamp lighted?

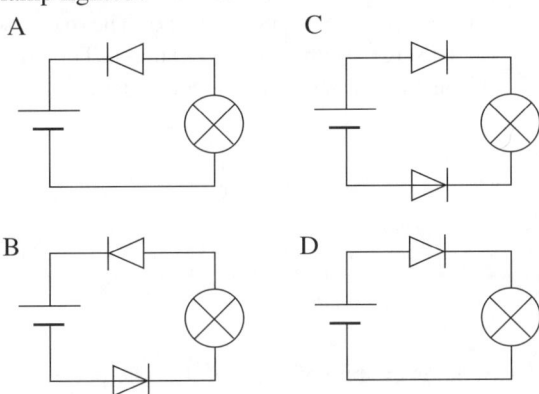

11. A rheostat X and a resistor Y are connected in series to a battery. Voltmeters V_1 and V_2 are connected across the rheostat and resistor respectively.

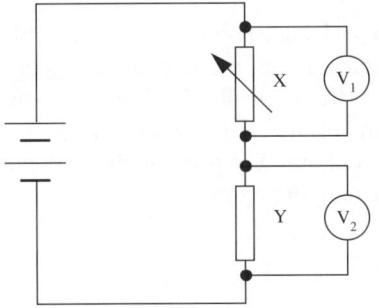

What happens to the readings of the voltmeters when the resistance of the rheostat X is reduced?

	Voltmeter V_1	Voltmeter V_2
A	Increases	Increases
B	Increases	Decreases
C	Decreases	Increases
D	Decreases	Decreases

12. In which circuits will the lamp glow more brightly when less light shines on the LDR?

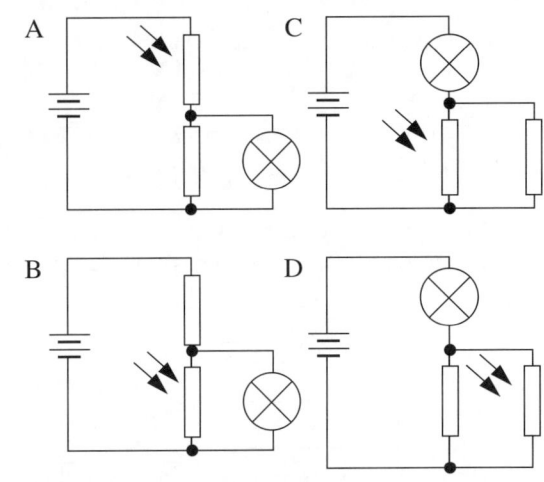

13. A thermistor is connected in a potential divider circuit as shown in the figure.

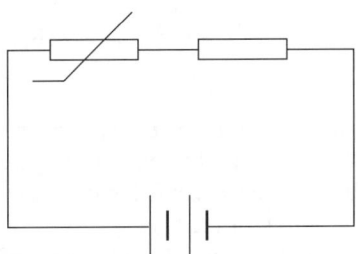

What happens to the current in the circuit and the potential difference across the thermistor when the thermistor is heated?

	Current	Potential difference
A	Increases	Increases
B	Increases	Decreases
C	Decreases	Increases
D	Decreases	Decreases

14. A LDR and a 100 Ω resistor are connected in series with a 6.0 V battery. The resistance of the LDR is 200 Ω in daylight and 2 kΩ in the dark.

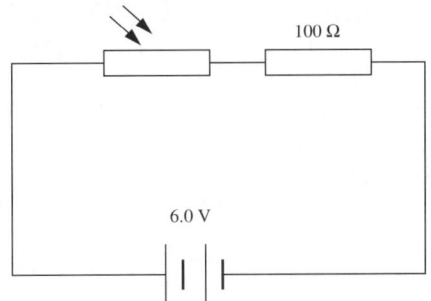

What is the potential difference across the LDR in daylight and in the dark?

	Daylight	Dark
A	2.0 V	0.1 V
B	2.0 V	0.3 V
C	4.0 V	5.7 V
D	4.0 V	6.0 V

15. The figure shows a rheostat used as a potential divider to control the brightness of a lamp.

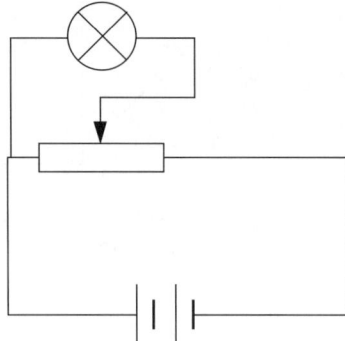

The function of the potential divider is to vary
A   the potential difference across the lamp.
B   the resistance of the lamp.
C   the e.m.f. of the battery.
D   the temperature of the filament of the lamp.

For questions 16 and 17, refer to the figure which shows the trace on the screen of a C.R.O. when an a.c. voltage is connected to Y-plates.

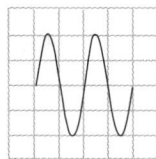

16. The timebase is set at 20 ms per division. What is the frequency of the a.c. voltage?
A   25 Hz   C   100 Hz
B   50 Hz   D   200 Hz

17. The voltage sensitivity is set at 2.0 V per division. What is the peak voltage?
A   1.0 V   C   4.0 V
B   2.0 V   D   8.0 V

18. When a cell of e.m.f. 1.5 V is connected to the Y-plates of a c.r.o., the light spot on the screen is deflected vertically from the centre of the screen as shown in figure 4(a). When an a.c. voltage is applied to the Y-plates, the trace on the screen of the c.r.o. is as shown in figure 4(b).

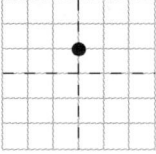 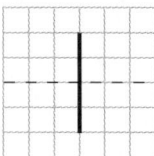

Figure 4(a)   Figure 4(b)

What is the peak voltage of the a.c.?
A   1.5 V   C   4.0 V
B   3.0 V   D   8.0 V

19. The electrodes from the chest of a patient are connected to the Y-input of a c.r.o.. The trace formed on the screen of the c.r.o. is as shown. The timebase of the c.r.o. is set as 0.50 s per division.

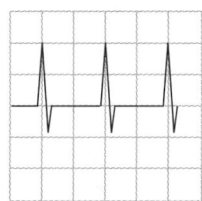

What is the rate of heart beat of the patient?
A   20 beats per minute
B   30 beats per minute
C   40 beats per minute
D   60 beats per minute

20. A microphone is connected to the Y-plates of a c.r.o. A student with the microphone is at a distance of 25 m from a wall. He clasps his hands once. The sound of the clasp and its echo are detected by the microphone. The trace on the screen of the c.r.o. is shown in the figure.

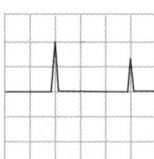

The timebase of the c.r.o. is set at 0.05 s per division. What is the speed of sound in air?
A   330 m s^{-1} C   500 m s^{-1}
B   450 m s^{-1} D   660 m s^{-1}

Structure Questions

Section A

1. A lamp is connected to a battery as shown. The current in the lamp is 0.32 A.

   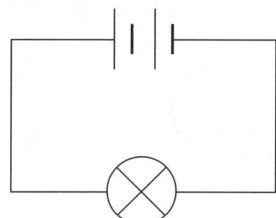

   (a) Mark
   - (i) the conventional direction of the current I in the circuit.
   - (ii) the direction of electron flow in the circuit.

   Label the directions clearly.

   (b) (i) Calculate the charge that flows through the lamp in 1.0 minute.

   (ii) The charge of an electron is 1.60×10^{-19} C. How many electrons flow through the lamp in 1.0 minute?

2. Two resistors P and Q are connected in series with a battery of negligible resistance as shown below.

   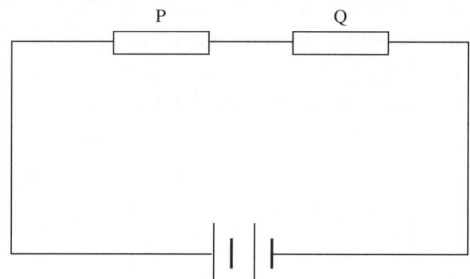

   In 5.0 s the work done by the battery to drive 2.0 C of charge through P and Q is 3.0 J and 5.0 J respectively.

   (a) What is the potential difference across the resistor P and Q?
   (b) What is the e.m.f. of the battery?
   (c) What is the current in the circuit?
   (d) Calculate the resistance of P and Q.

3. A number of 2 Ω resistors are available. Draw diagrams to show how you would connect a set of 2 Ω resistors to give the following effective resistances.

   (a) 6 Ω   (b) 1 Ω   (c) 5 Ω

4. The circuit below shows a lamp, a 5.0 Ω resistor and a component P are connected to a battery.

   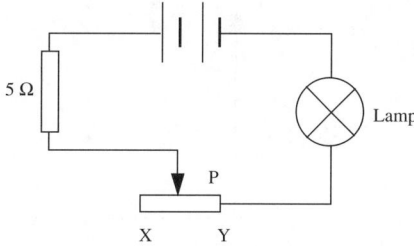

   (a) Name the component P and state its function in the circuit.
   (b) Describe and explain the variation in the brightness of the lamp when the sliding contact of P is moved from the end X to Y.
   (c) How does the resistance of the lamp vary when the brightness of the lamp changes?

5. The circuit shown in the figure is used to determine the resistance of a piece of constantan wire.

   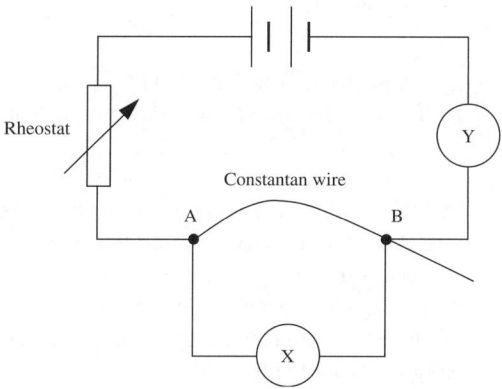

   (a) Name the types of measuring instrument at X and Y?
   (b) How is the resistance of the wire calculated from the readings of the measuring instruments at X and Y?
   (c) The experiment is repeated by changing the length l of the constantan wire connected between the points A and B. The corresponding resistance R of the wire is calculated.

   (i) On the axes provided, sketch the graph to show how the resistance R of the wire depends on its length l. Label this graph (i).

(ii) On the same axes, draw the graph for another piece of constantan wire of greater diameter. Label this graph (ii).

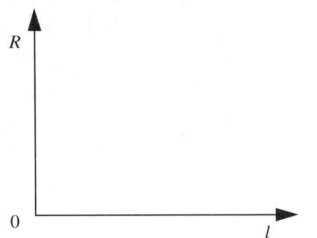

6. The figure shows the circuit symbols of four electrical components.

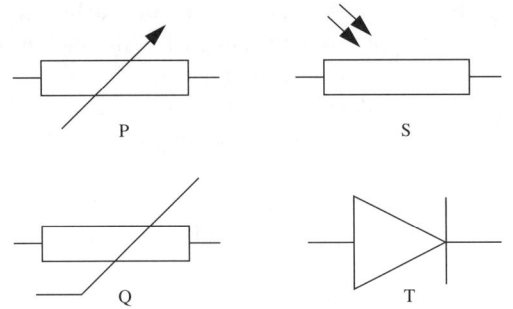

(a) Identify the components P, Q, S and T.
(b) Explain the conditions that would cause the resistance of P, Q and S to change.

7. The figure shows a uniform piece of constantan wire AB of length 100 cm and resistance 5.0 Ω connected in series with a battery of e.m.f. 2.0 V and negligible internal resistance. A high resistance voltmeter is connected across the points A and P using a crocodile clip at P.
(a) Calculate the current in the wire AB.
(b) What is the voltmeter reading when the length AP is
(i) 20 cm;
(ii) 50 cm;
(iii) 80 cm?

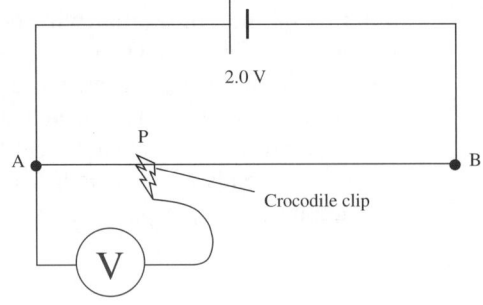

8. A resistor and a diode are connected in series with an a.c. supply as shown in the figure. A suitably adjusted cathode-ray oscilloscope (c.r.o.) is connected across (a) the a.c. supply, (b) the diode and (c) the resistor.

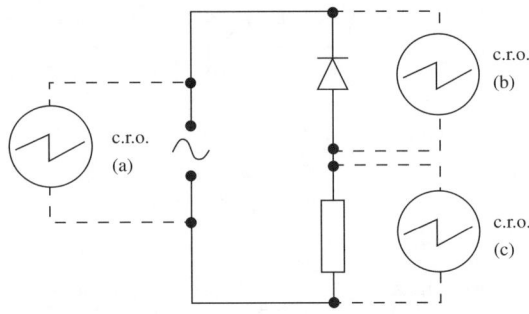

Draw in the space provided the trace on the screen of the c.r.o. in (a), (b) and (c).

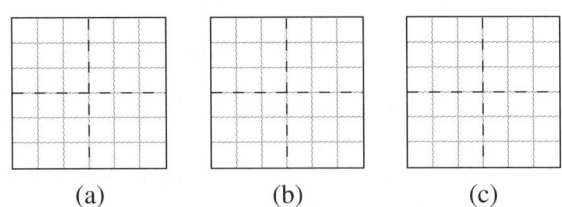

(a) (b) (c)

Section B

1. The figure shows how two resistors – one of resistance 6.0 Ω and another of resistance R, are connected in a circuit that consists of a rheostat, an ammeter, a voltmeter, a switch S and a battery of negligible internal resistance. The switch S is opened and the ammeter reading is 0.20 A.

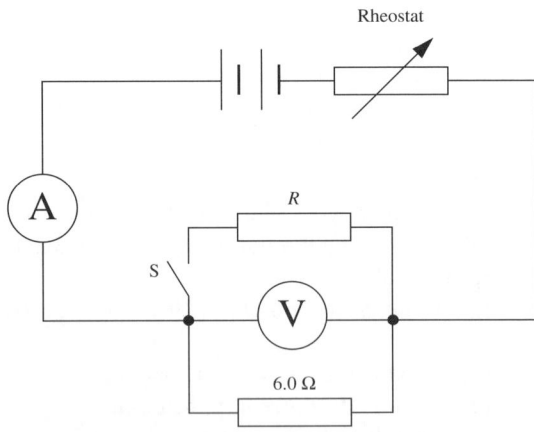

(a) What is the reading of voltmeter?
(b) The switch S is then closed. The ammeter reads 0.30 A and the voltmeter reads 0.60 V.
(i) Calculate the value of the resistance R.
(ii) Hence explain the changes in the readings of ammeter and voltmeter.

(c) With the switch S closed, the resistance of the rheostat is slowly increased. Explain what happens to
(i) the reading of the ammeter.
(ii) the reading of the voltmeter.

2. (a) A variable resistor XY of resistance 5 Ω to 15 Ω is connected in series with a 5 Ω resistor to a 6.0 V battery of negligible internal resistance. An ammeter of negligible resistance measures the current and a voltmeter measures the potential difference across the 5 Ω resistor.

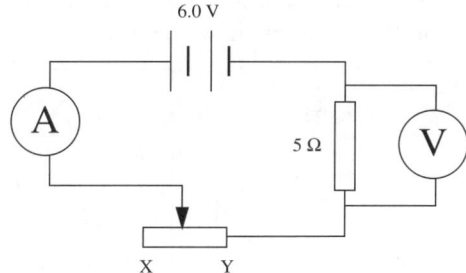

Calculate
(i) the maximum and minimun readings of the ammeter.
(ii) the maximum and minimum readings of the voltmeter.

(b) The 5 Ω resistor and the variable resistor are then reconnected as shown below.

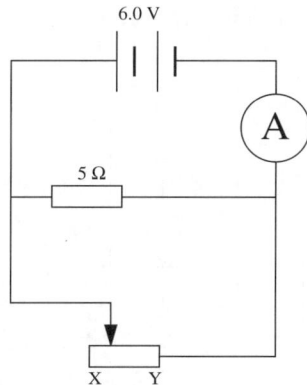

Calculate the maximum and minimum readings of the ammeter.

3. (a) On the axes below, draw the graph of current I against potential difference V across a semiconductor diode.

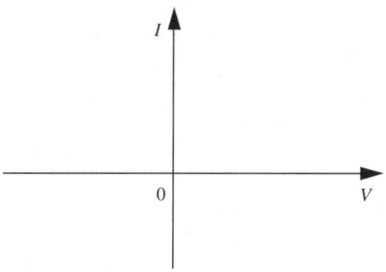

(b) From the graph you draw explain why the diode is suitable as a rectifier.
(c) The circuit shows how four diodes are used to rectify an alternating voltage V.

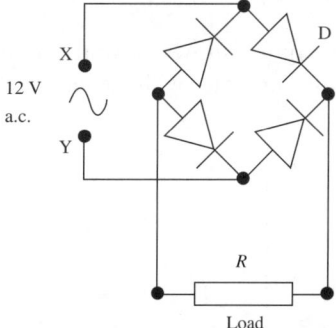

Mark with arrows on the various parts of the circuit to show the direction of the current for the half cycle of the a.c. when the terminal X is positive.

(d) On the axes provided draw graphs to show the variation of the following quantities with time.
(i) The 12 V a.c. supply
(ii) Voltage V_R across the load of resistance R
(iii) Voltage V_R across the load of resistance R if the diode D breaks down

(i)

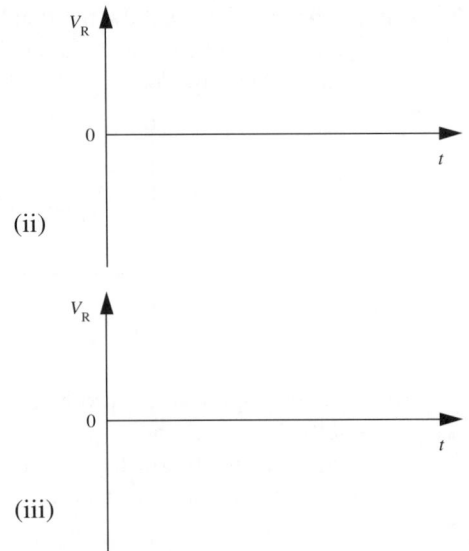

(ii)

(iii)

4. The figure shows how the resistance R of a thermistor varies with the temperature θ.

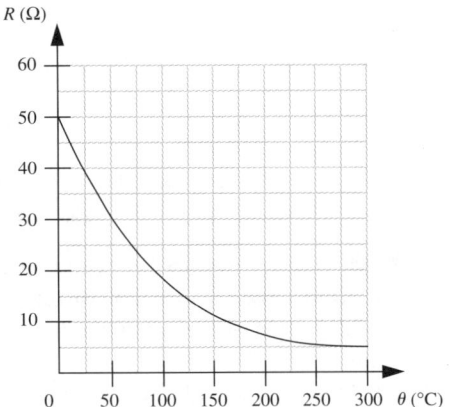

(a) Describe how the resistance of the thermistor varies as the temperature θ increases.
(b) Determine from the graph the resistance of the thermistor at (i) 50 °C and (ii) 200 °C.
(c) The thermistor and a lamp labelled 2.5 V, 0.20 A are then connected in series with a 6.0 V battery of negligible internal resistance as shown in the figure below. The thermistor is placed in an oven and the lamp is used as an indicator lamp.

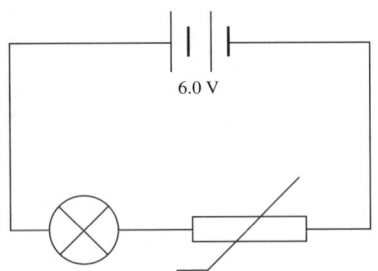

(i) Calculate the resistance of the lamp when the potential difference across is as labelled.
(ii) Calculate the current in the circuit when the temperature in the oven is 50 °C and 200 °C respectively.
(iii) Describe how the brightness of the lamp varies as the temperature in the oven increases.

5. A bicycle dynamo is connected to the Y-input of a cathode ray oscilloscope. The Y-sensitivity of the c.r.o. is set at 3.0 V per division and the timebase at 0.50 s per division. The waveform on the screen of the c.r.o. is as shown below.

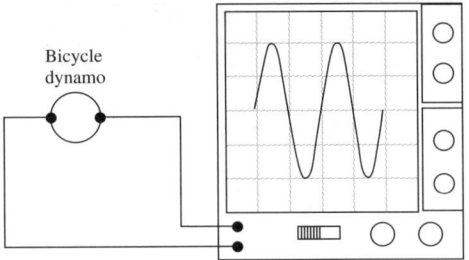

(a) Calculate
  (i) the peak voltage;
  (ii) the root-mean-square (r.m.s.) voltage;
  (iii) the frequency of the voltage generated by the dynamo.
(b) A diode is added to the circuit as shown in figure 5(a). In figure 5(b) there are two diodes. Draw the waveforms on the screen of the c.r.o. in figure 5(a) and 5(b).

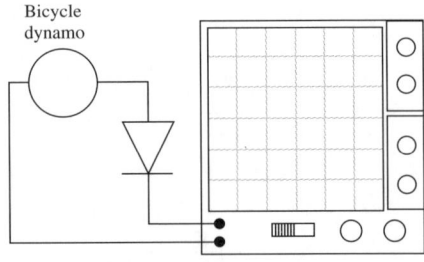

Figure 5(a)

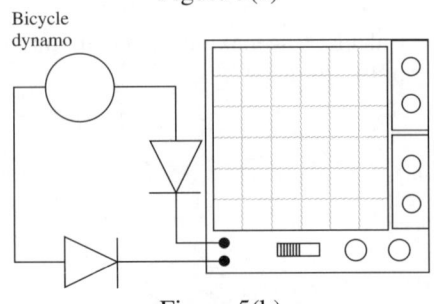

Figure 5(b)

CHAPTER 17
Practical Electricity

17.1 Electric Power and Energy

1. The heating effect of electricity is used in appliances, such as electric kettle, electric oven and electric heater.

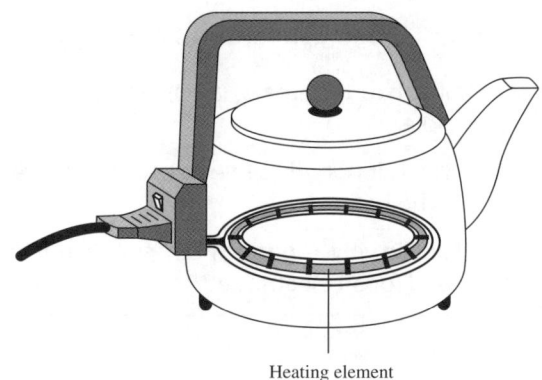

Heating element

Electric kettle

2. These electrical appliances have a heating element that converts electrical energy to heat.
3. The heating element usually consists of a nichrome wire, which has the following characteristics:
   - high melting point;
   - low resistance;
   - not easily oxidised;
   - not brittle when hot.
4. Potential difference is

$$V = \frac{\text{electrical energy}}{\text{charge}} = \frac{W}{Q}$$

Electrical energy $= QV$
$$= IVt \quad \text{where } Q = It$$
$$= I^2Rt \quad \text{where } V = IR$$
$$= \frac{V^2}{R}t \quad \text{where } I = \frac{V}{R}$$

5. Electrical power is

$$P = \frac{\text{electrical energy}}{\text{time}}$$
$$= IV$$
$$= I^2R$$
$$= \frac{V^2}{R}$$

6. From the equation, $P = \frac{V^2}{R}$, we can deduce that at fixed value of V, the electrical power P is higher if R, the resistance of the heating element is small.

Example

The resistance R of a 3 kW, 240 V kettle is given by

$$R = \frac{V^2}{P}$$
$$= \frac{240^2}{3000}$$
$$= 19.2 \, \Omega$$

The resistance R' of a 1 kW 240 V immersion heater is given by

$$R' = \frac{240^2}{1000}$$
$$= 57.6 \, \Omega$$

which is *three times* the resistance of the 3 kW 240 V kettle.

7. One unit of electrical energy $= 1$ kW h
   $= (1 \text{ kW})(1 \text{ h})$
   $= (1000 \text{ W})(3600 \text{ s})$
   $= 3\,600\,000$ J

8. Cost of electrical energy
   $=$ units of electricity used $\times$ cost per unit

175

Example

A house uses eight 60 W lamps for lighting. On the average each lamp is switched on for 6 hours each day. If the electricity tariff is 15 cents per unit, find the cost of the lighting the lamps
(a) for one day;
(b) for the month of January.

Solution

(a) Electrical energy used in one day
$$= 8(6 \text{ h})\left(\frac{60}{1000} \text{ kW}\right)$$
$= 2.88$ kW h.
Electricity cost per day
$= (2.88 \text{ kW h})(15 \text{ cents kW}^{-1} \text{ h}^{-1})$
$= 43.2$ cents

(ii) Electricity cost for the month of January
$= (31 \text{ days})(43.2 \text{ cents day}^{-1})$
$= \$13.39$

Self Evaluation 17.1

1. How many joules (J) is one unit of electrical energy equivalent to?

2. A 120 W lamp is switched on for 24 hours. How many units of electrical energy are consumed?

3. Water in a 1500 W 240 V kettle takes 8.0 minutes to boil. The electricity tariff is 15 cents per unit. How much does it cost to boil a kettle of water?

17.2 Dangers of Electricity

1. The voltage of the domestic mains supply is 240 V and the voltage of high tension transmission cables can reach up to 375 kV.
2. Although the electrical resistance of our body is high, electric current can still flow through it.
3. When the body is wet, the resistance of the body drops drastically.
4. A current of 0.01 A through the human body can produce a shock and a current of more than 0.1 A can cause death.
5. Situations that cause hazards in using electricity:
   (a) **Damaged insulation** – It causes wires or cables that carry current to be exposed. The exposed wire can cause electric shock when touched by somebody and a short circuit to occur when the live wire come into contact with the neutral wire. Short circuit can cause fire because of the large current that flows through the circuit.
   (b) **Overheating cables** – It occurs when the current in the cables exceeds the safe capacity. Overheating causes the insulation to burn, which can result in starting a fire.
   (c) **Damp conditions** – A wet switch or power point can cause leakage of electric current. When someone touches, it can cause an electric shock. Hence one should not switch on the electricity with wet fingers.

Self Evaluation 17.2

1. Give two hazards of a damaged electric cable.

2. Why is it not advisable to use a hair dryer in the bathroom?

3. Explain why a lighting point should not be used for an electric kettle.

17.3 Safe Use of Electricity at Home

Fuse

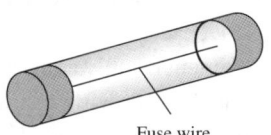

Fuse wire

1. A **fuse** consists of a short piece of wire, which becomes hot and melts when the current flowing through it *exceeds* a certain value. A fuse is used in a three-pin plug.
   E.g. A 13 A fuse will blow when current through it exceeds 13 A.
2. The fuse is connected in series with the live wire, so that when the fuse blows, power to the appliances is cut off. Damage to the electrical appliance is prevented and fire due to the overheating of cables is avoided.

Example

An electric oven is rated 5 kW 240 V. The fuses provided are rated 13 A, 20 A, 25 A and 30 A. Which is the most suitable fuse for the oven?

Solution

Power $P = IV$

Current $I = \dfrac{5000 \text{ W}}{240 \text{ V}}$

$= 20.8$ A

Most suitable fuse is the one that rates 25 A.

Switches and Earthing

3. A switch is connected to the live wire to stop current from flowing through the appliance when the appliance is not in use. When the switch is off, the appliance can be disconnected safely from the main supply.
4. Earthing of metal casing of an electrical appliance is done by connecting a wire from the metal casing to the ground.
5. If the live wire become loose inside the appliance that has a metal casing and make contact with the casing, the casing would become 'live'. Anyone who comes in contact with the casing can experience an electric shock because the body provides a low resistance path to the ground by becoming part of the circuit.
6. Without the earth wire, a person touching the 'live' metal casing can conduct a large current to the Earth. Thus the person can experience a fatal electric shock.
7. If this happens in a properly earthed appliance, a large current will flow to the ground and the fuse will blow to stop the supply.

Double Insulation

8. **Double insulation** is provided for electrical appliances such as radio, television and hair dryer. Only two wires, live and neutral, are used to connect to the appliances. There is no earth wire.

   □ Symbol of double insulation

9. There are two layers of insulation used for double insulation.
   (a) *Functional insulation* – around the internal electrical components.
   (b) *Protective insulation* – in the form of plastic casing for the electric appliance.

Circuit Breaker

10. Electrical appliances such as water heater use a **circuit breaker** to disconnect the appliances when a larger than normal current flows.
11. The extra large current can be due to a short circuit. The circuit can be reset after repair has been made.
12. Like the switch and fuse, the circuit breaker is wired to the live conductor.

Three-Pin Plug

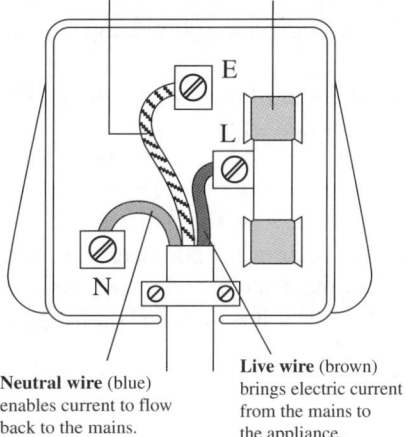

Earth wire (yellow-green) It is connected to the metal casing of the appliance. The earth wire conducts current to the Earth when there is a leakage.

Fuse would blow when the current exceeds the rated value.

Neutral wire (blue) enables current to flow back to the mains.

Live wire (brown) brings electric current from the mains to the appliance.

Self Evaluation 17.3

1. An electric kettle is connected to the mains supply using a three-pin plug as shown below.

   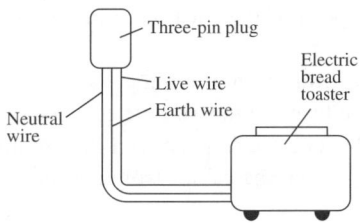

   (a) Which wire is connected to the fuse?
   (b) The earth wire is connected to which part of the bread toaster?
   (c) What is the colour of the neutral wire?

2. An electric hot-plate is rated 3.5 kW 240 V. The fuses available are rated 13 A, 15 A and 20 A. Which of the fuses is the most suitable?

REVISION EXERCISE 17

Multiple Choice Questions

1. An immersion heater of resistance 30 Ω is connected to a 240 V supply. What is the power dissipated from the heater?
   A 80 W   C 1920 W
   B 900 W   D 7200 W

2. Both a 60 W and a 100 W lamps are connected in series to a 240 V supply. Which of the following statements is correct?
   A The 100 W lamp is brighter.
   B The voltage across the 60 W lamp is greater.
   C The total power dissipated from the lamps is 160 W.
   D The current in the 100 W lamp is greater.

3. A filament lamp is rated 60 W 240 V. What is the resistance of filament?
   A 0.25 Ω   C 960 Ω
   B 4.0 Ω   D 14 400 Ω

4. The power of an air-conditioner unit is 1.50 kW. How many units of electricity are consumed by the air-conditioner if it is switched on for 12 hours?
   A 8.0 units
   B 18.0 units
   C 27.0 units
   D 96.0 units

5. Which of the following fuses is most suitable for a 5 kW 240 V electric oven?
   A 13 A   C 20 A
   B 15 A   D 22 A

6. The purpose of the earth wire in an electric kettle is
   A to prevent a short circuit.
   B to reduce the risk of an electric shock.
   C to reduce the resistance in the circuit.
   D to prevent the cables from overheating.

7. The figure shows a three-pin plug before the cables were connected.

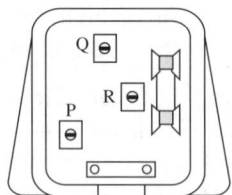

What colours are the wires of a three-core cable that are to be connected to the terminals P, Q and R?

	P	Q	R
A	Blue	Green & yellow	Brown
B	Brown	Green & yellow	Blue
C	Brown	Blue	Green & yellow
D	Green & yellow	Blue	Brown

8. A three-core cable runs from an electric iron. Due to the absence of a three-pin socket in a room, a student connects the brown and green & yellow wire to a lighting point. What would be the effect when the current is switched on?
   A The electric iron gets very hot.
   B The electric cables would catch fire.
   C The main fuse would blow.
   D The circuit breaker in of the house circuit would trip.

9. One unit of electricity costs 30 cents. What is the cost of running a 240 V 5 kW electric oven for 4 hours a day for the month of January?
   A $ 6   C $ 114
   B $ 37   D $ 186

10. A water heater for the shower has a circuit breaker. What is the purpose of the circuit breaker?
    A It cuts off the current when there is a short circuit.
    B It cuts off the current when the shower is turned off.
    C It cuts off the current when the water heater is switched off.
    D It cuts off the current when the water reaches the preset temperature.

Structure Questions

Section A

1. Calculate the electrical power consumed by a 2.5 V 0.2 A lamp when the potential difference across it is
   (a) 2.5 V;
   (b) 1.5 V.

2. The table below gives the details of the use of electricity in a household in a month.

Appliance	Time of usage	Units of electricity
Eight 60 W lamps	240 h	
Two 1.8 kW air-conditioners	320 h	
Three 2.5 kW heaters	120 h	
	Total	

(a) Complete the last column of the table.
(b) The electricity tariff is 30 cents per unit. What is the electricity bill for the month?

3. The figure shows the leads from the mains supply:
   Live (L), neutral (N) and earth (E)
(a) Complete the figure by showing how you would connect the leads to an electric iron. Your circuit should include a switch and a fuse.

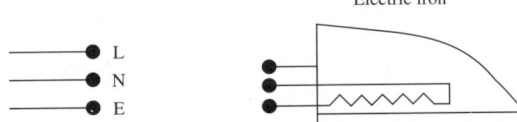

(b) The electric iron is rated 240 V 1.5 kW. Calculate the rating of the fuse required by the electric iron.

4. An electric toaster is connected to the mains supply using a three-pin plug.
(a) What is the purpose of the fuse in the three-pin plug?
(b) Why is the fuse connected to the live wire?
(c) To which part of the toaster is the earth wire connected to?
(d) Explain the purpose of the earth wire.

5. (a) Explain what is meant by a *short-circuit*?
(b) Explain how a short circuit may arise due to
   (i) damaged insulation;
   (ii) overloaded wires.

6. The electrical wiring system of a house uses three wires — live, neutral and earth. The mains supply is 240 V. What is the voltage between
(a) the live and neutral wires;
(b) the live and earth wires;
(c) the earth and neutral wires?

7. (a) Explain what is meant by an electrical appliance has *double insulation*.
(b) Why is an earth wire not required for an electrical appliance with double insulation?

Section B

1. (a) What is meant by the marking '60 W 240 V' on a lamp?
(b) A lamp P is rated 15 W 240 V and a lamp Q is rated 60 W 240 V. What is the resistance of lamp P and lamp Q?
(c) The lamps P and Q are connected in parallel to a 240 V mains supply. What is the total power dissipated from the lamps?
(d) If the lamps are connected in series with the 240 V supply, what is the power dissipated from lamp P and lamp Q?

2. The figure shows part of the lighting circuit in a house. The lamps are identical and all rated 120 W 240 V.

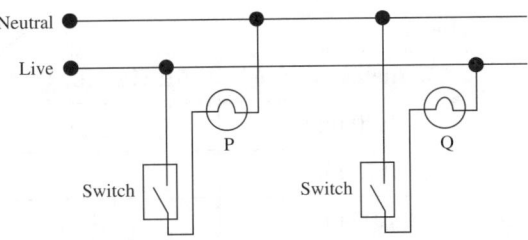

(a) Which of the lamps P or Q is wrongly wired? Give reason for your answer.
(b) A 5 A fuse is to be connected in the circuit.
   (i) Draw on the figure the position where the fuse should be connected.
   (ii) Calculate the maximum number of 120 W 240 V lamps that can be connected in the circuit and switched on simultaneously?
   (iii) Explain what would happens if the number of lamps connected to the circuit exceed the maximum number.
(c) Explain why an earth wire is not necessary for the circuit.

Data-based Questions

3. The figure shows a tungsten filament lamps P and an energy-saving lamp Q. The manufacturer of lamp Q claims that it is as bright as a 120 W filament lamp.

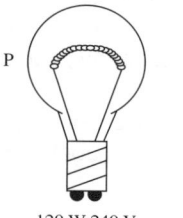 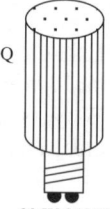

P — 120 W 240 V   Q — 23 W 240 V

(a) Calculate the resistance of the filament of lamp P.
(b) Why is tungsten used as the filament of the lamp?
(c) If 60% of the power consumed by lamp Q is dissipated as light, what is the rate of heat dissipated from lamp Q?
(d) The power dissipated as light from lamp P equals that from lamp Q.
  (i) What is the power dissipated as light?
  (ii) What other form of energy is emitted and at what rate is it dissipated from lamp P?

4. Table 1 shows the maximum current that may be carried safely by wires of different diameters.

Table 1

Diameter of wire	Maximum current
0.50 mm	3 A
0.75 mm	6 A
1.00 mm	10 A
1.25 mm	13 A

Table 2 shows the various electrical appliances, all rated 240 V but different power.

Table 2

Appliance	Current	Diameter of wire
100 W lamp		
1.2 kW heater		
2.5 kW kettle		

(a) Complete the table by calculating the current used by each appliance when connected to the 240 V mains supply and select the smallest diameter of the wire that can be used safely.
(b) Explain the danger of connecting the kettle to the leads meant for the 100 W lamp.

5. A filament lamp is rated 60 W 240 V and an electric kettle is rated 2 kW 240 V.
(a) Without making any calculation, explain which of them has
  (i) a larger current when connected to a 240 V supply;
  (ii) a higher resistance;
  (iii) a higher temperature.
(b) Tungsten is used for the filament of the lamp and nichrome is used for the heating element of the kettle.
  (i) Why is tungsten used as the filament?
  (ii) Why is tungsten not used for the heating element?

CHAPTER 18
Magnetism

18.1 Laws of Magnetism

1. Magnetic materials are materials that are attracted by a magnet. Examples are iron, steel, nickel, and cobalt.
2. Non-magnetic materials are not attracted by magnets. Glass, plastic, wood, and copper are some examples.
3. A magnet has two poles. They are the north-seeking pole (N-pole) and south-seeking pole (S-pole) where the magnetic forces are the strongest.

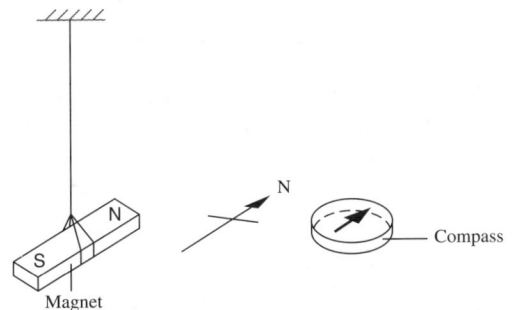

4. A freely suspended magnet comes to rest with its N-pole pointing north and its S-pole pointing south.
5. A compass needle is a magnet.
6. **Law of magnetism**

   Like poles repel, unlike poles attract.

7. A piece of magnetic material is magnetised when it is near to or in contact with a magnet. This is known as **induced magnetism**.

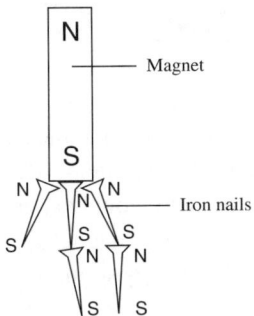

Induced magnetism

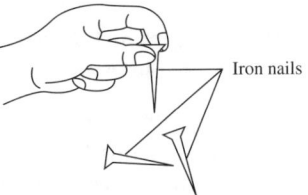

When the magnet is removed, the iron nails lose their magnetism.

8. Electrical methods of magnetisation.

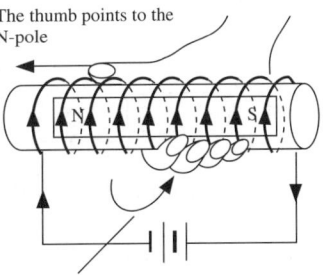

   (a) Place a piece of steel in a solenoid which is connected to a d.c. source.
   (b) The polarity of the magnet is determined using the **right hand grip rule**.
   The rule states that if the solenoid is gripped with the right hand such that the fingers curl in the direction of the current, then the thumb points to the N-pole and the direction of the magnetic field due to the solenoid.
   (c) When the current is switched off, the steel bar becomes a permanent magnet.

9. Methods of demagnetisation.
   (a) Place the magnet in a solenoid carrying an alternating current. Slowly withdraw the magnet from the solenoid in an east-west direction.
   (b) Place the magnet so that it is not in the N-S direction. When the magnet is hammered, it loses its magnetism.
   (c) When the magnet is heated, it loses its magnetism.

Self Evaluation 18.1

1. Two small plotting compasses are placed near the N-pole and S-pole of a bar magnet.

   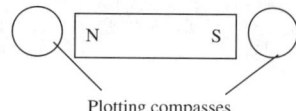

   Plotting compasses

   Draw the arrows in the figure to represent the compass needle in each compass.

2. (a) Figure 1(a) shows the end P of a bar magnet attracting to the S-pole of another magnet. What is the polarity of the end P?
   (b) Figure 1(b) shows the end P of a bar magnet repelling by the N-pole of another magnet. What is the polarity of the end P?

   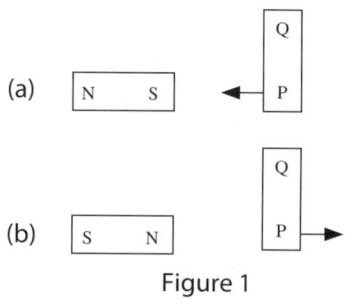

   Figure 1

18.2 Magnetic Properties of Matter

1. Permanent magnets are made from steel, alnico (aluminium, nickel, and cobalt) or fecal (ferrous, carbon, and aluminium). Permanent magnets do not lose their magnetism readily.
2. The different properties of iron and steel.

Iron	Steel
Easily magnetised	More difficult to magnetise
Temporary induced magnetism	Permanent magnet
Suitable as the core of an electromagnet	Suitable as a permanent magnet.

3. Permanent magnets are used in loudspeakers, electric motors, electric meters and dynamos.

4. Screw drivers are magnetised so that small screws can be placed in position easily.

   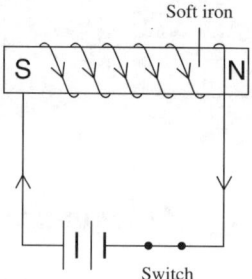

5. To make an electromagnet, wind a coil of insulated copper wire on a piece of soft iron and connect the coil to a battery. When the switch is closed, the soft iron becomes a magnet. The soft iron loses its magnetism when the switch is opened and current stops flowing in the circuit.
6. Electromagnets are used in electric bells, relay switches and telephone ear pieces.

Self Evaluation 18.2

1. Below are some common materials. Put a tick ✓ in the box for the magnetic material.

   ☐ Copper   ☐ Steel
   ☐ Iron   ☐ Carbon
   ☐ Aluminium ☐ Glass

2. With the aid of a diagram describe briefly how you would make an iron nail into an electromagnet.
3. Why is steel not suitable to be used as the core of an electromagnet?

18.3 Magnetic Fields

1. A magnetic field is the region where magnetic effects can be detected. Example the space surrounding a magnet is a magnetic field. Magnetic materials in this magnetic field would experience a force.
2. The pattern of the magnetic field around a bar magnet can be seen by sprinkling iron filings around the magnet.

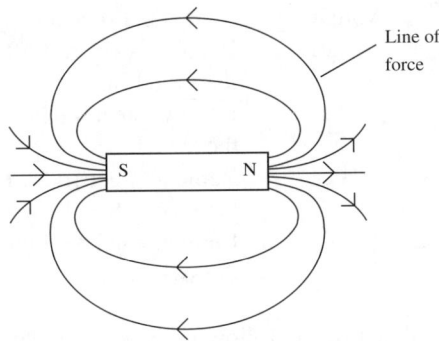

Magnetic field around a bar magnet

3. A magnetic field line is the path of a free N-pole in the field. The direction of the magnetic field at any location is the direction in which the needle of a compass points.
4. In a strong magnetic field, the field lines are close together, for example near the poles of a bar magnet,
5. A **plotting compass** can be used to plot the magnetic field lines around the magnet.

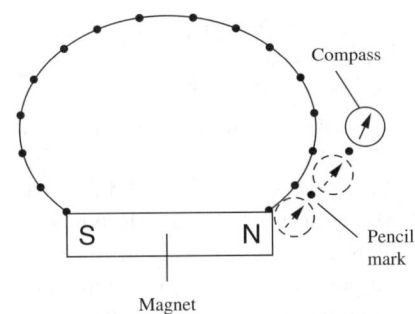

- Mark each end of the compass needle with a dot as the compass moves from the N-pole to the S-pole.
- Draw a smooth curve through these dots. Repeat the procedure with a different starting position of the compass.
- These lines represent the magnetic field of a bar magnet.

6. The figures below show the magnetic fields between the poles of two magnets.

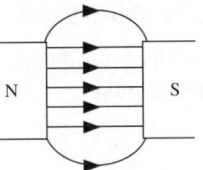

Magnetic field between N-pole and S-pole

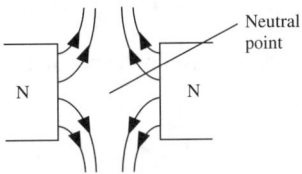

Magnetic field between two N-poles

Self Evaluation 18.3

1. (a) Draw the magnetic field pattern around a bar magnet. Mark the direction of the magnetic field.
   (b) Where is the strength of the magnetic field the strongest?

2. Two bar magnets are fixed in the positions shown.

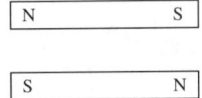

   (a) Draw the magnetic field pattern between the two magnets.
   (b) Explain what happens to the magnets if they are free to move.

REVISION EXERCISE 18

Multiple Choice Questions

1. Both P and Q are plotting compasses placed near a bar magnet as shown.

   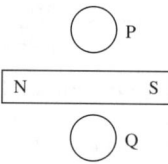

   In which directions do the needles of the compasses point?

   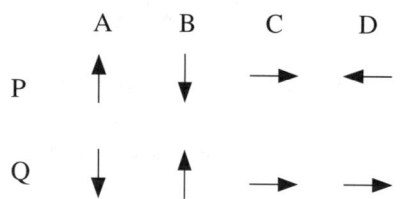

2. Which of the following materials is used to make permanent magnets?
   A Steel
   B Soft iron
   C Copper
   D Aluminium

3. Which figure correctly shows two iron nails hanging from a bar magnet?

   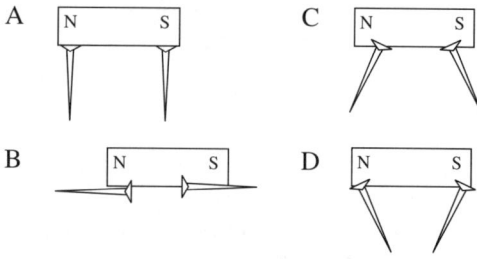

4. The figure shows a coil of insulated wire around a steel rod.

   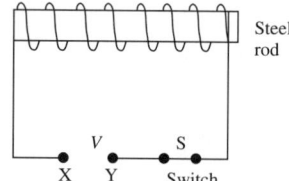

   Which of the following correctly states the voltage supply V across XY and the correct procedure required to magnetise the steel rod?

	Voltage V	Procedure
A	d.c.	Remove steel rod after opening the switch S.
B	d.c.	Remove steel rod before opening the switch S.
C	a.c.	Remove steel rod after opening the switch S.
D	a.c.	Remove steel rod before opening the switch S.

5. Which of the following is an example of induced magnetism?
   A A steel bar in a solenoid that carries a current is magnetised.
   B The soft iron core of an electromagnet is magnetised when the current is switched on.
   C The needle of a plotting compass is pointing to the S-pole of a magnet.
   D An iron nail attached to a bar magnet is able to attract another iron nail.

6. The figure shows two pieces of soft iron X and Y arranged in line with a bar magnet.

   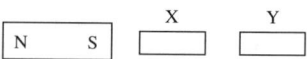

   What are the magnetic forces on X and Y?

	Force on X	Force on Y
A	Attraction	Repulsion
B	Attraction	Attraction
C	Repulsion	Repulsion
D	Repulsion	Attraction

7. Three electromagnets X, Y and Z are made using the same length of insulated wire and identical soft iron cores. X has 6 turns and is connected to two cells. Y has 6 turns and is connected to one cell. Z has 8 turns and is connected to two cells.

   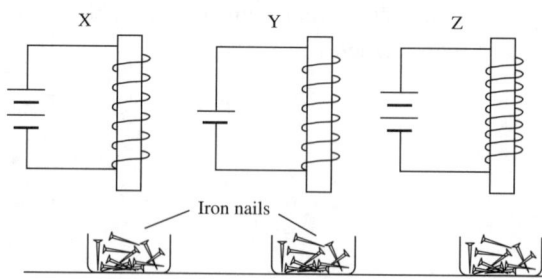

The electromagnets are brought near some iron nails. Six nails are attracted to X. The number of nails attracted to Y and Z is given by

	Y	Z
A	3	6
B	3	8
C	6	6
D	6	8

8. A steel rod is placed in a solenoid carrying a current. Which diagram correctly shows the magnetic poles of the rod?

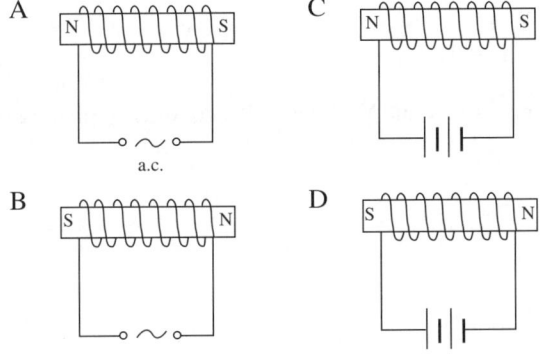

9. At which of the points close to a bar magnet is the magnetic field strength the strongest?

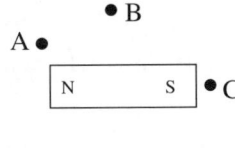

10. Which of the following actions will demagnetise a bar magnet?
    A Place it near another magnet.
    B Leave it inside a solenoid carrying an alternating current.
    C Break it into two pieces.
    D Hammer it when it hangs freely in the N-S direction

Structured Questions

Section A

1. The figure shows the magnetic field around two magnets.

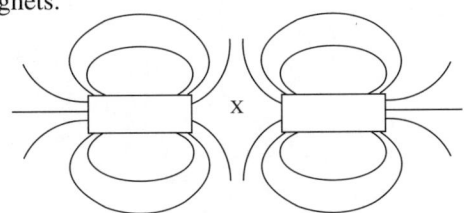

   (a) Label the poles of the magnets, N for N-pole and S for S-pole.
   (b) Mark with arrows to show the direction of magnetic field.
   (c) Name the point marked X.

2. (a) Give an example of (i) magnetic material and (ii) non-magnetic material.
   (b) Distinguish between the magnetic properties of iron and steel.

3. The figure shows two iron nails P and Q hanging from a magnet.

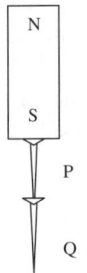

   (a) Why is the iron nail P attracted by the magnet?
   (b) Why is the nail P able to attract the nail Q?
   (c) Mark the poles on the nail P.
   (d) What happens to the nail Q if P slide off the end of the magnet slowly?

4. The figure shows an electromagnet made by winding insulated copper wire around a U-shaped core.

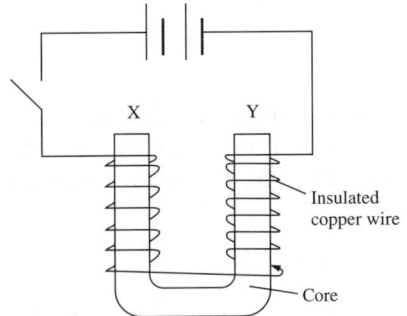

   (a) Why is the copper wire insulated?
   (b) Name a suitable material for the core. Give a reason for your choice.
   (c) What are the poles of the electromagnet at the ends X and Y?
   (d) State two uses of electromagnets.

Section B

1. The figure shows a simple compass made by a student.

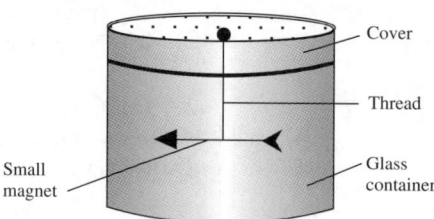

   (a) Is iron or steel is more suitable for making the small magnet. Why?
   (b) Besides glass, what other type of container can be used?
   (c) Give two reasons why a transparent plastic cover is used.
   (d) Why is the small magnet suspended from its centre of gravity?

2. The figure shows the view from above of two plotting compasses X and Y (the needles not drawn) placing near a soft iron bar in a solenoid. The switch S is opened.

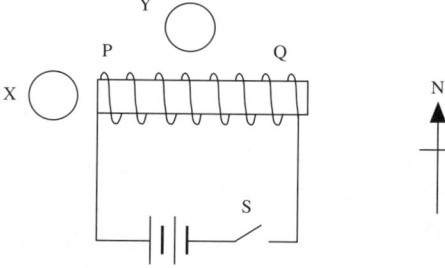

   (a) In the figure below, mark with an arrow to show the directions of the needles of the compasses X and Y.

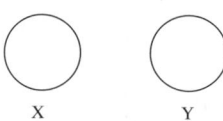

   (b) The switch S is then closed.
   (i) Mark the direction of the current in the wire.
   (ii) Show the directions of the needles of the compasses X and Y.

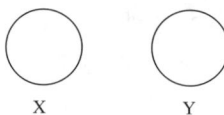

   (c) The switch S is opened again.
   Show the directions of the needles of the compasses X and Y.

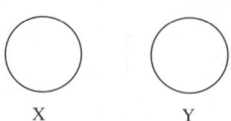

   Explain your answer.

CHAPTER 19
Electromagnetism

19.1 Magnetic Effect of a Current

1. When a current flows in a straight wire, a magnetic field is set up. The figure below shows the pattern of magnetic field around the wire.

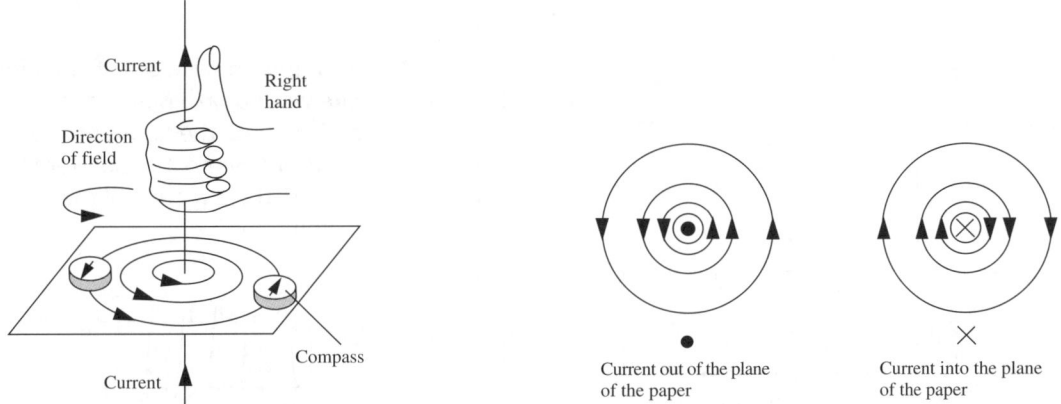

Right-hand grip rule

Magnetic field due to a current in a straight wire

2. The strength of the magnetic field due to a current-carrying wire at a point is:
   - directly proportional to the current in the wire;
   - inversely proportional to the distance of the point from the wire, i.e. the field strength decreases as the distance increases.
3. The direction of the magnetic field can be determined using a plotting compass or the **right-hand grip rule**. *Grip the wire with the right hand with the thumb pointing in the direction of the current. The other four fingers would then naturally curl around in the direction of the magnetic field lines.*
4. The direction of the magnetic field is reversed when the direction of the current is reversed.
5. The magnetic field due to a current in a solenoid is identical to that of a bar magnet.

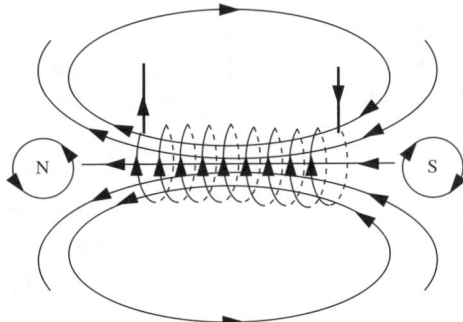

6. The pole at the ends of the solenoid can be determined from the direction of the current. The end is a N-pole if the current in the solenoid is in the anti-clockwise direction. The end is a S-pole if the current in the solenoid is in the clockwise direction.

Self Evaluation 19.1

1. Figure 1(a) shows a vertical wire carrying a large current downwards. P and Q are the plotting compasses.

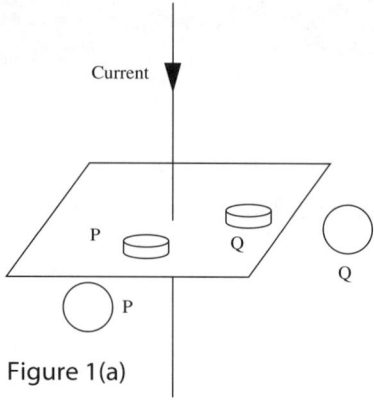

Figure 1(a)

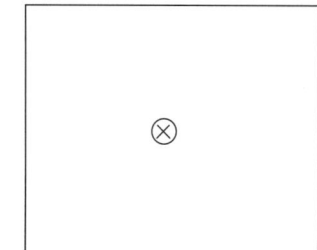

Figure 1(b)

   (a) In figure 1(a) mark in the circles the directions of the pointers in the compasses P and Q as observed from above.
   (b) In figure 1(b) draw the magnetic field pattern around the wire.

2. The figure shows a small plotting compass place above a copper wire.

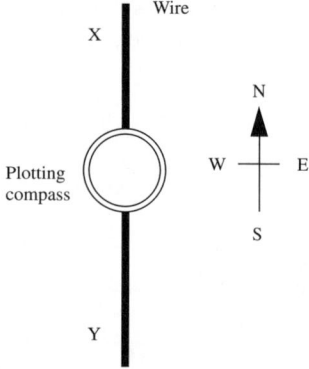

   (a) Mark in the figure the direction of the compass needle.

   (b) A large current then flows in the wire from X to Y. The magnetic field of the Earth is negligible compared to the magnetic field produced by the current in the wire.
   Mark in the circle below the direction of the compass needle when
   (i) the compass above the wire.

   (ii) the compass below the wire.

3. The figure shows a coil of insulated copper wire wound on a plastic tube.
   (a) Complete the figure to show how you would connect the battery to the coil. Mark the direction of the current in the coil.

   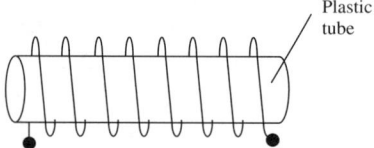

   (b) Draw the magnetic field pattern around the coil when the current flows.
   (c) What is the effect on the magnetic field when a soft iron bar is inserted into the plastic tube?

19.2 Applications of Magnetic Effect

Magnetic Relay

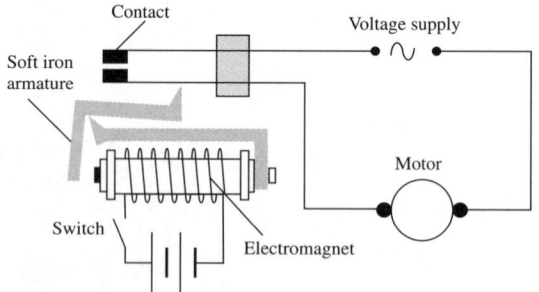

1. When the switch is closed, current flows in the electromagnet.
2. The soft iron armature is attracted by the electromagnet.

3. The contact is closed when the top end of the armature pushes it.
4. Motor is started where a large current flows in the second circuit.
5. Magnetic relay uses a small current to control a larger current in another circuit.

Circuit Breaker

6. A circuit breaker is an automatic switch that cuts off the current when the current exceeds a specified value.

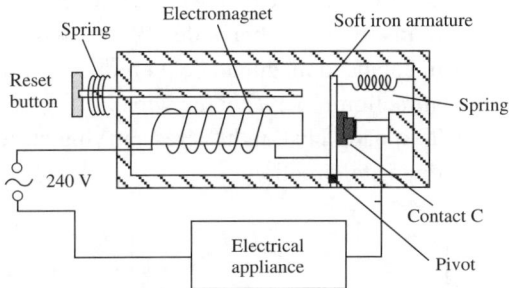

7. When the normal current flows through the electromagnet, the electromagnet is too weak to move the soft iron armature. The circuit is complete and the electrical appliance functions.
8. When a short circuit or overloading occurs, a large current flows through the electromagnet.
9. The electromagnet becomes powerful enough to pull the soft iron armature away from the contact.
10. The circuit is then broken and the appliance is switched off.

Self Evaluation 19.2

1. The figure shows a relay used to switch on a motor. The following is a list of materials: steel, soft iron, carbon, plastic

    (a) Pick the material that is most suitable for
      (i) the core of the electromagnet;
      (ii) the armature;
      (iii) the contacts.
    (b) Why is a relay used instead of connecting the switch directly to the motor?

19.3 Force on a Current-carrying Conductor

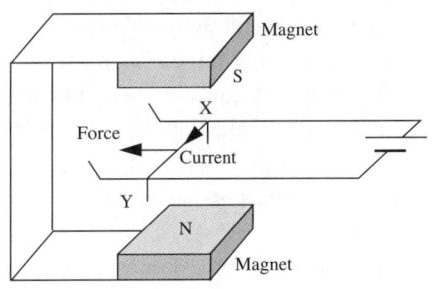

1. When a conductor XY carries a current is in a magnetic field, a magnetic force acts on the conductor as shown in the above figure.
2. This is due to the interaction between the two magnetic fields – magnetic fields between the poles of the magnets and the magnetic field due to the current-carrying conductor XY.
3. The figure(s) below show:
    (a) the magnetic field between the poles of the magnets;
    (b) the magnetic field due to a current-carrying conductor XY and;
    (c) the resultant magnetic field.

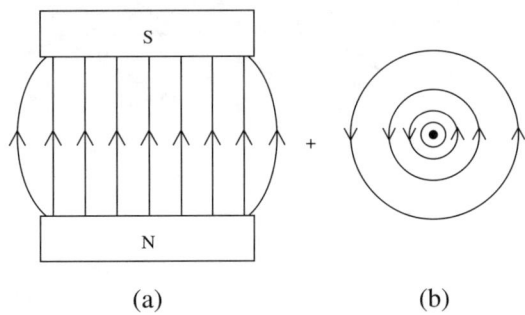

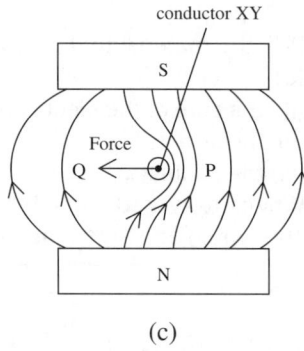

(c)

4. The resultant magnetic field is stronger on the right side of the conductor. This produces a force F on the conductor in the direction shown.
5. The magnitude of the force F increases if:
   (a) a larger current flows in the conductor;
   (b) the magnetic field between the poles of the magnets is stronger;
   (c) the length of the conductor in the magnetic field is longer.
6. The direction of the force F is reversed when:
   (a) the direction of current is reversed;
   (b) the direction of the magnetic field is reversed.
7. The relative directions of the force, current and the magnetic field can be deduced using **Fleming's left-hand rule**. *The rule states that when the thumb, first and second fingers of the left hand are held at right angles to each others, the first finger will points in the direction of the magnetic field and the second finger will point in the direction of the current and the thumb will point in the direction of the force* (see figure below).

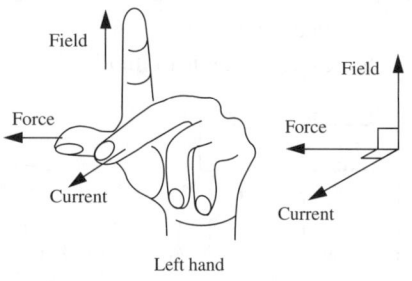

8. The figures below show the magnetic field patterns due to the current in two parallel wires.
   (a) Two parallel straight wires carrying currents in the same direction.

   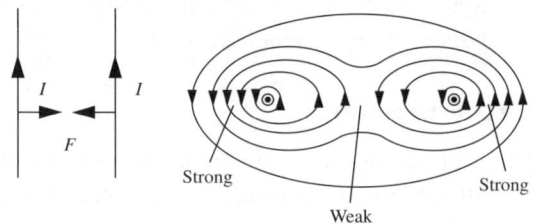

   The magnetic field between the wires is weaker than on the either sides of the wires. The unbalanced magnetic field produces a force of attraction F between the wires.
   (b) Two parallel straight wires carrying current in opposite direction.

   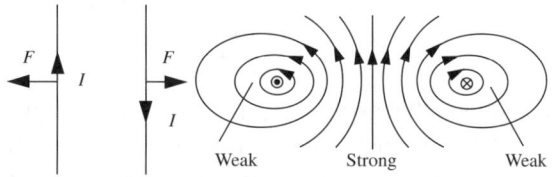

   The magnetic field between the wires is stronger than that on either side of the wires. This unbalanced magnetic field produces a force of repulsion F between the wires.
9. A charged particle moving in a magnetic field is subjected to a force F. If the velocity of the charged particle is at right angle to the magnetic field, the subsequent path of the particle is an arc of a circle.

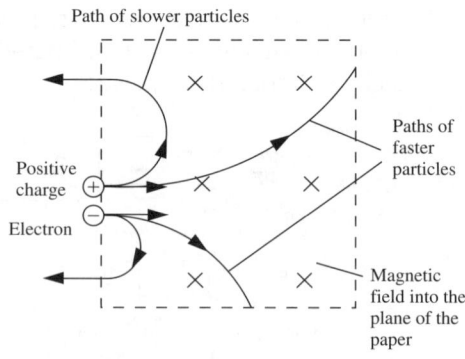

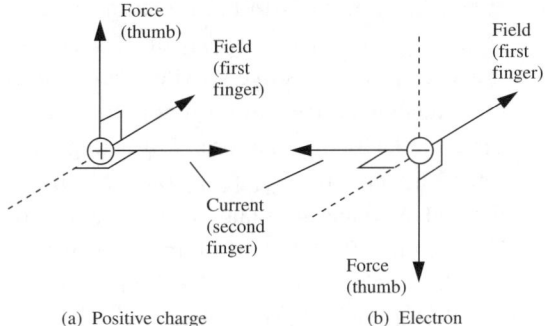

(a) Positive charge (b) Electron

10. Fleming's left-hand rule can be used to deduce the direction of the force on a charge moving in a magnetic field. For a negative charge such as an electron, the direction of the conventional current is opposite to the direction of motion of the electron.
11. When the same charged particle moves with a greater speed in the same magnetic field, the radius of curvature of the path is greater.
12. Magnetic fields are used to deflect the electron beam in a television set.

Self Evaluation 19.3

1. A current-carrying wire that is free to move is between the poles of a magnet. In the figures below, show the direction of the force on the wire.

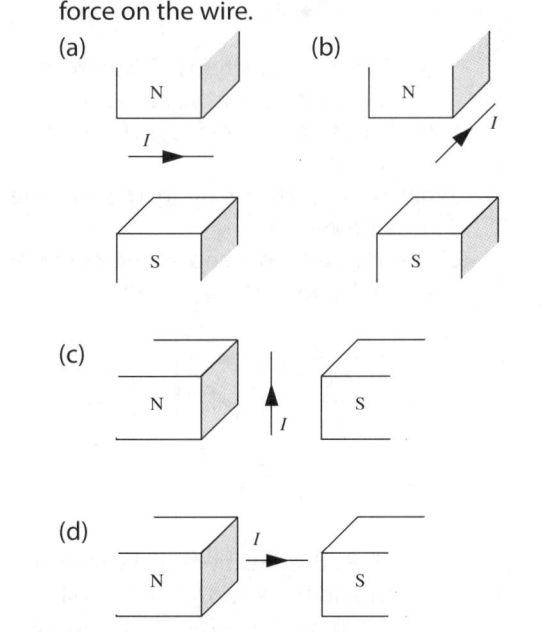

2. (a) A beam of positive ions enters a uniform magnetic field as shown in each of the figures. In each figure, draw the path of the beam.

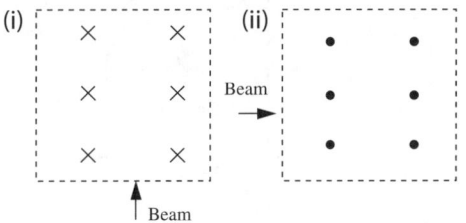

(b) A beam of electrons enters a uniform magnetic field as shown in each of the figures. In each figure draw the path of the beam.

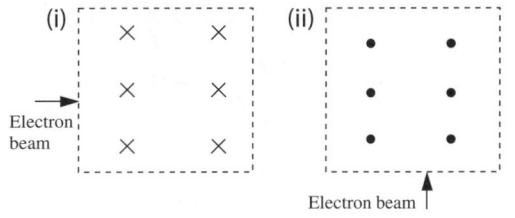

19.4 The D.C. Motor

Principle of the d.c. motor

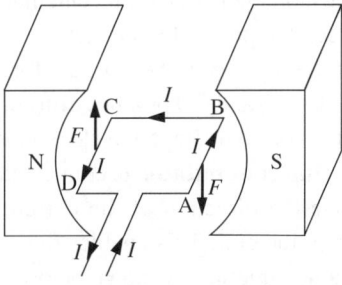

1. A force acts on a current-carrying conductor in a magnetic field. When a current-carrying coil ABCD is in a magnetic field, the forces F acting on the sides AB and CD of the coil produces a turning effect that causes the coil to rotate in the clockwise direction. This is the principle of the d.c. motor.

2. The figure below shows the resultant magnetic field produced when current flows in the coil.

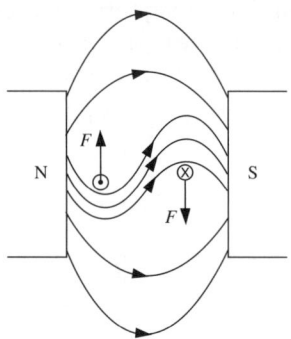

D.C. motor

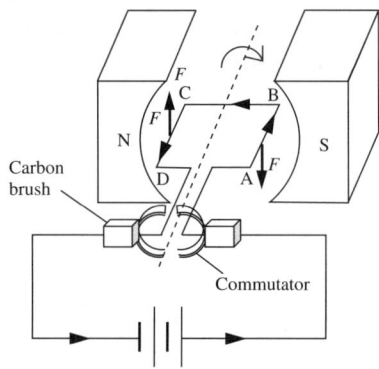

3. Electric motors are widely used in electrical appliances such as electric drills, hair dryers, electric fans, tape recorders, compact discs players and toy cars.
4. A simple motor consists of a rectangular coil ABCD in between the poles of a magnet.
5. When current flows in the coil, the forces F acting on the sides AB and CD produce a turning effect that causes the coil to rotate in the clockwise direction.
6. A **split-ring commutator** is connected to the coil to reverse the direction of the current every half rotation of the coil. This enables the coil to rotate in the same direction as shown below.

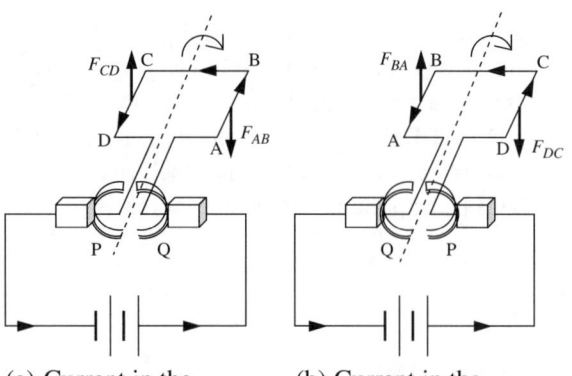

(a) Current in the direction ABCD
(b) Current in the direction DCBA

7. When the current is in the direction ABCD, the forces F_{AB} on AB and F_{CD} on CD are acting down and up respectively. After half a turn, the commutator reverses the current in the coil, in the direction DCBA, so the force F_{DC} acting on DC is down and the force F_{BA} acting on AB is up. Hence the coil continues to rotate in the same direction.
8. The turning effect on the coil increases when:
   - the number of turns in the coil increases;
   - the current in the coil increases.
9. In practical electric motors,
   - the coil has hundreds of turns wound around a soft iron cylinder known as the armature to increase the magnetic flux through the coil.
   - the poles of the magnet are curved to produce a radial magnetic field. This keeps the turning effect at the maximum as the coil rotates.

Self Evaluation 19.4

1. (a) The figure shows a rectangular coil carrying a current between the poles of the magnets.

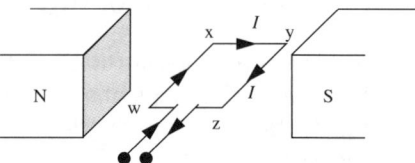

   (i) Show the directions of the forces on the sides wx and yz of the coil.
   (ii) What is the effect of the two forces?
   (iii) Why is there no force on the side xy?

   (b) The figure below shows the plane of the coil in its vertical position.

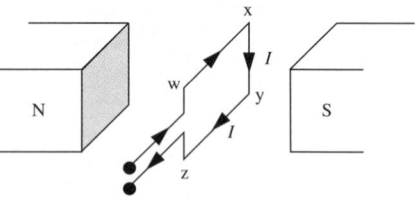

   (i) Show the directions of the forces on the sides wx and yz of the coil.
   (ii) What is the effect of the two forces?
   (iii) Is there a force on the side xy? If so, show its direction.

2. The figure shows a d.c. motor with a large number of turns in the coil. The coil has a soft iron core.

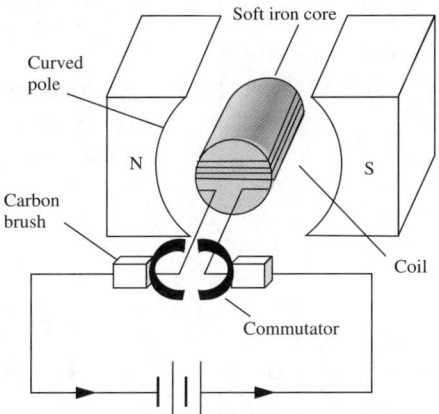

(a) Explain the rationale of the following features of the motor.
   (i) A large number of turns
   (ii) Magnet with curved pole
   (iii) Soft iron core
(b) What is the purpose of the commutator?

REVISION EXERCISE 19

Multiple Choice Questions

1. The figure shows a plotting compass P above a wire carrying a current and another compass Q below the wire.

   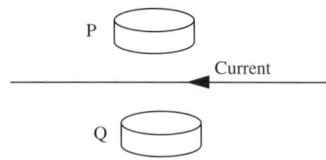

   Neglecting the Earth's magnetic field, when one observes from above, the pointers of the compass P and Q point in the directions shown in

   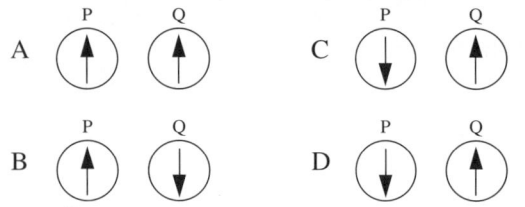

2. Which diagram correctly shows the magnetic field inside a current-carrying solenoid?

   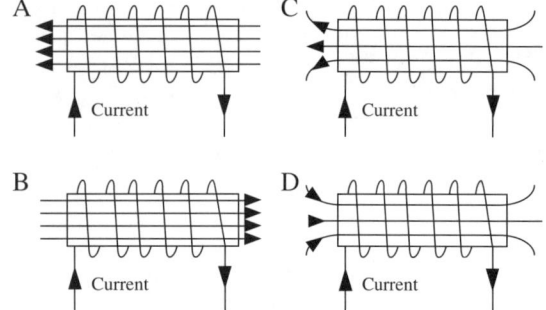

3. Which of the following will **not** produce a stronger magnetic field in a solenoid carrying a current?
   A Increase the number of turns of the solenoid.
   B Increase the diameter of the solenoid.
   C Increase the current in the solenoid.
   D Insert a piece of soft iron into the solenoid.

4. A rectangular coil abcd carrying a current is in between the poles of a magnet with its plane vertical.

   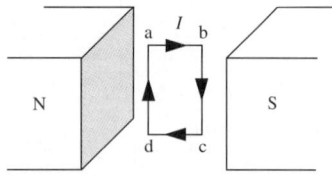

   There is a turning effect on the coil produced by the forces on the sides of
   A ad and bc.   C ab and cd.
   B ab and cd.   D ab and ad.

5. Which figures correctly shows the forces between two parallel wires carrying current in the same direction?

   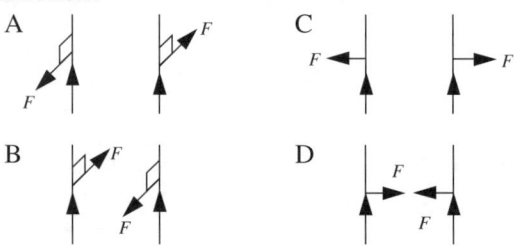

6. An electron beam enters a uniform magnetic field which is perpendicular and into the plane of the page. Which is the correct path of the electron beam?

   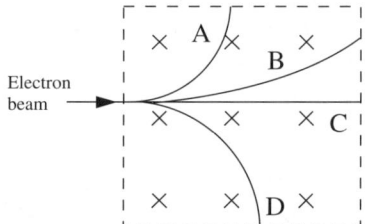

7. A current-carrying conductor in a magnetic field experiences a force F as shown in the figure. The direction of the magnetic field is

   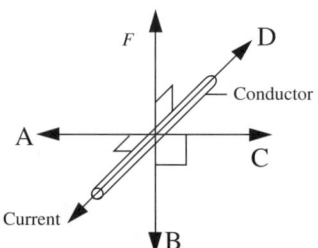

8. The purpose of the commutator in a d.c. motor is
   A to produce a stronger magnetic field.
   B to reverse the direction of the current in the coil.
   C to produce a greater turning effect.
   D to increase the speed of rotation of the coil.

9. The turning effect on the coil in a d.c. motor increases when
   A the current in the coil increases.
   B the coil is made of thinner wire.
   C the poles of the magnet are further apart.
   D the coil is connected to a commutator.

10. Which of the following appliances uses a motor?
    A An electric kettle
    B An electric bell
    C An electric drill
    D A circuit beaker

Structured Questions

Section A

1. The figure shows two parallel wires carrying current in opposite directions. The current creates strong magnetic field around the wires. P, Q and R are plotting compasses equally spaced with Q at the mid-way between the wires.

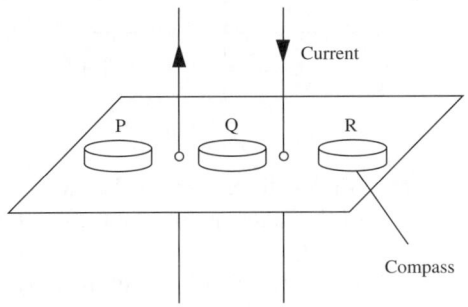

   (a) Draw the directions shown by the pointers of the compasses.

   P ◯   Q ◯   R ◯

   (b) Explain why the magnetic field between the wires is stronger than that on the outer sides of the wires.
   (c) Describe the motion of the wire if they were free to move.

2. Figure 2(a) shows a small bar magnet suspended freely from a thread at one end of a solenoid. There is no current in the solenoid.
   Figure 2(b) shows the final position the magnet when a large current flows in the solenoid.

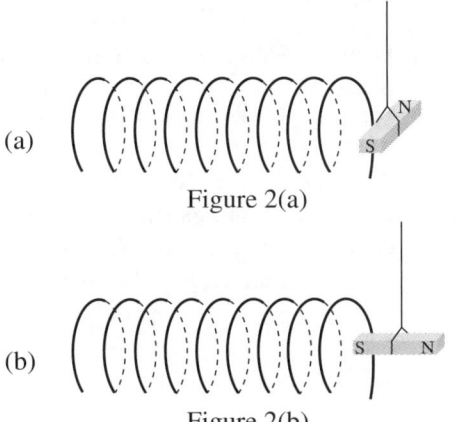

   (a) Mark in figure 2(b) the direction of the current in the solenoid.
   (b) The direction of the current is then reversed. Explain any changes to the position of the magnet.
   (c) With the direction of the current stays as in (b), the solenoid is slowly moved away from the magnet to the left. Describe and explain what happens to the magnet.

3. In the figures below, draw the magnetic field pattern and show the direction of the magnetic field.
   (a) Magnetic field between the poles of the magnets.

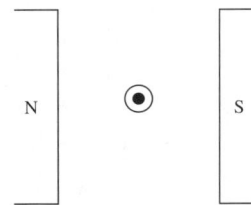

   (b) Magnetic field around a straight current-carrying wire out of the plane of the paper.

   ⊙

   (c) Magnetic field produced when a current-carrying conductor is in between the poles of a magnet.

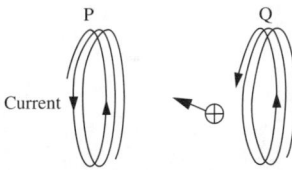

4. The figure shows current in two large plane circular coils. The magnetic field produced between the two coils may be assumed to be uniform.

   (a) Show with an arrow the direction of the magnetic field between the two coils.
   (b) A positive ion enters the magnetic field between the coils in the direction shown. Mark with an arrow the direction of the force on the positive ion.

5. The figure shows a coil carrying a current in the direction ABCD between the poles of a magnet.

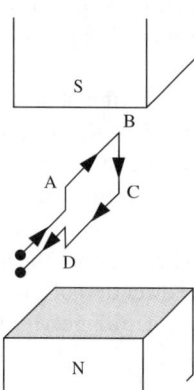

(a) Mark with arrows the directions of the forces on the sides AB and CD of the coil.
(b) These two forces produce a turning effect on the coil.
  (i) State two ways of increasing the turning effect.
  (ii) State two ways to make the coil turn in the opposite direction.

Section B

1. Figure 3(a) shows a vertical wire P carrying a large current upwards.

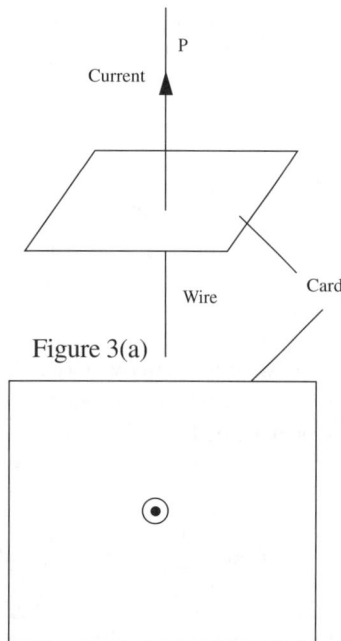

Figure 3(a)

Figure 3(b)

(a) Draw in figure 3(b) the magnetic field pattern produced by the current-carrying wire. Use arrows to mark the direction of the magnetic field.
(b) Describe how you would use a plotting compass to determine the direction of the magnetic field around the wire.
(c) Figure 3(c) shows another wire Q parallel to the wire P.

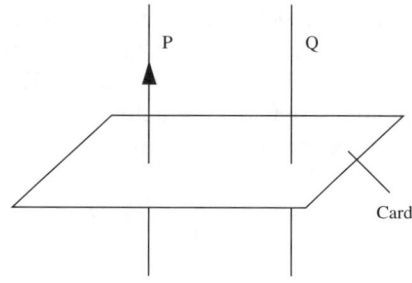

Figure 3(c)

  (i) Mark with an arrow on the card the direction of the magnetic field at the position of the wire Q.
  (ii) A current then flows in the wire Q in the same direction as the current in wire P. Mark with an arrow the direction of the force F on the wire Q.

2. An electron beam enters the space X and is deflected into Y then Z by the magnetic fields in X and Y.

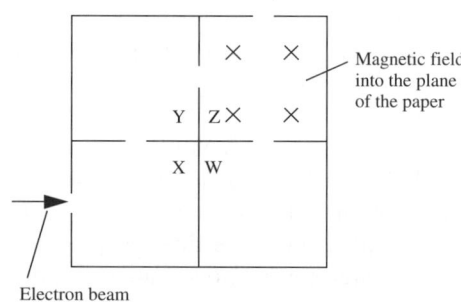

(a) Draw the paths of the electron beam in the space X and Y.
(b) What is the direction of the magnetic field in (i) X and (ii) Y?
(c) The magnetic field in the space Z is into the plane of the paper. Is the electron beam deflected into the space W or out of Z? Draw the path of the electron beam in Z.

3. The figure shows a coil with a number of turns in between the curved poles of a magnet.

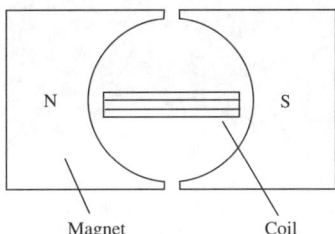

(a) Draw the magnetic field pattern between the poles of the magnet.
(b) Explain why the coil rotates when a current flows in it.
(c) What is the advantage of
   (i) the curved poles of the magnet?
   (ii) having a number of turns on the coil?
(d) Practical motors have the coil wound on a soft iron armature. What is the use of the soft iron armature?
(e) Name two appliances that use motor.

4. The figure shows plotting compasses X, Y and Z placing near a solenoid.

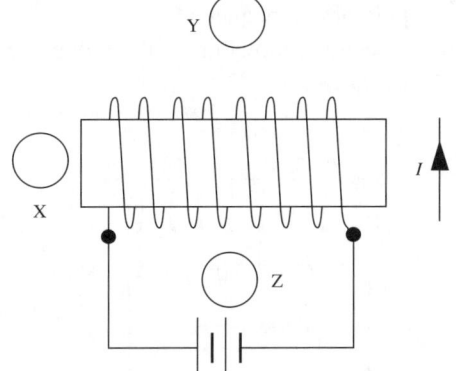

(a) Mark on the figure
   (i) the direction of the current in the solenoid.
   (ii) the directions of the compasses needles.
(b) A wire carrying a current I vertically upwards is placed at one end of the solenoid.
   (i) Show on the figure the direction of the force F on the wire.
   (ii) The current-carrying wire is then turned through 90° so that it is parallel to the axis of the solenoid. Does a force still act on the wire?

5. The figure shows a simple d.c. motor.

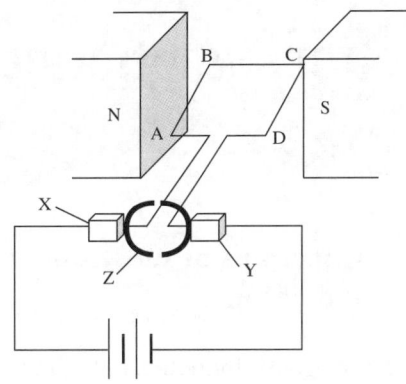

(a) Name and state the function of the parts labelled X, Y and Z.
(b) Explain what happens to the coil ABCD when a current flows in it.
(c) Suggest two modifications that would increase the speed of rotation of the coil.

CHAPTER 20
Electromagnetic Induction

20.1 Principles of Electromagnetic Induction

1. **Electromagnetic induction** is the production of an induced e.m.f. in a conductor when the magnetic flux linked with the conductor changes.
2. The apparatus shown in the figure below can be used to demonstrate electromagnetic induction.

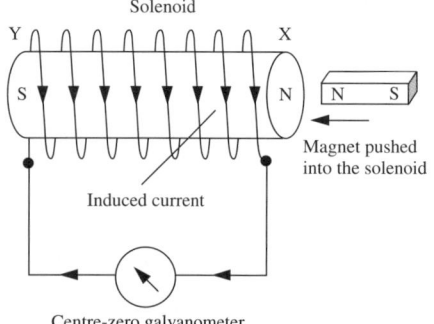

Figure 1

3. When there is relative motion between the magnet and the solenoid, the pointer of the centre-zero galvanometer is deflected. This shows that an e.m.f. is induced in the solenoid as the magnetic flux through the solenoid changes.
4. **Faraday's law of electromagnetic induction**
   The e.m.f. induced in a conductor is directly proportional to the rate of change of magnetic flux through the conductor.
5. This means that the induced e.m.f. increases when:
   – the relative speed between the magnet and the solenoid is increased;
   – a stronger magnet is used;
   – there are more turns per unit length on the solenoid.
6. No e.m.f. is induced in the solenoid when:
   – the magnet is stationary either outside or inside the solenoid;
   – there is no relative motion between the magnet and the solenoid, for instance when the magnet and solenoid move with the same speed in the same direction.
7. The direction of the induced current can be deduced using **Lenz's law**. *Lenz's law states that the direction of the induced current is such as to produce an effect that opposes the change that gives rise to it.*
8. In the figure 1 shown above,
   (a) the change that causes an e.m.f. to be induced in the solenoid is the N-pole of the magnet moving towards the end X of the of the solenoid.
   (b) To oppose the N-pole moving towards the end X, the current induced in the solenoid must produce a N-pole at the end X to repel the N-pole of the magnet.
   (c) Hence the direction of the induced current is as shown.

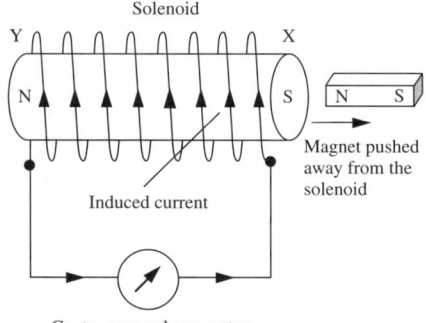

9. When the N-pole of the magnet moves away from the solenoid, the induced current would produce a S-pole at the end X to attract the N-pole back. Hence the induced current flows in the direction shown above.
10. When a straight wire is moved across a magnetic field, the magnetic flux is cut by the wire and a current is induced.

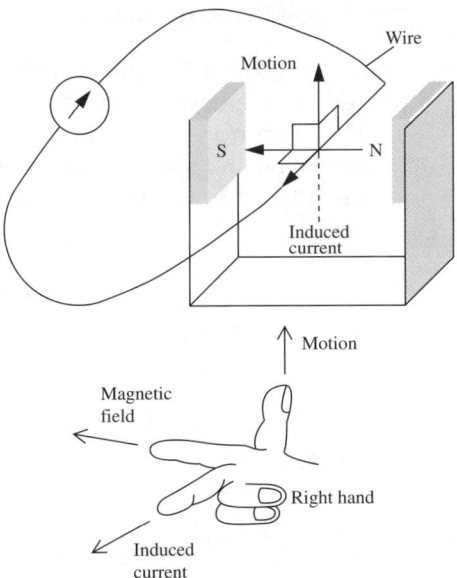

Fleming's right-hand rule

11. The relative directions of the magnetic field, motion of the wire and the induced current are given by **Fleming's right-hand rule** as shown above.

Self Evaluation 20.1

1. When a magnet is moved into the solenoid shown, the pointer of sensitive galvanometer shows a small deflection.

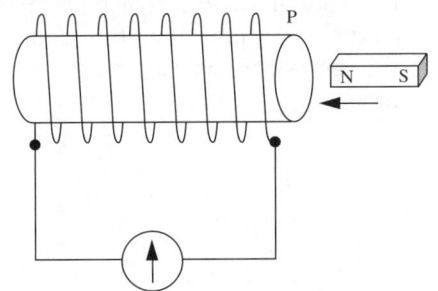

Which of the following would increase the size of the deflection?
A Pull the magnet out of the solenoid.
B Move the magnet through the solenoid.
C Push the S-pole into the solenoid.
D Reduce the separation between the coils by gathering them together at the end P.

2. Two coils X and Y are arranged coaxially. Coil X is free to move.

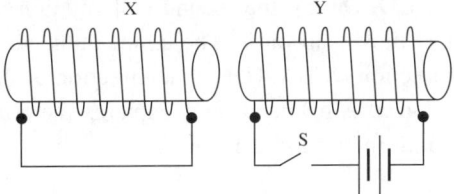

When the switch S is closed, the coil X
A is attracted to coil Y.
B moves away from coil Y.
C rotates clockwise.
D rotates anticlockwise.

3. When a rigid wire XY is moved between the poles of a magnet, the current induced flows from X to Y. In which direction is the wire moved?

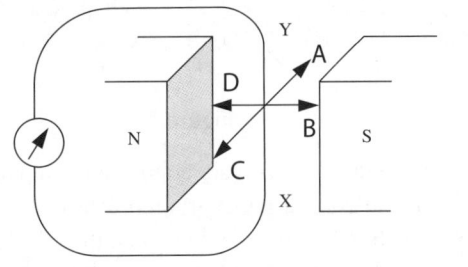

20.2 The A.C. Generator

1. The principle of electromagnetic induction is used in the generation of electricity.

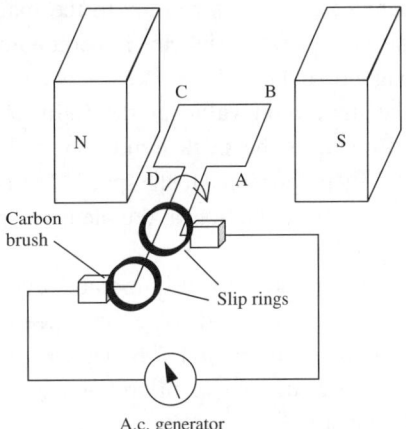

A.c. generator

2. The above figure shows a simple a.c. generator that consists of a coil between the poles of a magnet.
3. When the coil is rotated, the magnetic flux is cut by the coil and an alternating e.m.f. is induced in the coil.

4. Figure 2 shows that during the first half of a rotation, the side CD of the coil is moving downwards in the magnetic field. The e.m.f. induced is in the direction ABCD. During the second half rotation, the side CD moves upwards. The e.m.f. induced is in the direction OCBA. Hence the direction of the e.m.f. induced is reversed. This explains the alternating e.m.f. induced in the coil.

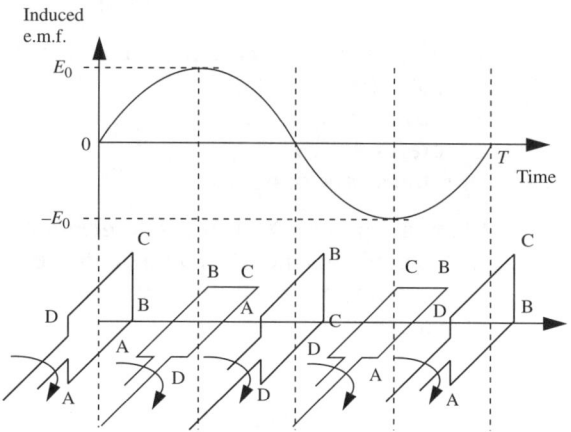

Figure 2

5. The ends of the coil are connected to a pair of slip-rings in contact with carbon brushes.
6. The slip-rings ensure that when the coil is rotated, the same end of the coil is constantly in contact with the same carbon brush.
7. The graph of induced e.m.f against time is shown in figure 2. The e.m.f induced is alternating because the direction of the current induced in the coil alternates.
8. The e.m.f. induced is at the maximum when the plane of the coil is parallel to the magnetic field and is zero when the coil is perpendicular to the magnetic field.
9. The maximum value of the induced e.m.f. E_0 is known as the **peak e.m.f**. The value of E_0 is directly proportional to the speed of rotation. When the speed of rotation is doubled, the peak e.m.f. is doubled.
10. The time taken for a complete revolution T is known as the period. When the speed of rotation is doubled, the period T is halved. The period T and the frequency of the rotation f is related by the equation:

$$\text{Period } T = \frac{1}{f}$$

Self Evaluation 20.2

1. Figure 3(a) shows a rectangular coil being rotated between two magnets.
   (a) Use Fleming's right-hand rule to determine and mark the directions of the induced e.m.f. along the sides ab and cd.

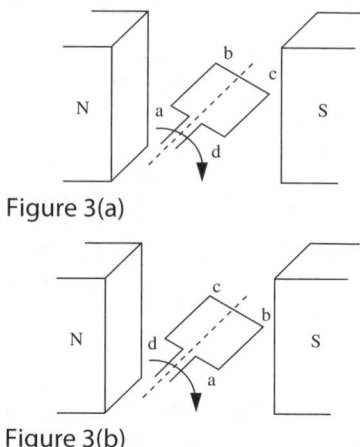

Figure 3(a)

Figure 3(b)

   (b) Figure 3(b) shows the coil after being rotated through half a revolution. Mark the directions of the induced e.m.f. and explain why the induced e.m.f. is alternating.

2. Figure 4(a) shows a coil being rotated in the magnetic filed between two magnets. Figure 4(b) shows how the reading V of the centre-zero galvanometer varies with time.

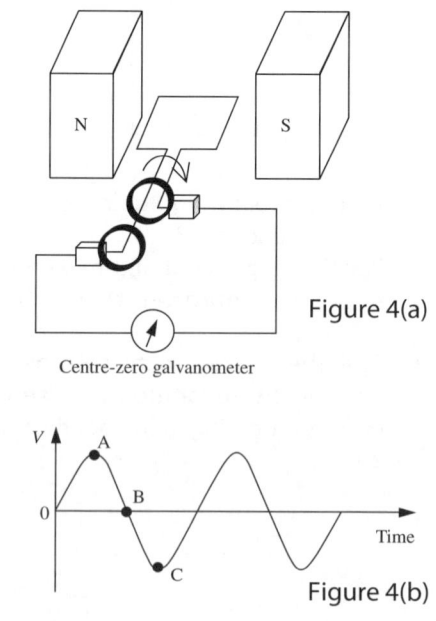

Figure 4(a)

Figure 4(b)

(a) Which of the points A, B or C represents the reading of the galvanometer
   (i) when the coil is horizontal as shown in figure 4(a)?
   (ii) when the coil has turned through 90° and its plane is vertical?
(b) Mark on figure 4(b), the period T of rotation of the coil.
(c) Draw in figure 4(b) the shape of the graph when the speed of rotation of the coil is doubled.

20.3 The Transformer

1. A transformer is used to step up or step down an alternating voltage.
2. Transformers are used to step down the mains voltage from 240 V to 12 V for appliances such as door chimes, radio and small electric pump.
3. Large transformers are used to step up voltages to 275 kV at power stations or to step down from 275 kV to 240 V at the substations.

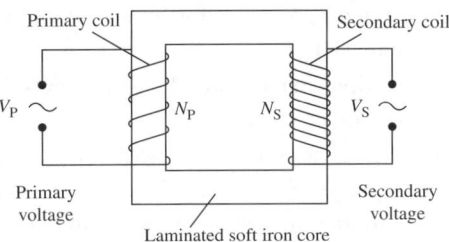

Transformer

4. A transformer consists of a primary coil and a secondary coil wound on a laminated soft iron core.
5. The principle used in the transformer is electromagnetic induction.
   (a) When an alternating voltage is connected to the transformer, an alternating current flows in the primary coil.
   (b) The alternating current produces a changing magnetic flux that is linked with the secondary coil.
   (c) The changing magnetic flux through the secondary coil induces an alternating voltage in the secondary coil.

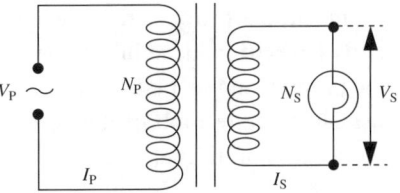

Circuit symbol of transformer

6. For an **ideal transformer**, no energy is lost.
   output power = input power
   $$I_S V_S = I_P V_P$$
   where I_P is the current in the primary coil,
   V_P is the primary voltage,
   I_S is the current in the secondary coil and
   V_S is the secondary voltage.
7. The secondary voltage V_S and the primary voltage V_P are related to the number of turns N_S and N_P in the secondary and primary coils by
   $$\frac{V_S}{V_P} = \frac{N_S}{N_P}$$
8. (a) If N_S is greater than N_P, the secondary voltage V_S is greater than the primary voltage V_P. The transformer is a step-up transformer.
   (b) If N_S is less than N_P, the secondary voltage V_S is less than the primary voltage V_P. The transformer is a step-down transformer
9. Most transformers are **not** 100% efficient because:
   – energy is lost in the form of heat in the primary and secondary coils and from the soft iron core;
   – there is a leakage of magnetic flux. Not all the magnetic flux produced by the current in the primary coil pass through the secondary coil.

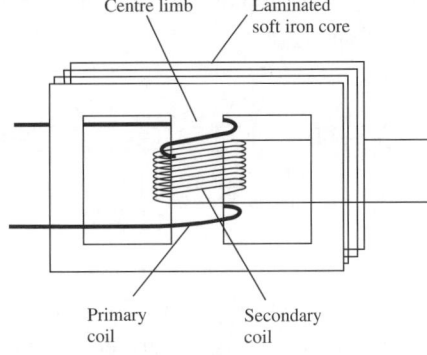

10. To increase the efficiency of the transformer:
    – thick copper wires are used for the primary and secondary coils to reduce the resistance of the coils. Hence the power dissipated as heat is reduced.

- a laminated soft-iron core is used to reduce the **eddy current** induced in the core.
- the primary and secondary coils are wound on the same centre limb of the soft-iron core to reduce loss of magnetic flux.

Example

An ideal transformer is used to light a lamp rated 36 W 12 V from a 240 V mains supply. If there are 4000 turns in the primary coil, calculate

(a) the number of turns in the secondary coil,
(b) the current in the primary coil.

Solution

(a)
$$\frac{N_S}{N_P} = \frac{V_S}{V_P}$$
$$N_S = \left(\frac{12\ V}{240\ V}\right)(4000)$$
$$= 200 \text{ turns}$$

(b) Since it is an ideal transformer,
input power = output power
$$I_P V_P = 36\ W$$
$$I_P = \frac{36\ W}{240\ V}$$
$$= 0.15\ A$$

Transmission of Electrical Energy

11. Electrical power generated in a power station is transmitted over long distances to consumers using cables.
12. The transmission cables have resistance. Energy in the form of heat is lost from the cables.
13. The figure below shows a model of electrical power transmission.

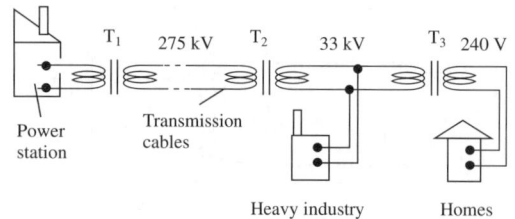

Transmission of electricity

14. Electrical power is generated in the form of alternating current (a.c.) because alternating voltage can be changed by means of electromagnetic induction using transformers.
15. The voltage generated in the power station is step up to a high voltage 275 kV using the step-up transformer T_1.
16. High voltage transmission reduces the power loss in the transmission cables.
    (a) Since electrical power = IV, when the voltage V is high, the current I in the transmission cables is small.
    (b) Power loss from the cable = $I^2 R$, where R is the resistance of the cables.
    (c) When the current I is small, the power lost from the cable is reduced.
17. For example if the current in the cable is reduced by a factor of $\frac{1}{100}$, the power lost from the cable is reduced by a factor of $\frac{1}{10\ 000}$.
18. Power lost from the cable is also reduced by using thick copper cables which have lower resistance R.
19. Before supplying the power to the homes, the voltage is step down in stages using step-down transformers T_2 and T_3. Heavy industries require high voltage 33 kV.
20. The various power stations and the consumers are connected by a network of cables, known as the **national grid**.
21. The advantages of having a national grid for the transmission of electricity are the following.
    (a) When a power station breaks down, consumers can still receive power from other power stations in the grid. Thus it prevents disruption of power supply.
    (b) The generation and distribution of electricity is more efficient. During low demand period, certain power stations can be shut down. These power stations will supply power during peak demand hours.
    (c) Power stations can take turns to shut down for maintenance.

Example

The power generated in a power station is 66 kW at a voltage of 1.2 kV. A transformer T_1 steps up the voltage to 132 kV. Power at this voltage is transmitted over cables that have a total resistance of 50 Ω.

(a) Explain whether the power generated is in the form of alternating current (a.c.) or direct current (d.c.)?
(b) Calculate
   (i) the current in the transmission cables;
   (ii) the power lost from the cables.

(c) What would have been the power lost from the cables if the voltage is not stepped up to 132 kV? Hence state the advantage of transmitting the power at high voltage.

(d) The voltage of 132 kV is stepped down by a series of transformers. A transformer T_2 steps down the voltage from 132 kV to 33 kV. Finally the voltage is stepped down to 240 V before being supplied to the homes.

Calculate

(i) the turn ratio $\dfrac{N_S}{N_P}$ of transformer T_2;

(ii) the number of turns in the secondary coil of T_2 if there are 3000 turns in the primary coil.

Solution

(a) Power is generated in the form of a.c. The alternating voltage can be stepped up or stepped down using transformers. Direct current (d.c.) voltage cannot be stepped up or stepped down by means of electromagnetic induction using transformers.

(b) (i)
$$\text{Power} = IV$$
$$\text{Current in the cables } I = \dfrac{66 \text{ kW}}{132 \text{ kV}}$$
$$= 0.50 \text{ A}$$

(ii) Power lost $= I^2 R$
$$= (0.50 \text{ A})^2 (50 \text{ Ω})$$
$$= 12.5 \text{ W}$$

(c) Current in the cable $= \dfrac{66 \text{ kW}}{3.6 \text{ kV}}$
$$= 18.3 \text{ A}$$
Power lost $= (18.3 \text{ A})^2 (50 \text{ Ω})$
$$= 16.7 \text{ kW}$$

Advantage: Power lost from the cables is greatly reduced if it is transmitted at high voltage.

(d) (i) Turn ratio $= \dfrac{N_S}{N_P}$
$$= \dfrac{V_S}{V_P}$$
$$= \dfrac{33 \text{ kV}}{132 \text{ kV}}$$
$$= 0.25$$

(ii) $N_S = \left(\dfrac{V_S N_P}{V_P}\right)$
$$= \dfrac{(33 \text{ kV})(3000)}{132 \text{ kV}}$$
$$= 750 \text{ turns}$$

Self Evaluation 20.3

1. The figure shows a step-down transformer with multiply output voltages. The primary coil has 2400 turns and the input voltage is 240 V.

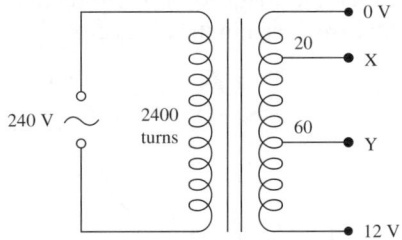

(a) How many turns are there between the 0 V and 12 V terminals in the secondary coil?

(b) How many volts should the terminals X and Y be labelled?

2. The power generated at a power station is 500 kW at 3.6 kV. A transformer steps up the voltage to 275 kV for transmission along cable of resistance 0.50 Ω m^{-1}.

(a) What is the current in the transmission cables? Assume that the transformer is ideal.

(b) What is the power loss per unit length of the cables?

(c) Suggest two ways of reducing the power loss from the transmission cables.

REVISION EXERCISE 20

Multiple Choice Questions

1. When a conductor which is connected to a galvanometer by flexible wires is moved down between the magnets in the direction shown, an e.m.f. is induced in the conductor.

   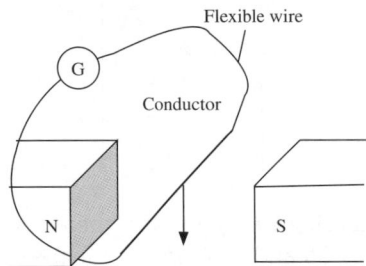

   Which of the following would induce an e.m.f. in the same direction?
   A Move the conductor upwards.
   B Move the conductor horizontally from left to right.
   C Move the conductor horizontally from right to left.
   D Move the magnets upwards.

2. A straight wire PQ that is connected to a sensitive galvanometer is moved between the magnets shown.

   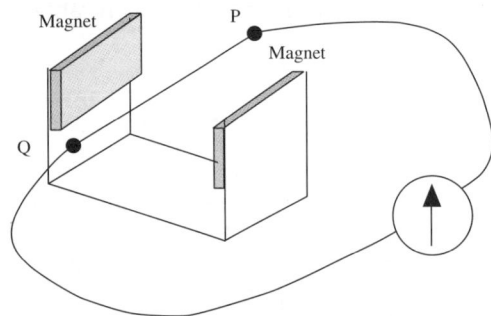

   Which of the following movements of the conductor would produce the largest deflection of the galvanometer pointer?
   A Sideway and quickly
   B Downwards and quickly
   C Upwards and slowly
   D Downwards and slowly

3. The figure shows a coil in a magnetic field. The coil is connected to a wire.

   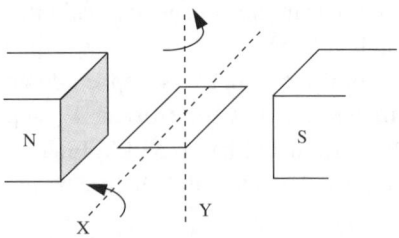

   How should the coil be moved so that an alternating voltage is induced in the coil?
   A Rotate the coil about the Y-axis.
   B Rotate the coil about the X-axis.
   C Move the coil vertically upwards.
   D Move the coil horizontally.

4. When the S-pole of magnet is pushed into the solenoid, the pointer of the galvanometer deflects slightly to the left.

   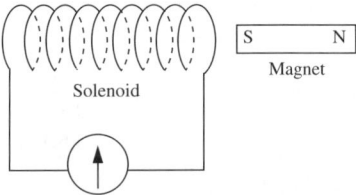

   Centre-zero galvanometer

   Which of the following would cause the pointer of the galvanometer to deflect to the right?
   A Move the solenoid towards the left.
   B Move the solenoid towards the right.
   C Move the magnet and solenoid at the same speed towards the right.
   D Move the magnet and solenoid at the same speed towards the left.

5. The figure shows a magnet at the end of a spring vibrating in and out of a solenoid.

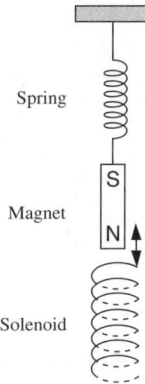

Which of the following would by itself increase the maximum magnitude of the e.m.f. induced in the solenoid?
A Use a spring of higher force constant.
B Decrease the number of turns in the solenoid.
C Use a heavier magnet.
D Increase the diameter of the solenoid.

6. An a.c. generator produces the voltage shown in the figure.

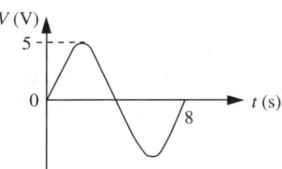

If the speed of rotation is doubled, which graph shows the voltage generated?

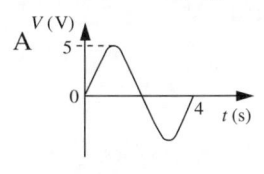 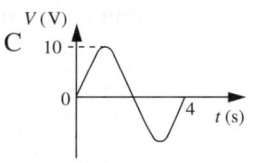

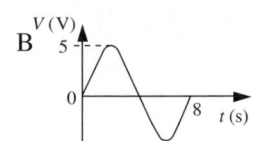 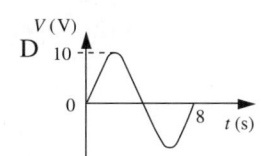

7. The graph below shows how the e.m.f. of an a.c. generator varies with time.

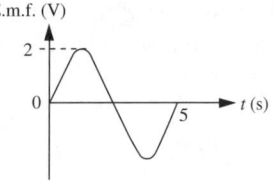

What are the peak e.m.f. and the frequency?

	Peak e.m.f.	Frequency
A	2.0 V	0.1 Hz
B	2.0 V	0.2 Hz
C	4.0 V	5 Hz
D	4.0 V	10 Hz

8. A transformer is connected to a 240 V a.c. supply to light up a 3 W 6.0 V lamp. What is the turn ratio $\dfrac{N_S}{N_P}$ of the transformer?

A 2   B 40   C $\dfrac{1}{2}$ D $\dfrac{1}{40}$

9. Why is soft iron used as the core of a transformer?
A Soft iron has a low resistance.
B Soft iron becomes a permanent magnet.
C Soft iron is easily magnetised and demagnetised.
D Soft iron is a better conductor than steel.

10. Which statement about a step-down transformer is correct?
A The output voltage is higher than the input voltage.
B The output power is greater than the input power.
C The output current is greater than the input current.
D The output current is lower than the input current.

Structured Questions

Section A

1. A coil P is connected to a battery and a switch S and a coil Q is connected to a sensitive centre-zero galvanometer.

   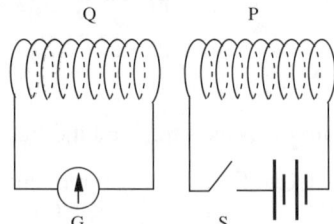

   (a) State and explain what happens to the pointer of the galvanometer
   (i) when the switch S is closed and then remains closed;
   (ii) when the switch S is opened again.
   (b) A soft iron rod is inserted through the coils P and Q. The switch S is then closed. Compare the observation with that in (a)(i) and explain if there is any changes.

2. The figure shows a soft iron bar wound with a coil which is connected to a centre-zero galvanometer. Magnets P and Q are placed on a conveyor belt that moves with uniform speed. As the magnet P moves below the soft iron the needle of the centre-zero galvanometer first deflects left then deflects right.

   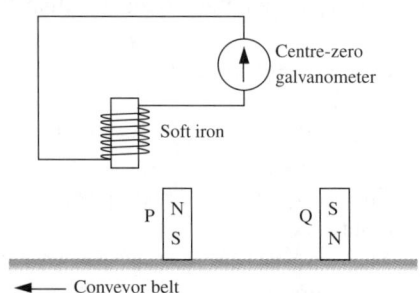

   (a) Explain why the needle of the galvanometer deflects.
   (b) Explain why the needle first deflects left then right.
   (c) Describe the change in the deflection when magnet Q moves below the soft iron bar.

3. The figure shows a coil rotating between two magnets.

   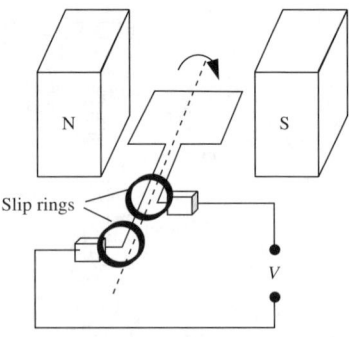

   (a) What is the purpose of the pair of slip rings?
   (b) On the axes provided below, sketch the graph to show how the output voltage V varies with time.

   (c) State two changes to the graph when the coil is rotated at twice the speed.

4. (a) State three sources of energy loss from a transformer.
   (b) Suggest the method of reducing the energy loss from each of the sources.

5. The primary coil of a transformer has 1200 turns and is connected to a 240 V a.c. supply. There are four terminals P, Q, R and S for the output. The number of turns between PQ is 30, QR is 60 and RS is 150. The terminal P is marked 0 V.

   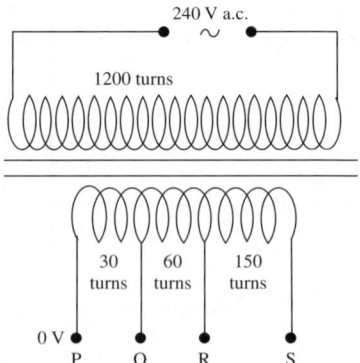

   Calculate the voltages that should be marked on the terminals Q, R and S.

Section B

1. The figure shows an experiment on electromagnetic induction. A coil X on a piece of soft iron is connected to a switch S, a battery and a rheostat. Another coil Y is connected to a centre-zero galvanometer.

   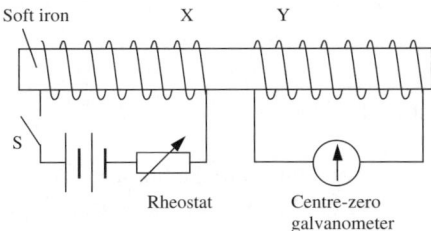

   (a) Explain why the pointer of the galvanometer deflects when the switch S is closed.
   (b) After the switch S is closed, the resistance of the rheostat is slowly reduced to zero. Compare the size and direction of deflection of the galvanometer pointer with that in (a).
   (c) When the resistance of the rheostat remains at zero, the pointer is not deflected. Explain.
   (d) The switch S is then opened. Compare the size and direction of deflection of the galvanometer pointer with that in (a).
   (e) The experiment is repeated with the piece of soft iron being replaced by a piece of aluminium. Explain any difference in the magnitude of the deflection of the pointer with that in (a).

2. A rectangular coil of copper wire moves across a uniform magnetic field at a constant speed.

   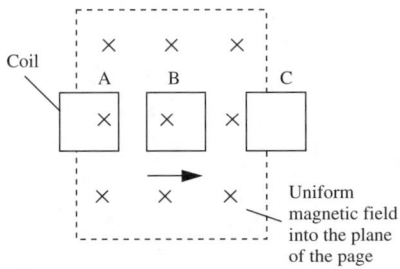

   (a) Mark the direction of the induced current in the coil when it is in the position (i) A and (ii) C.
   (b) Explain why there is no current induced in the coil when it is in the position B.
   (c) Suggest three modifications to the procedure so that a greater induced current is obtained when the coil is in the position A.

3. The figure shows three positions of a bar magnet which is released from rest and falls through a coil of copper wire

   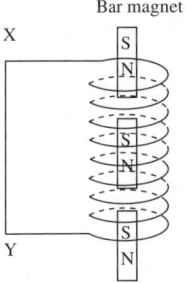

   (a) Describe the speed of the magnet as it falls through the coil.
   (b) Determine the direction of the induced current in the straight part XY
      (i) when the N-pole of the magnet enters the coil.
      (ii) when the N-pole of the magnet leaves the coil.
   (c) Compare the magnitudes of the induced current in (i) and (ii) above.
      Give reason for your answer.
   (d) The bar magnet is replaced by a piece of steel of identical dimensions.
      It is found that the piece of steel takes a shorter time to fall through the coil. Explain why.

4. The figure shows an ideal transformer connecting to a 240 V a.c. supply. The output voltage is 24 V a.c.

   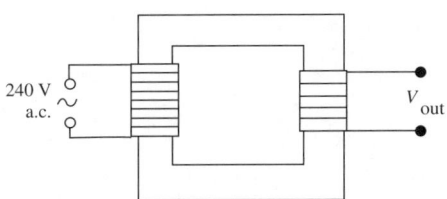

   (a) What is the type of transformer shown in the figure? Give a reason for your answer.
   (b) What is the value of the ratio

      $$\frac{\text{number of turns in the secondary coil}}{\text{number of turns in the primary soil}}?$$

   (c) Explain how the transformer works.

(d) On the axes provided, sketch a graph showing how the output voltage V_{out} varies with time.

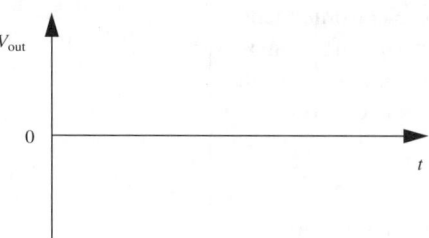

(e) If the current in the primary coil is 0.20 A, what is the current in the secondary coil?

5. The figure shows the transmission of electrical power from the power station to the home. The electrical power is generated at 250 kW of 50 kV and is transmitted at 300 kV to the transformer B.

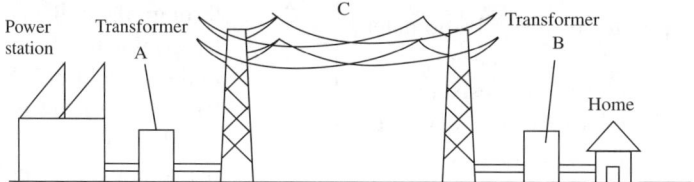

(a) (i) State the purpose of transformer A.
   (ii) If the transformer A is 100% efficient, calculate the ratio

   $$\frac{\text{number of turns in the secondary coil}}{\text{number of turns in the primary soil}}.$$

(b) (i) What is the current in the cable?
   (ii) If the total resistance of the cables is 50 Ω, calculate the power loss in the cables.
   (iii) Hence explain the advantage of transmitting power at high voltage.
(c) The output of transformer B is 240 V and there are 1800 turns in the secondary coil. Calculate the number of turns in the primary coil.

SPECIMEN EXAMINATION PAPER

Paper 1 (40 marks) (1 hour)

Answer **all** the questions.

1. Which of the following is most likely the radius of the Earth?
   A 6000 m
   B 600 km
   C 6000 km
   D 6 Gm

2. Which instruments should be used to measure the diameter of a wire and the diameter of a coin?

	Diameter of a wire	Diameter of a coin
A	Micrometer	Vernier caliper
B	Micrometer	Micrometer
C	Vernier caliper	Vernier caliper
D	Vernier caliper	Micrometer

3. Three vectors **u**, **v** and **w** are represented by the sides of a triangle as shown.

   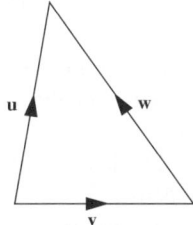

   The relationship between the three vectors is
   A **u** + **v** = **w**.
   B **v** + **w** = **u**.
   C **w** + **u** = **v**.
   D **u** + **v** + **w** = **0**.

4. Which is the distance-time graph of a body travelling under uniform acceleration?

   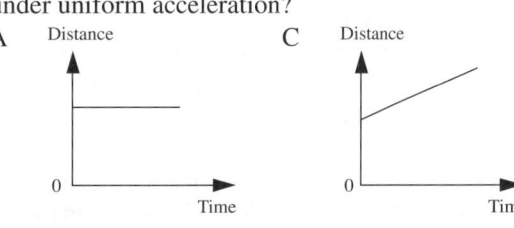
   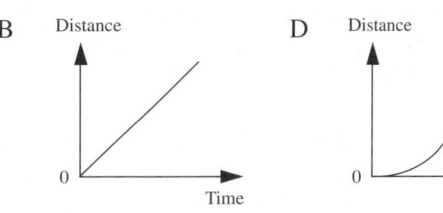

5. A car starts from rest and accelerates uniformly. After 12 s, the speed of the car is 18 m s^{-1}. What is the distance travelled by the car in 12 s?
   A 72 m   C 144 m
   B 108 m   D 216 m

6. When a sky-diver falls with the terminal velocity,
   A his speed is constant.
   B his speed is increasing.
   C his acceleration is less the acceleration of free fall.
   D his acceleration is increasing.

7. Two objects of equal mass m connected by an inextensible light string are pulled with a force F on a smooth surface. The objects move with uniform acceleration.

   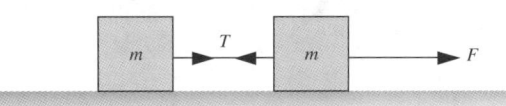

   If T is the tension in the string, then the F is
   A $0.5T$.   C $2T$.
   B T.   D $4T$.

8. A block initially at rest on a rough surface is pushed by a force *F* that increases from zero until the block moves with uniform acceleration.

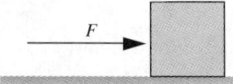

The friction between the block and the surface is the greatest
A when the force $F = 0$.
B just before the block starts to move.
C just when the block starts to move.
D when the speed of the block is the greatest.

9. The weight of an object of mass 5 kg on the surface of the Moon is 8.5 N. What is the gravitational field strength on the surface of the Moon?
A 0.6 N kg^{-1} C 10 N kg^{-1}
B 1.7 N kg^{-1} D 43 N kg^{-1}

10. A uniform rod of length 4 m is freely pivoted about its centre of gravity. Two forces act at the ends of the rod and another is one quarter of the way from one end. In which diagram is the rod in equilibrium?

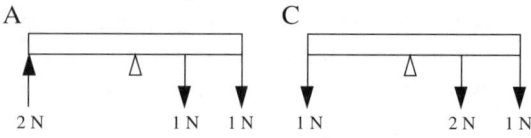

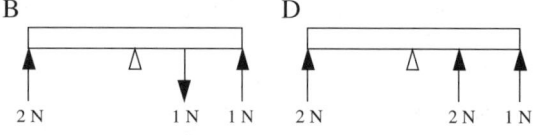

11. Three forces F_1, F_2 and F_3 act on a point O. Which diagram shows that the point O is in equilibrium?

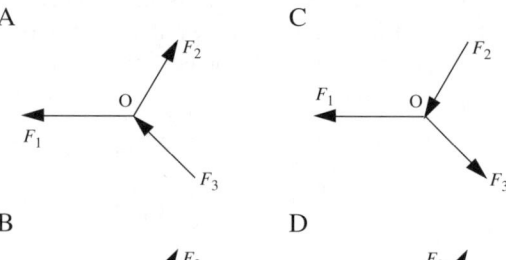

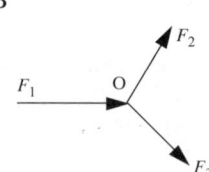 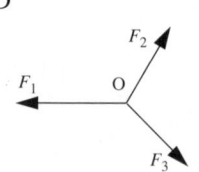

12. Some air is trapped in a glass tube by a column of mercury as shown in the figure.

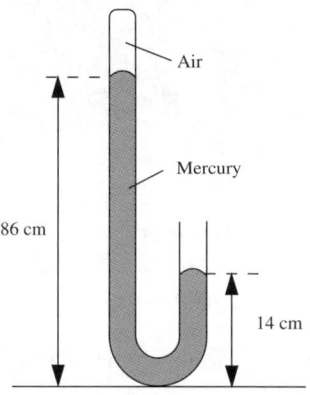

The atmospheric pressure equals the pressure of 76 cm of mercury. What is the pressure of the trapped air in cm mercury?
A 4.0   C 62.0
B 10.0   D 72.0

13. A body of mass 4.0 kg slides down from rest on an inclined plane. When it reaches the bottom of the incline, its speed is 6.0 m s^{-1}. What is the work done against the friction between the body and the incline?

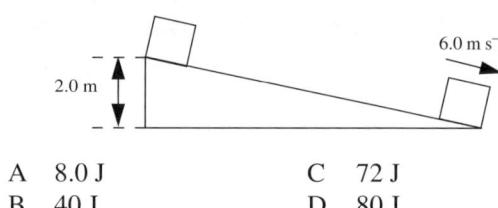

A 8.0 J   C 72 J
B 40 J   D 80 J

14. The pressure of a fixed mass of gas in an enclosed cylinder increases when the temperature increases. This is because
A the gas molecules collide into each other with greater speeds.
B the distance between gas molecules increases.
C the gas molecules collide more frequently with the walls of the cylinder.
D the number of gas molecules per unit volume increases.

15. Which of the following is the correct deduction from observations on Brownian motion?
A Gas molecules are in constant random motion.
B Gas molecules attract each other.
C Gas molecules collide elastically into each other.
D Gas molecules are visible under the microscope.

16. Which of the following graphs correctly shows the variation of the pressure *p* of a fixed mass of gas with volume *V* at constant temperature?

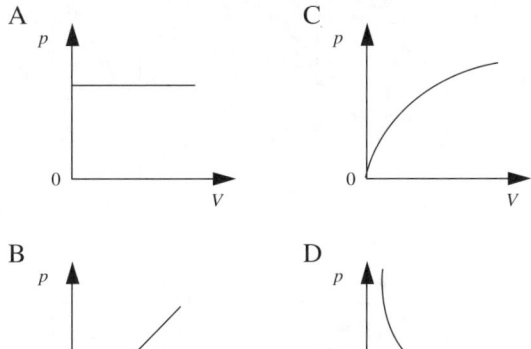

17. Figure 1(a) shows water in an electric kettle before the water starts to boil. Figure 1(b) shows two ice cubes melting in a glass of water initially at room temperature.

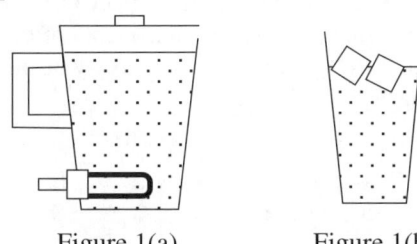

Figure 1(a)   Figure 1(b)

The temperature at which parts of the water in (a) and (b) are higher?

	In (a)	In (b)
A	At the top	At the top
B	At the top	At the bottom
C	At the bottom	At the bottom
D	At the bottom	At the top

18. Energy from the Sun is transferred to the Earth by
    A conduction.
    B radiation.
    C convection.
    D conduction and radiation.

19. When an object is in thermal equilibrium with its surroundings,
    A its temperature equals the temperature of the surroundings.
    B there is a net gain of heat from the surroundings.
    C there is a net loss of heat to the surroundings.
    D its temperature rises at a constant rate.

20. The amount of thermal energy required to increase the temperature of a body by 1 °C is known as
    A the specific heat capacity of the body.
    B the heat capacity of the body.
    C the latent heat of the body.
    D the specific latent heat of the body.

21. A substance in the solid state is heated until all of it turns into vapour. The temperature-time graph is as shown.

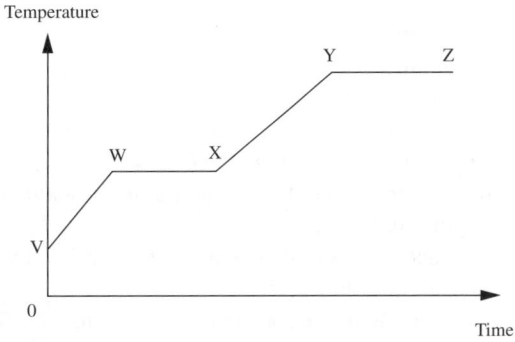

Along which section of the graph is the substance entirely in the liquid state?
A VW   C XY
B WX   D YZ

22. When salt is added to water and to ice, how do the boiling point of water and the melting point of ice change?

	Boiling point	Melting point
A	Increases	Increases
B	Increases	Decreases
C	Decreases	Decreases
D	Decreases	Increases

23. The figure shows a wave travelling along a spring of length 1.20 m.

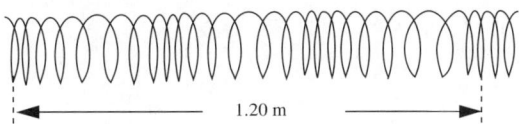

What is the wavelength of the wave?
A 0.20 m
B 0.40 m
C 0.60 m
D 1.20 m

24. When one end of a rope is waved up and down 5 times per second, the wave as shown in the figure travels along the rope.

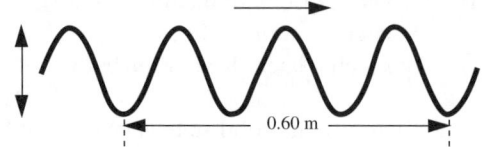

What is the speed of the wave?
A 1.0 m s^{-1}
B 2.0 m s^{-1}
C 3.0 m s^{-1}
D 6.0 m s^{-1}

25. Which of the following statements states correctly the difference between transverse wave and longitudinal wave?
A Speed of transverse wave is greater than that of longitudinal wave.
B Transverse can travel in a vacuum, longitudinal wave required a medium.
C Transverse wave has longer wavelength than longitudinal wave.
D Directions of oscillation in the waves relative to the direction of wave propagation are different.

26. An object O is placed between two plane mirrors which are arranged perpendicular to each other. Which diagram correctly shows the positions of the images in the mirrors?

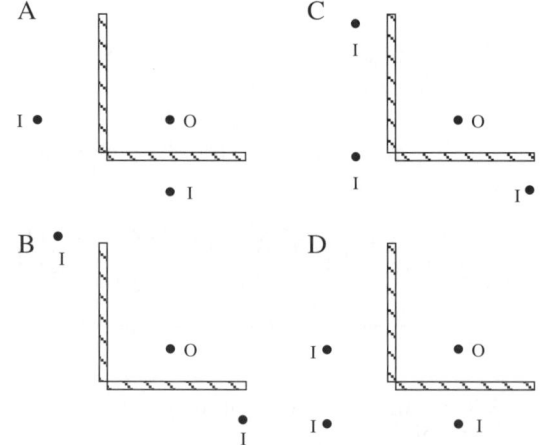

27. The critical angle of glass is 42°. Which diagram correctly shows the possible path of a light ray through a glass block?

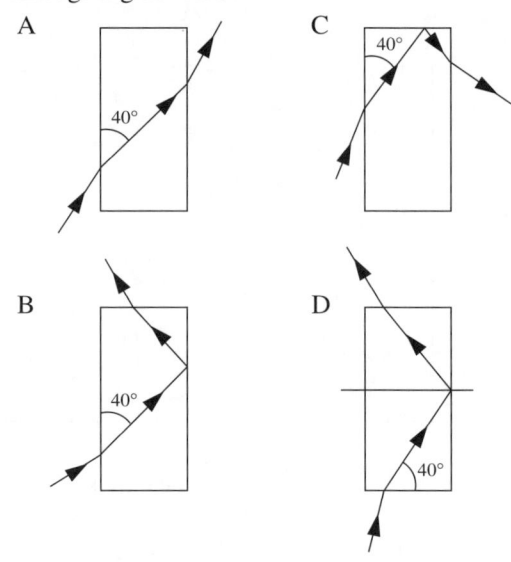

28. The figure shows a point object O in front of a converging lens. The principal foci of the lens are F_1 and F_2. Where is the most likely position of the image?

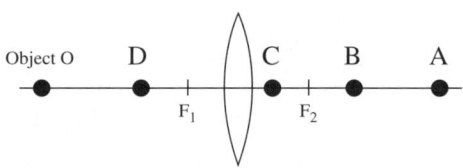

29. The image formed by a lens is inverted and magnified. Which of the following correctly describe the image and the lens used?

	Image	Lens
A	Real	Converging lens
B	Real	Diverging lens
C	Virtual	Converging lens
D	Virtual	Diverging lens

30. Which of the following is **not** a common property of electromagnetic waves?
A Electromagnetic waves are transverse waves.
B Electromagnetic waves can travel in vacuum.
C Electromagnetic waves have the same speed in glass
D Electromagnetic waves are refracted when they propagate from the air to the glass.

31. Which of the following is the effect produced by the absorption of microwaves?
   A Ionisation
   B Electromagnetic induction
   C Heating
   D Emission of light

32. The sound from a source has a high pitch but is not loud. Which is true about the frequency and the amplitude of the sound wave?

	Frequency	Amplitude
A	Low	Small
B	Low	Large
C	High	Large
D	High	Small

33. A positively charged sphere is lowered into an uncharged metal can which is on a piece of insulator. Which diagram correctly shows the charge distribution on the metal can?

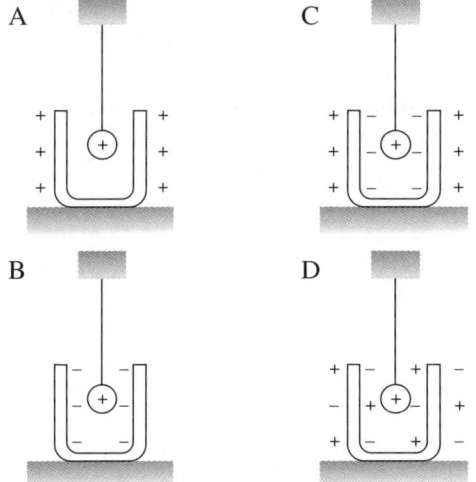

34. The resistance of filament lamp increases with temperature. Which graph correctly shows how the current I in the lamp varies when the voltage V across the lamp increases?

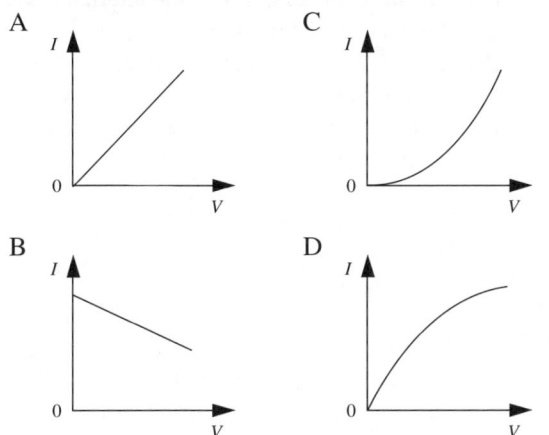

35. The resistance of a piece of nichrome wire of length 50 cm is 4.0 Ω. What is the resistance of another piece of nichrome wire of length 100 cm and twice the cross-sectional area?
   A 2.0 Ω
   B 4.0 Ω
   C 8.0 Ω
   D 16.0 Ω

36. A uniform resistance wire is stretched between the points P and Q as shown in the figure below. An ammeter is connected in series with a cell of negligible internal resistance and a sliding contact S. The sliding contact S is moved from P to Q.

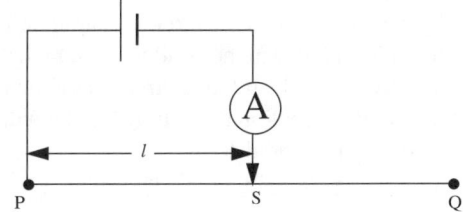

Which graph correctly shows the variation of the ammeter reading I with the length l of the wire between P and S?

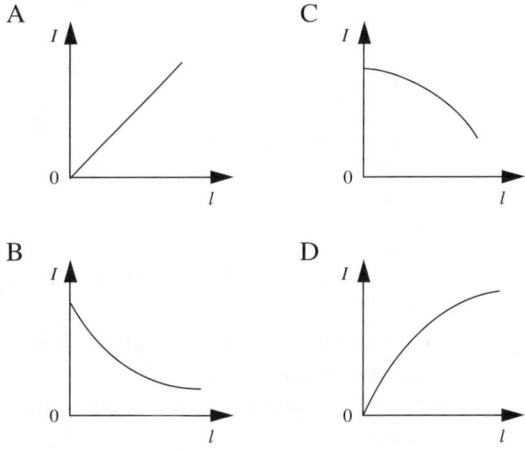

37. A filament lamp is rated 240 V 60 W. What is the power dissipated from the lamp when it is connected to a 120 V supply?
   A 15 W
   B 30 W
   C 60 W
   D 120 W

38. Three wires X, Y and Z carry equal current I in the directions shown. If the wire Y is free to move, in which direction will it move?

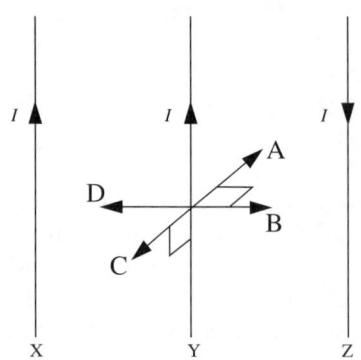

39. When a conductor is moved in a magnetic field, an e.m.f. E is induced in the conductor. Which diagram correctly shows the relative direction of the induced e.m.f. E, the direction of motion v and the direction of the magnetic field B?

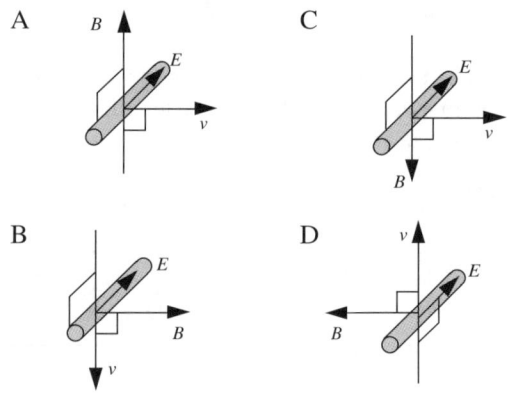

40. Which of the following is true for an ideal step-down transformer?
   A The secondary current is greater than the primary current.
   B The output voltage is greater than the input voltage.
   C The output power is less than the input power.
   D There are more turns in the secondary coil than the primary coil.

Paper 2 (80 marks) (1 h 45 min)

Section A (50 marks)

Answer **all** the questions in this section.

1. A car was 240 m from the stop-line of a traffic light when the driver steps on the brakes. The speed of the car was 20 m s^{-1}. The car decelerated uniformly and stopped at the stop-line.
   (a) What was the average speed of the car during the deceleration? [1]
   (b) Calculate the time taken for the car to stop. [2]
   (c) What was the deceleration of the car? [2]

2. A horizontal force F at the point P pulls the thread used to suspend a load of 5.0 N as shown in the figure. The tension in the inclined section of the thread is T. The point P is stationary.
   (a) Use a suitable scale to draw a triangle to represent the force F, tension T and the load of 5.0 N. [2]
   (b) Obtain from your diagram the magnitude of
       (i) the force F and (ii) tension T. [4]

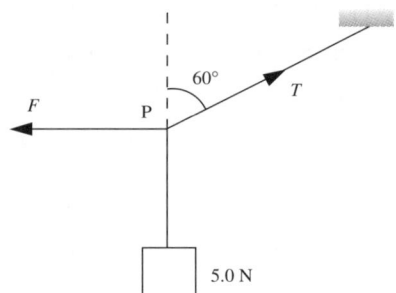

3. An electric kettle is rated 1.5 kW 240 V. The kettle takes 12 minutes to raise the temperature of 2.0 kg of water from 20 °C to 100 °C. The specific heat capacity of water is 4200 J kg^{-1} °C^{-1}.
   (a) Calculate the increase in the internal energy of the water in 12 minutes. [2]
   (b) Calculate the electrical energy supplied in 12 minutes. [2]
   (c) State two reasons why the answers to (i) and (ii) are different. [2]

4. The figure shows a ray of light entering a right-angled glass prism at P.

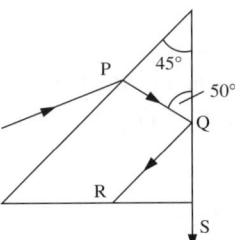

(a) State two properties of light that changes at P. [2]
(b) At Q the ray splits, with a ray along QS and another along QR.
   (i) What is the critical angle of the glass? [1]
   (ii) Calculate the refractive index of glass. [2]
(c) Explain what happens to the ray at R. [2]

5. The figure shows water waves travelling from the region X to the region Y in a ripple tank.

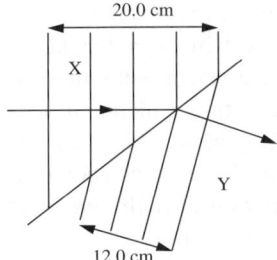

(a) Explain which part of the water – region X or Y is deeper. [2]
(b) What property of wave is illustrated in the figure? [1]
(c) What is the wavelength in the region X? [1]
(d) If the speed of the water waves in the region X is 32 cm s^{-1}, what is the speed in the region Y? [2]

6. An immersion heater of power 500 W is used to heat the water in a plastic cup until the water boils. The immersion heat is switched off 6.0 minutes later. The temperature-time graph of the water is as shown.

Figure 1(a)

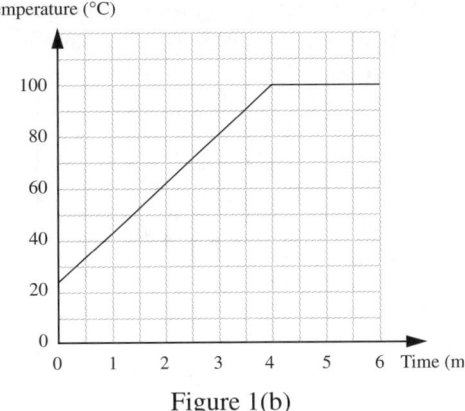

Figure 1(b)

(a) What is the initial temperature of the water in the cup? [1]
(b) Explain the shape of the graph. [2]
(c) Calculate the mass of water evaporated after the water boils. [2]
(d) Salt is dissolved in the water and the same mass of water is heated from the same initial temperature.
   (i) Neglecting heat lost to the surroundings, draw in figure 1(b) the new temperature-time graph. [2]
   (ii) Explain the differences in the two graphs. [2]

(Specific latent heat of vaporisation of water $= 2.26 \times 10^6$ J kg^{-1})

7. Figure 2(a) shows a magnet with a circular S-pole around a N-pole. When seen from above, the magnet is as shown in figure 2(b)

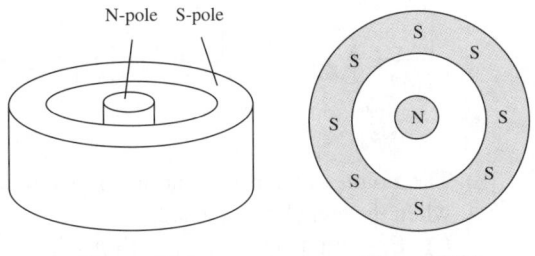

Figure 2(a)   Figure 2(b)

(a) Draw in figure 2(b) the magnetic field between the poles of the magnet. Mark the direction of the field. [2]

(b) A coil carrying a current is placed in the space between the poles of the magnet as shown below.

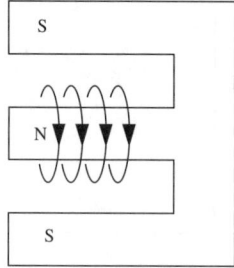

(i) Describe and explain what happens to the current-carrying coil in the magnetic field. [2]
(ii) If an alternating current flows in the coil, what would happen to the coil? [1]

8. The figure shows two circular coils placed side by side and they are coaxial with each other. Coil A is connected in series with a switch S and a battery while coil B is connected to a centre-zero galvanometer.
   (a) Draw the magnetic field produced by the current in coil A when the switch S is closed. Show the direction of the field. [1]

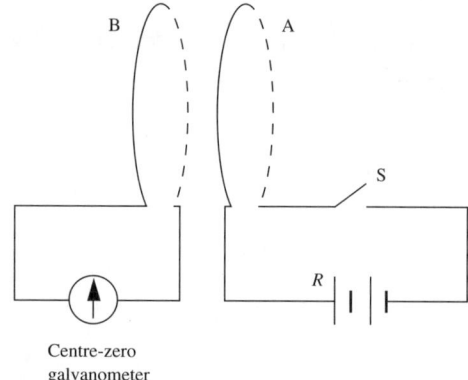

(b) The pointer of the galvanometer is deflected when the switch S is closed.
   (i) Explain why a current flows in coil B although there is no electrical contact between the two coils. [2]
   (ii) Show the direction of the current in coil B. [1]
(c) Explain why no current flows in coil B when the switch S remains closed. [2]

Section B

Answer **three** questions in this section.

1. (a) Figure 3(a) shows the gas molecules in a cylinder that is fitted with a smooth piston and there is a load on the piston.

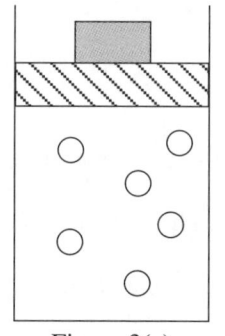

Figure 3(a)   Figure 3(b)

(i) Describe the motion of the gas molecules. [1]
(ii) Explain why the gas molecules are able to move, as described. [2]
(iii) Explain in molecular terms how the gas exerts a pressure in the cylinder. [3]

(b) An additional identical load is added on top of the piston. This causes the volume of the gas to decrease as shown in figure 3(b). The temperature of the gas remains unchanged. State the changes to
(i) the number of gas molecules per unit volume; [1]
(ii) the surface area of the walls of the cylinder; [1]
(iii) the rate of collision of the gas molecules with an unit area of the walls of the cylinder; [1]
(iv) the pressure of the gas. [1]

2. The figure is a multi-flash photograph of a ball falling under the action of gravity after being projected horizontally from the point P at time $t = 0$. The positions of the ball at an interval of one second are as shown. Each division on the grid represents a distance of 10 m.

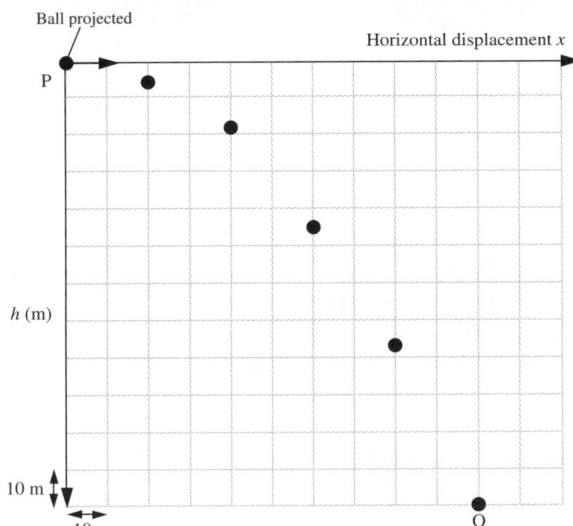

The motion of the ball may be considered to consist of
I. the horizontal component and
II. the vertical component.
(a) Consider the horizontal component of the ball's motion.
   (i) Record the horizontal displacement x of the ball in the table below. [2]

Time (s)	1	2	3	4	5
x (m)					

   (ii) Hence deduce the horizontal component of the velocity of the ball. [2]
(b) Consider the vertical component of motion of the ball as it falls.
   (i) Describe how the vertical displacement h vary with time in the successive time intervals of 2.0 s? [1]
   (ii) What can you deduce about the vertical speed of the ball as it falls? [1]
   If the vertical acceleration of the ball is uniform, use data from the above figure to find
   (iii) the time it takes to travel from P to Q. [1]
   (iv) the vertical distance of P from Q. [1]
   (v) the vertical acceleration of the ball. [2]

3. ANSWER EITHER
A carbon thermistor X and a light-dependent resistor Y together with two 5 kΩ resistors R_1 an R_2 are connected to a 6.0 V battery as shown in the circuit. A lamp is connected across the points A and B.

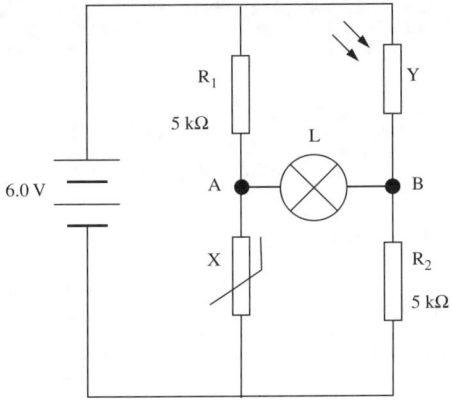

(a) State the characteristics of
   (i) the carbon thermistor X;
   (ii) the light-dependent resistor Y. [2]
(b) If both X and Y have resistance of 5 kΩ in darkness, explain whether the lamp L is lighted. [2]
(c) The circuit is then brought outside on a hot sunny day.
   (i) How do the resistances of X and Y change? [2]
   (ii) Is the lamp L lighted? [2]
(d) Explain whether the lamp L will be lighted on a cold night? [2]

OR
Parts of the electromagnetic spectrum, not in order of increasing frequency are: visible light, X-rays, microwaves, radio waves, gamma rays and ultra-violet.
(a) Name the missing part of the electromagnetic spectrum. [1]
(b) Arrange the components of the complete electromagnetic spectrum in the order of increasing frequency. [2]
(c) State two common properties of the electromagnetic radiations. [2]
(d) Give a value for the wavelength of visible light. [1]
(e) State two uses of microwaves. [2]
(f) State one hazard and one use of X-rays. [2]

Answers

Chapter 1 Physical Quantities, Units and Measurement

Self Evaluation 1.2

1. (a) kg s^{-1} (b) kg m^{-2} (c) m^3 s^{-1}
   (d) K kg^{-1} (e) A s (f) kg
   (g) m s^{-2}

Self Evaluation 1.3

1. (i) 4.00×10^5 mm^3
   (ii) 4.00×10^2 cm^3
   (iii) 4.00×10^{-4} m^3
2. (a) 1 light-year = 9.46×10^{15} m
   (b) 1 light-year = 6.31×10^4 AU

Self Evaluation 1.4

1.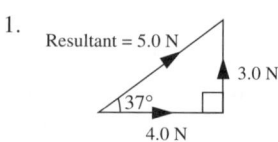

2.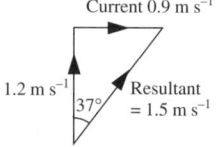

3. (a)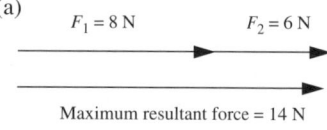

   (b)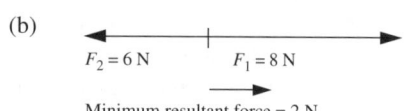

Self Evaluation 1.5

1. (a) Length: metre rule or mm scale
      Width: vernier calipers
      Thickness: micrometer screw gauge
   (b) Length = 20.0 cm
      Width = 2.00 cm
      Thickness = 2.00 mm
2. (a) 5.00 cm (b) 0.48 cm
3. (a) 0.01 mm (b) 3.51 mm
4. (a) B (b) C (c) A

Revision Exercise 1

Multiple Choice Questions

1. D   2. C   3. C   4. B   5. A
6. B   7. A   8. D   9. D   10. B

Structured Questions

Section A

1. (a) (i) 6 mm^3 (ii) 6×10^{-9} m^3
   (b) 2×10^8
2. 0.01 nm, 6 Mm, 0.2 mm, 10 m, 20 km
3. (a)

Reading	Instrument
20.0 cm	Metre rule
5.46 mm	Micrometer screw gauge
3.89 cm	Vernier calipers

   (b)

Physical Quantity	Instrument
Internal diameter of a test tube	Vernier calipers
Length of this book	Metre rule
Thickness of a pieces of paper	Micrometer screw gauge

4. (a) 3.1 cm
5. (a) 0.03 cm
   (b) 2.12 cm
   (c) For measuring internal diameters
   (d) Micrometer screw gauge

6. (a) (i) 0.03 mm (ii) 0.01 mm
   (b)

	Scale reading	Corrected reading
(i)	2.47 mm	2.44 mm
(ii)	5.04 mm	5.01 mm
(iii)	3.50 mm	3.47 mm

Section B

2. (b) Scalars: distance, energy, time.
      Vectors: velocity, acceleration, force.
   (c)

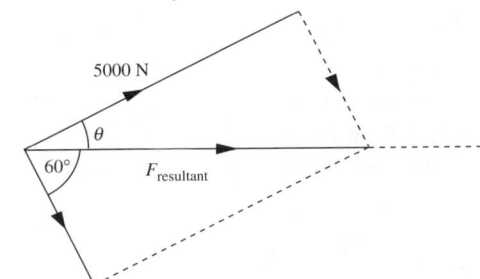

   (i) $\theta = 30°$
   (ii) $F = 2900$ N
   (iii) Resultant force = 6000 N

3. (a) Method 2 is most appropriate.
      Method 1: time for 5 oscillations too short and measurement less accurate.
      Method 3: time for 100 oscillations is too long. The experiment may not be completed in the time allotted.

Chapter 2 Kinematics

Self Evaluation 2.1

1. (a) 4.0 m s^{-2} (b) 8.0 m s^{-1} (c) 8.0 m
2. (a) 12 m
   (b) Deceleration = 2.0 m s^{-2}
   (c) No. Total distance travelled = 112 m < 120 m

Self Evaluation 2.2

2. (a) (i) 10 m s^{-1} (ii) 10 m s^{-1}
       (iii) 50 m   (iv) 0
   (b) (i) 7.5 m s^{-1} (ii) 7.5 m s^{-1}
       (iii) 37.5 m   (iv) -1.0 m s^{-2}
   (c) (i) 5.0 m s^{-1} (ii) 5.0 m s^{-1}
       (iii) 25 m   (iv) 2.0 m s^{-2}

Self Evaluation 2.3

1. (a) (i) 10 m s^{-1} (ii) 20 m s^{-1} (iii) 50 m s^{-1}
   (b) (i) 5.0 m (ii) 15.0 m
   (c) 125 m

2. (a) 90 m s^{-1} (b) 10 s
   (c) At the highest point, speed = 0
   (d) 50 m s^{-1} (e) 500 m

Self Evaluation 2.4

1. (a) (i) 9.5 m s^{-2} (ii) 5.5 m s^{-2}
   (b) The air resistance increases as the speed increases.
   (c) Terminal velocity = 23.0 m s^{-1}
   (d)

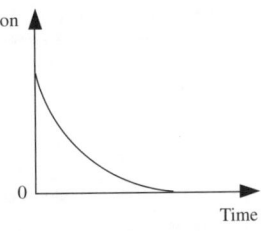

Revision Exercise 2

Multiple Choice Questions

1. A   2. C   3. D   4. C   5. A
6. C   7. D   8. B   9. D   10. C

Structured Questions

Section A

1. (a) (i) 40 s
       (ii) Distance travelled by P = 600 m
            Distance travelled by Q = 800 m
   (b) (i) 20.85 s
       (ii) Distance travelled by P = 313 m
            Distance travelled by R = 1087 m

2. (a) 50 m   (c) 18 m s^{-1}
   (d) 0   (e) 4 s

3. (a) (i) Gradient represents speed at $t = 2$ s.
       (ii) 5.0 m s^{-1}
   (b) 0.50 m s^{-1}
   (d)

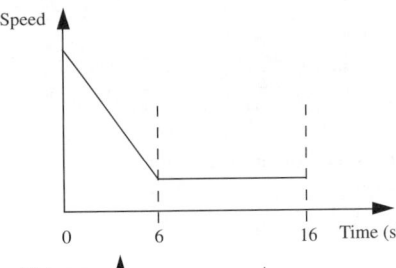

4. (a)

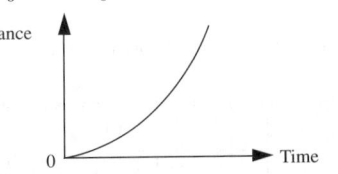

(b)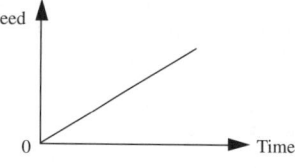

(c)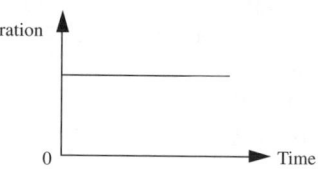

5. (b) Terminal velocity = 100 m s^{-1}
   (c) 1420 m
   (d)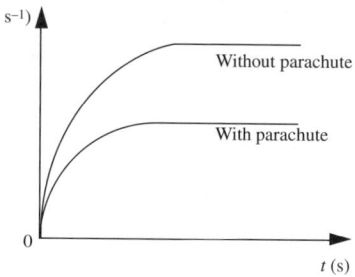

Section B

1. (a)

Pole number	0	1	2	3	4	5	6	7
Distance travelled (m)	0	20	40	60	80	100	120	140
Time taken (s)	0	3.2	4.5	5.5	6.3	7.1	7.7	8.4

(b)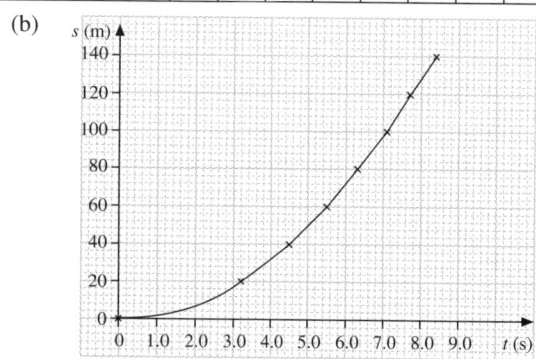

(c) The speed of the train increases.
(d) 28.6 m s^{-1}

2. (a) (i) 9 s   (ii) 486 m
   (b) 1944 m
   (c) L is directly proportional to v^2.

3. (a)

t (s)	0	1	2	3	4	5	6	7	8	9	10	11	12
x (m)	0	5	10	15	20	25	30	35	40	45	50	55	60
h (m)	0	55	100	135	160	175	180	175	160	135	100	55	0

(a) (i) Horizontal distance travelled in each 1 s interval remains constant.
    (ii) 5.0 m every 1 s
(c) (i) Vertical speed decreases.
    (ii) Gravity of the Earth retards the motion of the ball.
(b) (i) 5.0 m s^{-1}
    (ii) zero

Chapter 3   Dynamics

Self Evaluation 3.1

1. (a) Resultant force = 10 N
       Unbalanced forces
   (b) Resultant force = 0 N
       Balanced forces
   (c)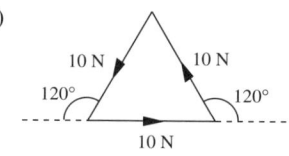

2. Balanced forces
   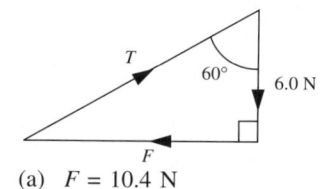
   (a) F = 10.4 N
   (b) T = 12 N

Self Evaluation 3.2

1. C   2. A   3. D

Self Evaluation 3.3

1. (a) Friction = 200 N   (b) 216 N
3. (a) a = 5.3 m s^{-2} (b) T = 18.6 N

Revision Exercise 3

Multiple Choice Questions

1. C   2. A   3. B   4. D   5. C
6. D   7. A   8. B   9. C   10. A

Structured Questions

Section A

1. (a) 40 N   (b) 48 N
2. (a) (i) Resultant force is zero.
       6 N ← • → 6 N
       (ii) Resultant force = 12 N
       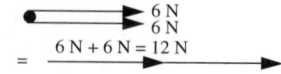
       = 6 N + 6 N = 12 N

(iii)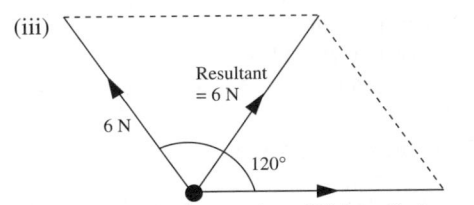

3. (a) No force to balance the weight of the traffic lights.

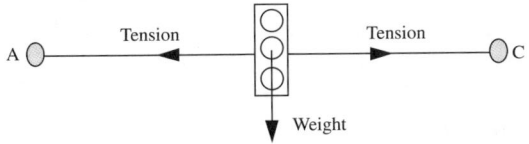

(b)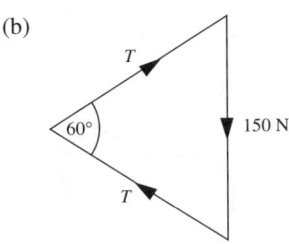

Tension $T = 150$ N

Section B

1. (a) 500 N
   (b) 0.50 m s^{-2}
   (c) (i) Gradient = acceleration
       Acceleration decreases as time passes.
       (ii) Terminal velocity = 25 m s^{-1}
       (iii) 900 N
       (iv) Shape: more streamline.
2. (a) (i) The frictional force is 12 N.
       (ii)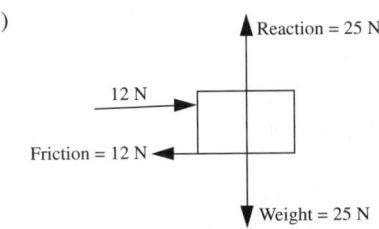

3. (a)

	Average speed in successive 1.0 s interval (m s^{-1})		
(i) Along AB	0.2	0.6	1.0
(ii) Along CD	0.9	0.7	0.5

   (b) (i) 0.4 m s^{-2}
       (ii) −0.2 m s^{-2}
   (c) Speed = 1.2 m s^{-1}

(d) (i)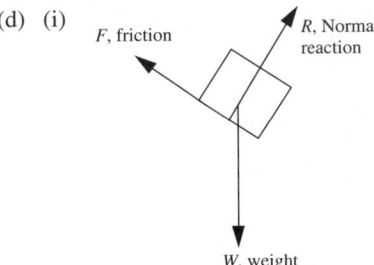

(ii)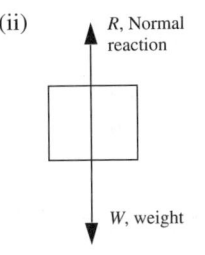

(iii)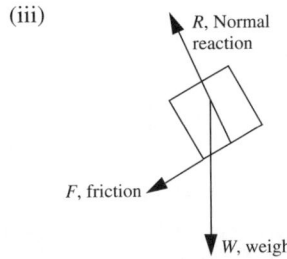

Chapter 4 Mass, Weight and Density

Self Evaluation 4.1
1. C   2. A   3. B   4. D

Self Evaluation 4.2
1. C   2. A   3. B   4. C   5. B
6. D

Self Evaluation 4.3
1. D
2. C
3. (a) (i) Metre rule   (ii) Vernier calipers
   (b) (i) 78.5 cm^3 (ii) 699 g

Revision Exercise 4
Multiple Choice Questions

1. A   2. B   3. C   4. A   5. D
6. D   7. C   8. B   9. C   10. B

Structured Questions

Section A

1. 6.3×10^{-4} g cm^{-3}
2. (a) 1.07 g cm^{-3}
3. $\rho_B > \rho_{wood} > \rho_A$
   $\rho_{wood} = \rho_C$
4. (a) (i) 12 cm^3 (ii) 0.77 g cm^{-3}
   (b) To submerge the piece of cork.

Section B

1. (a) (i) 4.0 g   (ii) 8.0 g
   (b) (i) 1.48 cm^3 (ii) 0.90 cm^3
2. (a)

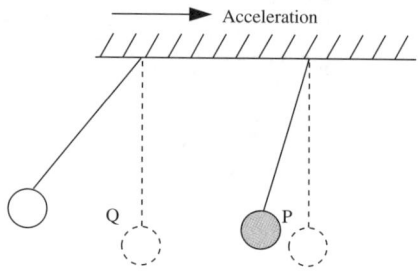

Figure (b)

(b)

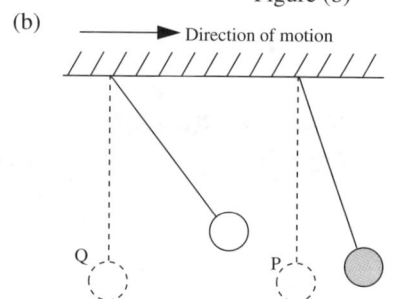

Figure (c)

3. (a)

Metal	Density (g cm^{-3})	Percentage by mass	Mass (g)	Volume (cm^3)
Gold	19.3	91.7%	18.34	0.950
Silver	10.5	5.5%	1.1	0.105
Copper	8.90	2.8%	0.56	0.063

(b) 17.9 g cm^{-3}

Chapter 5   Turning Effect of Forces

Self Evaluation 5.1

1. 2.5 N m
2. $R = \dfrac{2}{3}W$, $S = \dfrac{1}{3}W$

3. (a) $x = 0.727$ m
   (b) Reaction $R = 11.0$ N
4. (a) $F = 2460$ N   (b) $R = 3360$ N

Self Evaluation 5.2

1. (a) Circular   (b) Ellipse

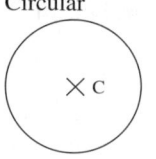 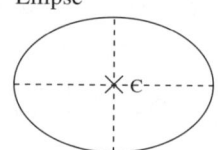

(c) Rectangle   (d) Triangle

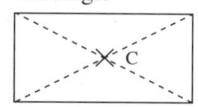 

2.

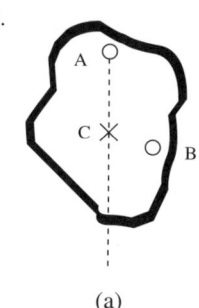 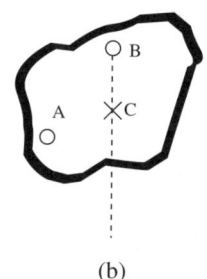

(a)   (b)

Self Evaluation 5.3

1. B

Revision Exercise 5

Multiple Choice Questions

1. B	2. A	3. D	4. C	5. D
6. B	7. C	8. C	9. A	10. D

Structured Questions

Section A

1. (a)

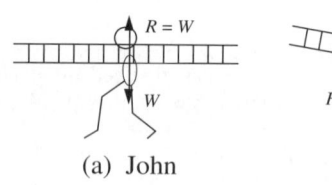

      (a) John   (b) Tom

(b) John's method is better.
2. (a) 4.8 N m
   (b) No
   (c) The rod rotates about C in the anti-clockwise direction.

3. (a)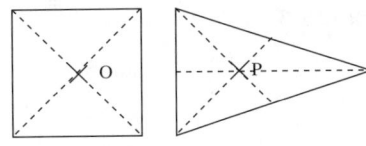

Figure (a)   Figure (b)

(b)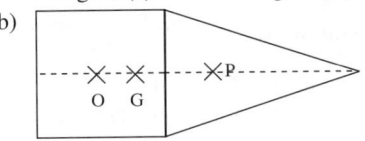

Figure (c)

Mass of square > mass of triangle
Hence G is closer to O.

4.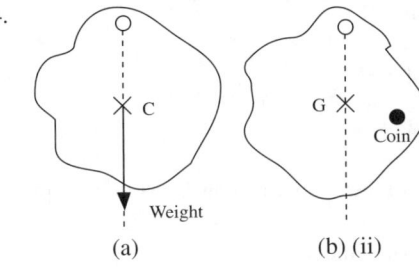

(a)   (b) (ii)

(b) (i) $M = 25$ g

Section B

1. (a) Forces on X and Y are equal.
   (b) No difference.
   (c) Force on X is larger because X is closer to the load.
3. (a) 50 g
   (b)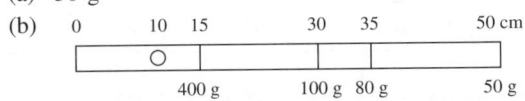
   (c) – Replace the 200 g mass with a smaller mass (say 100 g).
   – Shift the position of pivot to the left (say at 5 cm mark).

Chapter 6   Pressure

Self Evaluation 6.1

1. Maximum pressure = 0.40 N cm^{-2}
   Minimum pressure = 0.080 N cm^{-2}
2. (a) 52.5 N cm^{-2}
4. (a) $W = 1.20 \times 10^5$ N
   (b) $\dfrac{x}{y} = 600$

Self Evaluation 6.2

1. (a) $p = 936$ Pa   (b) $p = 960$ Pa
   (c) $p = 1896$ Pa

2. (a) $p = 3.0 \times 10^6$ Pa
   (b) $F = 7.92 \times 10^8$ N

Self Evaluation 6.3

1. (a) 75 cm Hg
   (b) 20 cm Hg
2. (a) $p_{atm} = p_{gas} + (35 - 15)$ cm Hg
       $p_{gas} = (76 - 20)$ cm Hg = 56 cm Hg
   (b) 7.62×10^4 Pa
3. (a) Pressure at P = pressure at Q
   (b) $p_Q = 2.0 \times 10^3$ Pa
   (c) $x = 0.25$ m

Revision Exercise 6

Multiple Choice Questions

1. C   2. D   3. B   4. D   5. B
6. C   7. A   8. A   9. A   10. D

Structured Questions

Section A

3. (b) $W = 20.0$ N   (c) 0.50 cm
4. (a) 1.02×10^5 N m^{-2}
   (b) 8.43×10^4 N m^{-2}

Section B

1. (d) 12 000 N
   (e) 6.0×10^6 N
2. (b) (i) Increased pressure = 0.20 N cm^{-2}
       (ii) $h = 20$ cm
   (c) (i) No change
       (ii) h is smaller.
3. (a) 1.03×10^5 Pa
   (b) 9.4×10^3 m
   (c) 74 mm of mercury

Chapter 7   Energy, Work and Power

Self Evaluation 7.1

1. (a) 7.2 J   (b) 1.8 J   (c) 5.4 J
   (d) 5.5 m s^{-1}
2. (a) 120 J
   (b) 76.8 J
3. (a) 600 J   (b) 10 m s^{-1}

Self Evaluation 7.2

1. (a) 2 J   (b) 20 N   (c) 0.04 m
2. 85.3 N
3. 4.03 m s^{-1}

Self Evaluation 7.3

1. 140 W
2. 10 kW
3. 15 s

Revision Exercise 7

Multiple Choice Questions

1. C 2. A 3. C 4. D 5. C
6. B 7. B 8. B 9. D 10. A

Structured Questions

Section A

1. (a) 2610 J (b) 1392 J (c) 1218 J
2. (a) KE = 12.8 J, PE = 48.0 J
   (b) 17.4 m s^{-1}
4. (a) Mass of the monkey m and the time taken t to raise the monkey through a height of 4.0 m.
   (b) 8.9 m s^{-1}
5. (a) (i) 1.12 × 10^4 J (ii) 5.60 × 10^4 N

Section B

1. (a) 25 m (b) 20 m s^{-1} (c) 1750 J
   (d) 50 m (e) 35 N
2. (c) (i) 1.2 × 10^4 kg
       (ii) 3.84 × 10^5 J
       (iii) 3.84 × 10^5 W
       (iv) 2.30 × 10^5 W
3. (a) Work done by
       (i) John = 2520 J
       (ii) Tommy = 1716 J
       (iii) Ben = 2240 J
   (b) Power delivered by
       (i) John = 42 W
       (ii) Tommy = 29 W
       (iii) Ben = 37 W
   (d) John

Chapter 8 Kinetic Model of Matter

Self Evaluation 8.1

1. (a) Ice   (b) Water and steam
   (c) Steam   (d) Steam

Self Evaluation 8.2

1. B 2. D
3. (c) Gas molecules are in constant random motion. Gas molecules collide with each other.

Self Evaluation 8.3

1. C 2. C 3. B 4. B 5. D
6. A 7. C 8. A

Revision Exercise 8

Multiple Choice Questions

1. C 2. A 3. D 4. B 5. C
6. B 7. D 8. A 9. D 10. B

Structured Questions

Section A

6. (a) 1.02 × 10^5 N m^{-2}
   (b) (i) 2.18 × 10^5 N m^{-2}
       (ii) 23.4 cm^3

Section B

2. (b) Pressure of the trapped air equals to the atmospheric pressure.
   (c) (i) Remains the same.
       (ii) Density is doubled.
       (iii) Mean speed remains unchanged.
       (iv) The pressure is doubled.
3. (a) (i) 1.0 × 10^5 Pa
       (ii) 2.0 × 10^5 Pa
   (b)

Weight (N)	0	2.5	10.0	15.0	30.0
p (10^5 Pa)	1.0	1.25	2.00	2.50	4.00
V (cm^3)	100	80	50	40	25

Chapter 9 Transfer of Thermal Energy

Self Evaluation 9.1

1. A 2. D 3. B 4. D

Self Evaluation 9.2

1. C 2. B 3. B 4. A

Self Evaluation 9.3

1. B 2. C 3. C 4. D

Revision Exercise 9

Multiple Choice Questions

1. D 2. B 3. C 4. A 5. C
6. B 7. A 8. B 9. D 10. A

(see page 238 for answers to Structured Questions)

Chapter 10 Temperature and Thermal Properties of Materials

Self Evaluation 10.1
1. D   2. C   3. C

Self Evaluation 10.2
1. B   2. D   3. A

Self Evaluation 10.3
1. C   2. B   3. D

Self Evaluation 10.4
1. (a) 240 J °C^{-1}
   (b) 33 °C
   (c) 16 800 J
2. (a) (i) 4.41×10^5 J
       (ii) 2.52×10^4 J
   (b) 233 s

Self Evaluation 10.6
1. (a) 3.13 J kg^{-1} °C^{-1}
2. (a) Rate of heat transferred = 1580 J s^{-1}
   (b) $t = \dfrac{ml}{P}$ = 106 s
3. (a) (i) $Q = mc\theta$ = 6300 J
       (ii) m = 18.9 g

Revision Exercise 10

Multiple Choice Questions
1. C   2. B   3. D   4. A   5. A
6. B   7. B   8. A   9. D   10. A

Structured Questions

Section A
3. (a) (i) CD   (ii) AB
   (b) T_2
   (c) Liquid state
5. (a) 0.50 °C s^{-1}
   (b) 80 °C
   (c) (i) C = 500 J °C^{-1} (ii) $L = 1.25 \times 10^5$ J

Section B
1. (a) Copper and constantan
       (or any two different metals)
   (b) 0 mV
   (c) 30 °C

3. (a) Pot made of metal Z is the heaviest.
       m_x = 2.16 kg, m_y = 1.44 kg,
       m_z = 6.40 kg
   (b) Y: Heat capacity of Y is lowest.
   (c) Z: It has the highest heat capacity, hence the most thermal energy.
   (d) Lightest, lowest heat capacity, high melting point

Chapter 11 General Wave Properties

Self Evaluation 11.1
1. (a) 5 Hz   (b) 5 cm   (c) 30 cm
   (d) 150 cm s^{-1}

Self Evaluation 11.2
2. (a) 20 cm   (b) 500 cm s^{-1} (c) 250 cm
3.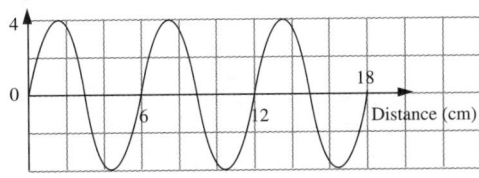

Revision Exercise 11

Multiple Choice Questions
1. A   2. B   3. B   4. A   5. C
6. B   7. D   8. A   9. A   10. C

Structured Questions

Section A
1. (a) Longitudinal wave. Reason: Vibration of the coils in the spring is along the direction of wave propagation.
   (c) 2 Hz
   (d) 12 cm s^{-1}
2. (a) (i) 15 mm   (ii) 2.5 s   (iii) 0.4 Hz
   (b) 70 mm
3. (a)

4. (a) (i) 8 cm   (ii) 4 s   (iii) 0.25 Hz
   (b)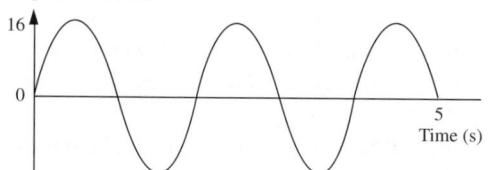

5. (a) (i) 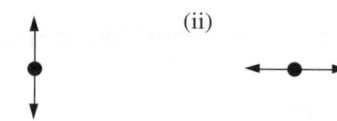 (ii)
   (b) Number of vertical vibrations in one second and amplitude of vibration are doubled.

Section B

1. (b)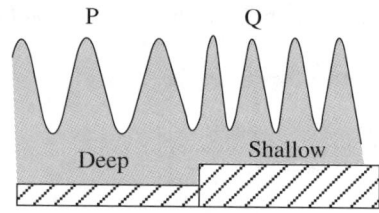
   (c) (i) 1.0 cm   (ii) 0.8 cm
   (d) (i) 8.0 cm s^{-1} (ii) 6.4 cm s^{-1}
   (e) Refraction

2. (b) (i) 6.0 Hz   (ii) $\frac{1}{6}$ s
   (c) (i)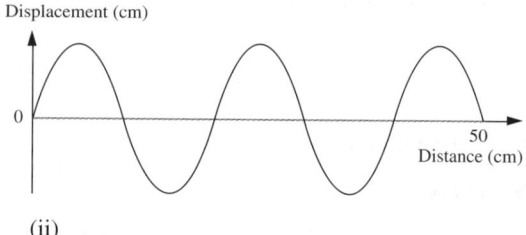
       (ii)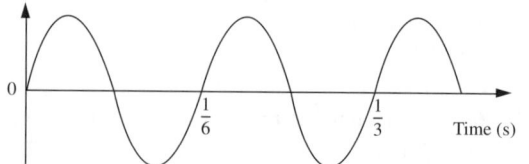

Chapter 12 Light

Self Evaluation 12.1

1. C   2. D
3.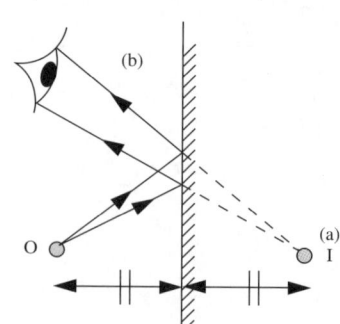

4. (a) (i) 4.0 m   (ii) 1.2 m   (b) 8l

Self Evaluation 12.2

1. C   2. D   3. B
4. (a) 60°   (b) 32°
   (c) 1.63
   (d)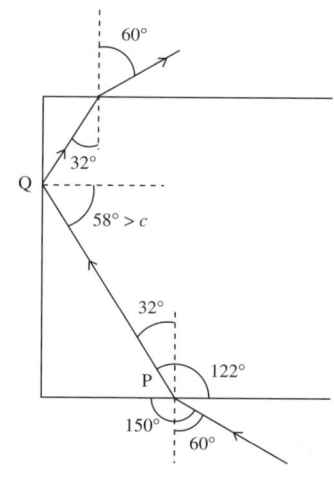

5. (a) (i) 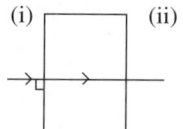 (ii) (iii)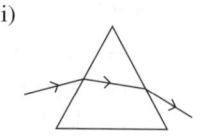
   (b) Speed of light in glass is less than that in air.

Self Evaluation 12.3

1. C 2. C 3. C 4. A 5. B

6.

Object's distance	Characteristics of image
(a) Infinity	Image is formed at the principal focus and it is real and inverted.
(b) 60.0 cm	Image is real, inverted and of the same size as the object.
(c) Between 30.0 cm and 60.0 cm	Image is real, inverted and magnified.
(d) 20.0 cm	Image is virtual, upright and magnified.
(e) 80.0 cm	Image is real, inverted and diminished.

Revision Exercise 12

Multiple Choice Questions

1. D 2. C 3. B 4. D 5. A
6. A 7. D 8. B 9. C 10. B

Structured Questions

Section A

1.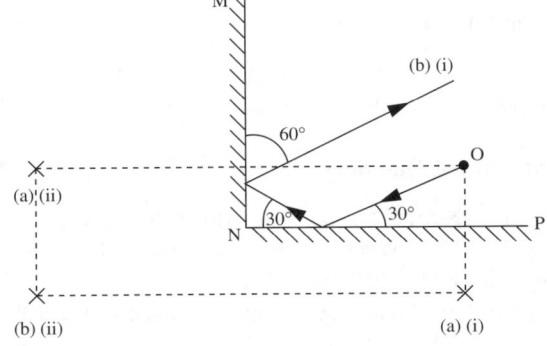

2. (a) $c = 39°\left(\sin c = \dfrac{1}{1.60}\right)$
   (b) (i) 0°   (ii) 45°
   (d)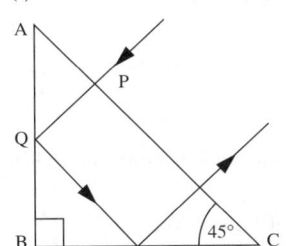

3.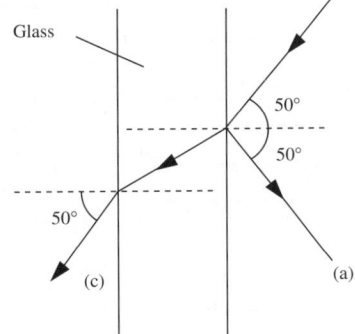
   (b) 40°

4. (a) and (b)
   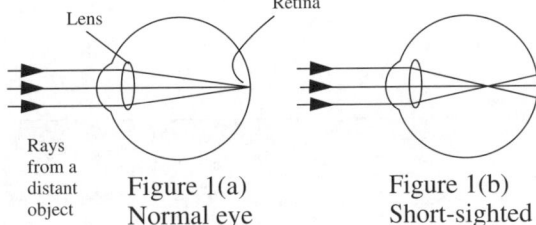
   Figure 1(a) Normal eye   Figure 1(b) Short-sighted
   (c) Diverging lens
   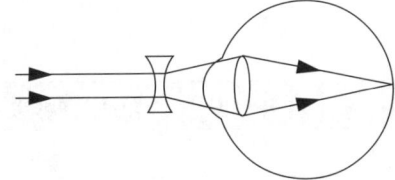
   Figure 1(c)

5. (a) (i)
   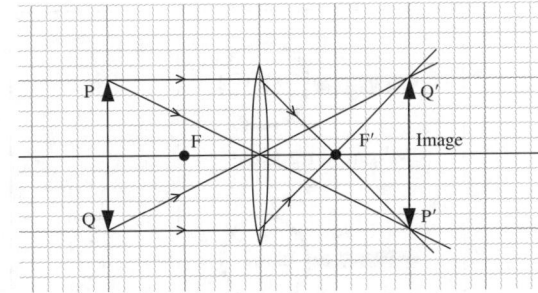
   (ii) Image is real, inverted and of the same size as the object.
   (b) Image is virtual, upright and smaller than the object.

Section B

1. (a) 0°
   (b) (i) $r = 22°$

(c) $c = 49°$

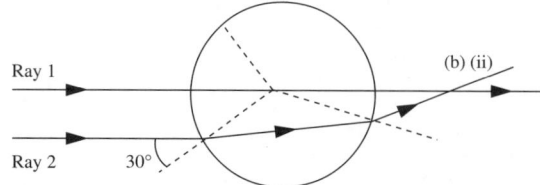

2. (a) $n = 1.41$
   (c) $1.52 = \dfrac{\sin 60°}{\sin a} \Rightarrow a = 35°$
   (d)

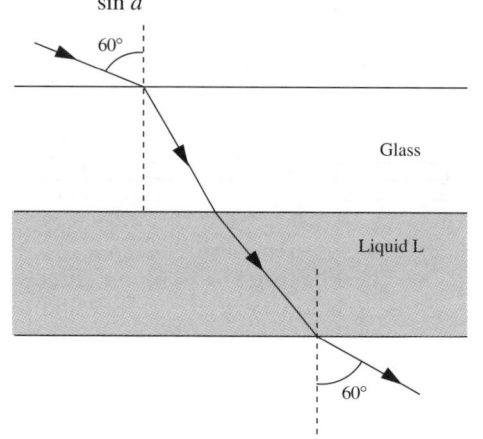

3. (a)

Lens	Power (D)	Focal length (cm)
X	+5	+20
Y	−5	−20
Z	+10	+10

Oct 2007 Magnifying glass	Lens Z
Oct 2007 Magnifying glass	Lens X
Glasses for a short-sightedness	Lens Y

(c) (i) Lens Y (ii) Lens X
    (iii) Lens Z (iv) Lens X

Chapter 13 Electromagnetic Spectrum

Self Evaluation 13.1

1. A: Microwaves
   B: Infra-red
   C: Ultra-violet
   D: Gamma ray
2. (a) Radio wave   (b) Gamma ray
   (c) Infra-red   (d) Gamma ray
3. (a) (i) 700 nm   (ii) 400 nm
   (b) (i) Neither, both have the same speed in vacuum.
       (ii) Red; speed in glass,
       $$v = \dfrac{\text{speed of light in vacuum}}{\text{refractive index}} = \dfrac{c}{n}$$
4. 1×10^{10} Hz, $f = \dfrac{c}{\lambda}$

Self Evaluation 13.2

1. (a) Infra-red   (b) Microwaves   (c) Ultra-violet
   (d) Visible light   (e) Microwaves

Self Evaluation 13.3

1. (i) X-rays and gamma rays
   (ii) Radio waves, microwaves, infra-red, light and ultra-violet

Revision Exercise 13

Multiple Choice Questions

1. B   2. C   3. C   4. D   5. A
6. A   7. B   8. D   9. D   10. B

Structured Questions

1. (a) X-rays   (b) Ultra-violet
   (c) Microwaves   (d) Infra-red
4. (a) 4.29×10^{14} Hz
   (b) (i) Frequency remains the same, 4.29×10^{14} Hz
       (ii) 2×10^{8} m s^{-1}
       (iii) 467 nm
5. (a) – Microwaves are used for transmission.
       – Heating effect of microwaves.
   (b) – Suntan is caused by ultra-violet radiation.
       – Glass absorbs ultra-violet radiation.
6. 1.3×10^{8} s
7. (a) Visible light
   (b) – Power of the light is concentrated in a small area.
       – Intensity of light is very high.
       – Heating effect of light causes damage to the tissue of the eyes.

Section B

1. (a) (i) From 400 nm to 700 nm
       (ii) From 1×10^{-5} m to 1×10^{-3} m
       (iii) From 1×10^{-7} m to 1×10^{-9} m
3. (a) (i) Speed = 3.0×10^8 m s^{-1}
       (ii) No
   (b) (i) Visible light   (iv) 6.0×10^{14} Hz
       (ii) Ultraviolet   (v) 1.0×10^{16} Hz
       (iii) 3.0×10^{-2} m   (vi) 3.0×10^{-10} m
   (c) (i) Electric transmitter or LC circuit
       (ii) X-ray tube
   (d) (i) Skin cancer or sun burn
       (ii) Cancer or genetic changes

Chapter 14 Sound

Self Evaluation 14.1

3. (a) 0.55 m
   (b) (i) 0.55 m (ii) 0.55 m   (iii) 0.275 m

Self Evaluation 14.2

1. Less by $\dfrac{100}{340} = 0.29$ s

2. (i) 300 m s^{-1} (ii) 1500 m s^{-1}
   (iii) 6000 m s^{-1}
   Speed of sound v in air < v in water < v in steel
3. 748 m

Self Evaluation 14.3

1. (a) (i) 1.0 s   (ii) 2.0 s
   (b) 1.0 s
2. (a)

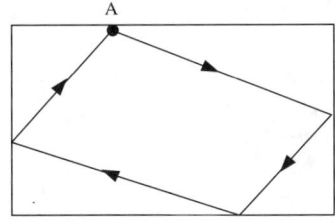

Self Evaluation 14.4

1. 4500 m
3. 450 m

Revision Exercise 14

Multiple Choice Questions

| 1. C | 2. C | 3. A | 4. B | 5. C |
| 6. B | 7. B | 8. D | 9. D | 10. C |

Structured Questions

1. (i)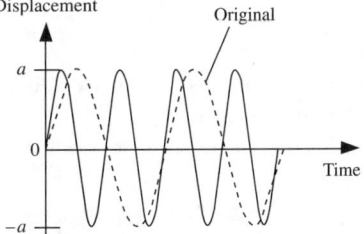

   (ii)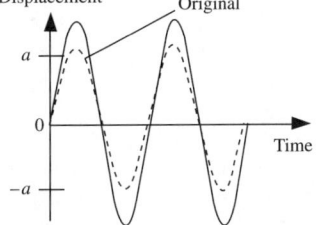

2. (a)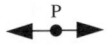
   (b) (i) 1.7 m
       (ii) Same frequency or same amplitude.
            Difference: in opposite directions.

   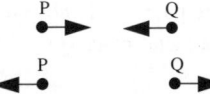

3. (a) Shortest wavelength = 0.017 m
       Longest wavelength = 17 m
   (b) Pitch increases as the frequency increases.
4. (a) Sound travels along the stethoscope.
   (b) Sound does not travel in vacuum.
   (c) Speed of sound is smaller than speed of light.

Section B

1. (a) Vibrating in the direction of propagation
   (b)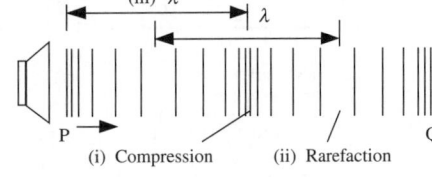
   (c) Amplitude of vibration is greater.
       Frequency of vibration is lower.
   (d)

2. (a) 325 m s^{-1}
3. (a) Sound of frequency greater that the audible frequency
   (b) 0.03 m

229

(c) (i) Ultrasound wave is not completely reflected from the shoal.
(ii) 0.50 s
(iii) 375 m
(d) Distance between pulses is shorter. Amplitude of second pulse is higher.
(e) Less diffraction, more accurate location

Chapter 15 Static Electricity

Self Evaluation 15.1
1. C 2. A 3. B

Self Evaluation 15.2
1. C 2. D 3. C

Self Evaluation 15.3
1. B 2. D 3. B 4. D 5. A
6. C

Self Evaluation 15.4
1. (c) No wastage of paint. All the paint droplets are attracted to the metal plate.

Revision Exercise 15

Multiple Choice Questions
1. D 2. A 3. C 4. D 5. B
6. A 7. D 8. B 9. B 10. B

Structure Questions

Section A

2. (b)

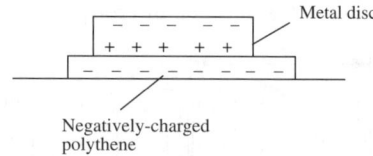

Figure 2(a)

(c)

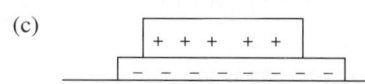

Figure 2(b)

3. (a) (i)   (ii)

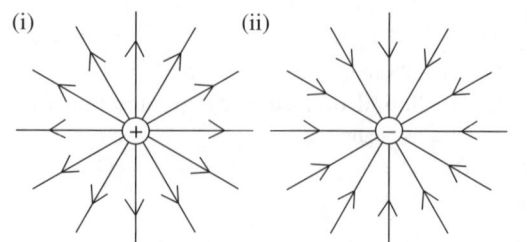

4. (a) (i)

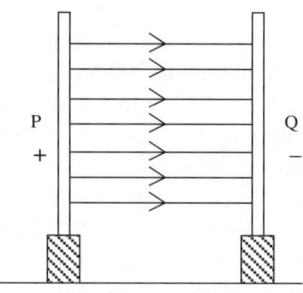

(b) (i) Negative
(iii) Electric force on the sphere is constant.

Section B

1. (a)

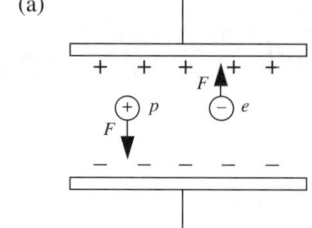

(b)

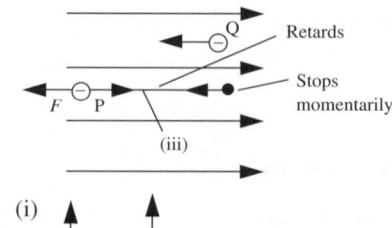

2. (a)

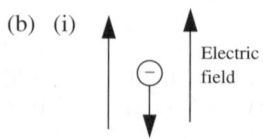

3. (a)

4. (a) (i) & (iii)

(b) (i)

Chapter 16 Current of Electricity and D.C. Circuits

Self Evaluation 16.1

1. (a) 40 C   (b) 1200 C
2. 4.0 A

Self Evaluation 16.2

1. (a) 7.5 J   (b) 0.03 J
2. 6.0 V

Self Evaluation 16.3

1. (a) 2.5 V
   (b) 12.0 J
   (c) 2.0 J required to drive the 4.0 C of charge through the battery.
2. (a) 7.5 C   (b) 18.8 J

Self Evaluation 16.4

1. (a) $3.0 \, \Omega$ (b) 3.6 V   (c) $1.0 \, \Omega$
2. (b) (i) 2.0 A   (ii) 6.0 A   (iii) $2.0 \, \Omega$
3. (a) $5.6 \, \Omega$ (b) $2.8 \, \Omega$

Revision Exercise 16

Multiple Choice Questions

1. D	2. C	3. A	4. A	5. A
6. C	7. B	8. B	9. B	10. D
11. C	12. B	13. B	14. C	15. A
16. A	17. C	18. B	19. D	20. A

Structure Questions

Section A

1. (a)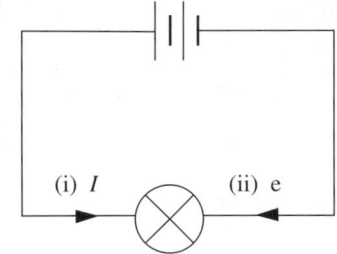
   (b) (i) 19.2 C
       (ii) $Q = Ne$
            Number of electrons $N = 1.20 \times 10^{20}$
2. (a) $V_P = 1.50$ V, $V_Q = 2.50$ V
   (b) $E = V_P + V_Q = 4.00$ V
   (c) 0.40 A
   (d) $R_P = 3.75 \, \Omega$, $R_Q = 6.25 \, \Omega$

3. (a)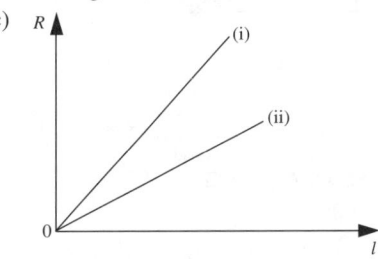
   (b)
   (c)

5. (a) X: Voltmeter
       Y: Ammeter
   (b) Resistance $R = \dfrac{V}{I}$
       where V is the reading of voltmeter and I is the reading of ammeter.
   (c)

6. (a) P: Variable resistor or rheostat
       Q: Thermistor
       S: Light dependent resistor
       T: Diode

7. (a) 0.4 A
   (b) (i) $V = \left(\dfrac{20 \text{ cm}}{100 \text{ cm}}\right)(2.0 \text{ V}) = 0.40$ V
       (ii) 1.0 V   (iii) 1.60 V

8.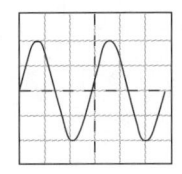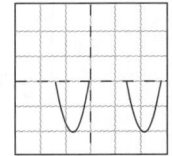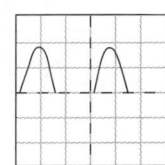

Section B

1. (a) 1.20 V
   (b) (i) $R = 3.0 \, \Omega$
   (c) (i) Ammeter's reading decreases.
       (ii) Voltmeter's reading decreases.
2. (a) (i) $I_{max} = 0.60$ A
           $I_{min} = 0.30$ A
       (ii) $V_{max} = 3.0$ V
            $V_{min} = 1.50$ V

(b) I_{max} = 2.40 A
I_{min} = 1.60 A

3. (a)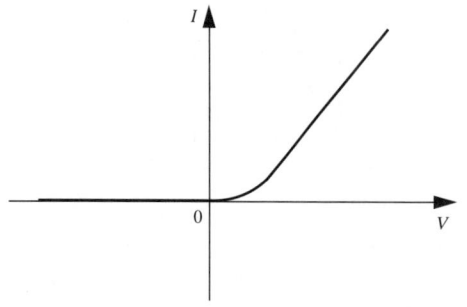

(b) The diode allows current to flow only in one direction.

(c)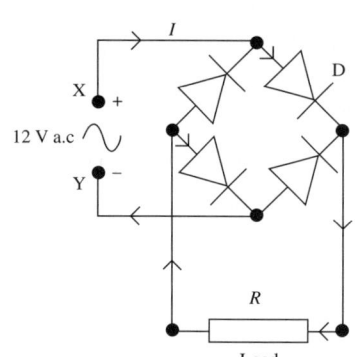

4. (b) (i) At 50°C, $R = 30\ \Omega$
   (ii) At 200°C, $R = 7\ \Omega$

(c) (i) $R = \dfrac{2.5\ V}{0.2\ A} = 12.5\ \Omega$

   (ii) At 50°C, $I = 0.14$ A
   At 200°C, $I = 0.31$ A

   (iii) The brightness of the lamp increases as the temperature increases.

5. (a) (i) Peak voltage $V_0 = 6.0$ V

   (ii) $V_{rms} = \dfrac{6.0\ V}{\sqrt{2}} = 4.24$ V

   (iii) $T = (2\ \text{div})(0.5\ \text{s div}^{-1}) = 1.0$ s
   $f = 1.0$ Hz

(b)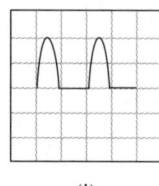

   (i)   (ii)

Chapter 17 Practical Electricity

Self Evaluation 17.1

1. 3 600 000 J
2. 2.88 units
3. 3 cents

Self Evaluation 17.3

1. (a) Live wire
   (b) Metal casing of the toaster
   (c) Blue
2. Most suitable fuse is the 15 A fuse.

Revision Exercise 17

Multiple Choice Questions

1. C 2. B 3. C 4. B 5. D
6. B 7. A 8. D 9. D 10. A

Structure Questions

Section A

1. (a) 0.5 W   (b) 0.18 W
2. (a)

Appliance	Time of usage	Units of electricity
Eight 60-W lamps	240 h	(8)(0.060)(240) = 115.2 units
Two 1.8-kW air-conditioners	320 h	(2)(1.8)(320) = 1152 units
Three 2.5-kW heaters	120 h	(3)(2.5)(120) = 900 units
	Total	2 167.2 units

(b) $650.16

3. (a)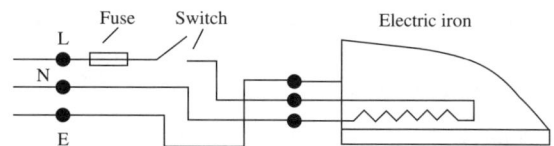

(b) $I = \dfrac{P}{V} = 6.25$ A
Fuse rating: 7 A

6. (a) 240 V   (b) 240 V   (c) 0 V

Section B

1. (b) $R_P = 3840\ \Omega$, $R_Q = 960\ \Omega$
   (c) 75 W
   (d) $P_P = 9.6$ W, $P_Q = 2.4$ W

2. (a) Lamp Q. The switch should be connected to the live wire and the lamp to the neutral wire.

(b) (i)

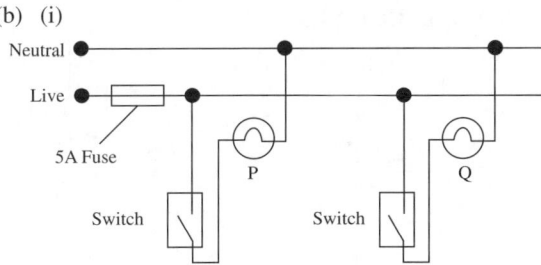

(ii) Current draws by a lamp is 0.5 A.
Maximum number of lamps = 10

Data-based Questions

3. (a) 480 Ω
   (b) Tungsten has high melting point.
   (c) 9.2 W
   (d) (i) 13.8 W
       (ii) Heat. Rate of dissipation is 120 W − 13.8 W = 106.2 W

4. (a)

Appliance	Current	Diameter of wire
100 W lamp	0.42 A	0.50 mm
1.2 kW heater	5.0 A	0.75 mm
2.5 kW kettle	10.4 A	1.25 mm

Chapter 18 Magnetism

Self Evaluation 18.1

1.

2. (a) N-pole   (b) N-pole

Self Evaluation 18.2

1. Iron, steel
3. When the current is switched off, steel retains its magnetism and becomes a permanent magnet.

Self Evaluation 18.3

1. (a)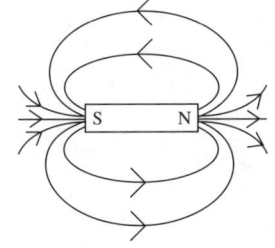

(b) At the ends of the bar magnet

2. (a)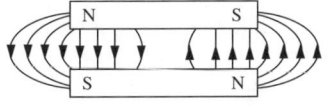

(b) The magnets move towards each other. Opposite poles attract.

Revision Exercise 18

Multiple Choice Questions

1. C   2. A   3. D   4. A   5. D
6. B   7. B   8. D   9. C   10. B

Structured Questions

Section A

1. (a) (b)

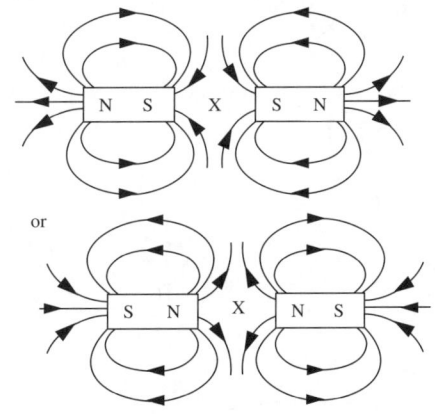

(c) X: neutral point

2. (a) (i) Iron or steel
       (ii) Glass, wood or copper

3. (c) N-pole on top, S-pole at the bottom
   (d) Q drops off. P loses its magnetism.

4. (a) There will be no short circuit.
   (b) Soft iron. It loses its magnetism when the current is switched off.
   (c) X: N-pole, Y: N-pole
   (d) Electric bell, relay

Section B

1. (a) Steel: Magnetism is permanent.
   (b) Plastic, cardboard
   (c) Non-magnetic, allow the compass to be viewed from above
   (d) So that it is balanced and horizontal.

2. (a)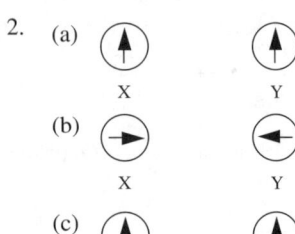

(b) (shown in image)

(c) (shown in image)

Soft iron core of electromagnet losses its magnetism when the current is switched off.

Chapter 19 Electromagnetism

Self Evaluation 19.1

1. (a) ←P ↓Q

   (b) (field lines around current into page)

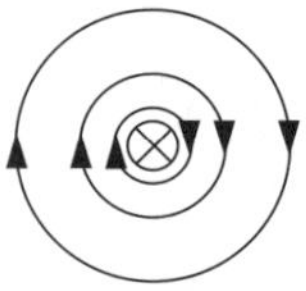

2. (a) ↑   (b) ← (i)   → (ii)

3. (a) (b)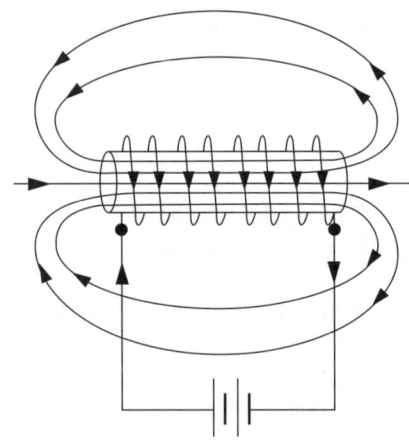

   (c) The magnetic field is stronger.

Self Evaluation 19.2

1. (a) (i) Soft iron   (ii) Soft iron
       (iii) Carbon

Self Evaluation 19.3

1. (a), (b), (c), (d)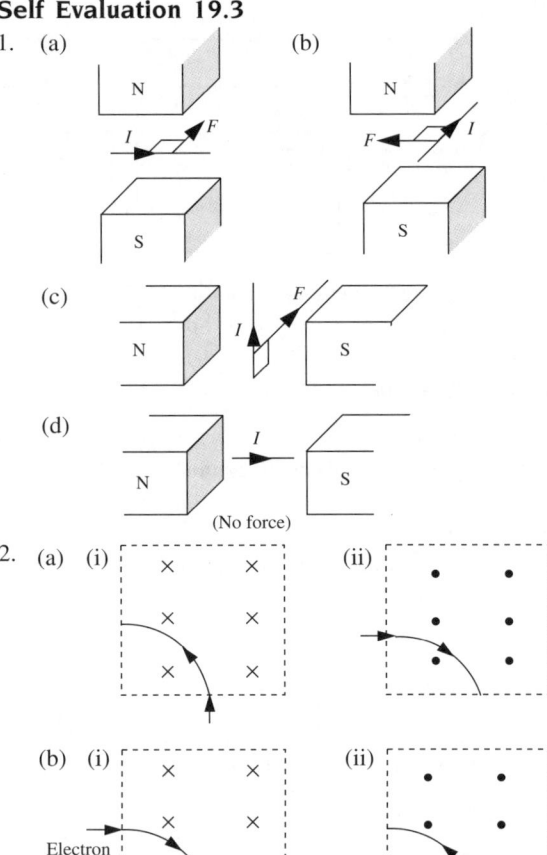
   (d) (No force)

2. (a) (i), (ii)
   (b) (i), (ii) Electron beam

Self Evaluation 19.4

1. (a) (i) wx: downwards
           yz: upwards

   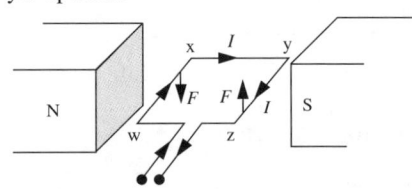

   (ii) Produce a turning effect which rotates the coil.
   (iii) xy is parallel to the magnetic field.

   (b) (i) wx: downwards
           yz: upwards

   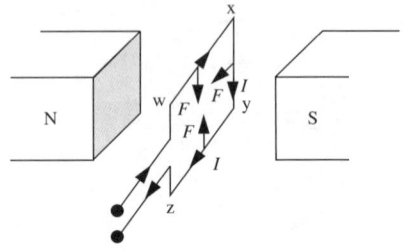

(ii) To change the shape of the coil.
(iii) Yes. Out of the plane of the paper (see figure).

Revision Exercise 19

Multiple Choice Questions

1. B   2. D   3. B   4. A   5. D
6. D   7. C   8. B   9. A   10. C

Structure Questions

1. (a)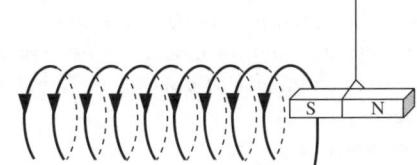

2. (a)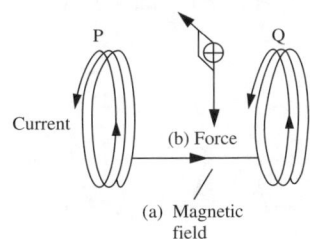

4.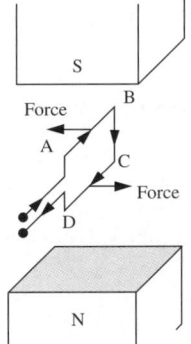

5. (a)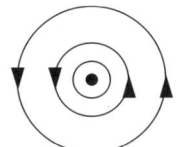

Section B

1. (a)

(c)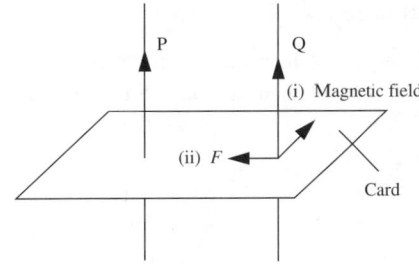

2. (a) (c)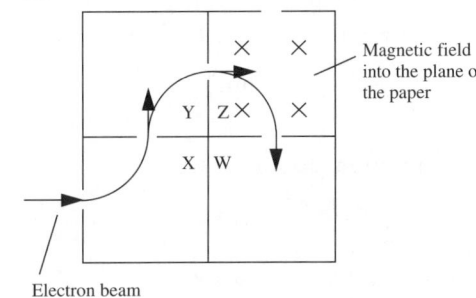

(b) X: Out of the plane of the paper.
Y: Into the plane of the paper.
(c) Into W

3. (a)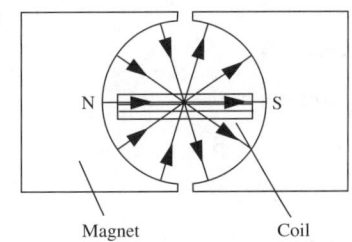

4. (a)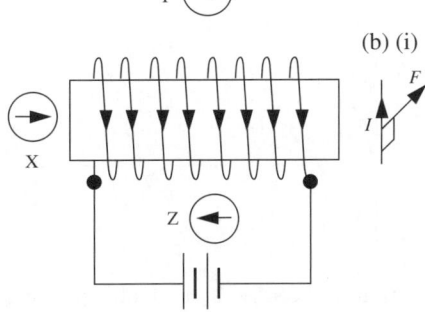

(b) (ii) No force acts on the wire. The wire is parallel to the magnetic field.

Chapter 20 Electromagnetic Induction

Self Evaluation 20.1

1. D   2. B   3. C

Self Evaluation 20.2

1. (a) Direction of induced e.m.f: a to b and c to d.
   (b) Direction of induced e.m.f: b to a and d to c.
2. (a) (i) A (ii) B

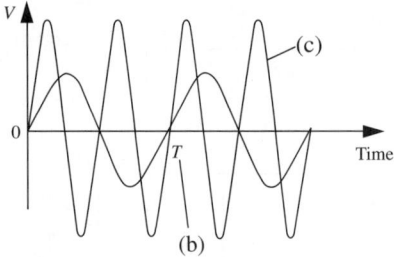

Self Evaluation 20.3

1. (a) $N_S = \dfrac{V_S N_P}{V_P} = 120$
   (b) $V_X = 2.0$ V, $V_Y = 8.0$ V
2. (a) $I_S = 1.82$ A
   (b) Power loss per metre $= I^2 R = 1.64$ W m^{-1}
   (c) – Step up the voltage to a higher value
       – Use thick copper cables of lower resistance

Revision Exercise 20

Multiple Choice Questions

1. D 2. B 3. B 4. A 5. A
6. C 7. B 8. D 9. C 10. C

Structured Questions

Section A

3. (b)

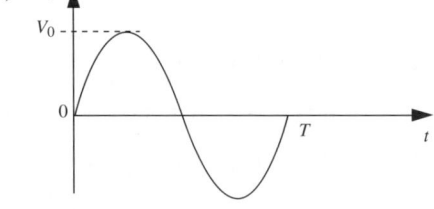

   (c) The peak voltage V_0 is doubled. The period is halved.
5. $V_Q = 6$ V, $V_R = 18$ V, $V_S = 48$ V

Section B

1. (b) Smaller deflection in the same direction
   (c) There is no change in the magnetic flux through coil Y. No e.m.f. induced in Y.
   (d) Larger deflection in the opposite direction
   (e) The deflections are smaller. Soft iron increases the magnetic flux but not aluminium.

2. (a) (i) (Anticlockwise direction)
       (ii) (Clockwise direction)
   (b) There is no change of magnetic flux through the coil.
   (c) – Move the coil at a greater speed
       – Use a stronger magnetic field
       – Use the same length of wire to form a rectangle that has longer left and right sides but shorter width
3. (a) The speed increases due to the pull of gravity.
   (b) (i) X to Y   (ii) X to Y
   (c) Magnitude of induced current in (ii) is greater because the speed of the magnet is greater than in (i).
   (d) Steel: No e.m.f. is induced in the coil.
       Magnet: Direction of induced current in the coil produces an effect that opposes the motion of the magnet.
4. (a) Step-down transformer
       Output voltage is less than the input voltage.
   (b) $\dfrac{N_S}{N_P} = \dfrac{V_S}{V_P} = \dfrac{1}{10}$
   (d)

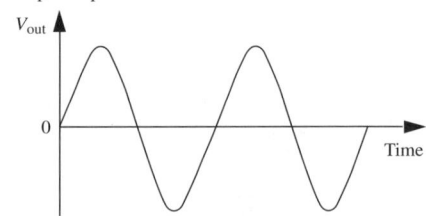

   (e) 2.0 A
5. (a) (i) To step up the voltage from 50 kV to 300 kV
       (ii) 6
   (b) (i) 0.83 A
       (ii) Power lost $= I^2 R = 34$ W
       (iii) Power lost from the cables through heating is reduced.
   (c) 2.25×10^6

Specimen Examination Paper

Paper 1

1. C   2. A   3. B   4. D   5. B
6. A   7. C   8. B   9. B   10. D
11. D 12. A 13. A 14. C 15. A
16. D 17. A 18. B 19. A 20. B
21. C 22. B 23. B 24. A 25. D
26. D 27. B 28. B 29. A 30. C
31. C 32. D 33. C 34. D 35. B
36. B 37. A 38. D 39. C 40. A

Paper 2

Section A

1. (a) 10 m s^{-1} (b) 24 s
   (c) Deceleration $= 0.833$ m s^{-2}
2. (a)

   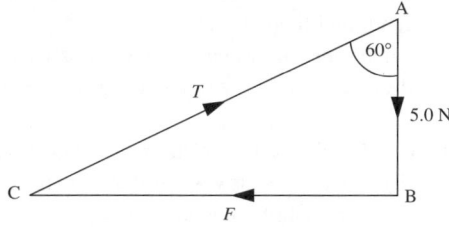

   (b) (i) $F = 8.7$ N (ii) $T = 10$ N
3. (a) 6.72×10^5 J (b) $Pt = 1.08 \times 10^6$ J
   (c) Electrical energy supplied is greater than gain in internal energy because:
   – heat is gained by the kettle
   – heat is lost to the surrounding by conduction, radiation and convention
4. (a) Speed, wavelength, direction of propagation. (Any two but not more than two)
   (b) (i) $40°$ (ii) Refractive index $= 1.56$
5. (a) Water in region X is deeper. Wavelength is greater in X, hence X is deeper.
   (b) Refraction (c) 5.0 cm (d) 25.6 cm s^{-1}
6. (a) $25\,°C$
   (b) Temperature of water increases until $100\,°C$ when it boils.
   (c) 0.0265 kg
   (d) (i)

   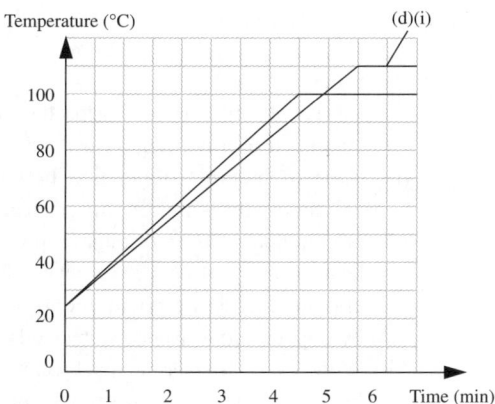

7. (a)

   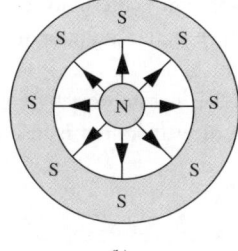

   (b) (i) The coil moves out of the magnet.
   (ii) The coil vibrates in and out of the magnet.

8. (a) and (b)(ii)

   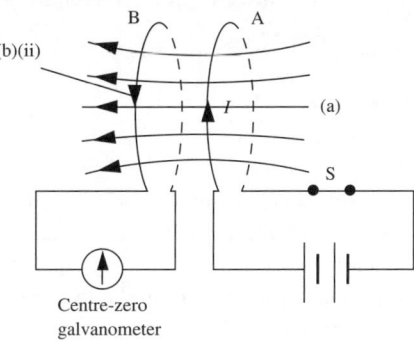

   (c) When S remains closed, the magnetic flux through coil B does not change. Thus no e.m.f. is induced in coil B.

Section B

2. (a) (i)

Time (s)	1	2	3	4	5
x (m)	20	40	60	80	100

   (ii) 20 m s^{-1}
   (b) (i) h increases with time.
   (ii) The speed increases.
   (iii) 5 s
   (iv) 120 m
   (v) 9.6 m s^{-2}

3. EITHER
   (a) X: Resistance of X decreases when the temperature increases.
   Y: Resistance of Y is low in bright lights and high in the dark.
   (b) Lamp L does not light up. Potentials at A and B are equal.
   (c) (i) Resistance of X decreases.
   Resistance of Y decreases.
   (ii) L is lighted.
   (Potential at B higher than at A.)
   (d) L does not light up. Potentials at A and B are equal.
   OR
   (a) Infra-red radiation
   (b) Radio waves, microwaves, infra-red, visible light, ultra-violet, X-rays and gamma-rays.
   (c) – Same speed of 3×10^8 m s^{-1} in vacuum
   – Are transverse wave
   (d) Any value between 4×10^{-7} m to 7×10^{-7} m
   (e) – Microwave oven: cooking
   – Telecommunication: satellite communication

Chapter 9 Transfer of Thermal Energy

Structured Questions

Section A

1. When the person stands barefoot, the thermal energy conducts away from the feet at a faster rate. Sock is made of wool which traps air and air is a poor conductor, so the rate of thermal energy loss from the feet is reduced when the person wears sock.

2. (a) Air trapped in expanded polystyrene cannot flow and air is a poor thermal conductor. Thus thermal energy loss by convection and conduction is reduced. White colour of the cup helps to reduce thermal energy loss by radiation.
   (b) The cover over the cup reduces thermal energy loss from the surface of the drink by convection and prevents steam from escaping.

3. (a) Air around the lamp is heated. Hot air rises and goes through the vents. Without the vents, temperature of the air below the cover keeps increasing. Plastic cover will melt.
   (b) Thermal energy is transferred to the bulb from the hot filament by radiation and conduction.
   (c) Thermal energy is transferred by radiation from the lamp, so the person feels warm.

4. (a) Air inside the bubbles cannot move, so no convection current is set up and thermal energy cannot be transferred by convection. Air is a poor conductor of thermal energy, so very little thermal energy is transferred from the hot oil to the ice cream.
   (b) Thermal energy is transferred by convection. When the less dense hot oil rises, the more dense cooler oil would replace it. This set up a convection current which distribute the thermal energy to all parts of the oil.

5. (a) Atoms in the copper are closely packed in an orderly manner. There are also many free electrons in the copper. When one end of a piece of copper is heated, the free electrons gain kinetic energy and diffuse to the cold end, colliding with atoms. Hence thermal energy is transferred to the cold end.
   (b) Air is a poor thermal conductor because
   - the distance between air molecules is large.
   - thermal energy is transferred when air molecules collide into each other.
   - time between collisions is large.

Section B

1. (a) Highly reflective surface is a poor absorber and poor emitter of thermal energy.
   (b) Air trapped by the fibre reduces thermal energy transfer by convection and conduction between the cabin and the exterior.
   (c) Air trapped between two pieces of glass prevents thermal energy transfer by convection and conduction.

2. (a) (i) Conduction, convention and radiation
   (ii) Thermal energy is transferred to the copper can and table by conduction.
   Thermal energy is transferred to the air by convection. Thermal energy is also transferred from the surface of the can to the surrounding by means of electromagnetic waves known as radiation.
   (b)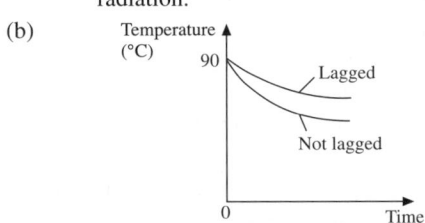

   Temperature of water in the lagged can drops at a lower rate because the felt is a poor conductor of thermal energy, so the rate of thermal energy lost due to conduction is reduced.

3. (a) (i) Conduction
   (ii) Convection
   (b) (i) Nature of surface
   Highly polished shiny surface – water boils faster
   Reason: less thermal energy lost due to radiation compared to a dull unpolished surface.
   (ii) Type of metal: Copper is a better thermal conductor than aluminium. Thermal energy is conducted faster through copper. Specific heat capacity of copper is lower than that of aluminium. Less thermal energy is absorbed by copper kettle. Hence water boils faster.
   (iii) With cover, less thermal lost by convection and less steam escape. Hence water boils faster.
   (c) Temperature of aluminium kettle is lower because
   – dull black surface better radiator than shiny polished surface
   – no cover – rate of thermal lost by convection is greater. Rate of evaporation is also greater.